Riven by Lust

Riven by Lust

Incest and Schism in Indian Buddhist Legend and Historiography

Jonathan A. Silk

University of Hawai'i Press
Honolulu

Printed in the United States of America
13 12 11 10 09 6 5 4 3 2 1

Library of Congress Cataloging-in-Publication Data

Silk, Jonathan A.
Riven by lust : incest and schism in Indian Buddhist legend and historiography / Jonathan A. Silk.
p. cm.
Includes bibliographical references and index.
ISBN 978-0-8248-3090-8 (hardcover : alk.paper)
1. Incest—Religious aspects—Buddhism. 2. Buddhist sects—Historiography. 3. Buddhist literature—History and criticism. I. Title.
BQ4570.I53S55 2008
294.3'563—dc22
2008014911

Publication of this book has been assisted by a grant from the J. Gonda Foundation.

University of Hawaiʻi Press books are printed on acid-free paper and meet the guidelines for permanence and durability of the Council on Library Resources.

Designed by University of Hawaiʻi Press production staff
Printed by The Maple-Vail Book Manufacturing Group

In Reverent Memory

Robert Hopkins Brower

(1923–1988)

and

Attipat Krishnaswami Ramanujan

(1929–1993)

Teachers, Friends

Contents

Preface

This is an ambitious book and at the same time a limited one. It attempts to stitch together a variety of sometimes quite diverse materials, aiming, ultimately, to create a quilt from them. If it ends up looking slightly less like the haphazardly sewn together contents of a ragbag and slightly more like Joseph's Coat of Many Colors, I will judge it a success. I would, then, like to think of this book as an *essay*, in that term's literal sense: an attempt, a try. The very endeavor itself is one aspect of this ambition. In addition, in the course of cutting up, laying out, and stitching together the swatches out of which the quilt will be created, the book attempts to come to grips with some of the most basic elements of human psychology, exploring along the way cross-cultural patterns of Oedipal tensions and tremors. This too is also an ambitious aim. At the same time, the book strives to expose—if that is an appropriate metaphor—the layers and valances of self-image and self-understanding associated with Buddhist conceptions of Buddhist history and sectarian legitimacy in India and beyond. In order to do this, I focus centrally on a single story and its implications. From one perspective, this book is narrowly intended as a historical and, in particular, rhetorical inquiry into one episode in Indian Buddhist historiography. As such it addresses issues of greatest concern to those interested in Buddhist Studies and ancient India, and by extension to those interested in the historiography and rhetoric of religious traditions in general. But the topic itself compels attention to another audience as well, one interested in these Buddhist stories not so much for what they may say about the history of Indian Buddhism or the deployment of religious rhetoric, but for what they may ultimately contribute to a picture of certain, possibly universal, human psychological modes.

To unpack the central story around which all else revolves, I attempt to survey all of Indian Buddhist literature, to take into account non-Buddhist Indian literature and to touch on Buddhist literature produced outside of India. This is ambitious, if not downright foolhardy. And therein lie some of the limitations of the book, since it has, naturally, proven impossible to fully contextualize and appreciate on their own terms all the sources upon which I have drawn, all the works I have referred to, all the ideas I have invoked. I would nevertheless maintain that the overall unity of the project is its own best apology.

There are, however, several issues that should be mentioned as specific limitations on this project. One problem that plagues any attempt to set Indian Buddhist materials in a coherent historical framework is our almost complete ignorance regarding the chronology and even geographical origins of many, if not almost all, of the relevant texts. The sectarian origins of texts may help us narrow down their geographic origins a bit. Theravāda materials in the Pāli language, as we now have them, have been transmitted for about 1,500 years in Sri Lanka and Southeast Asia, although some of the older materials may more directly reflect older mainland Indian sources. It is fairly certain that the materials belonging to the Mūlasarvāstivāda tradition, many of which survive only in Chinese or Tibetan translations, are products of the northwest of the Indian subcontinent, an area comprising what we now know as Pakistan and Afghanistan and that general region. Likewise, there are reasons to associate many of the Sarvāstivāda texts with nearby areas, especially Kashmir. The question of the localization of Mahāsāṁghika materials is considerably more complicated, and no good geographic specification is possible.

In a number of cases, the materials I studied led to lengthy considerations that did not find a place in this book. I have published a number of articles addressing certain related problems, and would direct interested readers to these more specialized publications for further details and materials. Likewise, it proved impossible to include editions of the many texts to which I refer, and with the exception of short passages, I have refrained from citing the originals of the many translations I offer. I plan to make available the texts I prepared on a website.

Acknowledgments

I have worked at this project, off and on, for about twenty years and have presented some of its tentative results several times at meetings during that time (a brief summary of one such presentation having been published in Silk 1990). Of the long delay from inception to completion, which transformed the work from a paper into a book, and from a narrow consideration of Buddhist history into a wide-ranging examination of cultural patterns, I regret only that it is now impossible to present the work to two of its early inspirations, my teachers and friends Robert Brower and A. K. Ramanujan.

Even more than his classes, which were exciting but difficult, I fondly remember the pleasant afternoons I spent with Professor Brower after his retirement, packing up his library for the move to a home he was able to enjoy only too briefly. That I am able to make use of materials in premodern Japanese I owe entirely to his relentless but gentle tutelage. The afternoons (and mornings and nights) I spent preparing for and participating in his course on classical Japanese have burned in my heart a model for the symbiosis of fine philology and poetic sense, a model still, and I fear likely forever, beyond me, but glowing like a beacon nonetheless. I would like to think that in particular Professor Brower's interest in the *Konjaku monogatarishū*, upon which he centered his doctoral dissertation, would have led him to find something in the present study to attract his attention.

I knew Professor Ramanujan more briefly. He taught a seminar on folktales during a one-term visit to Ann Arbor, when we became, I should like to think, not just student and teacher but friends. Even that short introduction to folklore studies, however, awakened me to an entirely new way of looking at the materials I study. I expect Raman would have appreciated that one result of my studies has been to suggest the expansion or revision of his own ideas of the Indian Oedipal complex, although I also strongly suspect that he would not have been surprised, and would moreover have had a great many more interesting things to say about these new sources than have I.

As happy as I am to bring this work to completion, and as joyous as I am that I can here honor the names and memories of two splendid scholars whom it was my great privilege to have known, I do remain ashamed, among other things, that the English style in which I present the materials I translate would probably have deeply disappointed both Professors Brower and Ramanujan, the beauty of whose own language both in translation and in exposition was always so perfectly displayed.

Although I am, of course, solely responsible for all the shortcomings of this book, of which I am confident there are many, that there are not many more I owe to the kindness of others, whose generosity has enabled me to improve my own efforts. A number of specific debts are acknowledged in the notes at appropriate places. In addition to the thanks offered there, I owe special gratitude to the following, in alphabetical order: Shayne Clarke, for carefully reading and correcting one incarnation of the manuscript with his eagle eye for detail; Byron Earhart, my former colleague at Western Michigan University, for his organizational and conceptual suggestions; Michael Hahn, for corrections of translations and philological suggestions; Satoshi Hiraoka, above all for what is probably the initial inspiration for this study, although neither of us recall precisely our discussions of twenty years ago, but also for his low-key yet inspirational model of humanity and friendship; Harunaga Isaacson, for his valiant efforts to make my translations from Sanskrit more accurate (read: less error filled!); Leonard van der Kujip, for his assistance with Tibetan materials, and general friendship, support, and guidance; Karen Muldoon-Hules, for reading of an earlier draft, and valuable suggestions; Shizuka Sasaki, for inspiration and encouragement early on. A special note of thanks is due the University of Hawai'i Press's two readers, who graciously allowed their names to become known to me. The generous comments of Wendy Doniger and John Strong reassured me that I had something interesting to say, while at the same time gently encouraging me to move it in a "shorter and sweeter" direction. The book is certainly shorter than it was when they read it, and I believe much better for it; whether it is sweet, others may judge for themselves. For felicitous suggestions and numerous improvements in wording I owe a debt to Margaret Black, who copyedited the manuscript for the press. Patricia Crosby (as always) and Ann Ludeman were patient and gentle (but firm!) in seeing the project through to publication.

Dare I mention, in such a book, which addresses inter alia issues of conflict between parent and child, the love and appreciation I have for my own parents, Larry and Ellen? Their patience with and support for their son's path has been exceptional, and only occasionally spiced with a certain degree of bafflement at the course he has chosen. For all of my own intergenerational struggles (now taken up in their turn by my own sons), as the years go by I grow ever more grateful for the opportunities and encouragement my parents have given me. Likewise, my debt to my wife Yoko and sons Oliver and Benjamin is profound. They have not directly contributed to this book; indeed, it might be fair to say that my domestic responsibilities slowed its completion. But every day and in every way they help me become a better person, in comparison to which, writing a mere book is inconsequential.

Technical Details and Abbreviations

Unless otherwise noted, all translations from classical and modern sources are my own. The accuracy of translations and all responsibility for errors of fact or heresies of opinion rests with me.

A translation can be no more accurate than its source. Therefore, I have endeavored to establish the best possible textual basis for the sources I cite.

For sources in Sanskrit I have referred to the best editions and to manuscripts when access to them is possible. When I cite manuscripts, I provide folio and line information. An asterisk (*) before Sanskrit terms indicates that while the name or term is not attested in Sanskrit, it can be reconstructed with reasonable certainty.

For Pāli, I have cited the standard editions of the Pali Text Society. However, these path-breaking works represent, from a text-critical point of view, provisional rather than final editions. I have, therefore, also consulted the Devanagari edition of the text established by the Sixth Sāsana Council (noted as DPG, Dhammagiri-Pāli-Ganthamālā). Although the result cannot yet be called critical in any sense, by referring also to this "official" Burmese edition, I hope to at least provide some check on the reliability of the Pali Text Society's editions.

For Chinese sources, I have referred to the standard Taishō edition of the Buddhist canon, and other standard editions for noncanonical or non-Buddhist sources. I am aware that the Taishō edition is not always entirely reliable, but a re-edition of every citation was not possible.

In the case of Tibetan materials, I have attempted to edit all passages I cite from canonical collections (Kanjur and Tanjur), except in the rare cases in which reliable editions already exist. For Kanjur texts I have had access to the sTog, Peking, and Derge editions, while for texts in the Tanjur to the Peking and Derge editions only. Such citations may therefore be considered as only minimally "critical." Since it has not been possible to reproduce my provisional editions of cited passages in this volume, I intend to make them available on a website in the near future. For noncanonical Tibetan sources, I have in most cases had access only to single editions.

Non-Buddhist sources are cited according to the best published editions, in the case of the *Mahābhārata*, for instance, the Poona critical edition.

A final note on the bibliography: family names are alphabetized according to the primary element. Thus de Jong is found under J, and von Hinüber under H, for instance.

Abbreviations

For Pāli sources:

DPG: Dhammagiri-Pāli-Ganthamālā. Publication of the Burmese Sixth Council edition of the Pāli canon in Devanāgarī script. Dhammagiri, Igatpuri: Vipasanna Research Institute, 1993–1998.

For Tibetan sources:

D: The Derge Kanjur and Tanjur. For the most part I have used the reproduction of the *par phud* (first edition) printing by the 16th Karmapa published on CD ROM by the Tibetan Buddhist Resource Center, New York.

P: The Peking Kanjur and Tanjur. I have used the reprint edition published in Kyoto by Otani University.

S: The sTog Kanjur. For the most part I have used the reproduction published on CD ROM by the Tibetan Buddhist Resource Center, New York.

For Chinese Buddhist texts:

T. 1234 (I) 123a12–13 (*juan* 1): The text numbered 1234 in the Taishō canon, found in volume I, on page 123, register b, lines 12–13, which is part of *juan* 1 of the text in question.

For some works not found in the Taishō edition I have used the following:

Zokuzōkyō: *Dainihon Zokuzōkyō* (Kyoto: Zōkyō shoin, 1905–1912).

I.83.3,218d15–16 refers to the first group of volumes (*daiippen*), case (*chitsu/kan*) or set (*tō*) 83, volume (*satsu*) 3, page 218, register d, lines 15 to 16.

Others:

Mahāvyutpatti: I have used Sakaki 1916, cited by entry number, but in every case the entries themselves were checked against Ishihama and Fukuda 1989.

Introduction

Our journey begins with a story—and I use the terms "narrative," "story," and "tale" more or less interchangeably, along with other words such as "account," rather than employing them as strict technical terms of folklorisitics or literary studies. The story at the core of this experiment is one of a man who has sex with his mother and kills his father. For some—to cite Hillel entirely out of context—all the rest is commentary. Psychoanalytically minded readers may find my interest in historical detail both overwhelming and ultimately irrelevant in light of the deeper psychological truths in play here. My own interests, however, lie more in the Buddhist traditions of India than they do in the abstractions of human psychology (if on a deep level these two can actually be fully separated). Hence, how and why Buddhist authors told their stories I see as questions not merely of Freudian import, but also as opening windows to Buddhist self-understandings. I will argue that Buddhist authors intentionally took up and deployed the story of an Oedipal antihero to prosecute a particular agenda of sectarian polemical propaganda. In order to understand what they did, why they might have done it, and how their tactic appears to have been received, I attempt to reconstruct ancient Indian—and particularly Buddhist—attitudes toward incest. In doing so I hope to visualize the environment within which the core story would have been received; further discussions of the wider significance of Indian attitudes may be reliably engaged in only upon this basis.

An introduction to the structure of the book will help to make clear its overall intentions. I have divided the work into twenty chapters, the first of which is dedicated to setting out the basic problematics with which the remainder attempts to come to terms. In Chapter 1 I introduce the core narrative of the man called Mahādeva, who has a love affair with his mother and kills his father. I then explore how and why this story provides a good point of departure for asking questions about the development of sectarian Buddhism in India on the one hand and the putative universality of social or psychological norms with respect to incest on the other.

Chapter 2 introduces the historical situation of early Indian Buddhist sectarianism and the explicit polemical context within which the story of Mahādeva is related in an important scholastic text, the **Abhidharma Mahāvibhāṣā*, while Chapter 3 offers a somewhat more detailed look at the story itself and its narration. Chapter 4 briefly discusses indigenous Indian Buddhist thinking about the stock set of crimes of which Mahādeva is accused, in which, interestingly, no great stress is put on his incest, the focus being rather on his murders (for having murdered his father, he goes on to kill a Buddhist saint and his mother as well). The overwhelmingly positive nature of Buddhist ethics is highlighted in this context by the fact that commission of even the worst imaginable crimes does not lead to eternal damnation, that idea playing essentially no role in Buddhist thought or mythology.

Chapter 5 investigates what other traditional Buddhist sources relate about the story of Mahādeva, and looks at how his story is told in East Asian and Tibetan Buddhist sources as well. Although these later traditions may represent developments of Indian thinking, rather than strictly reflecting Indian ideas or interpretations, as a sort of native commentary authored by those from within the tradition they serve as valuable resources for our understanding.

Since the story of Mahādeva is presented as a justification or rationale for the creation of the initial schism that split the previously unified monastic community, it is important to survey the ways this schism is portrayed in traditional sources. This is the task of Chapter 6, which introduces the accounts of Buddhist doxographies. Here, too, some attempt is made to understand why the character of Mahādeva may have been chosen for the role of instigator of the schism, with particular attention to the significance of his name.

Where did the authors or editors of the story of Mahādeva find their material? Is it a historical account or something else? Chapter 7 presents what I believe must represent the source of the story in the tale of Dharmaruci, as found in the *Divyāvadāna*, a collection of Buddhist stories transmitted separately from their original homes, but which are mostly traceable to the literature of monastic rules (Vinaya). In the story of Dharmaruci we find the same basic narrative of an Oedipal criminal, yet no connection with any sectarian or schismatic concerns. This sets the stage for my contention that the compilers of the **Abhidharma Mahāvibhāṣā* intentionally borrowed the story of Dharmaruci, fitting it to their own needs.

Chapter 8 explores the portrayal of the protagonist Mahādeva/Dharmaruci, and through an examination of the manner in which his moral culpability is presented begins to support the argument that the Dharmaruci story was intentionally and self-consciously adapted and transformed into the calumnious story of Mahādeva. In this context, issues related to sexual assault and psychological conditioning are considered and the applicability of modern discussions of these problems to ancient Indian society debated.

Chapter 9 briefly introduces a trope Indian Buddhist sources share with literatures from the classical Greek and Roman world to China—that of the "perverse Persians" for whom, it is alleged, incest was a religious obligation. The purpose of this survey is to establish that the ancient Indians, like their neighbors, strongly disapproved of incest, notwithstanding the fact that the explicit objections to Mahādeva's behavior all center on his murders and demonstrate no overt concern with his incest. Part of my overall argument is that although Indian Buddhists may not discuss it in the context of the Mahādeva story, they certainly were concerned with incest, which they did find objectionable, although not unimaginable. Buddhist treatments of incest nevertheless appear to stand is contrast to those of ancient Indian Hindu sources, an issue considered in Chapters 15, 16, and 17.

Chapter 10 explores the motif of the bedtrick, the literary device in which sexual partners are portrayed as unaware of their mutual identities or where one partner is unaware of the identity of the other. Here I argue, once again, that a crucial transformation took place when the story of Dharmaruci was altered into that of Mahādeva, a reorientation in which the protagonist was intentionally made culpable.

Chapter 11 introduces a second Indian telling of the story of Dharmaruci, that of the eleventh-century Kashmiri poet Kṣemendra. Kṣemendra's presentation, which is directly based on that in the *Divyāvadāna*, gives us a rare opportunity to see how a traditional reader understood and retold the story of Dharmaruci.

In Chapter 12 we turn to other presentations of the same basic plot, in many of which the central character is differently named. This survey allows us to gauge the popularity of the story in surviving Buddhist literature and to further the argument that a pre-existing story was taken over by the compilers of the **Abhidharma Mahāvibhāṣā* with self-conscious intent. Chapter 13 widens the scope by taking cognizance of a range of incest stories in Indian Buddhist literature, with the goal of gaining some appreciation for the extent of this motif in Indian Buddhist culture. We find, somewhat surprisingly, that the motif exists here and there in Indian Buddhist texts, a presence the important further implications of which are explored later. Chapter 14 focuses on a lengthy tale of a woman named Utpalavarṇā, later to become a famous nun, and the multiple instances of incest that punctuate her life story. This is followed in Chapter 15 by a broader look at the Oedipal in ancient Indian society in general framed by an examination of the ideas of A. K. Ramanujan and Robert Goldman concerning what Ramanujan has called the "Indian Oedipus." Here we enter a more theoretical realm, one dealing with cross-cultural patterns of thought and the nature of the human psyche.

The Buddhist evidence uncovered in the earlier chapters, I argue, may challenge the hypotheses of Ramanujan and Goldman, but additional evidence may also be found in other sources. Some of this evidence forms the focus of Chapter 16, which studies the motif of Joseph and the wife of Potiphar, stories of a mother-figure's attempts to seduce a son-figure. Examples of both Buddhist and non-Buddhist stories demonstrate that the motif of mother-son incest, one crucial leg of the Oedipal tripod, is relatively widely found in classical Indian literature, albeit in slightly displaced fashion. Further evidence for the presence of the Oedipal in ancient India, overlooked by Ramanujan and Goldman, may be discovered even in several Purāṇas, scriptures highly valued by Hindu traditions. Two instances are studied in Chapter 17, which explores their differences from and similarities to Buddhist presentations of the same theme.

Chapter 18 is devoted to a contrastive case from medieval Europe, in which we find in the tale of the Oedipal Judas a presentation structurally remarkably similar to, but ultimately conceptually quite different from, that of the Indian Buddhist Mahādeva. The starkest contrast comes from the work the respective tales were made or expected to do: the Judas tale was a more or less popular recounting one clear purpose of which was antisemitic incitement, while the Mahādeva story was always focused internally, on intra-Buddhist sectarian concerns and quarrels.

In Chapter 19 I turn to the basic question of what may have inspired its authors to deploy the Oedipal tale of Mahādeva. Here I investigate the hold that incest has on human mentality and try to trace the social and biological bases of that fascination. Modern scientific thinking sees the roots of incest abhorrence in both biological and psychological causes, and I suggest that an understanding of these factors helps us see how ancient Indian attitudes, Buddhist and non-Buddhist alike, fit into larger human concerns.

The final chapter, "Forging Mahādeva," argues that the authors of the Mahādeva story self-consciously utilized a pre-existing story of an Oedipal criminal, the story we now know as the tale of Dharmaruci, in order to promote their own sectarian agendas and demonize their opponents. This story and others we have encountered not only challenge the picture Ramanujan and Goldman have painted of an Indian Oedipus, a picture based solely on non-Buddhist sources, but they also illuminate the diversity of ancient Indian worlds of thought. This in turn raises questions with regard to some of the ways ancient Indian evidence has been used in comparativist universal and theoretical discussions of the Oedipal. Finally, my "essay" ends—for here perhaps "concludes" is not the best word—with an appreciation of the position in which the ancient Indian Buddhist historians found themselves as they tried to understand Mahādeva's history, both in the sense of a chronicle of what happened and as a lesson for how to understand and appropriate the past. In this sense, I suggest, our job as modern historians does not fundamentally differ from that of the historians of old.

1
Incest and Schism

Long ago there was a merchant in the kingdom of Mathurā. He married while still a youth and soon his wife gave birth to a baby boy. The child, who had a pleasing appearance, was given the name Mahādeva.

Before long, the merchant went on a long journey to another country, taking with him rich treasure. Engaging in commercial ventures as he wended his way, a long time passed without his return. The son, meanwhile, had grown up and defiled his mother. Later on, he heard that his father was returning and he became fearful at heart. Together with his mother, he contrived a plan whereby he murdered his father.

This deed of his gradually came to light, whereupon, taking his mother, he fled to the city of Pāṭaliputra, where they secluded themselves. Later, he encountered a saint-monk from his native land who had previously been patronized by his family. Fearing that his crime would be exposed, he devised a plan whereby he murdered the monk.

Mahādeva became despondent. Later still, when he saw that his mother was having sexual relations with another, he said to her in raging anger: "Because of this affair, I have committed two serious crimes. Drifting about in an alien land, I am forlorn and ill at ease. Now you have abandoned me and fallen in love with another man. How could anyone endure such harlotry as this?" With this excuse, he also murdered his mother.

Inasmuch as he had not entirely cut off the strength of his roots of goodness, Mahādeva grew deeply and morosely regretful. Whenever he tried to sleep, he became ill at ease. He considered by what means his serious crimes might be eradicated. Later, he heard that the Buddhist monks were in possession of a method for eradicating crimes, and so he went to the Kukkuṭārāma monastery. Outside its gate he saw a monk engaged in slow walking practice, reciting a hymn:

> If someone has committed a serious crime,
> He can eradicate it by cultivating goodness;

> He could then illuminate the world,
> Like the moon coming out from behind a screen of clouds.

When Mahādeva heard this, he jumped for joy. He knew that by taking refuge in the Buddha's teachings his crimes could certainly be eradicated. Therefore he went to visit the monk. Earnestly and persistently, Mahādeva entreated the monk to ordain him. When the monk saw how persistent Mahādeva's entreaties were, he ordained him without making an investigation or asking any questions. He allowed him to retain the name Mahādeva and offered him admonitions and instructions.

THIS STORY from a nearly two-thousand-year-old Buddhist text, composed by Mahādeva's sectarian rivals, continues by describing how, after rising to prominence, he preaches a heretical doctrine and thus forces a schism in the previously unified monastic community. When I first encountered it more than two decades ago, while fascinated I pigeonholed it for myself as a transparent attempt to dismiss an opponent and his teachings by vilifying him with a calumnious, ad hominem attack. But the story stayed with me. And as I continued to study it, it kept raising question after question in my mind: Where did it come from? Did ancient Indian authors borrow the motif from the Greeks? Just who is this Mahādeva—was he a historical personage? Was he really responsible for the basic schism that brought about the first two sects of Indian Buddhism? How did the story function as polemical rhetoric? And from another point of view, is it possible that I misread, or over-read, the story, perhaps because of my own assumptions about the Oedipal? Might ancient Indians, I began to wonder, have thought about incest and patricide[1] significantly differently than we moderns are wont to, and if so, how would this have affected the meaning the story held for its authors? With this doubt in mind, I began to wonder whether it is even acceptable to speak of an Oedipus complex in India at all, and if not, what this might mean for its alleged universality. These are questions of Buddhist and Indian Studies, of history, of comparative folklore, and of psychology. As such, they might seem not only to belong to separate disciplines, but also to be best treated by separate authors. I have come to see all these questions, however, as intimately related to one another, and their answers equally mutually informative. In the pages that follow, I hope to demonstrate the connections I have detected and to portray as clearly as I can how Indian Buddhist sectarian polemics and the institutional development of organized Buddhism, Indian thinking on sexual morality and intergenerational relations, and cross-cultural and theoretical speculations about some of our most basic human urges and dispositions toward sex and violence together illuminate, and are illuminated by, the ancient Indian Buddhist story of Mahādeva.

Several tasks confront us if we wish to carry out an informed and contextualized investigation of this Mahādeva story. We must first understand how the story is told, and how it is retold, for in these tellings and retellings we will find the basic stuff out of which to build our model of how the tale functions. We must likewise understand its contexts in Buddhist literature and history and doctrinal disputes. And we must understand how its key elements would have been perceived by traditional audiences, something we can learn only by familiarizing ourselves with some of the things readers of the story would themselves have known. To anticipate a basic conclusion, I will argue that the story of Mahādeva represents an intentional modification of an earlier tale, in particular through an intensified and refocused depiction of the protagonist's evil character. The tale of a victimized youth seduced by his mother was transformed into the story of a sexually and physically violent aggressor. I will explore both how and why this was done, and in the process ponder why incest is so frequently considered, in India as elsewhere, the paradigm of immorality. But there are many forms or configurations of incest; are some worse than others? If we can demonstrate that ancient Indians felt they were (and we can), does this help us to understand how the tale of Mahādeva was constructed? For these, ultimately, are basic questions: how was the tale of Mahādeva created, to what ends, and what about it assured its authors that it would be capable of executing the task with which they entrusted it, the task of discrediting their adversaries?

Insofar as we can separate them from our other concerns, questions with a specifically Buddhist Studies focus include those regarding the details of the sources within which we find our information, the interrelationships among these sources, and what roles they may have played in the ideological history of Indian Buddhism. Such discussions run the risk of becoming tangled and sometimes overly technical. Yet if we do not set the stage, little of what will be acted upon it will make sense, and whatever conclusions we might want to draw will rest on flimsy foundations. So some attention must be directed to fairly detailed collections of evidence and the clear establishment of chains of reasoning.

I think it is obvious that we are primarily interested in learning about the past for what it can tell us about ourselves. This is why certain things about the past interest us more than others, and why what may appear to us as most significant may not have seemed so to those whose lives and ideas we study. An ancient story of incest and patricide, for instance, may hold a particular attraction for us because we have been conditioned by a century of psychological thinking to accept that there is something universal in the trope of the "Oedipal fantasy."

But are we not assuming our conclusion when we presume that a story so distant from us in time and in cultural presuppositions nevertheless has something to say to us, and thus about us, today?

To make any story meaningful, we must distinguish between what we read *in* the story and what we read *into* it. Both kinds of readings are necessary. If we do more reading *into* than we do reading, we do not permit the past to teach us, while if we do not read ourselves into a story at all, we do not allow it to reach us. Creative discovery emerges from a balanced interaction between facts and the imaginative ways we organize them. When historians attempt to narrate the past for a present audience, their success or failure depends (among other things) on the internal consistency of their story and on its correspondence with other stories believed to be true. In this regard at least, we can expect from traditional Buddhist historians the same approach we can expect from contemporary scholars. How, then, are Buddhist authors telling their stories? What they are reading into their sources? And how they are fashioning their past in ways meaningful to them in their present?

This approach to sources and their interpretation is valid and necessary for any historical enterprise, but tracing the history of religious traditions can present particular problems for modern scholarship. It is especially difficult when the tradition in question has often been treated as a special case, and all the more so when the object of study brings with it its own theoretical, and more importantly emotional, complications. Our story, about Buddhism, incest, and internecine conflict, has such complications in abundance.

Buddhism, as perhaps all religions, is often imagined to stand with only one foot on the ground in the world of history, the other leg somehow floating in a transhistorical, preternatural, and indeed supramundane void. Many inside such traditions, and not a few outside them as well, see Truth and its embodiment as an—or even *the* unique—integral element of a religious tradition, and thus understand the essential core of a religion to lie outside the realm of the senses. In this light, the historian faces a challenge if he would attempt to address that tradition according to the canons of historical criticism applicable to all other sorts of mundane phenomena. Therefore, the historian of religion has two stools between which to fall: he must honor the facts, but he must animate them. If he merely collects and adds up the facts of the world he cannot make those facts speak, or at least say anything of interest. As Alain Boureau warns us, "The historian tends to sketch, in ever increasing detail, with the vain hope that the series, the accumulation will shape itself into a cause, asymptotically. But facts remain mute, or return only a simple echo."[2] This leaves no story to tell, for piling up facts has them merely recited without plot or narrative. By reading only "on the lines," the historian ignores those aspects of the tradition he seeks to chronicle that, while real, lie beneath the surface and are able to yield themselves only to an imaginative decoding. At the same time, historians of religion have a special temptation they must avoid. If in reading between the lines they allow themselves to imagine the transcendent elements of a religious tradition as if they have the same reality as facts that can be seen and verified in this world, their work cannot help but move from the realm of careful, justifiable reconstruction to that of fiction—interesting, even stimulating, but ephemeral and imaginary.[3]

Buddhism has been subjected, over the years, to a grandiose amount of mystification. Myriad are the books, for example, which profess to explain how and why Buddhism is a technology conducive to the attainment of human perfection. Such investigations are almost by definition ahistorical and synchronic. The present study, in contrast, is intended as a historical investigation: it sets out to explore one aspect of the Buddhism of ancient India in a human context. At the same time, it is a meta-history or critical historiography. Therefore, as we investigate a set of stories, some of which explicitly claim themselves to be histories, ostensibly concerning the background of the originary and fundamental division within the institutional organization of Indian Buddhism—an event claimed to have taken place somewhat more than a century after the Buddha's death, perhaps in the fourth or third century B.C.E.—our questions will be historical. But as we ask how the story tellers narrate their tales, and how they attempt to accomplish their ideological goals rhetorically and otherwise, our focus shifts to the historiographical.

What, then, of the psychology of our investigations? Some of the greatest intellectual debates of the past century have revolved around the legacy of Sigmund Freud. No one, certainly, can deny the tremendous impact of his thought; indeed, much of the way we now think, much of what we consider "modern thought," tacitly assumes and constantly takes for granted ideas pioneered or promoted by Freud. None is more important than the basic notion that there exists an unconscious, or that human beings have drives of which they themselves are often not fully aware. Not all of Freud's legacy deserves to be preserved, however. One of his most central theories has also proved to be one of the most consistently controversial, namely, his concept of the so-called Oedipus complex, which speaks to some of our most basic urges and emotions. The theory is sometimes understood to say that, although they repress such feelings, all sons hate and really want to kill their fathers and desire to have sex with their mothers—or for women, the inverse (although this aspect is even more controversial). While this may not be an entirely fair and accurate characterization of Freud's actual ideas, the full theory (assuming for the moment that Freud himself maintained a single theory, which he plainly did not) has its weaknesses and even its absurdities.[4]

There are big questions in play here, about what it means to be human and the commonalities we humans all share, whether by virtue of our nature or through universal aspects of our nurturing. Since it is beyond doubt that a great deal of who we are we owe to the psychological dynamics that sculpt our early lives, we must wonder whether some of the same forces are at work on every human being in every time and in every social setting, and if they are, how we might explain them.

In a nutshell—if one will pardon the expression in a psychological context—the central question regarding the universal validity of the Oedipus complex comes down to this: do all sons in all societies feel the same basic way about all fathers and all mothers? Now, there is no reason we should limit our considerations of any theory to the particular form in which it was propounded by its originator; to do so would be to give the first expression of the theory a quasi-religious, canonical status, something completely antithetical to the scientific spirit. Consequently, since we are not engaged in a history of psychoanalysis, we need not concern ourselves with how Freud himself may have conceived of "the" Oedipus complex. Instead, we should direct our attention to the forms under which the theory has been, and might further be, modified to take into account the full range of relevant evidence. From this perspective we may ignore the fact that the details of Freud's ideas regarding infantile development have been thoroughly disproved. A suitably modified version of a universal Oedipal complex might be able to address general patterns of intergenerational tensions and take into account all configurations of the intergenerational relations which are held to characterize it, including especially those in social and historical contexts not envisioned by the original articulations of the theory. Such an accounting will be necessary if the theory as a whole is to claim comprehensive validity. Our aim, however, is significantly more limited, and shifts the focus solidly from universal claims to local identities. We will examine regional and, as I will argue, subcultural patterns, primarily those that appear in ancient Indian Buddhist literature. Scholars have already spoken about Oedipal patterns in India and have offered some general hypotheses regarding the place of Indian evidence in comparison with classical models. I aim to refine and revise these generic claims about India in light of Buddhist evidence previously not taken into account, and to place this new evidence in a meaningful framework, in both an Indian and a comparative light.

Previous studies of Indian materials have suggested the need for regional modifications to the pattern of the Oedipus complex as Freud proposed it, or as it can be schematized on the basis of its Greek presentation. Despite earlier suggestions that India lacked such a complex altogether, more than thirty years ago the folklorist A. K. Ramanujan, and following him the Sanskritist Robert Goldman, forcefully suggested its existence in both ancient and modern Indian sources. What they found, however, is not the classically patterned Oedipus complex of Sophocles (and Freud), but a variant with a particular architecture which Ramanujan dubbed "The Indian Oedipus." This suggestion fits into a more global approach, which recognizes variant, transformed, or even suppressed expressions of the complex in different (especially non-European) cultural contexts.[5] Just how such contexts are defined, however, is a key point, and the mere localization of evidence in time and space a rather blunt tool. In particular, there is not now, nor has there ever been, only one "India," and thus we should be wary from the outset of the idea of a single Indian Oedipus.

If general patterns of intergenerational tensions are indeed universal, expressing themselves differently in variant contexts, there is no reason to think that such contexts are necessarily grossly circumscribed by geography or language, for instance. But because Ramanujan dealt primarily with contemporary oral folktales of southwestern India, we cannot expect to bring our ancient Indian sources into direct contact with his modern materials. Of more immediate interest is the opinion of Robert Goldman, who, in responding to suggestions that the Oedipus complex is unknown to ancient Indian sources, maintained the following:[6]

> If the scope of inquiry in this matter [of Oedipal conflict in the Sanskrit epics, the *Mahābhārata* and the *Rāmāyaṇa*] is restricted to materials that conform closely to the classical legend of Oedipus, i.e., a legend in which a son actually kills his own father and marries his mother, then indeed one is hard put to find any such episodes in all of the Sanskrit literature. Even if one allows for the extraordinarily strongly expressed taboo on maternal incest that is characteristic of Indo-Aryan culture and excludes or represses this part of the story, it is still difficult to find Indian myths or legends in which a son kills or even shows any significant aggressive behavior towards his actual father.

The conclusion Goldman draws from this (as we shall see, alleged) absence is the following:[7]

> [I]n traditional India's strictly hierarchical and rigidly repressive family, representation of a son actually attacking his own father or entertaining sexual thoughts about his own mother is subject to the strictest sort of taboo. . . . [T]he rule is that active oedipal aggression must, in general, whether in the law books, the epics or the conscious mind, be displaced onto father and mother surrogates.

Goldman is willing, even eager, to defend the position that India knows an Oedipus complex, but for him this is a transformed, displaced complex, one that does not directly resemble the Greek model and thus differs from the constellation imagined by Freud as well. It is also a complex that concentrates on the aggression a (surrogate) son demonstrates for and toward his (surrogate) father, with little room for the mother-son relation of desire and its physical fulfillment. Goldman, then, believes that the classically structured Oedipal triangle is absent from Sanskrit literature and, he implies, it is therefore unknown to classical or ancient India in toto, thus mirroring Ramanujan, who makes much the same claim for present-day India. Goldman seeks instead to substitute a widespread pattern of a differently shaped Oedipus complex, in which displaced sons display their aggression for displaced fathers. For Goldman, Indian sons really *did* hate their fathers, but the taboo structures of Indian society were such that the cultural artifacts embodied in the Hindu epic literature could not countenance such anti-filiality, and thus served to suppress and displace these patterns into other, more socially acceptable forms.

Goldman's reliance on the Hindu epic literature has important implications. Since we are talking about cultural patterns and generalities of large groups of people, our questions about attitudes may best be approached through an empirical study of cultural artifacts, sources from which we may generalize to draw conclusions of a broader social scope. If we are willing to grant that there is such a thing as a group or community character, that a collection of people, if not each and every individual, can hold certain characteristic patterns of thought, then we need to find sources that allow us to generalize from a cultural artifact to some widely held (subconscious) attitude. The idea of a bridge between the individual subconscious and cultural artifacts and the value of communal lore is expressed by the comparativist Wendy Doniger as follows:[8]

> Out of context, anything can symbolize anything; the context of a dream is provided by the personal associations of the individual dreamer, and the context of a myth by the associations of the culture. And because the culture is embodied in people, we must search for the associations of the culture in the cumulative glosses offered by a group, rather than by an individual, within the culture.

To find the patterns that are the property of a group, individual evidence does not suffice. Rather, we need to seek a group product or legacy, which we will then contextualize within a culture. Myth and legend, for Doniger as for Goldman, provide us this needed window into the (sub)conscious of a culture, and the best source of for these is a culture's literary traditions. A revered source for such generalizations is so-called folk literature. From at least the early nineteenth century and the Grimm brothers, Jakob and Wilhelm, it was believed that stories and tales ("fairy tales") might reveal the inner mentality of a people. If the Grimms, or those who made use of their materials, sought, first in an age of nascent nation building and subsequently in ages of renewed nationalism, to discover a truly German spirit, in this they failed. But their failure was not one of misunderstanding the role of folk literature and its ability to reveal cultural archetypes; rather, they misapprehended the borders of the community whose mythology they sought to map and catalogue. One thing that folkloric investigations by the Grimms and others revealed was the vast extent of common stories, told and retold across national, linguistic, and cultural boundaries. Succeeding generations of folklore investigations and other studies have confirmed that stories, tales, legends, and myths preserve and can present and represent the ideology and the spirit of a culture in such a way that an investigation of such materials can indeed open a window into the "subconscious" of that culture. One issue central to this study is precisely the proper delineation of the borders of a culture or subculture. In the case of European folklore, it is clear that geopolitical boundaries do not necessarily conform to the boundaries of folk cultures. This was also the case in ancient India, where linguistic and religious distinctions were at least as important as other types of divisions. In view of this fact, I argue that certain stated or unstated assumptions about subcultural boundaries within ancient India, most particularly that between Buddhism and "Hinduism," may be fruitfully (re)mapped through patterns of myth and legend, and that the stories we will study provide an excellent set of relevant materials.

Goldman's arguments for a reformulation of an Indian Oedipus complex are primarily based on his explorations of the iconic literary corpora of Hindu India, the two epics, the *Rāmāyaṇa* and the encyclopedic *Mahābhārata*, materials entirely appropriate to investigate as paradigmatic representations of classical Hindu culture. The ancient India of this study, in contrast, is the India of Buddhism, not Hinduism. These traditions overlap in time and place, but their respective cultural loci are, in part, distinct.[9] The region I, for the sake of convenience, call "India" might more properly be called the South Asian subcontinent, since it encompasses areas from what is now Afghanistan to Sri Lanka. And since we are concerned with Buddhism, our inquiries ideally span the period from the time of the Buddha in roughly the fifth or fourth century B.C.E. until its virtual disappearance from the subcontinent in something like the thirteenth century C.E. In practice, most of our sources belong to perhaps the first century B.C.E. through the eighth century C.E.[10] It was during this same time and in this same general geographical region that the Hindu epics came to achieve virtually canonical cultural status. In contrast, some of the passages I will adduce from Buddhist literature were apparently not well-known even within the Buddhist traditions, Indian or otherwise, much less within the broader culture of ancient India. Indeed, it would appear that very little of Indian Buddhist culture left a significant impact on the broader Indian society or culture. In this respect, the materials studied below are not even remotely as representative of wider ancient Indian culture as are the epics.

And this is precisely the point. For broadly influential or not, Indian Buddhist texts most certainly form part of the overall cultural heritage and literary record of "traditional India." As such, their evidence bears on the subject of Goldman's inquiries. Goldman, as Ramanujan before him, suggests that the Indian Oedipal complex has a number of features that differentiate it from the classical, particularly Greek, pattern. Part of the following is devoted to a refinement of this broad contrast of Indian and Greek patterns, through the search for variant architectures within Indian traditions themselves. Once discovered, these different Indian presentations may then in their turn be compared with the Greek archetype (without, however, assuming its chronological or logical priority). I believe this effort to further nuance a monolithic view of Indian sources by looking not only at Hindu but also at Buddhist India will prove valuable not only narrowly (and "emically") for Indian and Buddhist Studies, but more broadly (and "etically") for folkloric, anthropological, and psychological investigations as well.

The historicity of stories that depict remarkable behavior is a concern we must acknowledge at the outset. Need we assume the historical facticity of such stories to view them as valuable cultural informants? Among the most primitive and least controversial of the lessons we have learned from Freud is that, in fact, the very opposite is the case: cultures, like individuals, reveal their "true feelings" only in veiled forms. The study of a culture's stories and myths is comparable to a psychological investigation of an individual, in which hidden motives and unconscious agendas may be discerned beneath the surface. Stories often talk about the past, and many such tales are historical in the sense that they depict actual events, although some distortion, intentional or not, is inevitable. We can, on occasion, discover the traces of willful misrepresentation and peel back the concealing façade to reveal the subsurface beneath. But this step does not absolve us from the responsibility of moving even deeper into the background assumptions and presumptions of the text. By the same token, we know that façades are often more interesting than what they cover over, and an examination of the ways in which they are formed, and the reasons for their application, can reveal much, not only about the underlying structures they ornament, but also about the architects who designed them and the artists who created them.[11]

The central pivot of the present study is a story of incest and murder, of deceit and betrayal, a universal drama to be sure, but one in which each performance remains unique and fascinating. It requires us to travel through the history of the early Buddhist communities to try to understand how later Buddhists understood the antecedents of their tradition, to explore their attitudes toward morality and deviance, and to go beyond Buddhist traditions to frame their place in wider Indian society and indeed within the context of humanity as a whole.

2

The Creation of Sects in Early Buddhism

THE PARTICULAR stage upon which the drama of Mahādeva is set belongs to a crucial time in Indian Buddhist history. Buddhist legends tell us that during his lifetime the Buddha Śākyamuni established a monastic community, his *saṁgha*, which has survived down to the present day. The members of this community—monks, and eventually nuns—were ordained directly by the Buddha himself and later by his immediate disciples, the Buddha remaining both de jure and de facto head of the community until his death. But even during the forty-five years of the Buddha's teaching career, and certainly increasingly thereafter, the original unitary community gradually diversified, for reasons no doubt in part connected with the geographic expansion of Buddhism within the Indian subcontinent itself. The exact relation between such geographically inspired diversity and doctrinal diversity—whether communities grew apart in thought and practice because they lived apart, or whether they lived apart because they grew apart—is an unanswerable question. Regardless of the mechanisms which brought about the process, at a certain point the divisions between various elements of the once-unified monastic community grew profound enough that the community split into what are generally termed "sects" or "schools." These are organizationally and institutionally distinct units that, while naturally intimately related in a variety of respects, nevertheless considered themselves as separate.[1] A word or two is in order here regarding this vocabulary.

In classical Weberian usage, terms such as "sect" and "schism" presuppose a structure in which there is an existing, established Church, from which smaller groups split off. The groups that originate through a schism with the mother Church are termed sects—they are "schismatic" in the sense that they have deviated from the center.[2] In the case of Indian Buddhism in the period with which we are concerned, this model does not apply. There is no central Church, no single normative Buddhist community. When the putative original, unitary monastic community of the Buddha splits some time after his death, it divides, like a cell, into two—one part does not secede from the other, but rather the single entity bifurcates. The resultant groups, although we term them "sects" in

English (with similar usages in other languages of modern scholarship), are not hierarchically related, with one emergent from the other. We may perhaps usefully think, then, of the original community "bisecting," with the resultant two "sections" becoming the first two sects. One way to think of the general task of this book is as an exploration of some traditionally recounted details of this process of bisection.

Debates over the origins of Buddhist sects (or schools, when a distinction is made between the two) occur not only in the modern period of Buddhist Studies, but already in traditional Buddhist scholasticism, since traditional scholars and thinkers were often concerned to justify themselves from a historical perspective. At stake for the modern scholar are questions of how organized Buddhism evolved, in what ways and over what issues some Buddhists chose to distinguish themselves from others. For traditional Buddhists, the same kind of question tends to revolve around issues of the very identity of a particular group and its own self-definition. Looked at in their broadest historical context, such debates over self-identity and the overall organizational structure of Buddhist communities encompass a range of discussions. These extend from the ninth-century Tibetan "Council of Lhasa," traditionally understood as the determining event that led Tibet to follow an Indian gradualist rather than a Chinese subitist (Chan/Zen-type) model, to twentieth-century Japanese internecine conflicts between Lotus-Sūtra-centered groups, the priestly Nichiren-shū, and the lay-led Sōka Gakkai. In the context of the oldest Indian Buddhism, the discussions generally center on problems of the so-called Councils (*saṁgīti*—literally, communal recitation), variously enumerated as two, three, or sometimes four.[3]

Buddhist traditional histories tell us that immediately after the death of the Buddha a meeting or council was held in order to codify the Buddha's authentic teachings. Five hundred of his eminent disciples gathered and, through a process elaborated in myth and legend, recited (hence the "communal recitation") and thus canonized the Buddha's teachings, which came to be transmitted as the discourses (*sūtra*) and monastic code (*vinaya*).[4] This meeting is referred to as the Council of Rājagṛha, after the town outside of which it is said to have been held. Critical modern scholarship makes it virtually certain that there is little or nothing historical in this account. Or, to put it more cautiously, we now know that even if such a meeting indeed ever took place, and even if such a codification was carried out in anything like the traditionally recounted manner, the later Buddhist textual traditions do not represent or transmit the results of that codification in any meaningful or recoverable form or fashion. What is, however, quite certain is that at some point and for some reason, or more likely for multiple reasons, the Buddhist community did split into what were initially apparently only two groups. This fundamental division that created two sects, in the sense

I have just described, is said in some sources to have been the result of the so-called Council of Pāṭaliputra, named once again after the town at which the meeting (or here we had perhaps better term it "confrontation") is alleged to have taken place. All subsequent sectarian evolutions of Indian Buddhism may be traced back, through a sort of family tree, to this fundamental split into two branches, each of which went on to produce further subdivisions. The overall historical importance of the subsects of the Mahāsāṁghika, the "majority monastic community," is not nearly as great as that of the offshoots of the other branch, the Sthavira line, the "Elders." The descendents of the latter include such well-known lineages as the Sarvāstivāda, Mūlasarvāstivāda, Dharmaguptaka, and what we now know as the Sri Lankan and Southeast Asian Theravāda.[5]

It has long been maintained, in both traditional lore and upon that basis in most modern scholarship, that the break between these two basic groups arose over a disagreement concerning the Five Theses or Points of Mahādeva, the *pañca-vastūni*. These are the allegedly heretical theses he is said to have propounded. The Sthaviras accuse the Mahāsāṁghikas of having been innovative and unorthodox, and of setting forth ideas contradictory to the traditional and correct doctrines—those upheld by the Sthaviras, who remained true to the Buddha's teachings. (In this sense, the Sthavira side may be said to have accused the Mahāsāṁghikas of schism in a Weberian sense after all.) The putative essence of the Five Points alleged to have been proposed by the Mahāsāṁghika founder Mahādeva seems to be to devalue the perfection of the arhat, the Buddhist saint considered second in his accomplishment only to the Buddha himself.[6] The precise meaning of these Five Theses has occasioned considerable discussion, and nothing even close to a consensus over their proper interpretation has yet emerged.[7] Since, however, it is the fifth and final point that is most relevant for what is to follow, we may content ourselves with a rough sketch of one version of the first four theses. Mahādeva and the Mahāsāṁghikas are alleged to have believed and insisted on the truth of the following:[8]

(1) Arhats can be led astray by others.
(2) Arhats are still subject to ignorance (despite their awakened state).
(3) Arhats are subject to doubt.
(4) Arhats can be taught by others (and are therefore not omniscient).

In the Sthavira view, the arhat is a perfect being whose awakening ("enlightenment") is equivalent to that of a buddha. For Mahādeva, an arhat is in some respects incomplete and, indeed, imperfect, a stance that was apparently a serious challenge to the traditional view of orthodox Buddhism. For the fifth and final "thesis," let us refer to the perhaps second-century C.E. compendium of Sarvāstivāda doctrine called **Abhidharma-Mahāvibhāṣā* (Great Commentary on the Abhidharma; henceforth *Vibhāṣā*). This is the source of the account of Mahādeva that began Chapter 1. The following continues the story:[9]

> Mahādeva had, indeed, committed a host of crimes. However, since he had not destroyed his roots of good, during the middle of the night he would reflect upon the seriousness of his crimes and upon where he would eventually undergo bitter sufferings. Beset by worry and fright, he would often cry out, "Oh, how painful it is!"[10] His disciples who were dwelling nearby were startled when they heard this and, in the early morning, came to ask him whether he was out of sorts.
>
> Mahādeva replied, "I am feeling very much at ease."
>
> "But why," asked his disciples, "did you cry out last night, 'Oh, how painful it is!' "
>
> He proceeded to inform them: "I was proclaiming the noble path [**āryamārga*]. You should not think this strange. In speaking of the noble path, if one is not utterly sincere in the anguish with which he heralds it, it will never become manifest at that moment when one's life reaches its end. Therefore, last night I cried out several times, 'Oh, how painful it is!' "
>
> This is termed the "origins of the fifth false view."

"Mahādeva had," the text says, "indeed, committed a host of crimes." We learned in Chapter 1 what these crimes are alleged to have been, allegations that should arouse our suspicions. The mere association of the advocate of the controversial Five Theses with a host of crimes cannot help but raise doubt that at least part of the "argument" inherent in the *Vibhāṣā*'s presentation of these theses may be an assumption of the prima facie inadmissibility of positions set forth by an individual who is otherwise known to be unreliable. It is most natural to read the text as implying that the positions attributed to Mahādeva are entirely unacceptable ab initio, since their author is morally disreputable, and in fact depicted as a fundamentally flawed, if not basically evil, figure.

Now, the "official" Buddhist position, found expressed even in rather early sources, holds that the veracity and authenticity of any teaching must be evaluated not only in light of its conformity to scripture but on its own terms as well, with regard to whether the ideas conform to reality as otherwise known. This approach is promoted in doctrinal treatises in the context of evaluations of categories such as the *mahāpadeśa*s, the "great authorities," the bases upon which the acceptability of doctrines are judged. This well-developed theory attempts to allow the evaluation of Buddhist truth claims in as objective a framework as possible. However, in fact the real acceptability of ideas and doctrines has probably always been grounded not in abstract appeals to conformability with known reality but rather in the authority of a reliable, trustworthy teacher.[11] If Mahādeva is not a reliable, trustworthy individual (because he is a horrific criminal, for instance), it fits with the general approach to authority in Indian Buddhism that any ideas attributable to him are ipso facto to be viewed with great skepticism or even rejected out of hand.

Whether or not we accept the validity of such reasoning, we need to recognize the ubiquity of the association between bad character and suspect ideas. Therefore, in a quest to understand this process of aspersion, the *Vibhāṣā*'s Oedipal calumny, we must begin by investigating the narrative structure and rhetoric of the relevant passages in those texts that present accounts of Mahādeva as the author of the Five Theses. Our chief goal will be to trace the story of the "evil" Mahādeva and—to anticipate one conclusion—to try to understand how a preexisting story of moral depravity came to be associated with an account of the fundamental schism in the early Indian Buddhist monastic community. Since it seems almost obvious *why* such an association might have been forged, given the polemical value of an ad hominem attack, we may concentrate instead on the *how*.

In the first place, we should ask what materials Sthavira authors, such as the authors of the *Vibhāṣā*, may have had available to them, what the pieces were out of which they stitched together the complex tapestry they ultimately present. How might they have manipulated and recast these sources? What can we learn about the environment within which this rhetorical strategy would have been expected to function? The directions these inquiries take will be determined by what we learn of the alleged crimes of Mahādeva, and thus it is to these that we now turn.

3
The Story of Mahādeva

The most detailed and commonly cited account of Mahādeva and his contentious theses is contained in the Chinese translation of the *Vibhāṣā*. While the theses themselves, summarized in Chapter 2, are expounded in an earlier Sarvāstivāda Abhidharma work, the *Jñānaprasthāna*, upon which the *Vibhāṣā* itself is a voluminous commentary, no Mahādeva is mentioned in that text or associated with the Five Theses.[1] The *Vibhāṣā*'s detailed background story can be divided into roughly two parts, the first being the life of Mahādeva before he entered the monkhood, the second consisting of his exploits as a schismatic monk. We will limit our attention to accounts of Mahādeva's exploits before his entry into the monastic community,[2] since it is here that his character is established and therefore here that the imputations of unreliability are made.

Scholars who have compared the *Vibhāṣā*'s account of Mahādeva to those in other texts, including later Chinese and Japanese accounts, have generally assumed the latter to be based on the former.[3] While there are significant differences among the various versions of the story of Mahādeva, differences that reveal much about how the *Vibhāṣā*'s authors worked, in many respects the *Vibhāṣā*'s account is of fundamental importance. Since the recounting of Mahādeva's story cited at the beginning of Chapter 1 is slightly free, here is the *Vibhāṣā*'s narration of the pre-monastic life of Mahādeva translated as carefully as possible:[4]

> Long ago there was a merchant in the kingdom of Mathurā. He married while still a youth and soon his wife gave birth to a baby boy. The child, who had a pleasing appearance, was given the name Mahādeva.
>
> Before long, the merchant went on a long journey to another country taking with him rich treasure. Engaging in commercial ventures as he wended his way, a long time passed without his return. The son, meanwhile, had grown up and defiled his mother. Later on, he heard that his father was returning and he became fearful at heart. Together with his mother, he contrived a plan whereby he murdered his father.

Thus did he commit his first sin of immediate retribution.

This deed of his gradually came to light, whereupon, taking his mother, he fled to the city of Pāṭaliputra, where they secluded themselves. Later, he encountered a monk-arhat from his native land who had received the support of his family. Again, fearing that his crime would be exposed, he devised a plan whereby he murdered the monk. Thus did he commit his second sin of immediate retribution.

[Mahādeva] became despondent. Later when he saw that his mother was having sexual relations with another, he said to her in raging anger: "Because of this affair, I have committed two serious crimes. Drifting about in an alien land, I am forlorn and ill-at-ease. Now you have abandoned me and fallen in love with another man. How could anyone endure such harlotry as this?" With this excuse he also murdered his mother. He had committed his third sin of immediate retribution.

Inasmuch as he had not entirely cut off the strength of his roots of goodness, [Mahādeva] grew deeply and morosely regretful. Whenever he tried to sleep, he became ill-at-ease. He considered by what means his serious crimes might be eradicated. Later, he heard that the Śākyaputra śramaṇas [Buddhist monks] were in possession of a method for eradicating crimes. So he went to the Kukkuṭārāma monastery. Outside its gate he saw a monk engaged in slow walking practice. The monk was reciting a hymn:

If someone has committed a serious crime,
He can eradicate it by cultivating goodness;
He could then illuminate the world,
Like the moon coming out from behind a screen of clouds.[5]

When [Mahādeva] heard this, he jumped for joy. He knew that, by taking refuge in the Buddha's teachings his crimes could certainly be eradicated. Therefore he went to visit the monk. Earnestly and persistently, [Mahādeva] entreated the monk to ordain him.[6] When the monk saw how persistent [Mahādeva's] entreaties were, he ordained him without making an investigation or asking any questions.[7] He allowed him to retain the name Mahādeva and offered him admonitions and instructions.

The text then goes on to note how, due to his natural aptitude, Mahādeva became a well-known and respected monk. But of course he was not an arhat as he claimed himself to be. He therefore had to explain away, as in accord with correct doctrine, the various failings to which he was prey. These explanations or rationalizations came to constitute the Five Points or Theses, to which the group that became the Sthavira order objected.[8]

The aspersions of monstrous deviance cast on Mahādeva's character cannot help but work to discredit the ideas attributed to him, a circumstance that in and of itself should arouse our suspicions. We do not have to be radical skeptics to wonder about the authenticity of an extremely convenient claim that the proponent of a set of ideas objectionable to the author(s) of a certain text is a thoroughly despicable individual. This should be as transparently suspect to us in the context of ancient Indian religious history as it is in our contemporary world, in which we would be unlikely and unwise to accept at face value, or even to credit at all, the claim of one politician that his opponent has a sexual relationship with his mother and is a serial killer. But of course, the sheer implausibility of a claim is no proof of its falsity.[9] Some people do sleep with their mothers, and some people do kill their fathers, and some perhaps even do both. There is a vast divide between sheer possibility and real probability, to be sure, but we cannot reject out of hand the hypothetical possibility of an incestuous patricide having played a prominent role in Buddhist sectarian history. Therefore, if we wish to argue against the facticity of the story, and more importantly if we wish to maintain that it represents an intentionally crafted polemic, we must elicit evidence that might refute its historicity or, better yet, positively establish the story to be a calumnious fictional account of Mahādeva's antecedents.

Since our ultimate task is to understand how the *Vibhāṣā* presents its story, it is crucial to learn how this text understands the crimes it attributes to Mahādeva. One of the first things that struck me when I initially met this story is the casual way the *Vibhāṣā* deals with what must strike many readers as the most indecent, if not the most heinous, of Mahādeva's offenses, his sexual relationship with his mother. The *Vibhāṣā* dispenses with Mahādeva's incest with a laconic statement: "The son had grown up and defiled his mother." Given the importance placed on this expression in the arguments developed below, it is worthwhile emphasizing that the key vocabulary and syntax are quite clear.[10] Mahādeva is explicitly stated to have defiled his mother, the sexual sense of the expression being incontestable. The crime for which he is forced to flee his hometown, however, is the murder of his father, not his incest with his mother. Subsequently he murders an arhat in order to conceal his incestuous relations with his mother; when he finally does murder his mother, he is, to be sure, indeed motivated by sexual jealousy. Aside, then, from its explicit mention in a single clause, and implicit reference once more, the deviant sexuality that underlies this story, that for us places it in a class separate from the masses of other stories of "mere" murder and mayhem, is ignored by the *Vibhāṣā* itself. For this text it is Mahādeva's murders of his parents and an arhat, as well as his subsequent instigation of a schism in the Buddhist monastic community, which are of greatest concern.

To understand what the authors of the *Vibhāṣā* may have been up to, we should begin by familiarizing ourselves with how Indian Buddhists thought about crimes such as incest and murder. It is to this topic that we now turn.

4
The Buddhist Context of Sin

ALMOST EVERYONE regards crimes such as the murder of one's parents as terrible. But the Buddhist scholastic tradition goes further (as it often does, for it is nothing if not systematic), and speaks of a classification of five "sins of immediate retribution" (*ānantarya-karma*): killing one's father, mother, or an arhat, drawing the blood of a buddha, and creating a schism in the monastic community. These are crimes so heinous that their inevitable karmic result of descent into hell takes place immediately and necessarily in the next life, rather than at some unspecified vague point in the future, as is usual for generic karmic results.[1] In other words, upon the death in this life of an individual who has committed one of these crimes, his or her fate will necessarily, directly, and immediately be that of hell.[2] It is for this reason that they are termed "sins of immediate retribution." These are the most serious crimes catalogued and studied within Indian Buddhist literature.[3]

Discussions of this set of five transgressions are found through the schematic and classificatory Abhidharma literature, although like many such ideas, an awareness of the concept permeates the generalized Buddhist worldview and is not restricted to the realm of abstract doctrinal speculations.[4] The five crimes make an invariable set, though the order of their presentation can vary.[5] In the *Aṅguttara-Nikāya* (Gradual Sayings of the Buddha), for instance, we find them listed as matricide, patricide, murder of an arhat,[6] drawing the blood of a buddha, and creating a schism.[7] When the *Abhidharmakośa* (Treasury of the Abhidharma) speaks of the hierarchy of severity of the items, it offers in ascending order:[8] patricide, matricide, murder of an arhat, drawing the blood of buddha, and creating a schism. The text goes out of its way to specify that of the five, patricide is the least heinous and the instigation of a schism the most severe.[9] Thus, while there is general agreement that the most serious crime is the instigation of a schism—almost certainly to be understood as motivated by the fact that this crime directly challenges the Buddhist monastic institution itself, rather than affecting a specific individual—there is less agreement over the first two items. This issue is important for us, since we want to understand how Indian Buddhist authors and audiences would have understood Mahādeva's crimes. The *Manorathapūraṇī* (The Wish-Fulfiller), the Ceylonese commentary to the *Aṅguttara-Nikāya*, explains the relative hierarchy of the two items as follows:[10]

> If the father is principled and the mother unprincipled, or simply not [particularly] principled, patricide weighs more heavily in karmic terms. If the mother is principled, matricide [is worse]. If both are equally principled or equally unprincipled, matricide weighs more heavily in karmic terms, for the mother is responsible for difficult tasks, and is very attentive to her sons.[11]

On the basis of this commentary, we might judge Mahādeva's murder of his father to be worse than the murder of his mother, since his mother's behavior was plainly immoral. This Ceylonese opinion, however, stands in at least partial opposition to one strongly stated Indian view, which sees the murder of any woman, not just the mother, as a particularly serious offense. Already the *Śatapatha-Brāhmaṇa*, a late Vedic text, states:[12]

> Prajāpati created Śrī; she was resplendent. The gods said to Prajāpati, "Let us kill her and take [all] this from her." He said "Surely, that Śrī is a woman, and people do not kill a woman, but rather take [anything] from her [leaving her] alive."

Later literatures, the Indian epics the *Mahābhārata* and the *Rāmāyaṇa*, as well as law books and proverbial literature, stress the sinfulness of killing a woman. "Women are not to be slain!" both epics repeatedly and categorically rule, comparing the killer of a woman even to the killer of a brahmin, the worst criminal (from the point of view of the elite brahmins, of course).[13] The murder of a woman is one of the four transgressions for which there is no expiation, and such a crime leads to horrible retribution in hell and subsequent rebirth as a worm.[14] The mother is a very special case for all Indians, Buddhists included, and in this regard the story of Maitrakanyaka is most instructive.[15] This extremely popular tale, known in Southern Pāli and Northern Sanskrit Buddhist sources alike, recounts the events that lead the protagonist to bear upon his head a blazing wheel of iron, a punishment which, it turns out, is undergone by sons who have struck their mothers. The notions of filiality that underlie this story clearly imply that actually killing one's mother is hardly imaginable, although, as we shall see, a number of episodes in Indian Buddhist literature do explicitly depict just such an act. In sum, the special status accorded women in general, and the mother in particular, in ancient Indian culture at large plainly informed Buddhist scholastics and led them almost uniformly to rank the murder of a mother more severely than that of a father.[16]

What have the five sins of immediate retribution to do with the case of Mahādeva? Our central source, the *Vibhāṣā*, is above all a dogmatic scholastic treatise, and in the course of its narration of Mahādeva's story it explicitly itemizes those three of the five sins of immediate retribution that Mahādeva commits, namely, the murder of his father, of an arhat, and of his mother. After mentioning each crime, the text says, "Thus did he commit his first/second/third sin of immediate retribution." This pattern appears consistently in those texts that address the issue in this context. The *Vibhāṣā* and other texts do not accuse Mahādeva of creating a schism in the monastic community, the most serious of the five sins of immediate retribution. Instead, referring to the royal decision to provide sponsorship for the schismatic group, the *Vibhāṣā* relates:[17] "The king followed the majority and supported Mahādeva's group. . . . Afterwards, according to their different views [those at the Kukkuṭārāma monastery] split into two groups, Sthaviras and Mahāsāṁghikas." The bisection of the community is described here impersonally, without implication of an agent of this separation. Why is Mahādeva not accused of this fourth sin of immediate retribution?

It is possible, although not certain, that the *Vibhāṣā* fails to do so, despite a detailed description of his schismatic activities, because it was technically impossible for him to actually cause a schism, as legally defined in this tradition. The key lies in the determination of who is legally qualified to motivate a schism. According to a number of central Sthavira lineage texts, including both the Pāli Theravāda Vinaya and the Sarvāstivāda *Abhidharmakośabhāṣya* (Commentary on the Treasury of Abhidharma), a monastic community can be split only by one who is a genuine monk in good standing within a regular monastic community. The Pāli *Cullavagga* (Lesser Division of the Vinaya) tells us, for instance, "Only a regular monk in good standing,[18] belonging to the same community, dwelling together within the same monastic boundary, splits a monastic community."[19] The *Abhidharmakośa*'s idea is quite similar:[20]

> Who is the one who splits a monastic community?
>
> > A monk who acts virtuously based on his discernment splits [the monastic community].
>
> A monk splits [the monastic community], not a layman, a nun or any other. And he is one whose acts are based on his discernment, not one whose acts are based on his impulses. He is one who is virtuous, not one

whose virtue is compromised, since the utterances of such a person are inadmissible.

The same idea is found in other Abhidharma treatises, including, importantly, the *Vibhāṣā* itself.[21] The principle appears to be rather simple: Buddhist technical literature acknowledges the possibility that schism may occur within a monastic community. In fact, it seems to accept this as an inevitability. It insists, however, that any action to instigate such a schism must be brought about by a legitimate, indeed a respected and honorable, member of the community in question, and only upon reflection, never impulsively. This cannot but strike us as peculiar, since the same literature that sets these conditions holds the instigation of a schism to be the most serious of the five sins of immediate retribution. Be this as it may, since the *Vibhāṣā* and, as we shall see, a number of other texts suggest that Mahādeva's ordination was irregular, and since he was thus according to the legal criteria most emphatically *not* a genuine monk in good standing, Mahādeva cannot be accused of this crime, at least formally.[22]

Finally, Mahādeva is not accused of the remaining transgression, drawing the blood of a buddha, but this time for a different reason. Without the presence of a buddha one cannot do him any injury, and thus one cannot accuse anyone in the period after the lifetime of the Buddha of this particular offense, regardless of his or her degree of depravity.[23] Eighty years after his birth the Buddha died and was thenceforth no longer present. Practically no one disputes this, and even those who might reject it on the essentially docetic ground that the Buddha is thoroughly transcendent and transmundane would correspondingly be constrained to admit the impossibility of harm coming to such a transcendent being.[24] Traditional Buddhist scholars, nonetheless, can always find a way to preserve every category and every list inherited from the tradition, even if it means transforming and modifying the inherited material in ways that may look to us suspiciously like innovation.

What drawing the blood of a buddha is thus understood to mean, in a buddhaless world, is the destruction or damaging of a stūpa, the memorial mound that encases relics of a buddha.[25] This makes perfect sense from the perspective of Buddhist doctrine, once one understands the stūpa as equivalent, legally and otherwise, to the absent Buddha, as recent scholarship has demonstrated is the case.[26] Commentaries and inscriptional references make clear that the destruction of a stūpa is not, itself, exactly a sin of immediate retribution, but rather "resembles" such a sin, or is functionally equivalent to it.[27] Now, our texts never raise against Mahādeva the charge of the destruction of a stūpa. The scholastic tradition, however, extends the entire list of five sins of immediate retribution by means of a new set of equivalences. Conforming to its systemic and systematizing nature, immediately following its discussion of the five sins of immediate retribution the *Abhidharmakośabhāṣya* asks:[28]

> Is it only through [one of] the sins of immediate retribution that one is necessarily reborn in the hells? [No,] one is necessarily reborn [there] also through sins of the same category as the sins of immediate retribution (*ānantaryasabhāga*). Others say: But just not immediately. What are they?
>
> > Defilement of one's mother [when she is] an arhat; murder of one certain [to become a buddha]; murder of a practitioner who has not yet reached the stage of becoming an arhat; theft of the wealth of the monastic community; and the destruction of a stūpa as the fifth: [these are] the sins of the same category as the sins of immediate retribution.
>
> These five belong to the same category as the five sins of immediate retribution, in corresponding order. One defiles one's mother who is an arhat through the performance of unchaste acts; one murders a bodhisattva who is certain [to become a buddha]; one murders a practitioner who has not yet reached the stage of becoming an arhat; one steals the wealth of the monastic community;[29] one destroys a stūpa.

Yaśomitra's commentary to this passage makes explicit the equivalences implied by the expression "in corresponding order": defilement of one's mother who is an arhat belongs to the same category as matricide; murder of a bodhisattva certain to become a buddha belongs to the same category as patricide; murder of a practitioner who has not yet reached the stage of becoming an arhat belongs to the same category as the murder of an arhat himself; theft of the wealth of the monastic community belongs to the same category as creating a schism in that same community; and the destruction of a stūpa belongs to the same category as drawing the blood of a buddha.[30] We can hardly fail to notice here that the very first item refers to incest with one's own mother, although the terms in which this text states the nature of this offense are odd.

I have translated in accord with the Sanskrit text of the *Abhidharmakośabhāṣya* and Yaśomitra's commentary thereon, and in agreement with the interpretation of the Chinese and Tibetan translators.[31] Still, there are certain peculiarities that cannot help but draw our notice, and not only with regard to the first item. Some help might come from a parallel list in the encyclopedic *Yogācārabhūmi* (Stages of the Yoga Practitioner). In the list in the *Abhidharmakośabhāṣya*, it is not clear why it should be a crime equally as serious as one meriting immediate retribution to have sexual relations with one's own mother only if she happens to be a saint. As far as I know, commentaries are silent on this point. This is doubly peculiar since the same literature has already made it abundantly clear that sexual relations with one's own mother are forbidden.[32] Moreover, in the *Abhidharmakośabhāṣya*'s discussion of the possibility of double culpability for the murder of one's father who is an arhat, we read:[33] "Who would kill his father, an arhat, would be [guilty of] only one sin of immediate retribution, because the bodily basis [of the act of murder] is singular." So in this light too the text's wording of the rape item looks odd. When we look at the parallel in the *Yogācārabhūmi*, moreover, we find the first item of the five sins of the same category as the sins of immediate retribution stated quite clearly to be sexually approaching a female arhat *or* one's mother,[34] which makes considerably better sense. The crime of incest with one's mother is thus listed as the first of the supplementary sins of immediate retribution. So at least within the sphere of influence of this doctrinal classification, Mahādeva's incestuous relations with his mother, though evidently not viewed as seriously as his homicidal crimes in a systematic classificatory sense, would not have been ignored. (It is nevertheless true that the *Vibhāṣā* itself never invokes this category of sins similar to those of immediate retribution, either in direct relation to Mahādeva or anywhere else.)

The doctrinal framework of Mahādeva's crimes is clearly provided by these five sins of immediate retribution, the "sin" side of which we have just investigated. What, then, of their "immediate retribution"? The performance of even one of the sins leads to necessary and immediate suffering in hell. That suffering, however, is inevitably *temporary*, and never eternal (although the term in hell may last a very long time). The punishment even for multiple occurrences of these gravest of sins is emphatically not damnation as such, although some sources suggest that multiple transgressions require correspondingly longer periods of suffering to recompense. The one possible exception to the claim that (at least Indian) Buddhism knows no idea of eternal damnation is the doctrine of the *icchantika*. The core concept is, however, actually quite distinct.

The *icchantika*, as most sources understand the idea, is either one who rejects the truth of Buddhism or the individual who lacks the inborn, innate capacity to become a buddha, a capacity which, according to the so-called Tathāgatagarbha philosophical tradition, almost all beings possess. Such an individual is therefore doomed to eternal rebirth in the realms of transmigration (*saṁsāra*), from which liberation in nirvāṇa is impossible. One fundamental difference between this concept and that of Christian eternal damnation, however, is that the *icchantika* does not reach this state as a result of some action on his part, and most sources very clearly distinguish the *icchantika* even from one who commits the five sins of immediate retribution. Rather, this state is, so to speak, his birthright, the way he is constructed; he lacks an essential component from the beginning of beginningless time.[35] This component, the buddha-nature (*buddhagotra, buddhatva,* and so on), is what allows almost all beings to eventually—and according to this doctrine, inevitably—attain awakening. The *icchantika* is, on the other hand, in no way fated to rebirth in hell or any other unfavorable rebirth, as is the sinner who commits one or more of the transgressions of immediate retribution. The sinner must suffer in an unfavorable rebirth, which the *icchantika* need not do, but his ultimate liberation is quite possible, while for the *icchantika* the impossibility of his liberation is what defines him.[36]

To illustrate this principle, and in keeping with our focus on potentially Oedipal relations, we may notice a rather peculiar story about the eminent monk and direct disciple of the Buddha, Mahā-Moggallāna, in which it is related that in a former life he murdered both of his parents. The story, offered in explanation for his murder by robbers in the present life, is found in Pāli in both the commentary to the *Dhammapada* (Words of the Teaching) and that to the *Jātaka* (Stories of the Buddha's Former Lives), the former version being importantly different from the latter. The *Dhammapada* commentary version reads as follows:[37]

> Once upon a time there was a young man of social status, a resident of Benares, who looked after his parents by himself, taking care of the household duties such as pounding rice, cooking, and so on. One day his parents said to him: "My dear, you're exhausting yourself taking care of the household and outside duties all by yourself; we'll bring a young woman for you."
>
> He refused them, saying: "Mom, Dad, there's no need to do such a thing for my sake. I'll serve you with my own hands as long as you both live." Again and again they begged him, [and in the end] they brought him a young woman [for his wife].
>
> She served them for only a few days, but from then on was unwilling to bear even the sight of them, telling him with annoyance "I can't live together in the same place with your parents."

The wife then tricks the husband into thinking that his aged, blind parents are littering the house with dirt and bits of food, which she cannot tolerate, such that

> even such a one as he, who had fulfilled the Perfections, broke off relations with his parents. "Let it be!" he said. "I'll discover what's to be done with them." And having fed [his parents], he said: "Mom, Dad, in such-and-such a place relations of yours are asking for you to come for a visit. Let's go there." And putting them in a cart, he went along with them. When

> they reached the middle of the woods, he said: "Dad, take the reins. The oxen will go [by themselves as if they were] aware of the goad. Robbers dwell in these parts. I am going to alight." And giving the reins into his father's hands, he alit. As he went away, he made noises, producing a yell like [a band of] robbers. His parents heard the sounds, and thinking "There are robbers," said "Dear, we are old, just protect yourself!" Making the robbers' yell, he beat his parents who were crying out to him like that, and killed them, throwing [their bodies] into the forest and going home.

This version is presented without ambiguity: in a former life the great monk Mahā-Moggallāna, one of the chief disciples of the Buddha, renowned for his magical powers as well as his wisdom, murdered his parents deliberately, in cold blood, and with premeditation. Perhaps demonstrating some discomfort with this directness, the more compact version of the same story recounted in the commentary to the *Jātaka* has Mahā-Moggallāna repent at the last minute:[38]

> Once long ago, harkening to what his wife said, he wanted to kill his parents. Leading them into the woods in a cart, he made it seem as if robbers had appeared, and he beat and struck his parents. Deprived of their ability to see shapes by their poor eyesight, they did not recognize that he was their own son, and thinking "Robbers have come!" they wailed only for his sake: "Dear, some robbers are killing us. Get away!" He thought to himself: "Although they are being beaten by me, they wail only for my sake. What I'm doing is not right." Then taking care of them he pretended that the robbers had fled. He rubbed their hands and feet and said: "Mom, Dad, don't be afraid. The robbers have fled." And he led them back home.

The context within which both accounts are presented, and the fact they are meant to explain, involve what we might call the "karmic fruit loop." Mahā-Moggallāna is beaten to death by robbers in the story of the present in recompense for his beating of his own parents, related as a story of the past. This pattern—of a present fact being explained by a past circumstance—is the standard formula that essentially defines the Jātaka and Avadāna story literature. In the commentary to the *Dhammapada*, it is explicitly stated that his repeated experience of being beaten to death through hundreds of lives is in addition to, not instead of, his suffering numberless rebirths in hells. This is a typical application of the idea we may term "conformable multiplied recompense," wherein the karmic fruit of an action resembles the action itself (a sort of *lex talionis*), but in much increased intensity, so that even a small act of generosity produces later wealth, for instance, or causing a certain form of harm results in one's suffering a much multiplied reflex of that harm oneself. This sort of narrative illustration of the laws of karma, in both positive and negative forms, is ubiquitous in the story literature, and in no way unique to this case. What I would emphasize here, however, is the fact that even a sin so grave as the murder of one's parents, constituting two of the sins of immediate retribution (one for each parent), does not prompt the application of principles other than those already in general use. This is merely one instance of a widespread pattern.[39]

This story simultaneously illustrates two things: first, we see an example of the limited effects of even the worst sort of karma. Once the fruits of any act have ripened, to borrow an Indian metaphor, the seeds that gave rise to that fruit vanish. Second, we see here an example of a type of story we shall meet several more times, namely, that of a son's murder of his parents.

It is true that these stories, or two versions of the same story, are not Indian but Ceylonese, and I have so far been unable to discover a parallel in other sources. They do demonstrate, nevertheless, that at least in the context of the Ceylonese Theravāda commentarial tradition, the commission of such sins of immediate retribution as matricide and patricide does not debar one from subsequent high spiritual attainments.[40] Mahā-Moggallāna is a great and spiritually adept disciple of the Buddha. No matter what great crimes he may have committed in the past, by dint of his own efforts he achieved profound insight into the Buddhist truth. The central point here is the temporary nature of karmic fruit, and the salvific fact that over time the results of even the most heinous of crimes can and will be overcome. The key to appreciating this certainty is the notion of rebirth: the limitations placed on an individual as a result of his actions may follow him into a future life, but not into all future lives, for they follow him only until the "karmic retributive energy" of an act has spent itself. Since personal identity is not something limited to one physical incarnation in one life (even in the absence of a "self"), restrictions placed upon an individual do not follow him into death, and thus are not permanent in this "long view."[41]

Another illustration of this principle, again with narrative relevance to our larger project, appears in what may at first seem an unlikely context. The five sins of immediate retribution find a place in the rules and rituals of monastic ordination, since in all traditions of Buddhist monasticism it is forbidden to ordain a specified variety of individuals. A general principle tacitly imposes restrictions on any individual who has either a previous social or economic responsibility, who may damage the reputation of the monastic community, or who may become a burden to that community. Therefore, slaves, royal servants, and soldiers, for example, must not be ordained, since they owe an obligation to their owners, to the king, or to some other individual, respectively.[42] Likewise, those who are ill and whose ordination would tend to turn the monastic community into a vast hospice for the sick and dying are to be denied admission. Even the ugly, who may discourage supporters from drawing near and offering their generosity, are to be denied ordination.[43] If it is discovered after ordination that a monk does, in fact, belong to one of the banned categories, the appropriate response differs, but in the more serious cases it is stipulated that the offender be expelled, if for no other reason than that the presence of those who belonged to such groups will tend to bring the monastic community into disrepute. The five sins of immediate retribution are offenses that impede ordination and, if discovered later, call for expulsion. Or at least this is what the framework sketched above stipulates.

It is one of the conceits of the literature of the Buddhist monastic codes, the Vinayas, that they record case law. They cite a story of the paradigmatic event that precipitated the promulgation of the rule in question; the story illustrating the rule is usually the story of the first offense.[44] The attribution of such stories sometimes appears to be fictitious, and Vinaya texts of the different sects sometimes attribute to the same rule different origin stories. Most of the many Vinaya rules are shared in common between the Vinayas of the different sects, but not all of the stories attached to these rules overlap in any significant way. Caution suggests, then, that such stories be read and interpreted in terms other than as reports of actual incidents that historically led to the promulgation of particular rules. With this understanding, we may turn to the following origination story presented in the *Pravrajyāvastu* (Section on Monastic Ordination) of the Mūlasarvāstivāda Vinaya in illustration of the prohibition of matricides from ordination. This is one of the five most serious transgressions, and the same text's narrative treatment of patricide is identical, so the following depiction should tell us much. The text reads:[45]

> [Once] there was a certain householder in Śrāvastī. He took a wife from a suitable family, and he had sex, made love, and coupled with his wife, and from that sex, lovemaking, and coupling, a son was born.
>
> He said to his wife: "Dear, we have had born to us a remover of our [spiritual] debt and a taker of our [material] wealth. I will take my wares and go to another county [to conduct my business of trade, so that we may survive]."
>
> She said: "Lord, do so."
>
> So taking his wares he went to another country, and there met with disaster. And [his wife] raised, nourished, and fostered her son with the aid of her relatives and with her own hands.

On one occasion, accompanied by a friend, [the son] went to someone's nearby house. A young girl was living in that house, and she threw down a garland wreath to him.[46] And he saw her.

His friend said to him: "Friend, I hope you have not made an assignation in this house."

He said: "Yes, I have made an assignation."

He said: "Friend, this house is dangerous. You must not go in, lest we meet with disaster."

After being made to wander around for the whole day, [the boy] was led [by his friend] before his mother.

"Madam, this son of yours has made an assignation at that house. I have watched over him for the whole day. Now you watch over him for the night. That house is dangerous. He must not go into it, lest the two of you meet with disaster."

She said: "Young man, you did right to tell me about this."

She provided [her son] with a bed in an inner apartment of the house, and she brought two vessels, and placing water and earth in that inner apartment arranged her own bed at the door, and went to sleep.

[Half-way through the night][47] he said: "Mother, open the door!"

"Why, son?"

"I have to urinate."

She said: "Son, I put out a jar; urinate in that."

After a short time he said: "Mother, open the door!"

"Why?"

"I've got to go to the toilet."

She said: "Son, I put out a jar and water and earth;[48] go in that."

Again, after a short time, he said: "Mother, open the door!"

She said: "Son, do you think I don't know where you want to go? There's no way I'm going to open the door."

"Mother, I'm going to kill you."

She said: "Son, I'd rather be dead than watch my son be killed."

—There is no evil act that one giving himself up to lust will not commit.—[49]

With a pitiless heart, forsaking the other world, he unsheathed his sword and cut her head off from her neck, and it fell to the ground. Having killed her he left. The evil being was shaking,[50] and that young girl said to him: "Good sir, do not be afraid! There is no one else here but this young woman."

He thought, "I'm going to tell her what happened, and I'll become her favorite," and so he said: "Dear, for your sake I killed my mother."

She said: "The wet nurse or your birth mother?"[51]

He said: "My birth mother."

She thought, "Good god, if this guy is so oblivious to moral character that he would kill his own mother, what'll happen to me when he gets mad at me?" And so she said: "Good sir, stay here—I'm just going to run upstairs and I'll be right back."

He said: "Okay."

She went upstairs, and yelled "Thief! Thief!"

He got scared and fled in fear. Going to his own house, he threw down the sword at his door and cried: "This one's the thief who killed my mother and fled."[52]

He performed the obsequies for his mother, and went away.

But the performer of evil deeds found no rest, and he visited a number of holy spots, groves of ascetics, and asked them: "Honored ones, what action might one perform to destroy evil karma?"

To this one said: "Enter the fire,"[53] another "Fall down a cliff," another "[Throw yourself] into water," another "Hang yourself with a rope and die." All of them pointed out means to kill oneself, but none a means to salvation. Then on another occasion he went to the Jetavana, and saw there a monk reciting to himself:

> Whose evil action is covered over by good
> Shines here in the world like the moon released from clouds.

He thought, "It is possible to cover over one's evil actions. I will renounce the world in this [community]."[54]

He approached a monk, and said: "Noble, I want to become initiated."

[The monk] initiated and ordained him,[55] and he began to recite with the excessive energy of a beginner; and through that recitation and rehearsal he learned by heart the Tripiṭaka, and became a Tripiṭaka master, a reciter of the teachings, one quick and ready in eloquence.[56]

The monks asked him: "Reverend, why do you strive with such energy?"

He said: "I will get rid of evil karma."

"What evil karma have you done?"

"I killed my mother."

"Your wet nurse or your birth mother?"

He said: "My birth mother."

The text continues by presenting the Buddha's order that the offender be expelled from the monastic community, and his subsequent promulgation of the prohibition against ordaining a matricide.[57] It is remarkable that the story then goes on, however, to narrate how the monk, apparently on his own volition, does not in fact return to lay life, but instead travels to a remote region.[58] He converts a householder, who is so taken with him that he has a monastery constructed for the matricide, which must have been a sizable establishment rather than a mere hut since monks come from far and wide to dwell there. "Many," the text goes on, "directly realized the state of arhatship through his instruction."[59] The story continues with the eventual illness and death of this matricide. One of his disciples, who is an arhat and therefore endowed with various supernatural powers, begins to wonder where his preceptor (*upādhyāya*) has been reborn. Using his supernatural sight he is able to survey the realms of transmigration, beginning with that of the gods and, when he does not locate him there, then descending through the realms of humans, animals, and hungry ghosts. It is only when he examines the lowest realm, that of hell, that he discovers his teacher in the great Avīci hell. Seeking the cause of his fate, the disciple learns of his master's crime of matricide. Upon the matricide's death in that hell, however—for as we have seen, no fate within the realms of transmigration is permanent—he is, thanks to his positive state of mind (*kuśalacitta*) at the moment of his death,[60] reborn among the gods. He goes to hear the Buddha preach and, in the formulaic fashion common in this literature, thanks to a sermon on the Four Noble Truths "smashes with the cudgel of wisdom the stone mountain of the mistaken philosophical view of belief in a real self,"[61] thereby attaining the stage of "Stream Winner," *srotāpattiphala*, the initial and lowest of the advanced stages of the path to complete awakening, which culminates in arhatship. When his erstwhile disciple the arhat once again surveys the realms of transmigration in search of his former teacher, he this time finds him vanished from his former abode in hell, as from the realms of animals, hungry ghosts, and men, and instead dwelling now among the gods. The disciple then proclaims: "How wonderful is the Buddha, how wonderful the Dharma, how wonderful the Saṁgha, how wonderful the recitation of the Teachings, such that now even such evildoers as these, who have experienced descent [into hell], attain a collection of virtues conducive to awakening such as this!"[62]

There is much of interest in this story, not least the odd way in which the Buddha's edict of expulsion is depicted as being, essentially, altogether ignored, not only by the monk at whom it is directed, but apparently by the remainder of the monastic community as well. It is true that the problem of the status of monks subject to expulsion is more complicated than it may at first appear and than has usually been presented in modern scholarship. In fact "expulsion" does not always and necessarily entail a complete and total return to lay life. Even in the Pāli tradition, whose monastic code is sometimes at variance with the common interpretations of the other sects, it is now clear that the most severe form of expulsion (called *liṅga-nāsanā*) renders one not a lay person, thoroughly unconnected to the monastic community, but rather places one into a liminal status in which one retains the monastic robes (hence, the emblem, *liṅga*, of the monastic state), but does not participate in normal monastic life; it is stated in Pāli texts that this is precisely the type of expulsion that should apply to a matricide if his crime is discovered after his ordination.[63] What appears to be basically the same idea is found in the Mūlasarvāstivāda tradition, as well as in the Vinayas of other sects, in which committing any of the four *pārājika* or dire offenses (sexual activity, theft, murder, and falsely boasting of one's spiritual prowess) makes a monk liable to being placed in the status of *śikṣādattaka*, subject to life-long penance, causing him to be barred from participation in all ecclesiastical procedures, rather than expelled as such.[64] At least in the Pāli Vinaya, it is explicitly stated that it is an offense to ordain one whose preceptor (*upajjhāya*, in Sanskrit *upādhyāya*) is a matricide.[65] In the story just cited, at least some of the monks who come to join the matricide—and the text is careful never to call him a monk, *bhikṣu*—in his monastery, and take him as their preceptor, have already been ordained elsewhere; the text says that *bhikṣus*, ordained monks, came from far and wide. But *upādhyāya* in Buddhism (in contrast to its more general Indian usage) denotes a technical category that refers to the monk responsible for a particular ordinand; it has no independent meaning, but signifies only within the context of a relationship of teacher and disciple. An *upādhyāya* is the preceptor of a novice monk, whom he looks after, the Pāli Vinaya tells us, as a father looks after a son, the pupil correspondingly taking great care of his teacher.[66] If this interpretation is correct, and applies equally to the Mūlasarvāstivāda tradition as it does to the Theravāda, we must conclude that the legally responsible preceptor of the arhat monk in our story is a banished matricide, who ignores his expulsion and continues to teach, run a monastery, and generally act just like an ordinary monk, if not more so, since he has in addition a host of special responsibilities, including some reserved for senior monks. One of the peculiar conclusions to draw from this is that, since the legal status of the matricide would be questionable in the context of canon law (even though the crime was committed before ordination), we may have here the case of an individual who should be technically and legally a nonmonk acting as preceptor. This situation, even if we set aside the complication of the pupil becoming an arhat, would naturally be, prima facie, extremely problematic from the point of view of that very same normative legal tradition. As irregular as this may be, the central point to stress here is what comes afterward; this story, like the story of Mahā-Moggallāna, does not make a commotion over the thorough redemption of the matricide. And this is precisely what general Buddhist doctrine would lead us to expect. Once the offender has died, he serves his time in hell, which the text mentions here quite routinely, and then, thanks to a mere (or we had better say, crucial) positive mental state at the time of his death in hell, our antihero the matricide manages to be reborn in one of the highest realms of transmigration, whence he is able to hear the Buddha preach and steadfastly set out himself on the correct path. The results of even severely evil actions are, yet again, depicted as strictly temporary.

The Abhidharma literature provides an explanation of why it is possible for even such a criminal as a matricide to transcend his sin and attain to spiritual heights. While Vasubandhu's *Abhidharmakośa* and its autocommentary assert that one guilty of a sin of immediate retribution has thereby forfeited the opportunity to create further merit during the lifetime in which he committed the crime, the text then goes on to quote a scripture (so far not positively identified), as saying:[67]

> This person is not fit to connect himself to the roots of goodness in this present life, but he will certainly connect himself to those roots of goodness when he has died [and been reborn] in the hells, or upon being born [in the intermediate state between lives].

Once the karmic seeds of an evil deed, even so severe as one of the sins of immediate retribution, have borne fruit, the evil doer is thoroughly freed from that deed, and able to turn himself to the good. We recall that for the *Vibhāṣā*, despite his having committed three of the sins of immediate retribution, Mahādeva "had not entirely cut off the strength of his roots of goodness." One might, in fact, even be tempted to see traces of a radical idea here. Unlike other karmic seeds, which may lay dormant, as it were, for any number of lifetimes, the sin of immediate retribution must bear fruit directly after death. The process from sin to redemption, then, in these five most severe cases is promised to be quicker than the equivalent process might be for less serious offenses, although the punishment is also correspondingly more acute.[68]

In contrast to the generally positive attitude toward the possibilities of spiritual progress evident in texts like the *Abhidharmakośa*, other sources, while not contradicting the doctrinal stance adopted there, nevertheless put a slightly different spin on matters. There can hardly be any doubt that the story of the matricide we studied from the *Pravrajyāvastu* of the Mūlasarvāstivāda Vinaya is directly related to a tale fragment found in the **Aśokarājāvadāna* and **Aśokarājasūtra* (Scripture on King Aśoka), both texts (or better, two versions of the same text) that likewise almost certainly belong to the Mūlasarvāstivāda, and are products, like the Mūlasarvāstivāda Vinaya, of the northwest of the Indian subcontinent. In the **Aśokarājasūtra*, the tale reads as follows:[69]

> In South India there was a man who had sexual relations with the wife of another, and used to always go to her house. His mother did not approve,

> and said to him: "If someone does such evil acts, there is no evil he will not do." The man got angry, and immediately killed his mother, and after killing her he went to another country. In that other country he could not get his fill of the pleasures of the five senses, and because of this he became deeply troubled, and renounced the world into the Buddhist community. He mastered the Tripiṭaka and became very learned. Surrounded by his disciples, together they went to Mathurā, to the Naṭabhaṭikā monastery, where Upagupta was. At that time Upagupta reflected on and thought about [the man], and saw that because he had murdered his mother and incurred a heavy sin, he would be unable to see the truths, and obtain the fruit of the path. Although [the man] had come from a great distance, [Upagupta] would not meet him or greet him. Then that monk was much ashamed, and went far away from there.

In light of the sequel to our story in the *Pravrajyāvastu* version, it is remarkable to notice that the authors of the Aśoka texts are pursuing a different doctrinal agenda. Upagupta, the famous and eminent monk, is made to proclaim that one who has committed such a serious crime will be incapable of making spiritual progress. This may not technically contradict the stance of the *Pravrajyāvastu*, since in that text it is only *after* the matricide has suffered for his crime in hell that he is able to be redeemed. For all intents and purposes the nameless criminal in the Aśoka texts would indeed be unable to profit from any teaching Upagupta might give, since such teaching would have to take place in this life, before the miscreant's death, karmic retribution, and subsequent, as it were, new start with a clean slate.[70] The stress here, however, seems to differ, suggesting a different approach to the same basic situation.

We have now seen how, and perhaps to some extent why, Mahādeva's crimes are detailed and emphasized as they are, since the triad of murders situates Mahādeva's criminality within a well-established category of paradigmatic ultimate transgressions. But there is more to the *Vibhāṣā*'s presentation than a narrative elaboration of a schematic categorization. Let us take just a moment to reflect on the manner and the style in which the *Vibhāṣā* presents the crimes of Mahādeva. The three crucial passages read as follows:

> The son, meanwhile, had grown up and defiled his mother. Later on, he heard that his father was returning and he became fearful at heart. Together with his mother, he contrived a plan whereby he murdered his father. . . .

> He encountered a monk-arhat from his native land. . . . Again, fearing that his crime would be exposed, he devised a plan whereby he murdered the monk. . . .
>
> When he saw that his mother was having sexual relations with another, he said to her in raging anger: "Because of this affair, I have committed two serious crimes. Drifting about in an alien land, I am forlorn and ill at ease. Now you have abandoned me and fallen in love with another man. How could anyone endure such harlotry as this?" With this excuse he also murdered his mother.

In this exposition, it is quite plain that the culpability for these crimes—not only the three murders, but also the mother-son incest—is laid entirely at Mahādeva's feet. It is he who defiled his mother, expressed in syntax and vocabulary that make it clear that Mahādeva is the aggressor and his mother the victim. While the authors can hardly have approved of the mother's actions, her sexual activities are described in less inflammatory language. While he "defiles," she "has sexual relations with another"[71] and has "fallen in love with another man,"[72] both relatively value-free descriptions. In contrast, when Mahādeva is made to describe this behavior, he labels it "harlotry."[73] Culpability for the three murders likewise is entirely attributed to Mahādeva, although the text does admit that he planned the murder of his father "together with his mother." Mahādeva's total responsibility for each of his crimes is, I will argue, a crucial element in the *Vibhāṣā*'s presentation.

This polemical agenda of the *Vibhāṣā* will become clearer through an examination of other depictions of the same basic history. For the story of Mahādeva appears repeatedly in Buddhist literature, sometimes in texts that place it in the same "historical" context as does the *Vibhāṣā*, namely, as antecedent to the initial schism between the Sthaviras and Mahāsāṁghikas, and sometimes in narrations seemingly without much context at all. In the following chapter, we will survey both types, while in Chapter 6 we will have a glance at depictions of the schism narrative that parallel the Mahādeva story, including some in which he himself does not figure.

5
Mahādeva in Other Sources

GIVEN THE importance of questions of sectarian identity and the legitimacy and orthodoxy of one's own teachings and traditions, it is not surprising that a number of Indian Buddhist texts directly relate the story of Mahādeva and his Five Theses. Although not all of these texts may be considered "histories" as such, by organizing their presentations of Buddhist doctrines as they do, even the more programmatic treatises assume an implicit historical framework, which must therefore attract our attention. Equally important and interesting are those works that narrate the story without such a historical context.

One of the basic questions I posed at the outset concerns the historicity of the story of Mahādeva: was he really responsible for the schism for which he is blamed? This is important because, if he is not, we must approach quite differently the question of how his story functions. A crucial task, then, must be to examine the bases upon which traditional sources other than the *Vibhāṣā* blame Mahādeva for the schism.

One of the fundamental sources for the various doctrines and ideas held by the sects of Indian Buddhism, as well as the mutual relations of those sects, is Vasumitra's *Samayabhedoparacanacakra* (Wheel of the Formation of the Divisions of Buddhist Monastic Assemblies), the lost Sanskrit original of which we have access to only through one Tibetan and three Chinese translations. The Chinese versions were translated by an unknown translator in the fourth century (perhaps Kumārajīva), by Paramārtha in the sixth century, and by Xuanzang in the seventh.[1] Of these, only the newest Chinese translation, that of Xuanzang, contains a reference connecting the initial schism between the Mahāsāṁghikas and the Sthaviras with the Five Theses and with Mahādeva, about whom, however, no information is provided:[2]

> This is heard according to tradition: About one hundred years after the parinirvāṇa of the Bhagavat, the time after the sage had gone was dark as if the sun had long ago set. In the land of Magadha in the town of Kusumapura [=Pāṭaliputra] there was a king named Aśoka. He ruled over Jambudvīpa [=India], (his protection like) a white umbrella, converting

> gods and men everywhere. At that time the great community of the Buddhist Teachings split for the first time. It is said that the reason is that the four communities argued among themselves over the Five Theses of Mahādeva, and because they could not agree, they split into two groups: the Mahāsāṁghikas and the Sthaviras.[3]

The other versions of Vasumitra's text contain basically the same information, save for the mention of Mahādeva, although Paramārtha's translation does say that the Five Theses were established by a "heretic" (*wàidào*).[4] All versions of Vasumitra's *Wheel* do, however, mention that two hundred years after the Buddha's nirvāṇa—that is, a further century after the events just cited in Xuanzang's version—a "heretic"[5] Mahādeva founded several subsects within the Mahāsāṁghika order. According to the Tibetan translation:[6]

> When two hundred years had passed [since the Buddha's death] a wandering ascetic (**parivrājaka*) named *Mahādeva renounced the world (**pravrajya*) and dwelt at *Caityaśaila; he taught the Five Theses of the Mahāsāṁghikas, and having publicized them thoroughly, he created the division into three sects called *Caityaka, *Aparaśaila, and *Uttaraśaila.

When Xuanzang renders this same episode, his account perforce contrasts this Mahādeva with the one he had mentioned previously:[7]

> When the second century [after the Buddha's death] was complete, there was a renunciant wandering ascetic who had given up heresy and returned to the truth; he too was called Mahādeva. He renounced the world into the Mahāsāṁghika community and was ordained. Learned and diligent, he dwelt at Caityaśaila. Together with the monks of that order he once again fully detailed the Five Theses, and for this reason a dispute broke out which resulted in the division into three orders: (1) *Caityaśailas. (2) *Aparaśailas. (3) *Uttaraśailas.

Here Mahādeva is not credited with (nor blamed for) the foundation of the Mahāsāṁghika sect itself, and only Xuanzang, who mentions a first Mahādeva, feels the need to distinguish this "second" Mahādeva from any other, which he does plainly when he uses the words "he *too* was called," and "*once again* fully detailed."[8] Moreover, although traditions preserved in Pāli sources, most notably the doxographical *Kathāvatthu* (Points of Controversy), know the Five Theses, they do not associate them with any Mahādeva, of whom they are, in fact, quite ignorant.[9] Because it is only in the newest Chinese translation of the *Wheel* of

Vasumitra that we find mention of this first Mahādeva, it is generally presumed that Vasumitra's original text contained no such reference. However, Xuanzang translated the *Vibhāṣā* from Sanskrit into Chinese several years before he rendered Vasumitra's treatise.[10] This sequence makes it certain that Xuanzang himself knew the story of Mahādeva as associated with the Mahāsāṁghika-Sthavira schism before he translated Vasumitra's text. The most likely scenario appears to be that Xuanzang added to his Chinese rendering of Vasumitra's *Wheel* a reference to the story of this first Mahādeva as a sort of gloss or historical background, even though no such reference occurred in the treatise as it was transmitted in and from India, or in the source from which he worked.[11] If this is correct, the evidence of Mahādeva's involvement in the schism in Vasumitra's work is not independent of that in the *Vibhāṣā* and thus cannot confirm it.

This raises a very interesting and important question for the sectarian history of Indian Buddhism. If Vasumitra knew Mahādeva only as the founder of, or party responsible for the emergence of, several subsects within the larger Mahāsāṁghika sect, what grounds are there for associating him with the fundamental first schism? Partly in response to such problems, it has been suggested that only Xuanzang's second Mahādeva, the Mahādeva he shares with other versions of Vasumitra's treatise, had any historical reality, and the association of the first Mahādeva with the Mahāsāṁghika–Sthavira schism is based on a confusion of accounts; Mahādeva and his Five Theses are to be correctly associated only with the later intra-Mahāsāṁghika schism. Nattier and Prebish state the case clearly:[12]

> The name of Mahādeva (who was known to be involved with a schism affecting the Mahāsāṁghikas), and with him the Five Theses, was only later read back into the original schism by subsequent sources. As a result, the later texts attribute the original schism of the Mahāsāṁghikas from the Sthaviras to the activities of Mahādeva, when in fact he was involved only with the second. . . . Mahādeva and his Five Theses should be associated not with the original Mahāsāṁghika–Sthavira schism, but rather with a later schism which developed among the ranks of the Mahāsāṁghikas themselves, resulting in the founding of the Cetīya sect (which later produced the Śailas or Andhakas, and the rest of the southern schools) by the followers of Mahādeva.

While the *Wheel* of Vasumitra does not itself provide many details of Mahādeva and this second schism, and in its original Indic form was most likely ignorant of the story associating Mahādeva with the first schism, several commentaries on the text are more forthcoming. For once Xuanzang attached

Mahādeva to the initial schism, later traditions elaborated on this connection, preserving some accounts that indeed do seem to be independent of the *Vibhāṣā*'s narration. However, the commentary closest to Xuanzang, that of his disciple Kuiji (632–682),[13] serves to support the hypothesis that Xuanzang based his association of the schism with Mahādeva on the *Vibhāṣā*. Kuiji recorded his teacher's oral commentary on Vasumitra's *Wheel*, available to us as the *Yibuzonglunlun shuji* (Expository Account of the Treatise [called] The Wheel of Tenets of Diverse Sects),[14] at the same time stating that he is broadly summarizing an earlier commentary by Parmārtha, a mid-sixth-century Indian scholar resident in China.[15] The version of the Mahādeva story cited by Kuiji in his commentary is merely a quotation of the version found in Xuanzang's translation of the *Vibhāṣā* and is therefore of no independent significance in this regard.[16] It does strongly suggest, however, that Xuanzang, in lecturing on Vasumitra's *Wheel*, referred directly to the *Vibhāṣā* for his account of Mahādeva.

But independent versions are available elsewhere. The *Sanron gengi kennyūshū* (Profound Collection of Investigations on the Mysterious Meaning of the Three Treatises) of the Japanese monk Chōzen (1227–1307)[17] is a commentary on the *Sanlun xuanyi* (Mysterious Meaning of the Three Treatises) of the Chinese Sanlun master Jizang (549–623). In his *Sanlun xuanyi* Jizang says the following about Mahādeva:[18] "After the 116th year [after the Buddha's nirvāṇa], there was a ship captain's son named Mahādeva; handsome and intelligent, he entered the Buddhist order after committing three sins of immediate retribution." The direct source of this nondescript version of the story is not clear, and when we come to the commentary of Chōzen, we find that it relies, according to Chōzen himself, on the story transmitted in Paramārtha's now-lost commentary on Vasumitra's *Wheel*, a version which, Chōzen notes, differs from that recorded in the *Vibhāṣā*.[19] The story recorded in Chōzen's text reads as follows:[20]

> Before this Mahādeva had been ordained, he was the son of a merchant. He was named Mahādeva; this is translated [into Chinese] as Datian [great god].[21] His surname was Kauśika. His father, whose trade was vast, went to another country, leaving his son at home. Reaching twenty years of age, his son was very handsome. [The boy's] mother was attracted to him with impure affections, and through secret means joined together with her son in stealthy liaison.[22] Ultimately six years passed without him knowing that [his partner] was his mother. Later, although he became aware of the fact, he did not renounce his affections.
>
> His father was returning from the foreign lands, having acquired a great amount of goods. When he was about to reach his home, [Mahādeva's] mother heard that her husband was returning, and fearing

that he would come to know of these matters [of her relations with her son], straightaway took some poison and ordered her son to kill [his father with it]. Mahādeva took the poison and, meeting him on the road, killed him. He took the goods and returned to living together with his mother.

Having passed much time together with his mother in this way, he began to worry that others knew, and so he took his mother and fled furtively to the land of Pāṭaliputra. There he met an arhat-monk whom [his family] had in the past patronized in their native land. And fearing again that the facts would be disclosed, he ultimately killed him.

Later, seeing his mother having a stealthy liaison with another, he also killed his mother. Having committed three sins of immediate retribution, he was deeply regretful and sought to wipe out his crimes by means of ordination. But the monks knew that he was an evildoer, and none would ordain him. Nevertheless, he ordained himself and studied the Tripiṭaka. Being of bright intelligence, within a short time he was able to recite from memory the [whole] Tripiṭaka.[23] But there were fools who followed him and received his teachings, and thus he gained a group of followers, who themselves claimed to have already attained arhatship.

We find here that Chōzen attributes to Paramārtha an important clarification in comparison with the version in the *Vibhāṣā*. As Sasaki Shizuka has pointed out in this context,[24] and as I have remarked above, from a normative point of view monastic ordination may not be conferred on one who has committed any of the five sins of immediate retribution. While the *Vibhāṣā* makes a point of saying that the ordination procedure did not include the (requisite) inquiry concerning such disqualification (and the failure to make this inquiry itself may invalidate the ordination), Paramārtha's version takes note of and compensates for this same fact by making explicit Mahādeva's self-ordination.

There is a further correspondence between these versions of the story of Mahādeva and that presented by Xuanzang: these texts know both an earlier and a later Mahādeva. Jizang speaks of a Mahādeva whom he dates to 116 years after the death of the Buddha. Slightly later in his *Sanlun xuanyi*, however, he says the following:[25]

A full two hundred years [after the Buddha's nirvāṇa], there was a heretic named Mahādeva. At that time, there was a lay follower (**upāsaka*) in the kingdom of Magadha who widely propagated the teachings of the Buddha. In order to profit materially, the heretics all shaved their heads and renounced the world, and they became "thief-monks."[26] Mahādeva was the head of the thief-monks. Mahādeva had ordained himself, and those disciples he converted were initiated and ordained by his community. At that time, everyone was arguing about this situation. The Sthaviras said: "If the preceptor (**upādhyāya*) has not undertaken the vows of monastic restraint (**śīla*) or has violated those vows (**duḥśīla*), but the instructor (**ācārya*) upholds the vows, and the monastic assembly upholds the vows, then it is permissible to undertake the vows [that is, be ordained, in that community], since vows are obtained from the monastic community. But if the monastic community is aware that the preceptor has not undertaken the vows, but nevertheless communally grants the vows, the monastic community is guilty of a **duṣkṛta* offense [against the monastic code]."

Question: "If the vows are not obtained from the preceptor, why mention the preceptor's name?"

Answer: "[First] someone wants to undertake the vows; later on, the preceptor records [his name together with that of the disciple] and educates the disciple. [The name must be recorded in order to have a record of the disciple's standing.]" The Sarvāstivādins adopt this understanding.

Other schools say: "If the preceptor has not undertaken the vows of monastic restraint or has violated those vows, then even if the monastic community upholds the vows it is not permissible for it to convey the vows, since the vows come from the preceptor [not the community]." Therefore they disputed these points, and ultimately they did not accept [the legitimacy of] Mahādeva. For this reason his followers then took up separate residence in the mountains. And among these mountain dwellers themselves there arose again differences, hence [developed] the *Caityaśaila school and the *Uttaraśaila school.

The fundamental point behind the legal issues raised here revolves around the status of individuals who, in good faith, undertake ordination from a preceptor who, it transpires, was either himself initially not entirely qualified to offer such ordination, or who, although technically qualified at one point, subsequently violated his vows in such a way as to disqualify himself. The crux of the problem is illustrated by the recorded fact of Mahādeva's having produced disciples, who then went on to develop schools of Buddhist thought and practice—subsects of the Mahāsāṁghika order. Since Mahādeva was not qualified to offer ordination, the text considers the question of whether the lineages that resulted from the ordinations he offered are legitimate; in doing so, it provides one piece of evidence of how some might have viewed the authenticity of the lineages that traced themselves, or were traced by others, back to Mahādeva. The implication here is that, in addition to other doctrinal or philosophical reasons, the traditions associated with Mahādeva are to be rejected for legal reasons having to do with the authenticity of the monastic status of those who subsequently propagated those traditions, even if their ex post facto disqualification is due to no fault of their own. It is interesting and important that this dispute is linked not to the fundamental schism between the Sthaviras and Mahāsāṁghikas, but to the emergence of breakaway groups within the Mahāsāṁghika itself.[27]

The author Chōzen, although he appears to be citing a significantly older authority, belongs to thirteenth-century Japan. And his is not the only source from that milieu that bears on our present question. We possess several other Japanese versions of the same tale, one from the *Konjaku monogatarishū* (Tales of Long Ago), an eleventh-century collection of Buddhist tales, another from the twelfth century *Hōbutsushū* (Collection of Treasures), and a third from the early fifteenth century *Sangoku denki* (Traditional Account [of Buddhism] in the Three Countries [India, China, and Japan]). Since these versions differ in important respects from those we have examined so far, as well as among themselves, it is worthwhile to notice them here despite their chronological and geographical distance from their ultimate Indian sources. The most important difference is that they do not connect the story of Mahādeva with the "historical" context envisioned by the *Vibhāṣā*. The version in the *Konjaku monogatarishū* is incomplete, a portion of the text having been lost early on. What remains reads as follows:[28]

> At a time now long ago, in India, four hundred years after the Buddha entered Nirvāṇa, there was a man named Mahādeva in the land called Mathurā. His father had gone off across the ocean to another land on a commercial venture. In the interim, Mahādeva thought: "I will take for my wife the woman who is the fairest of face and most surpassingly beautiful in the world," and though he sought her, he could not find her. He returned home, and seeing there his mother, fair of face and surpassingly beautiful, he thought: "There is no woman in the world finer than she." And he took his mother to be his wife.
>
> When they had lived together for several months, his father returned after having spent many months overseas and was about to land. It occurred to Mahādeva: "Since I have taken my mother as my wife, should my father return he will certainly not think well of me." And so Mahādeva went forth and meeting him even before he had stepped on shore, killed his father.
>
> After this, while they were living together without concern, Mahādeva went away for a short time, and it happened that his mother

> went over to a neighbor's for a spell. Mahādeva returned, and thinking: "She's gone to the neighbor's secretly and had intercourse with another man!" he flew into a great rage and, seizing his mother, beat her to death. And so it was that he murdered both his father and his mother.
>
> Fearful of the ignominy which such conduct would bring him, Mahādeva left his native home and journeyed to a distant place where he took up residence. At that time it so happened that there was [at that place] an arhat-monk from his native land. When that arhat came to the place where Mahādeva was presently dwelling, Mahādeva looked at him and thought: "When I was in my native home, I killed my father and mother. Fearing the ignominy which such conduct would bring me, I came and dwelled here. Here I stealthily concealed the matter of the murder of my father and mother. However, this arhat has come around and he will certainly make it known to people. The best thing for me to do would be to get rid of this arhat." And so he killed the arhat, and thus he committed his third sin of immediate retribution. After that, Mahādeva. . . . [29]

The *Hōbutsushū*, attributed to Taira Yasuyori (1145?–1200 or after),[30] differs from the *Konjaku* collection in a number of respects in terms of the overall characteristics of the two works. Here we are concerned only with the content of one small story, however, and in this the *Hōbutsushū* presents an unusual, if not unique, configuration of our narrative:[31]

> [Once] there was a brahmin in Śrāvasti. In order to find an attractive woman, after he searched throughout the city, [he found that] there was no woman as beautiful as his [own] mother. Therefore, he lured his mother into a deserted place where he attempted to rape her, and although his mother tried to resist, since women are helpless creatures, ultimately she surrendered. After that encounter, things did not go as he wished, and as his affection was deep, beyond bounds, in order to be together with her whenever he wished, he killed his father. After the death of his father, for a long time they lived together as he wished. Thus those who learned of this grew disgusted with them,[32] and so his mother, being embarrassed by this, found another man in a neighboring country. When it came to his notice that she had tried to go away, he said: "Long ago, you were my mother, and now you are my wife. How dare you try to embrace another man!" He grew so terribly angry that he hit her, and beat his mother to death.
>
> One day when the brahmin was passing by the Jetavana monastery, and the Buddha's disciples were disgusted and would not look at him, he

> became angry, set fire to the monastery and burned it down. Many scriptures were burned up. The Buddha felt compassion for his grave sins and was saddened by them, became his spiritual guide, and saved him. Even such an evil one as this can be rescued by the power of a spiritual guide—how much more, then, one without such grave sins, who has met a spiritual guide and vows to be reborn in the Land of Bliss. Let there be no doubt about this!
>
> The brahmin spoken about here was Mahādeva. A certain scripture says: "After his death when he was cremated, because of his grave sin [his corpse] did not burn. After it was sprinkled with dog feces, it burned," and so on.[33] Again, it seems to be recorded that when he set fire to the Jetavana monastery, many disciples of the Buddha were killed. Given the alternate versions [of this story] preserved in the scriptures, we should strictly pay careful attention to determine a standard version.

It is hard to account historically for some of the elements in this version of the story, which we might guess could have been hardly coherent or understandable to an audience not familiar with any other telling of the tale. To be sure, although different from that presented in other versions, the initial motivation of Mahādeva is not narratively impossible: the young brahmin wants a lovely woman, decides his mother is the most beautiful available and, when she naturally will not agree to his idea, he waylays and rapes her. Further, although the reasons are not elaborated upon, it is not inconceivable in this context that he should then kill his father in order to further his possession of his mother. This, interestingly, makes the story perfectly Freudian, even as it removes it from its obviously Indian roots. Still, even in light of the coherence of the narrative logic thus far, what is one to make of the brahmin's mother, shamed by talk about their relationship, taking a lover from a neighboring land, or of her trying to go away? Why is the neighboring land introduced? Does the teller wish to imply that she would go, by herself and without her son, to another country, to escape the rumors swirling about her, but that she needs the protection of a man to do so, since her husband and protector is dead? This is not impossible, but it requires the reader him- or herself to supply large elements of plot development. Similarly, the motivation for the brahmin's arson of the monastery (here specified as the Jetavana, perhaps because this was the most famous Indian monastery in Japan) makes a certain sense, even though it bears no resemblance to the logic of any other known version of the story. In this reading, it is well known that this brahmin (subsequently identified as Mahādeva) has killed his mother, with whom he previously lived as man and wife, although why the monks, shunning him, should particularly spark (so to speak) his ire remains unexplained. Finally, it is interesting to note that the Buddha's salvific actions, and the lessons to be learned from the salvation of the sinner, are placed, probably in a broader medieval Japanese context as well but certainly in the context of the *Hōbutsushū* itself, in an Amidist light, with the easy accessibility of rebirth in the Land of Bliss emphasized as a reward available to the pious aspirant. The considerable number of points at which the *Hōbutsushū*'s recension of the story differs from the core versions we are studying permits us to postulate it as considerably altered from its ultimate Indic source, rather than transmitting an otherwise unknown Indian variant.[34]

The final Japanese version we will consider here, the *Sangoku denki*, was compiled some two centuries later, in the first half of the fifteenth century, by the monk Gentō,[35] and records the following:[36]

> In the Sanskrit, it is said: One hundred years after the extinction of the Tathāgata, to the southeast of the country of Magadha, in a land called the land of Mathurā,[37] there was a man named Mahādeva, the son of a merchant. His name is translated into Chinese as Datian. When his father was on a distant journey, he became impurely attached to his mother. Upon his father's return, thinking that his wicked conduct would be exposed, he waited along the road and killed his father. Taking his mother with him, he fled to the city of Pāṭaliputra. While dwelling there, he met a monk-arhat of his native land who had always received the patronage of his father. Fearing that the arhat would reproach him for his wicked conduct, he murdered him. Later on, suspecting his mother also of being untrue to him, ultimately he murdered his mother as well.
>
> Because he had already committed three crimes of immediate retribution, naturally he felt vaguely apprehensive. He paid a visit to the monastery called Kukkuṭārāma and spoke with the monks there. Subsequently he heard the exposition of a hymn from the sūtras:
>
> Even though one commits serious crimes
> If he would cultivate goodness, then his crimes would be
> extinguished.
> It would be like the moon illuminating the world
> After the clouds have been brushed away.[38]
>
> Hearing this brought great joy to Mahādeva's heart and thus he sought to renounce the world, whereupon the monks pardoned him.[39] Before long he became versed in the profundities of the Tripiṭaka and conversant with all the twelve-fold divisions of the teaching.[40]

One of the most important facts about these versions is not readily apparent in the isolated extracts just translated. All other versions of the story of Mahādeva cited so far were drawn from "historical" or polemical contexts, from narrative or dogmatic textual environments in which the story is made to illustrate or support one argument or another. In contrast, in these three Japanese examples, the story is radically decontextualized. The *Konjaku monogatarishū*, *Hōbutsushū*, and *Sangoku denki* belong to what scholars of Japanese literature classify as "story literature" (*setsuwa bungaku*). The *Konjaku* and *Sangoku denki* collections are divided into sections of stories set, respectively, in India, China, and Japan, and are free of any overall "argument" or unifying polemical structure, save perhaps that of nominally illustrating the ubiquity of Buddhism in those three lands. This is not to deny that there may also be organizational principles governing the internal structure and arrangement of such works; in the *Hōbutsushū*, for instance, our story is placed amid others likewise concerned with the role of the spiritual guide (*zenchishiki= kalyāṇamitra*).[41] While it would be going too far, then, to say that these stories are presented without *any* context, their contexts are nothing like the "historical" context provided by the Indic sources we have examined, and the principles underlying the organization of these *setsuwa* collections do not include any detectable historical or doctrinal frame for the Mahādeva story. I will return to this issue below.

Turning from context, or lack thereof, to the texts' actual presentation, we see that the story in the *Konjaku monogatarishū* differs significantly from the other versions we have noticed so far. Among other things, it entirely rearranges the narrative sequence, and thus the logic of the actions, through which Mahādeva carries out his crimes. Since he is made to kill his mother before he kills the arhat, the motivation for the arhat's murder is also altered. In addition, the initiation of the incestuous relations between Mahādeva and his mother is depicted entirely differently, a crucial fact. Rather than merely "defiling" his mother in a contextless sort of way, as the *Vibhāṣā* presents the matter, the *Konjaku* and the *Hōbutsushū* depict Mahādeva as quite aggressively searching the world for a suitable sexual partner. It is only when he is entirely unable to find such a woman that he returns home and realizes that his mother is the woman he has been seeking from the very beginning. Her reaction to his desire and her role in their relationship remain unelaborated. Moreover, Mahādeva's culpability in the three murders is, in the *Konjaku* version, not shared with his mother at all, even with respect to planning; everything from the very beginning is attributed to his own instigation and responsibility. It is also especially noteworthy that in this version Mahādeva's mother is not said to have "cheated" on her son by engaging in a sexual relationship with anyone else; rather, he merely suspects her of having done so, since she is not at home when he returns. In his rage at her suspected infidelity, he beats her to death. This depiction emphasizes the author's intent for his audience to blame Mahādeva for all the evil in the account: there is no space to blame anyone else, not even the mother, who is on the one hand a stick figure, in that she is lovely but has no voice and no volition, and on the other hand a complete victim, who is murdered even though she has done nothing to provoke Mahādeva's suspicions or to incite his wrath. In comparing the two works, we may be justified in seeing the *Konjaku*'s influence on certain elements in the *Hōbutsushū*, even if the *Hōbutsushū* does not follow the *Konjaku* in an even greater number of cases, including some of the greatest interest to us, since in the *Hōbutsushū* Mahādeva is not even a monk.

Since the *Konjaku* account as transmitted breaks off immediately after Mahādeva's murder of the arhat, we do not know how its authors might have treated Mahādeva's subsequent career. In the *Sangoku denki* version, however, the irregularity of Mahādeva's ordination is noticed, and accounted for by having the monks forgive his transgressions, something quite impossible according to the nominally normative Indian monastic codes and which other sources do not mention, probably for this very reason.

These Japanese variants are interesting and potentially quite important. But it is not only in East Asia that we find recitations of this story in medieval times. In early thirteenth-century Tibet several sources preserve versions of the tale, some of which place it in its "historical" context, while others decontextualize it as do the Japanese sources. Although I earlier disavowed any intention to treat Mahādeva's complete career, restricting the scope of inquiry to his life prior to his ordination, when we come to the Tibetan accounts, their manner of presentation prevents us from ignoring Mahādeva's history after ordination.[42]

The story of Mahādeva was evidently known in Tibet from at least the end of the twelfth century. The first Tibetan notice I have come across appears in the **Subhāṣitaratnanidhi* (Treasury of Aphoristic Jewels), a popular collection of moralistic sayings composed between 1215 and 1225 by the patriarch of the Sa skya school, and one of the greatest scholars in the history of Tibetan Buddhism, Sa skya Paṇḍita Kun dga' rgyal mtshan (1182–1251).[43] In this work, popular both in being aimed at a lay audience and in having been widely circulated, we find the following verse:[44]

> Fully realizing their error,
> The crafty will [nevertheless] entice others with words.
> When Mahādeva uttered a wail,
> He said that he [merely] declared the Truth of Suffering.

These four short lines in themselves quite unambiguously allude to one element of the story, namely, Mahādeva's excuse for his failure to have transcended suffering. There is no doubt that this is the correct interpretation, since Sa skya Paṇḍita himself provides an extended version of the story in one of his major works, the *Sdom pa gsum gyi rab tu dbye ba* (A Clear Differentiation of the Three Codes), in which, moreover, the account is explicitly connected with its "historical moment" as the instigation for the Third Council:[45]

> After the completion of the First Council [during which was compiled] the Buddha's stainless preaching, while his teaching remained pure, the monks of Vaiśālī created ten incorrect points in contradiction to the Buddha's teaching. Then, in order to refute that inverted teaching seven hundred nobles convened the Second Council, it is said. After [the teaching] was thus purified, there appeared a monk named Mahādeva, a thief in this teaching. He killed his own mother and father, murdered a saint who was his teacher, and became a monk without preceptor or sponsor.[46] Later, he dwelt in a monastery and consumed the offerings made in faith by lay devotees. He served as preceptor and sponsor for fools [who ordained and trained under him], and the food and wealth given to him by rich fools fell like rain. He was surrounded by a monastic community of many hundreds of thousands gathered from the unfortunate devout. Then that great liar claimed that he was a saint. When his retinue requested a display of magical powers, he said "My magical powers became impaired this morning at dawn."
>
> Because he was mindful of his own [previous] sins, when he uttered a great wail, he declared "I was proclaiming the Truth of Suffering." With such lies he made the heads of his followers spin, and even those gifts of faith that ought to have been given to the nobles went to him. A great number of the foolish renunciants forsook the Saints and gathered around him. It is said that after the nirvāṇa of the Buddha, there was no assembly gathered by an ordinary person greater than his. Since students followed his instruction of the inverted teaching, there arose many competing doxographical systems. It is said that after that fool Mahādeva died, he fell into hell. I have heard that the Saints refuted those inverted teachings of his and convened a Third Council.

Very close to this version both in the time of its composition and in terms of its content is the account in the *Rgya bod kyi chos 'byung rgyas pa* (Extensive History of Buddhism in India and Tibet) of the Rnying ma pa author Mkhas pa lde'u, dated in its present form to "later than 1261."[47] The account in this text reads as follows:[48]

> Then, 110 years after the passing of the Teacher, there was a Venerable Mahādeva who was born in a merchant family. While his father was gone on trade, he slept with his mother. When his father returned, having deliberated with his mother, he killed his father. Concerned about their bad reputation, they fled to another country. There was an arhat-monk whom they had earlier patronized. When they met him there, out of concern that he might have spread their bad reputation, through a stratagem they offered him an invitation and killed him by giving him poison. Then after the mother slept with another, [Mahādeva] became jealous, and killed his mother as well. Thus did he commit three of the sins of immediate retribution. Still, his outlook was not inverted.
>
> Having removed the impediments to his serious religious practice, going to another country he then requested initiation in the monastic communities, and this being given he was fully ordained [as a monk]. Since his intelligence and drive were great, he applied himself to religion, and thus he grew full of wisdom, such that the king of the land and all of the people honored him greatly.
>
> He then became lustful, and pridefully he lied, saying: "I have obtained the fruit of arhatship." His merit increased, and the king offered him an invitation [to attend him]. There [at court] he became enamored of the king's consort. Since [she] saw him ejaculate, [she] asked: "If one is a saint, one has cut off the defilements, and thus does not produce semen, yet how is it that you produce semen?"
>
> "I am tormented by Māra. Even though I have become an arhat [**aśaikṣa*], Devaputramāra places obstacles in the way of my goodness." Because his disciples were given to idle chatter, he said to several of them: "You have obtained the status of Stream Winner, or Arhat, Lone Buddha or Renunciant."
>
> Since he said that, his retinue asked: "We don't know anything at all, so how are we able to obtain these great fruits?"
>
> [He replied] "Sure you have obtained them!" and said many such things.
>
> On another occasion, having repented since he had lied in giving inverted teachings to his disciples, at night he was afflicted, and called out, "Alas, alack, the great suffering!"
>
> The assembly heard this, and said "What is the trouble?"

> "There is no trouble at all."
> "Then why did you say 'alas, alack,'" they asked.
> He said: "I was thinking of the Noble Path. If one does not call out, it will not be clear to one." Then he summarized his inverted teaching in verse for his disciples:
>
> [Arhats] are gods beguiled by ignorance,
> Possess doubt, are manipulated by others.
> [For them] the path emerges out of verbal flow.
> This is the teaching of the Buddha.
>
> When Mahādeva said this on the occasion of expounding the meaning of the Prātimokṣa [core monastic rules] at the time of the Uposatha [bimonthly confession] rite, there were a few who were listening at that spot near to obtaining wisdom and the fruit [of the path], and they inquired into that expression [in the verse] saying: "This expression contravenes the [Buddha's] word. What you say does not put his intention in a good light. Mahādeva, don't say things like this! This is not the teaching[49] preached by the Buddha." Engaging in discussion about the wording in that [verse], they argued the whole night long. After the king, his ministers and others [tried] in turns to reconcile them, but were unable to, they said: "Didn't the Buddha formerly say anything about the means to solve a dispute?" Someone said: "Yes, he did." So, [the king] said "Please, those who did not agree with the Elders go to one side, and those who did not agree with Mahādeva go to the other."
> At that time, the side of the great Elders was left with a small number of the senior [monks], while on Mahādeva's side the monastic community swelled in numbers with young, arrogant [monks]. [Thus the monastic community] split into two, the Sthavira and the Mahāsāṁghika.

Both this and the version related by Sa skya Paṇḍita himself, relying at least in part on the same tradition, present a number of interesting features.[50] Before we explore these, however, we should also notice an even more detailed version found in the oldest known commentary to Sa skya Paṇḍita's *Treasury of Aphoristic Jewels*, that composed, sometime before 1245,[51] by his disciple Dmar ston Chos kyi rgyal po (ca. 1197–ca. 1258).[52] There we find the following rendition of our story:[53]

> Previously in southern India there was a great city called Varuṇa.[54] A certain rich householder had no son, and hence he fell to entreating the

gods. So after ten months, a son was born to his wife, and they gave him the name Mahādeva. In order to provide for a great celebration of his birth, his father went to sea in search of wealth, and he was gone on his journey for twelve years.

During that time the boy thoroughly grew up, and turned into a young man. He developed an unnatural desire for his mother, and then his mother bid him: "Son, if you want me to have sex with you and join up with you, after your father comes back from sea, when he is about to arrive, lie in wait on the road and kill your father." The son did as he was told, and concealing himself he killed his father on the road. A little while later, his mother got together with some other man, and so Mahādeva got upset, and killed his mother too. Later, there was an arhat who was his teacher, and while he was listening to some teachings from him he feared that due to his profound insight [the arhat] would make known to others [Mahādeva's] earlier sins, so he murdered him too.

Then he became weary of the things he should not have done, and not wishing to stay in his hometown, he gave his household goods to someone who wanted them and went to a place near to Central India. At that time, there had arisen a great famine in that land, and being unable to obtain a livelihood as a layman and seeing that monks were venerated and had their needs fully met, he found a rag robe in a charnel ground. Independent of any masters, he ordained himself, and adopting the guise of a monk, he settled in an outlying region.

When he went into the city to beg for his needs, owing to his previous circumstances he was not happy, and he dwelt with a displeased countenance. Over time, herdsmen who kept buffalo, goats, and sheep saw him and approached him. Mahādeva taught the Teachings to the herdsmen, making them profound and easy to listen to. When he told them that his appearance was due to his disgust with transmigration, they said: "This great meditator is cultivating his awareness of the impurity of the world. He is one who is a sincere true aspirant after the Teaching." And they had faith in him, and honored him.

Through his renown based on his false front, he came to the notice of the townspeople, and at first the women and children made offerings to him, but gradually throngs of people gathered and offered great alms to him. At that time Mahādeva accepted things from those who had and stored them up, then donating them to those who had not.

Since he flattered the people, curried their favor, and abundantly agreed with their way of doing things, the people said: "The teacher is a person endowed with both religious and mundane knowledge, and truly compassionate—he is far greater than even a saintly arhat." And so saying, they zealously and wholeheartedly made offerings to him of all the wealth they had. Even the rich opened their storehouses filled with the possessions accumulated by their ancestors, and gave them to him. He in turn gave them what they needed in the way of food, vegetables and clothing.

Although he had not obtained those qualities, he said: "I am an arhat. I have eliminated all defilements, done what needs doing." And he seduced everyone with the deception that he had thoroughly surpassed the mundane state, and everyone thought: "He is truly perfect." Some people motivated by faith, and a majority in order to procure a livelihood, requested ordination, and he consented. A crowd of people ordained, and gathered around him. Monks from elsewhere who had gathered for the sake of their livelihood vowed themselves to him, and he came to be surrounded by a retinue of some many hundreds of thousands of monks.

At that time, when he was there preaching the Teachings to his followers, in the early predawn hours, he thought to himself: "Previously I had illicit sexual relations with my mother; because of that I killed my father; later I killed my mother; I killed an arhat, and I ordained myself, wasted gifts of faith,[55] and lied about having surpassed the mundane state." Mindful of the sufferings he would endure in hell as punishment for taking advantage of many ignorant people, he thought about it and said three time: "Oh, how painful it is [oh, suffering]! How painful it is!"

Some of the students in the huts [in his monastery] heard him speaking like this, and the next morning they asked him: "Master, if an arhat is free of suffering, why did you loudly complain this morning at daybreak?"

The master said: "What are you talking about?"

They said: "You spoke in such-and-such a manner."

The master said: "Didn't you hear the rest?"

They said: "No, we did not hear."

The master said: "I was naming the truths; I proclaimed: 'Oh, its arisal! Oh, its cessation! Oh, the path!' You did not hear the others."

Even though the students were ignorant, they had some doubt because of all his different facial expressions, and one said: "Well then, master, if you are an arhat, why didn't you know the answer to our question about the Teachings?"

He was worried, and said: "There are those like Śāriputra too, disciples who are messengers of the Teacher who are like this. The teacher alone has passed beyond doubt."[56]

Everyone gathered there asked the master to show them a display of his magical powers.

"My arhatship was destroyed early this morning; I don't have any magical powers."

"Can they be destroyed?'

"Certainly. It is said that 'Destruction is a quality of an arhat.'[57] In the same way, an arhat has the quality of ignorance mentioned earlier. He has the quality of looking after others. He has the quality of admonishing people."

And although he curried favor with them in this way, to the dissatisfied assembly he said: "Nevertheless, I do have magical powers. There are mistaken interpolations and omissions in the scriptures preached by the Blessed One."

It is said that after he died, he fell into hell.

Dmar ston's version of this story clearly belongs to the same tradition as that recorded by his teacher, Sa skya Paṇḍita, and by Mkhas pa lde'u; probably the elaborations Dmar ston records are elements he heard from Sa skya Paṇḍita or obtained from some source parallel to Sa skya Paṇḍita's own. While the precise ultimate source(s) of this version are not yet clear, commentators belonging to the Sa skya school several centuries later specify that Sa skya Paṇḍita did not have a written source, but rather relied on oral accounts.[58] Studies of other tales transmitted by Dmar ston also indicate that he relied very heavily on oral traditions, something that is suggested not only by the content of his tales but by their very language, which is more akin to the colloquial than to the formulaic "translationese" characteristic especially of works rendered from Sanskrit.[59] Sa skya Paṇḍita's own version, perhaps in part because of the constraints of its metrical form (erased in my English translation), is less flowery and considerably less detailed.

Speculation about the mode of transmission of Dmar ston's version of the story raises an interesting issue. As with the Japanese texts, Dmar ston's story is decontextualized, or one might better say recontextualized, since Sa skya Paṇḍita both provides an environment for his pithy single-verse version by placing it in a section of his collection of aphorisms devoted to "bad conduct,"[60] and a context for his more extended version in "A Clear Differentiation of the Three Codes," within which it fits into an overall "historical" argument for the necessity of his own work.[61] It is also located in a historical narrative of the early Buddhist Councils, but not specifically associated with the schism between the Sthaviras and Mahāsāṁghikas. Among the Japanese and Tibetan retellings, only in the *History* of Mkhas pa lde'u is there any connection, explicit or even implicit, to the Mahāsāṁghika-Sthavira schism. On the other hand, in several of these versions the name Mahādeva is either explicitly or by implication connected with the exclamation "Oh, how painful it is!" Moreover, in the versions directly associated with Sa skya Paṇḍita, his own and that of his disciple Dmar ston, and only slightly less explicitly in the version of Mkhas pa lde'u, Mahādeva is made to take advantage of the ambiguity of this expression. In these versions Mahādeva claims that the words his students took (and as we the audience know, took rightly) to mean "Oh, how painful it is!" should have been understood instead as a proclamation of the first of the Four Noble Truths in the form "Oh, suffering!" Since Mahādeva is not really an arhat, but only pretending to be, he must make excuses for his inability to behave as an arhat should, demonstrating precisely the pattern we saw in the *Vibhāṣā*, in which the Five Theses are generated as a result of Mahādeva's attempts to explain away those of his actions that deviate from what is expected of an arhat.

The content of these Tibetan versions is not related solely to the account in the *Vibhāṣā*. In the first part of the story, there are interesting connections with the *Konjaku* version, most particularly in regard to the reordering of events. In both Sa skya Paṇḍita's and Dmar ston's texts, the murder of the arhat takes place after the murder of the mother, and the revised motive for this third murder is the same. I do not necessarily wish to suggest any direct connection between thirteenth-century Tibetan versions of the story and that in the perhaps two centuries older Japanese *Konjaku monogatarishū*. Since, however, the source(s) of the story in both of these traditions remain(s) unknown, there is ample scope for the speculation that they might ultimately have shared a common inspiration, perhaps in a version of the tale that circulated in China but is now lost to us (or simply remains undiscovered). Japan's near complete reliance on China for its Buddhism, including its Buddhist lore, either directly or through Korean intermediaries, is too well known to require recital here. In contrast, only wholesale adoption of the thoroughly polemical claim that all the vital sources of Tibetan Buddhism stem directly from India allows one to overlook the profound influences flowing, from the earliest periods, into Tibet from the east. Contrary to what the common Indophilic Tibetan self-understanding would suggest, there is nothing whatsoever unusual or problematic in imagining possible proximate Chinese origins for narratives or doctrines found in Tibetan Buddhist sources, even in cases in which we can be quite sure that the ultimate origins of the stories or ideas in question do indeed lie in India. In other words, there is no prima facie reason to doubt that originally Indian Buddhist materials might have reached Tibet by way of China—we have voluminous evidence that precisely this did often happen. This, of course, does not suggest, much less prove, that the particular story transmitted by Sa skya Paṇḍita, Mkhas pa lde'u, and Dmar ston came from or through China. It does remind us, however, of this possibility, and thus of the possibility that Japanese versions of the Mahādeva story may share elements with Tibetan tellings because they share a common Chinese source.

I have collected versions of the story of Mahādeva parallel to that in the *Vibhāṣā*, but in at least some cases evidently independent of it, since crucial elements often differ. As the next step in our efforts to understand this story, we must notice how traditional sources speak of the initial Sthavira-Mahāsāṁghika schism when they do not associate it with Mahādeva.

6
Schism Accounts in Buddhist Doxographies

Some versions of the Mahādeva story we have studied treat it as a tale, either uncontextualized or placed within an apparently unrelated narrative frame. At the same time, there exists a group of texts that recount a schism story squarely within a "historical" frame, without, however, attributing its instigation to Mahādeva. And although the character of the schismatic monk in these sources is touched upon only briefly, with no discussion of his life before ordination, there can be little doubt that the same fundamental episode lies behind these accounts as well. The earliest known version of such a historically framed schism account is probably that in the *Tarkajvālā* (Blaze of Reasoning) of Bhāviveka,[1] in the fourth chapter of the text, which also has an independent existence under the title *Nikāya-bhedavibhaṅgavyākhyāna* (Commentary on the Classification of the Divisions of Buddhist Monastic Communities). In the *Tarkajvālā* we find the following:[2]

> Again, others say that 137 years after the parinirvāṇa of the Blessed One, King Nanda and Mahāpadma[3] convened an assembly of the āryas in the city of Pāṭaliputra, and when they had attained the state of calm emancipation free from clinging, Ārya Mahākāśyapa, Ārya Mahāloma, Mahātyāga, Uttara, Revata, and so on constituted a monastic community of arhats who had obtained perfect knowledge. When they were thus gathered, Māra the evil one [as] *Bhadra opposed them all.[4] Taking up the guise of a monk,[5] he performed various feats of magic and with five propositions caused a great schism in the monastic community. Sthavira *Nāga and *Sthiramati,[6] both of whom were very learned, praised these five propositions and taught in accord with them, namely: . . . [7] This, they claimed, is the teaching of the Buddha. Then, the two sects [**nikāya*] split, the Sthavira and the Mahāsāṁghika. Thus for a period of sixty-three years was the monastic community split by a quarrel.

Here we have an account of the fundamental schism in the early Buddhist community, which resulted in the Mahāsāṁghika and Sthavira orders, with the cause for this schism identified as five contentious points. The author of those points, however, is not called Mahādeva but rather apparently *Bhadra. Relevant Indian historical sources are unfortunately almost nonexistent. The most detailed and reliable surviving traditional histories of Indian Buddhism are those authored by Tibetans, although these are clearly based ultimately on Indian sources. Among them, a number of important works repeat the *Tarkajvālā*'s account, sometimes with variations that suggest some confusion in the historical and doxographical tradition.[8] Special attention should be paid to the great Tibetan historian Tāranātha (1575–1635), who recorded two interesting accounts in his seminal work, *Rgya gar chos 'byung* (History of Buddhism in India), perhaps the most important history of Indian Buddhism ever written. The first of his accounts reads as follows:[9]

> When the Ārya Mahātyāga was upholding the teaching in Madhyadeśa, King Nanda's son Mahāpadma did honor to the entire monastic community in the town of Kusumapura [=Pāṭaliputra]. The monk *Sthiramati, who was a follower of the Sthavira *Nāga, proclaimed five propositions, and by provoking a great argument, the four sects gradually began to be divided into eighteen.

Here it appears that the monk *Sthiramati is taken as the author of the five propositions, although according to Bhāviveka and those who follow him most closely, *Sthiramati is an adherent of these theses, but not their author. In addition, the schism alluded to appears not to be the initial one dividing the community into two sects, the Mahāsāṁghika and the Sthavira, but another, which led to the development of the (legendary) eighteen sects of mature Indian sectarian Buddhism. At the same time, just a few pages earlier, Tāranātha also reports the following tradition, which on the whole accords with the version in the *Vibhāṣā*:[10]

> In Mathurā there lived the son of a merchant called Mahādeva. He committed the three deadly sins, namely, killing his father, killing his mother, and killing an *arhat*. Depressed in mind, he left for Kashmir where, carefully concealing his misdeeds, he became a monk. As he had a keen intellect, he acquired mastery of the three Piṭaka-s, felt remorse for his sins, and strove by himself after meditation in a monastery. Being blessed by the power of Māra, he was taken by all for an arhat, and thus his prestige grew more and more.

Although certainly much briefer than the version in the *Vibhāṣā*, this recounting agrees with it in virtually all particulars, including the visit to

Kashmir, an episode I omitted above because, although it plays an important role in Mahādeva's subsequent monastic career, our attention here is limited to his life before he became a monk. A few lines further along, Tāranātha's text continues:[11]

> After his death, another monk called *Bhadra, who is considered to have been an incarnation of the evil Māra himself, raised many objections and doubts to the sayings [of the Buddha].

This *Bhadra is then said to have propagated five theses. Tāranātha's report here effectively merges into a single account the Mahādeva and *Bhadra stories. Elsewhere, however, Tāranātha explicitly indicates his belief that there were two distinct individuals, Mahādeva and *Bhadra, whose influence brought about the degeneration of the monastic community. In sum, if we survey all the versions of such apparently related stories in Tāranātha's text, we are forced to conclude that we meet here a considerably confused and varied transmission of what was, originally, one basic story.[12] What, then, is the connection between Bhadra and Mahādeva?

Despite the importance of Mahādeva's mythology in Buddhist sectarian history, only a few scholars have attempted to discuss and interpret his character. Among them, the pioneering Dutch Indologist and scholar of Buddhism Johan Hendrik Caspar Kern (1833–1917) was probably the first. Although many of Kern's suggestions, based as they often are on his notions of "astronomical" mythology linking myth and natural phenomena, have, justifiably, been met with considerable skepticism, if not derision,[13] they are nevertheless indicative of his willingness to engage the material on a level that later writers have on the whole avoided. In the present case, our appreciation of Kern's attempt at interpretation is complicated by the fact that for him the Mahādeva of Tāranātha, the Tibetan historian (and, as he calls them, the "northern" sources), is identical with another Mahādeva, a monk who ordains Aśoka's son Mahinda and subsequently becomes a missionary spreading Buddhism in the Āndhra region.[14] For Kern, however, Mahādeva was obviously not a historical monk, but rather a symbol:[15]

> Although the legend that we have just summarized may be far from clear, it is nevertheless known however that Mahādeva and Bhadra are names of Śiva who, in his capacity as the god of Time, may be called the Genie of destruction. . . . When one considers the diversity of the nature of Śiva, one is not astonished that the southern Mahādeva plays an entirely different role from that of the heretic.

It is true that one cannot read Kern nowadays without some puzzlement at his promiscuous appeal to mythological tropes. Still, as an Indologist he could not help but notice that the name Mahādeva refers, first and foremost, to the Hindu god of destruction, Śiva. Moreover, the Sanskrit words *śiva* and *bhadra*, as common nouns rather than proper names, are virtually synonymous, a fact well known, of course, to Indian authors, Buddhist and otherwise. There is thus a strong link between the two words and hence between the two names. In his appreciation of a conceptual link between Mahādeva and Bhadra, one that extends beyond the common narrative and attempts to account for their similarity through the associations the names are likely to evoke, Kern zeroed in on an important point.

One of the few to have taken Kern seriously in this regard is Constantin Régamey, a superb scholar of Buddhist philology and philosophy much better known as an important twentieth-century composer.[16] In his discussion of the problematic role of the juggler Bhadra in the Mahāyāna sūtra *Bhadramāyākāravyākaraṇa* (Prediction to Buddhahood of the Magician Bhadra), Régamey wrote:[17]

> The name given to the juggler does not seem fortuitous. In the Buddhist tradition the names Bhadra or its variant Subhadra are connected with the spreaders of schisms and doubts. In the Southern tradition we find a legend[18] which relates that, when the monks were lamenting Buddha's recent death, one of them, Subhadda by name, stood up in the assembly and cried: "Do not grieve, we are now delivered from the Great *Śramaṇa* who oppressed us saying: 'this beseems ye' and 'that beseems ye not!' Now we shall do what we like, and we shall not do what we do not like." These words, so dangerous for the keeping up of the unity and the continuity of Buddhist tradition, were one of the reasons for which Mahākassapa insisted on calling the Council.[19] . . .
>
> Considering that in the . . . story [from Tāranātha] Bhadra appears as the continuator of another spreader of troubles Mahādeva, Kern's opinion . . . that in the Buddhist tradition both these figures represent Śiva, the god of destruction, has some foundation, since we are aware that both Bhadra and Mahādeva are names for Śiva.

Although suggestive, there are some problems with these speculations. Even assuming, for the moment, that Bhadra may be equated with Subhadra, which is itself far from obvious, the most serious problem may be that the name Subhadda is applied to more than one individual in Buddhist traditions, and the individual to whom Régamey refers is far from the best known of these. Rather, most of those familiar with Indian Buddhist lore would have been likely to first associate the name Subhadra with the legend of Śākyamuni's last disciple, the brahmin Subhadra, who came to the Buddha on his death bed, asked about the teaching, and was ordained.[20] In fact, the legend of the monk who rejoices at the death of Śākyamuni, celebrating the freedom from onerous restriction this will bring, while itself well and widely known, appears to be connected with the name Subhadda only in Pāli Theravāda literature, and not in any of the traditions likely to have been known to Bhāviveka, Tāranātha, and others who in their histories name the schismatic monk Bhadra.[21]

Régamey has, nonetheless, put his finger on a key point suggested by Kern's interpretation: while Mahādeva and Bhadra are defined and connected to each other by the legends they are given in our sources—by the acts they are said to have performed—they are more deeply positioned in a broad cultural context by their names. Neither "Mahādeva" nor "Bhadra" are likely to have been selected entirely at random by the authors of their tales. As Kern so incisively realized, for those Indians who composed and heard these texts, steeped in an Indic world of lore and legend, the name Mahādeva, even in a Buddhist context, could not but have also, if not indeed primarily, brought to mind images of Śiva, the destroyer, especially when the tale of Mahādeva's destructive deeds was told. To be sure, as with most major Hindu deities, any list of the names of Śiva would be quite lengthy. Although inclusion in such a list would not automatically ensure association with Śiva first and foremost, the name Mahādeva is among his most common epithets.[22] As for Bhadra, it is possible that the literal meaning of the word—which, like *śiva,* means "auspicious"—is evoked here sarcastically or ironically, since this character's role is anything but auspicious; as a parallel, the apotropaic intent of calling the inauspicious deity Śiva "The Auspicious One" is well known.[23] In sum, both Mahādeva and Bhadra are names that may very well have been selected precisely for their associations with danger and destruction.

The "historical" accounts of the schism, whether attributed to Bhadra or another, seem on the whole to reflect the same basic situation as that depicted in the *Vibhāṣā* and allied sources, which blame Mahādeva for the split. That sources as important as Bhāviveka's *Tarkajvālā* transmit an account of this schism that omits any mention of the story of murder and incest is significant. But this text does allude to the very bad character of an individual it names Bhadra, labeling him nothing less than an incarnation of Māra, the Buddhist Satan. Evidence such as this cannot help but lead us to wonder whether the

Vibhāṣā's authors did not meld together some less specific outlines of the initial Sthavira-Mahāsāṁghika schism with an otherwise unrelated narrative in an effort to assign responsibility for the community's division. I believe not only that this was indeed the case, but that I can identify the very source upon which these authors drew.

7
The Story of Dharmaruci

I HAVE argued that an originally and factually later intra-Mahāsāṁghika squabble was, in various sources, transferred and predated in such a way that at least one central name, that of Mahādeva, was applied to an entirely unrelated earlier dispute, that between the Sthaviras and the Mahāsāṁghikas. While this transference may have been due to some misinterpretation of internal Mahāsāṁghika dialectics, our understanding of this process does not yet include an appreciation of why and how the opponents of the Mahāsāṁghikas told and retold the story of Mahādeva. It is now possible to begin to approach these questions by examining the antecedents of the Mahādeva narrative.

To formalize the central hypothesis I have alluded to several times already: those who attacked the Five Theses added to their criticisms of the content of those theses an ad hominem attack upon their putative author. The substance of this attack can have had nothing at all to do historically with the polemical circumstances to which it was attached. It would be optimal in this respect, then, to locate the calumnious story of Mahādeva's preordination life in some other context, and it would be close to decisive if we could actually demonstrate that the critics of the Five Theses borrowed and made use of that story for their own ends. What I would most like to show is that in the process of objecting to a set of doctrinal assertions with which they could not agree, the opponents of that individual (or group) whom they identified by the name Mahādeva did not simply react to his ideas, did not report an actual history, and did not merely invent a story about this so-called heretic. Rather, they adopted and adapted a pre-existing source or sources for this purpose. An investigation of the fashion in which they did so can teach us much not only about the aims and methods of these polemicists, but also about the range of Indian Buddhist thinking about the kinds of crimes described in such tales, Indian Buddhist attitudes toward sexual (im)morality, and perhaps even ultimately something about the universality of certain types of human thought—the very goals I set at the outset of this study.

Referring only to the stories in the *Vibhāṣā*, the *Konjaku monogatarishū*, and the *Sangoku denki*, all of which he translates so elegantly, Victor Mair writes:[1] "The series of three stories . . . is derived from an Indian source that is no longer extant." We have seen above that these three tellings cannot, in fact, be traced directly to a single archetype, since there are very important differences between them. In making this statement, Mair probably assumes that the Chinese translation of the *Vibhāṣā* and the Japanese tales relied directly or ultimately on the Indian prototype of the *Vibhāṣā*. That is, rather than intending to hypothesize an independent origin for the tale found in the *Vibhāṣā*, he means to state the fact that no Indic language version of the *Vibhāṣā* is extant, and in this he is correct.[2] If, however, Mair means that the story of Mahādeva is not found in an Indic language, he is mistaken.[3] The story itself does exist in Sanskrit, but told in a manner free of any association with the name Mahādeva.[4]

Sanskrit Buddhist sources preserve two versions of the story. The primary version is that found in the *Divyāvadāna*, a collection of uncertain date (but existing in some form already in the fifth century or so). This compilation for the most part consists of excerpts from the Vinaya of the Mūlasarvāstivāda school, although the section in question here is not found in any of the extant versions of that Vinaya. The second version appears in the eleventh-century Kashmiri poet Kṣemendra's literary recasting of the *Divyāvadāna*, his *Bodhisattvāvadānakalpalatā* (Wish-Granting Garland of Tales of the Bodhisattva), which I will treat separately in Chapter 11. In the *Divyāvadāna* the tale occurs in the story of Dharmaruci, the *Dharmarucy-avadāna*, as the third part of chapter 18 of the collection. As will soon become clear, there can be very little doubt that the tale we encounter here is intimately connected to the story of Mahādeva. It reads as follows:[5]

> Later still, in the third infinite [aeon] there arose in the world a perfect Buddha named Krakucchanda, perfected in knowledge and good conduct, a Sugata, world-knower, unsurpassed, a charioteer of people to be tamed, a teacher of gods and men, a Buddha, a blessed one. [He dwelt near the metropolis of Śobhāvatī.][6] And in that metropolis dwelt a certain great merchant. He took a wife from a suitable family, and he had sex, made love, and coupled with his wife, and from that sex, lovemaking, and coupling, a son was born. That householder [the merchant] was a believer, and he had as spiritual advisor to his family a monk who was a saint.
>
> [Once] that householder spoke to his wife as follows: "We have had born to us a remover of our [spiritual] debt and a taker of our [material] wealth; with my merchandise I will go now, dear, to another country, as is the merchants' way." And so the merchant, filled with greed, took his merchandise and went far away. And for an exceedingly long time no tidings came from him.
>
> Now, in the course of time that boy of his had grown big and full, good-looking and attractive. Thereupon he asked his mother, "Mother,

what is the business followed by our family?" And she explained, "My boy, your father used to engage in commercial trade."[7] So the boy began to engage in commercial trade.[8]

Now, his mother, being afflicted by passions,[9] began to think: "I wonder what way there might be for me to dispel my passions, and yet for no one to find me out?" Thinking about it, she resolved the following: "That's it—my son! In order to fulfill my desire, I'll have sex, and so dispel my lust with him alone. And certainly none of my relatives will have any suspicion." So she invited an old procuress, fed her twice or three times, and afterwards clothed her in new garments. That old woman said to her: "Just *why* are you strategically pursuing me like this, giving me presents and the like?"

Emboldened, she spoke to that old woman thus: "Mother, listen to what I have to tell you. I am severely afflicted by passions. Have affection for me, and look for a man who could be an intimate and would not arouse people's suspicions." The old woman said: "There is no such man here in this house, nor could any lover come in who would not arouse people's suspicions. What man will there be to whom I should address myself?"

Then the merchant's wife said to the old woman, "If there's no other man suitable for such an approach, it must be this very own son of mine. No one will suspect him." The old woman said to her: "How can you possibly engage in sex play with your son? It would [rather] be proper for you to enjoy sex play with another man." Then the merchant's wife said, "If there is no other intimately available man, then it must be this very own son of mine." The old woman said to her: "Well, do what you like." Then the old procuress approached that very same merchant's son and asked: "My dear, you're young and handsome. Are you already pretty well set, or no?"[10] He responded to her: "What do you mean?" So the old woman said: "Sir, handsome and young as you are, now in the prime of your life, you should be happy, playing, making love, and sporting amorously with a young woman. Why on earth should you be deprived of the enjoyment of desires?" Hearing that, the merchant's son, shrinking in modesty and bashfulness, did not accept the old woman's suggestion.

Then the old woman spoke to the boy repeatedly, saying "A young woman is afflicted by passions on your account."[11] Being repeatedly importuned, the merchant's son spoke to the old woman, saying: "Mother, did you say something to that young woman about me?" Then the old woman said, "I spoke to her about you, and she agreed, thanks to my suggestion. Gripped by timidity and bashfulness, that girl won't say anything. She won't reveal her body, neither should you make an effort to ask her who she is." So the merchant's son said to the old woman: "Where will our liaison be?" She said: "In my own house." He said: "Where's your house located?" Then the old woman pointed out the house to him. And the old woman went to the merchant's wife and said: "I got this boy of yours to agree." She said: "Where will our liaison be?" "In my own house."

After the son completed his business, he went home. When he had, in due course, finished eating, he said to his mother, "I'm going—I'll sleep at a friend's house." His mother permitted him, saying "Go!" Having obtained permission, the boy went to that old woman's house. When he arrived there, he waited in expectation of a time of sex play. In the night time, at the time when forms are not recognizable, his mother went right to that very house in which the merchant's son was waiting in order to enjoy sex play. Arriving at the house, in the evening when things are discerned indistinctly, when shapes do not appear, secretly step by step she began to enjoy sex play together with her son, sinfully and illicitly. And having enjoyed her sex play, at the end of the night, in the black, still hours of blind darkness, when the undiscerned shapes of forms do not appear, she went back to her own house.

And when the night began to grow light, the merchant's son, too, having enjoyed the sex play, went to their goods shop and took care of the family business. He enjoyed the sex play a number of times there in the old woman's house in that manner, and a long time passing in that fashion with a series of sexual encounters, the mother began to think about that boy: "For how long shall I go to another house, and in this way in undisclosed shape enjoy sex play? What if I were to make known to him this manner of our sex play gradually, in such a way that we could have our sex play here in this very house?" So thinking she went right to the house of the old woman, and after having enjoyed sex play with her son, just as she had planned, at the end of the night, in the time of deepest darkness, she went home having put on the boy's upper garment and having left her own head covering. In the early morning time, the boy spied that cloth lying on the top part of the bedstead, and not finding his own upper garment, he recognized that cloth. Getting rid of it, he went to their shop, and dressing in another pair,[12] he went home. When he got there he saw his very own garment being worn on his mother's head. Seeing that he asked his mother: "Mother, how did this cloth come to be on your head?"

She responded, "I'm still your mother. It's true that for a long time you've been enjoying sex with me, but I'm still your self-same mother."

At that the merchant's son, hearing such words from his mother, dropped to the ground stunned and shaken. Then his mother sprinkled him with water from a jar, and after a long while the boy, having been sprinkled with water, recovered his breath. He was consoled by his mother: "Why are you so depressed, hearing my words? Be strong, don't be despondent!" The boy said to her: "How shall I not be mindful of my depression, or my bewilderment, by which I have done such an evil act?" Then she said to him: "Don't distress yourself over this. The female sex is like a road: for that upon which the father goes, the son too goes upon just the same. And this road is not the agent of fault to the son who follows it—it is rather the female sex [which is the agent of the fault]. And the female sex is also like a bathing spot, for at just that bathing spot in which the father bathes, the son too bathes, and the bathing spot is not the agent of fault of the son who is bathing—it is rather the female sex. Moreover, in a bordering country, just this is the normal way things are done: the son also approaches that same woman whom the father approaches for illicit purposes." The merchant's son, with his distress thus removed by his mother through many conciliatory words, was aroused by intense lust and engaged again and again in that illicit sin with his mother.

[There came a time when] the master sent a letter to the house: "My dear! Be firm, gallant, and strong! I will come following right after this very letter!" The merchant's wife, hearing that this was the sense of the letter,[13] grew dejected and began to think. "For a very long time while I was waiting for him to come back he did not come. Now that I have sported in this way with my son, he will come back. What strategy might there be for me to remove him from the living before he gets back here at all?" Having thought it through like this, she called her son and said: "You know that your father sent a letter saying that he will come back. What shall we do now? Go and kill your father without him ever getting back." He said: "How will I kill my father?" When he did not dare to commit the murder of his father, his mother addressed him repeatedly with appeasing words. And being addressed with appeasing words, and inflamed with lust, he resolved himself on the murder of his father.

"Certainly for one who indulges in lust there is no evil act which is forbidden," I say.[14]

Then he said, "By what means will I kill him?" She answered, "I myself shall arrange the means," and so she cooked sweetmeats, mixing poison with the wheat flour, and she also cooked others without poison. Then she called the boy and said, "Go. These sweetmeats are poisonous, and these nonpoisonous. Take them and go to your father. And when he is unsuspectingly eating some place, offer him these poisonous sweetmeats, and you yourself eat the nonpoisonous ones."

Then the boy, accompanied by the servant who had brought [the father's] letter, took those sweetmeats and went off.

When he approached his father, his father saw that son of his, surpassingly handsome, lovely, and distinguished, and he was filled with joy. Asking after his welfare, he said to the merchants, "This, gentlemen, is my son." When the son observed this, he thought, "Everywhere my father recognizes me," and so he said "Father, mother sent a gift of sweetmeats which you, father, should eat." Later while eating together with his father atop a cargo crate, he gave his father the poisonous sweetmeats, and he himself ate those without the poison.

And eating those poisonous sweetmeats his father died. When his father was yoked by the law of time, no one suspected or recognized that the son had done an evil deed. Later those merchants, beloved loving friends, mourned, and gave whatsoever merchandise or gold or valuables that merchant had to his son. The boy took that merchandise and gold and valuables that had belonged to his father and returned home. But when he had come home, his mother did not experience passion while having sex with her son in their secret, illicit way, and with an unsatisfied look said to her son: "For how long will we enjoy our sex play in this secret way? Why don't we leave this country and go to another country where we may dwell happily and openly in the avowed state of husband and wife, without being secretive?"

So the two of them abandoned their house, quit their friends, kin, and relations, and gave up the slave women, slave men, and workers who had long served them, and even their possessions, and just taking their gold and valuables went to another region. When they had arrived there in those foreign lands, avowing that they were husband and wife, they dwelt there enjoying sex play. Then after some time had passed, a saint-monk wandering in the land came to that neighborhood. He roamed through there for alms, and resting on the road saw that boy doing business in the fashion of a merchant. Seeing him and greeting him, he addressed him saying: "Is your mother well?" Hearing the saint addressing him in these terms, the boy was very shaken and anxious because of the wicked acts he had committed, and he began to think. Pondering what to do, he went to his mother and informed her: "An ascetic has come—it's the one who [formerly used to] visit our house. And now that he's here in this neighborhood, he will recognize that "she is this boy's mother." But we are known around here as husband and wife, so how can we succeed in getting him killed?"

And they considered, thinking that they would invite him to their house, and kill him while he was eating. Having thought about it in this way, the two of them invited the saint-monk inside the house and began to feed him. Having concealed a knife on himself, the boy fed the saint together with his mother. Having dismissed the servants, when the saint-monk finished eating he departed from that house, striding with a confident gait. Then the boy seeing the saint striding confidently from within the house, turning his back and departing, he plunged his knife into his body and took his life.

And lusts are just like salt water—
The more they are enjoyed, the more they are craved.

That boy's mother, while still engaged in the illicit pursuit of her son, also had a secret affair with a guildman's son in that very same neighborhood, and she became obsessed with those philanderings. But those exploits of hers were discovered by her son, and he said to his mother, "Mother, turn back from this sin!" But she with her mind enamored with that guildman's son did not turn back even though she was repeatedly asked to. So unsheathing his sword he deprived his mother of life.

When his three sins of immediate retribution were accomplished, the local gods declared to the people: "This one is evil—he is a patricide, an arhat killer, and a matricide. He has performed and piled up three deeds of immediate retribution which lead to the karma of hell." Then when the people of that neighborhood heard that, they drove him out from that neighborhood. When he was driven out from the neighborhood, he began to think: "In the Buddha's teaching there is certainly some expiation of this [situation]." Thus he considered. "I will go now and become ordained." And he went to a monastery and, approaching a monk, he said: "Noble One, I would take ordination." So the monk said, "First of all, you aren't a patricide, are you?" He told the monk, "I did kill my father." Then he asked again, "You're not a matricide, are you?" He said, "Noble One, I killed my mother." He asked once again, "You didn't kill a saint, did you?" And he said, "I killed a saint too." Then that monk said, "Doing these acts one by one would disqualify you from ordination into the ascetic life—how much more all of them together! Get out of here, boy, I won't ordain you!" Then that man approached another monk and said, "Noble One, I would become ordained." And that monk too, having questioned him in the appropriate sequence, refused. After that he approached another monk and implored him, too, for ordination in the same manner. But he, too, questioning in the same way in the appropriate sequence, also refused. When, although he had begged repeatedly for ordination, the monks still did not grant it to him, he became angry and began to think: "Although I beg for that ordination common to all, I don't receive it.'

Then he set fire to the monks asleep in that monastery. Having set the fire in that monastery, he went to another monastery. And there, too, he approached the monks and begged for ordination. They, too, questioned him in the very same way in the appropriate sequence and then refused. And there again in the same way with hostile intention he set [the monastery] on fire. And in that monastery, too, he burned many monks, common monks and saints.[15] When he had burned countless monasteries in this way, everywhere the word spread: "In such-and-such a fashion a man, a doer of evil deeds, upon not receiving ordination from the monks, burns down monasteries and their monks." And the man set out for another monastery.

In that monastery dwelt a monk who was a bodhisattva,[16] a knower of the Tripiṭaka. He heard that that man, a doer of such wicked deeds, was on his way there, and so the monk went forth to meet that person even before he had reached the monastery. Approaching the man, he said: "Good sir, what's going on?" So the man said to him, "Noble One, I can't obtain ordination." Then the monk said, "Come boy, I will ordain you." Later the monk shaved the man's head and gave him ochre robes. Then the man said, "Noble One, confer the rules of training on me!"[17] But the monk said, "Of what use are the rules of training to you? Always speak thus:[18] 'Homage to the Buddha! Homage to the Dharma! Homage to the Saṁgha!'" Then the monk began to sermonize to the man: "You have done such-and-such evil deeds. If you ever hear the word 'Buddha,' you must retain it in your awareness." Then that monk, a knower of the Tripiṭaka, died and was reborn among the gods, and that man also died, and was reborn among the hells.

Then the Blessed One spoke: "What do you think, monks? The one who was in the past the monk, the knower of the Tripiṭaka, he was none other than I at that time and on that occasion. The being who was the doer of evil deeds, the killer of mother, father, and saint, he was none other than Dharmaruci. This is my demonstration of [the life of] this Dharmaruci in the third infinite period. In this respect I say, Dharmaruci, it was a long time ago, Dharmaruci, it was a very long time ago,

> Dharmaruci, it was a very, very long time ago.[19] And for as long as it took me, monks, through three infinite periods practicing the six perfections and hundreds of thousands of other difficult practices to attain unexcelled perfect awakening, so long this Dharmaruci was for the most part fallen among the hells and beasts. When the Blessed One had said this, glad at heart, those monks rejoiced in what the Blessed One had proclaimed.

There can be virtually no doubt that the Mahādeva stories we have examined are, if not based directly upon this specific version of the tale of Dharmaruci, at least ultimately dependent on precisely the same narrative tradition. This Dharmaruci story contains a level of detail far beyond that in any of the known Mahādeva tales, particularly with regard to the portrayal of the sexual relationship between mother and son and the psychological dynamics of the story's character development as a whole.[20] I will explore these aspects below, but one of the first things we can conclude from the very existence of this story is that the account of the sins of the schismatic Mahādeva in the *Vibhāṣā* and similar sources must, virtually without question, be recognized as a borrowing, an abbreviated and simplified adaptation of a previously existing account, dropped or thrust into a completely foreign narrative and polemical context. A potential alternative hypothesis—that the Dharmaruci story is an expanded and elaborated version of some tale that looked much more like the Mahādeva tale—is so unlikely as to be nearly completely out of the question.

This discovery of the Dharmaruci story serves, among other things, as a strong confirmation of the supposition I offered above regarding the fictitious and constructed, and therefore thoroughly ahistorical, nature of the Mahādeva narrative. The *Vibhāṣā*, of course, is a text of the Sarvāstivāda school, and the *Divyāvadāna* belongs to the Mūlasarvāstivāda tradition. The relation between these two traditions, while not entirely clear, is certainly intimate, and thus for all intents and purposes we may consider the sectarian location of the two texts to be identical, or very nearly so. In this regard, we might want to venture as a working hypothesis that the Sarvāstivādin compilers of the *Vibhāṣā* utilized the resources of their own literary tradition when they constructed the calumnious and defamatory tale of the background of the proponent of the Five Theses, to which they so strenuously objected. I will return to assess the validity of this hypothesis in Chapter 12.

In contrast to the various versions of the Mahādeva story, the *Divyāvadāna* tale is elaborate in its detail, and indeed in drama. This greater degree of detail enables us to explore this narration in a number of different ways, and to discover in it perhaps unexpected depths. Despite the moral simplicity of the story of Mahādeva in the *Vibhāṣā* and elsewhere (particularly in the *Konjaku monogatarishū*, not to mention the *Hōbutsushū*), in which the actions of Mahādeva are painted in thoroughly negative and unsympathetic hues, the story of Dharmaruci is an ambiguous tale: the son is both victim and victimizer. The mother, who in the Mahādeva tales is nothing more than a shadow, is here a more complex figure, likewise both victimizer and then herself victim. The father, arhat, and monks all remain simply victims, characters who here, as in the Mahādeva stories, undergo no narrative development to speak of. Both central characters, then, the son and the mother, are depicted in morally equivocal terms, and it is in large part the relation between them that motivates the story's ethical complexity. Dharmaruci himself, however, is naturally the central figure, not only from the narrative but from a moral point of view as well.

Let us begin with the question of responsibility. When the *Vibhāṣā* and other texts radically abbreviate the story they borrow, their transformation of Dharmaruci into Mahādeva erases the evidence of his victimization. This can hardly be incidental. Rather, in choosing how to abridge the long drama, the authors or compilers of these texts opted to portray their protagonist, (re)named Mahādeva,[21] in a radically monochromatic fashion. There are no shades of grey for him, only black and white.[22] Dharmaruci, on the other hand, the Ur-Mahādeva, is not only a villain but also a victim many times over: as a young boy, his father abandons him, going off to sea in search of profit. Left at home with his mother, he is seduced, or perhaps even raped, by his mother. Having been manipulated into unwitting sex with his mother, Dharmaruci, despite his resistance, is then further provoked by her to murder his father who, as is apparent from the scene of their reunion, clearly loves and is proud of his son, despite their lengthy separation. Under his mother's influence, Dharmaruci flees with her, the two then living incestuously in a foreign land. Together they arrange the further murder of an arhat, and later still, enraged with jealousy at his mother's sexual infidelity, he murders her as well. When he desires, finally, to escape this horrible cycle and seeks a path to redemption, he is once again victimized when he is refused assistance by the very religious body to which he turns, the Buddhist monastic community, the same group that everywhere in its own literature is constantly proclaiming itself to be a refuge.

A number of these elements have survived the adaptation of the story in the versions we have examined—or, with an excess of caution, we may say that parallel characterizations are found in apparently allied texts. The *Vibhāṣā* itself says that Mahādeva planned the murder of his father "together with his mother," thus implying that his mother is at least partially responsible for this crime, although the degree of individual culpability is left unaddressed. In addition, certainly the depiction of Mahādeva's murder of his mother in a number of sources seems to track very closely the portrayal of Dharmaruci's own crime. So while one cannot say that Dharmaruci is depicted in the *Divyāvadāna* thoroughly sympathetically, and Mahādeva thoroughly unsympathetically in all the sources that recount his tale, the tendency to demonize Mahādeva is clearly evident. Even in the final major story element, the ordination episode, the account of Dharmaruci portrays him as denied by the monastic community to which he turns, until the future Buddha intervenes, while in the *Vibhāṣā*'s version the evil Mahādeva is immediately ordained "without question." This failure to ask any of the requisite questions of the prospective monk signals a clear violation of the normal procedures of canon law. Even if one were to argue that in the narrative time of the text such procedures had not yet been laid down as such, from any reader's perspective these violations of established procedure must surely have been obvious. But the failure to ask the necessary questions prior to ordination has a double meaning. Not only does it mark Mahādeva's ordination as improper, and Mahādeva then as not, after all, a Buddhist monk (just as Mahādeva's doppelgänger Bhadra is clearly stated not to have been a real monk), it simultaneously suggests the openness and generosity of the monastic community toward the sinner; it "devictimizes" Mahādeva by not denying him what was withheld from Dharmaruci. This leaves an impression of Mahādeva's ingratitude and willfulness that even an audience unaware of Mahādeva's story as an adaptation of Dharmaruci's tale would have sensed. This devictimization has the effect of further criminalizing Mahādeva while simultaneously promoting the moral superiority of the (legitimate) monastic community, namely, the *saṁgha* of those opposed to Mahādeva's legacy—the Sarvāstivādins representing the Sthaviras who opposed the Mahāsāṁghikas. Mahādeva is painted as particularly ungrateful in light of the monastic community's willingness to accept him, and his betrayal is therefore all the worse.[23] On the other hand, in both the *Vibhāṣā* and the *Divyāvadāna*, Dharmaruci/Mahādeva does not become a monk for a bad reason, but rather for a very good one. And in both accounts it is the monastic community's failure to accept his sincerity, their rejection of his aspiration toward repentance, contrition, and spiritual rebirth, which pushes him further back in the direction from which he sought to flee.[24] When in the *Vibhāṣā* Mahādeva does eventually become a monk, it is suggested that, after all, nature triumphs over intention, for having become a monk and gained access to the "liberative technology" of Buddhist monasticism, Mahādeva nevertheless creates, or at the very least inspires, a schism in the monastic community. The

Dharmarucy-avadāna is willing to rescue the sinner, while the *Vibhāṣā* wants only to demonize him.

Although it is always dangerous to read the past through modern filters, I believe that it is often worthwhile to look at ancient materials from different points of view. And with that in mind, it is interesting to think for a moment about how Dharmaruci and Mahādeva are depicted.

8

Abuse and Victimhood

Our appreciation of the morally ambiguous portrayal of Dharmaruci and its contrast with the comparatively monochromatic depiction of Mahādeva may be enriched by a more general consideration of the types of experiences these characters are depicted as having undergone. While it is necessary to try to understand these experiences in an Indian context, it may also prove valuable to approach them from a more generalized point of view. It is thus of some interest to note what contemporary specialists have to say regarding mothers who sexually abuse their sons. For long the accepted dogma was that such behavior was profoundly rare and occurred only under the most unusual circumstances. Some twenty years ago, for instance, one observer wrote:[1]

> Mother-son incest seems to be extremely rare. It appears to occur only under extremely pathological conditions, generally where there has been an absence of early closeness between mother and son. The following conditions are generally present in mother-son incest: (1) a loss of the father, through absence or extreme weakness, at an early age; (2) overt seduction by the mother; (3) loss of other sexual outlets to the adult son. . . .[2]

A number of explanations are offered in the psychological and anthropological literature to account for the rarity of mother-son incest. For instance, it has been hypothesized that since women traditionally have greater contact with children than do men, and are intimately involved in their genital and excretory functions, whatever mystery and fascination there may be in children's bodies is diffused by familiarity. It has also been suggested that the protective role that women take with regard to children may make them more sensitive to the potential damage sexual relations may cause.[3] These ideas are not unrelated to hypotheses concerning the origins of the incest taboo itself, an issue I will take up in due course. To anticipate that discussion a bit, however, we may note that some speculation concerns what has been called the "incest barrier," which refers to the biological bases of incest avoidance from an ethological or animal behavior point of view. Of course, humans are animals, and at least some scholars believe there to be evidence that "the human patterns of separation-individuation and dominance that are so crucial in establishing incest barriers (as well as so much else that is integral to being human) to a large extent parallel, and are derived from, those observed in animals."[4] This is partially related to the so-called Westermarck hypothesis, which holds that incest avoidance is based on close familiarity. As Edward Westermarck wrote in 1891:[5]

> What I maintain is, that there is an innate aversion to sexual intercourse between persons living very closely together from early youth, and that, as such persons are in most cases related, this feeling displays itself chiefly as a horror of intercourse between near kin.

Precisely how this might work remains an unanswered question, but most scholars look to some recognition of the evolutionary or genetic disadvantages of inbreeding, the loss of overall fitness technically called "inbreeding depression." Naturally, no one claims that the incest taboo evolved through a knowledge of scientific genetics; rather, those who follow this argument suggest that the causality of patterns of decreased fertility or mutation produced by incestuous unions was recognized, and taboos arose to avoid this. On the other hand, our human aversion to incest is neither purely biological nor the result of evolutionary adaptation to facts such as decreased fertility or cumulative genetic damage caused by the expression of recessive genes:[6]

> Human psychology has converted an incest barrier inherent in our pattern of family structure into an incest taboo—a rich and complex, deeply meaningful symbolization and reinforcement of the behavior in families we, as humans, inherited from our forbearers. It is part of our destiny, as determined by natural selection, that we are creatures that live in monogamous or small polygamous nuclear families, that we have a long dependency period before maturation, and that steps of detachment and dominance result in a relatively strong barrier to incest. But it is another part of our destiny to have a highly sophisticated psychological and intellectual apparatus that greatly elaborates and enriches this behavior and gives it a particularly human coloring and meaning—the stuff of our myths and tragedies.

In light of approaches such as this, it is easy to see how the question of the alleged rarity of mother-son incest may be fundamentally related to the general question of the origins of the incest barrier and of incest taboos themselves. If incest taboos arose originally in primitive societies through an avoidance of sexual contact between those who in early life spend significant amounts of time together, it should not surprise us that father-daughter incest might be less strongly tabooed than mother-son incest, since fathers would generally speaking have been a more distant presence in the early life of daughters than mothers were to sons. But this can hardly be the only important factor. Moreover, we know that historically there did exist (albeit rare and isolated) socially sanctioned incestuous relations between mothers and sons, in Iran for instance, as I will discuss in Chapter 9.[7] But even in these cases, where the powerful desire to maintain the "purity of the lineage" was a motivation for procreation within the family, there are negative pressures favoring father-daughter or sibling relations instead. That is to say, when the motivation is reproductive, simple demographics militate against mother-son relations. Even if we assume a bride of, say, fourteen, who has a son as a firstborn, by the time that boy is pubescent and able to reproduce, at let us assume the same age, the mother will be twenty-eight.[8] When we compare the procreative possibilities of a father-daughter or sibling relationship, the demographic advantages of the latter two are obvious.[9]

Given this reasoning and the alleged absence of evidence for mother-son incest, we might feel justified in concluding that there is indeed a close correspondence between the opprobrium with which such relations are viewed in general and their rarity in actual fact. In the past couple of decades, however, thinking about mother-son incest has undergone some revision. It has been shown, for instance, that this form of incest may not be as rare as had been thought, one reason for which is that "the taboo against disclosure is far stronger than the taboo against the behavior itself."[10] A more comprehensive explanation suggests the following possibilities for the lack of attention paid to this topic:[11]

> (1) males do not get pregnant, and the evidence of sexual abuse has not been present; (2) a double standard in belief systems has existed in which fathers have the potential for evil and mothers are "all good;" (3) adult males have been too embarrassed to reveal their sexual activity with and arousal by their mothers; (4) male children have been presumed to be unaffected by sexual abuse, and reports by sons have been ignored; and/or (5) patients and therapists alike have been unaware of the connection between the sexual abuse of males by mothers and later interpersonal relationship problems.

These suggestions cannot, however, be taken as indicative of any widespread occurrence of mother-son incest or even of female sexual activity with male children not their own (as might occur in a daycare setting, for example). In addition, there is a lack of agreement over what sorts of behaviors are to be included in the category of mother-son incest or child sexual abuse by females in general, since plainly the category as generally evoked in such discussions in no way limits the relevant behavior to intercourse. In part this is due, as we noted, to the fact that women in their traditional role as caregiver are allowed a variety of kinds of contact with children, including nursing, bathing, supervision of excretion, or cosleeping. These activities are less commonly performed by men, at least in the societies that are generally the subject of modern studies. It is problematic, therefore, to simply transfer to women notions of what might constitute sexual abuse between an adult male and a child (of either gender), even assuming general agreement on the definition of such abuse. Scholars, social workers, and therapists do seem to agree that it is sometimes difficult to judge when such activities cross the line, and there is a wide recognition (except, perhaps, among politicians and religious zealots) of great cultural variability in such notions. An additional factor complicating an appreciation of female sexual abuse of male children is the notion that some males "may reframe sexual activities with older females as sexual initiation or sexual exploration in order to maintain their role as sexual initiators,"[12] thus contributing to an underappreciation of the frequency with which such behavior occurs. All of this allows us to say, then, that while anecdotal evidence would support a confident assertion that mother-son incest is exceedingly rare, as was formerly thought, it is more common than is generally imagined. There is no reason to think that this was not also the case in ancient India.[13]

Notwithstanding, we should not assume, nor do I mean to suggest, that the Indian stories under our lens reflect a real-world situation, or that their authors conceptualized mother-son incest as do modern researchers. Still, the correspondence between clinical appraisals of the conditions under which mother-son incest actually takes place and the dramatic setting of the Dharmaruci story is, despite the vast temporal and cultural divide between the sources, quite striking. Our story begins by making clear the long-term absence of the father and continues by emphasizing that it is the mother who secretly seduces the unwitting son. At the same time, it is not entirely clear whether the son is an adult, and there is no suggestion that he is otherwise lacking in sexual opportunities. His description, it is true, does suggest him to be at least a teenager, for the *Dharmarucy-avadāna* says "in the course of time that boy . . . had grown big and full, good-looking, and attractive," a description it shares, perhaps not incidentally, with the *Vibhāṣā*, which explicitly states that "the son had grown up." On the other hand, it is also clear that the young man Dharmaruci has never even considered becoming sexually active, a possibility that he countenances only when it is repeatedly put to him by the go-between, a fact strongly suggesting his psychological or social, although not necessarily physical, immaturity.[14]

Another domain in which some recent reevaluation has taken place concerns the mental states of those involved in adult female–male child sexual abuse. An older formulation ran as follows:[15]

> One of the interesting themes that emerges . . . is that serious psychopathology seems to rest with the participant who initiates the incest. While father-daughter incest is generally coercive in nature and acted out against the will of the child, the initiator of mother-son incest may be the son, and in those cases in which that is true, he is invariably described as severely mentally ill. Conversely, when the mother initiates the incest, she is usually portrayed as more disturbed than her son who is then likely to later develop serious psychopathology as a consequence of the incest. As a result of this theme, the consideration of who was responsible for the initiation of the incest joins the variables of the type of sexual abuse, the degree of coercion, and the frequency and the duration in defining the nature of the incestuous experience and its impact on the son.

Although this description is based on clinical observations of more or less contemporary situations (apparently exclusively in North America), it might appear to shed remarkable light on our ancient Indian tale. Despite the fact that the mother in our story is not anywhere described in any way that could lead us to see her as mentally ill (unless through the circular reasoning that she is unbalanced since she initiates an incestuous relationship with her own son), it can hardly be questioned that the son develops what today we would judge to be serious psychopathology, which expresses itself in multiple murders and in some versions arson. More recent research, however, has suggested that the posited link between female sexual abuse and psychosis (a problematic category in itself) is far from clear, and again may be little more than an artifact of the systems of reportage and the fact that the mentally ill may be much less able to conceal their socially unacceptable behaviors than those who are otherwise "normal."[16] We may also note that virtually all modern sources concur in maintaining that the actual rate of mother-son incest *initiated by the son* appears to be virtually nil, an important fact to which I will return.

With regard to the question of violence, our Indian authors fail to even suggest any connection between childhood abuse and later criminality. Perhaps their message was less subtle: this criminal, their protagonist, is simply involved in all sorts of despicable acts, including incest and murder. How he came to have such a horrible character is an issue they did not need to address, and they were entirely uninterested in approaching the question from a standpoint that might seem to us, in our Freudian world, psychologically convincing.[17] Moreover, recent research indicates that childhood sexual victimization is a negatively correlated predictor of later violent criminality. While there is strong correlation between being a victim of childhood physical abuse and later becoming an adult perpetrator of violence, victims of sexual abuse were noticeably less likely to engage in violent criminal behavior than nonabused children in a control group,[18] although the same studies do recognize some tendency toward higher rates of violence toward family members.[19]

The possible importance of the absent father has been noted. Indeed, at least one therapist sees a possible link between the absence of the father and mother-son incest, in a study in which he imaginatively links modern clinical experiences with the classical story of Phaedra and Theseus.[20] In the case of the Dharmaruci story, however, I am inclined to disregard the possible influence of the absent father, for the simple reason that so many stories belonging to the same genre of Indian Buddhist narrative literature begin in precisely the same manner, with the father departing for a period of years to a foreign land in search of wealth through trade.[21] We can hardly see this as anything more profound than a literary cliché, and are therefore neither able to use it as proof that most Buddhist householders were involved in trade, nor does it allow us to assume any particular psychological circumstances in the Dharmaruci story that we would not wish to assume elsewhere. Since there is no evidence in other Buddhist stories with the same formulaic opening of any psychological significance to the absence of the father, we are correspondingly precluded from asserting its importance in Dharmaruci's story as well.

These comparative materials are of more than merely intrinsic interest. They may also assist us in our efforts to understand our Indian materials in a broader context, which in turn will help us comprehend the psychology of the Mahādeva story. In terms of our evaluation of the Indian evidence, however, more important than what modern social scientists believe or speculate may be the case in the real (modern, and generally Western) world is what ancient Indian authors, who spoke as representatives of their tradition, thought.[22] Fortunately, and perhaps unexpectedly, we possess some very clear information regarding Indian attitudes toward incest, including that between mother and son.

9
Persian Perversities

In its presentation of Mahādeva's offenses, the *Vibhāṣā* objects explicitly only to the murders he committed, framing his crimes in terms of the five sins of immediate retribution. Yet at least for me, what is so striking in that context is not so much what the text says as what it does not say: while Mahādeva's three murders are serious crimes, no doubt, the *Vibhāṣā* gives no special emphasis to Mahādeva's incest with his mother. Moreover, although there is a classification of transgressions "belonging to the same category" as the five sins of immediate retribution, but subsidiary to them, in which sexual relations with one's mother holds first place, the *Vibhāṣā* does not invoke it or even appear to know of it. Since Mahādeva's incest with his mother is bound to strike many modern readers as it struck me, as the most remarkable and unexpected form of deviance, the most unusual and perhaps even the most outrageous of Mahādeva's transgressions, we may well wonder whether Indian Buddhists saw such a relationship differently. Perhaps mother-son incest was not such an objectionable practice, and perhaps for an Indian Buddhist audience the absence of emphasis that so strikes us may have made little or no impact. However, having familiarized ourselves with the category of the five sins equivalent to those of immediate retribution, and with the *Dharmarucy-avadāna*, in which the sexual relationship of Dharmaruci with his mother is given considerable attention, we have some grounds for affirming that Indian Buddhist attitudes toward this type of liaison probably did not differ so very much from our own. Further strong evidence comes from the manner in which Indian Buddhist sources treat a well-known example of culturally sanctioned mother-son incest, one to which the *Dharmarucy-avadāna* itself alludes. It is important to understand these materials, since the linchpin of my overall argument for the *Vibhāṣā*'s polemical transformation of Dharmaruci into Mahādeva is the intentional and purposive nature of that text's Oedipal calumny.

In several places in the Pāli scriptures we find the following verse:[1]

> As a river, road, tavern, assembly hall or roadside drinking-water shed,
> So indeed are women in the world—Wise men are not angry at their evil.

A commentary explains the verse as follows:[2]

> There [in the verse] *as a river* means as a river with multiple bathing spots, to which outcastes and kṣatriyas and the like all come to bathe in common. And with regard to expressions like *road* and so on, as a highway is common to all people, everyone is permitted to go on it. A *tavern* or wine house is common to all; whoever wants to drink just goes in there. An *assembly hall* is constructed, by those in search of merit, any place at all, for people to stay together in common, and everyone is welcome to enter. A *roadside drinking-water shed* is constructed for all to use in common, having been set up on a highway and outfitted with drinking cups. Everyone is welcome to drink water there. *So indeed are women in the world* means that in this very way, my dear young man, in this world women are common to all, to be used in common just as a river, road, tavern, assembly hall, or roadside drinking-water shed. Therefore *wise men are not angry at their evil*, meaning that thinking "this sinful misconduct, misbehavior, of these women is common to all," wise men clever and endowed with wisdom do not become angry.

This verse and its commentary express a broad sentiment about women, fully in concert with generalized Indian Buddhist misogynistic notions, which among other things see women as sexually dangerous and inconstant beings. When we find an echo of this expression in the *Dharmarucy-avadāna*, however, it takes the form of the following aphoristic justification for the acceptability of a son having a sexual relationship with his mother:[3]

> The female sex is like a road. For that upon which the father goes, the son too goes upon just the same. And this road is not the agent of fault to the son who follows it—it is rather the female sex [that is the agent of the fault]. And the female sex is also like a bathing spot, for at just that bathing spot in which the father bathes, the son too bathes, and the bathing spot is not the agent of fault of the son who is bathing—it is rather the female sex. Moreover, in a bordering country, just this is the normal way things are done: the son also approaches that same woman whom the father approaches for illicit purposes.

The authors of this text, with a rhetorical tour de force, turn a well-known cliché on its head. Women are accessible to all, the mother argues, so son and father may share a woman, even the son's mother. That the appeal here is not only to the idea found in the verse cited above becomes clear from a look at other sources. For although apparently presented in a nonspecific fashion, the second portion of the aphoristic or proverbial appeal in the *Dharmarucy-avadāna* is more than a stereotyped criticism of immoral behavior, attributed here to nameless foreigners—the depraved, degenerate, and obscene Other—although it is certainly that as well. It is this second element of the argument that gives us our key. For it refers to an actual practice, to which allusion is made many times in various Indian texts, Buddhist and non-Buddhist, as well as in other ancient sources from East and West. A familiarity with these sources will allow us both to more fully appreciate the *Dharmarucy-avadāna*'s aspersions and their rhetorical force, and to better gauge general Indian Buddhist attitudes toward incest. We will notice in the following that the stock example of incest is invoked to illustrate the very worst immorality, strong evidence that Indian Buddhists also found such practices entirely unacceptable.[4]

One of the earliest sources helpful to our appreciation of the rhetoric of the *Dharmarucy-avadāna* is found in the *Karmaprajñapti* (Elucidation of the Workings of Karma), a Sarvāstivāda Abhidharma text. There we read as follows:[5]

> In the West there are those called Maga-Brahmins, and they speak as follows: "No sin comes about from the practice of perverted lustful behavior toward a mother, a daughter, a sister, or a friend, a kinsman, or the aged." Why? They say: "Women are like cooked rice: just as cooked rice is to be enjoyed [by all in common], so too are women to be copulated with [by all in common]. Women are like pestles: just as pestles are to be used for pounding [by all in common], so too are women to be copulated with [by all in common]. Women are like roads: just as roads are to be traveled on back and forth [by all in common], so too are women to be copulated with [by all in common]. Women are like river banks: just as river banks are for [all to communally] gather at to bathe, so too are women to be copulated with [by all in common]. Women are like flowers and fruit: just as flowers and fruit are to be enjoyed [by all in common], so too are women to be copulated with [by all in common]."
>
> Having made this claim, they go on to say: "For [such] people there is no engaging in incestuous intercourse." Why? With the claim that because there are no distinctions for [such] people between different types of individuals, they say that that action [of incestuous intercourse] has no manifestation or any fruit. And seeing things in this light, they say: "This action has no [karmic result, thus karmically speaking it is a nonaction]. This action does not bring about full fruition (**phalavipāka*)." Making this claim, non-Buddhists (**tīrthika*) who engage in incestuous intercourse engender [this type of] karma.

We see here a fusion of the characterization of women seen in the verse cited above with a claim that therefore incestuous intercourse is permissible. The text goes so far as to dramatize the defense of these actions that their practitioners would or might offer. Similar presentations are not rare in Indian Buddhist literature. Without doubt based on the same idea or tradition, the *Vibhāṣā* itself says the following:[6]

> In the West there are barbarians (*mleccha*) called Maga who produce such views as these and establish such theories: There is absolutely no sin in behaving lustily with one's mother, daughter, elder or younger sister, daughter-in-law, or the like. Why? All women-kind are like ripe fruit, like prepared food and drink, a road, a bridge, a boat, a bathing spot, a mortar, and so on. It is the custom that beings use these in common, and therefore there is no sin in behaving lustily toward them.

In a very similar passage in a later philosophical text, the *Tarkajvālā*, the author Bhāviveka criticizes the Maga and others of perverse behavior, including in this category Persians and attributing to them the following view:[7]

> In the same way: since all women are similar to a wooden mortar, a flower, fruit, cooked food, bathing steps, a road, and so on, it is no good to claim that it is not proper to sexually approach a mother, sister, daughter, and so on.

These Indian Maga-Brahmins, the ancestors of whom were in fact Persian Zoroastrians, are often conflated with the Persian Magi, and with Persians in general. Given the not uncommon association, or even outright identification, of Persians with Magi, it is not surprising to find Indian Buddhist sources attributing to Persians in general the very same practices attributed elsewhere to Indian Magas. The *Abhidharmakośabhāṣya* of Vasubandhu, for instance, says:[8]

> [Illicit love is] produced by delusion, as with the Persians who consort with their mothers and other women, . . . And [so too are] those who say "Women resemble a wooden mortar, a flower, fruit, cooked food, a bathing spot, and a road."

Similar references are repeated in later Buddhist philosophical literature as examples of archetypical immoral behavior. Parallel references also appear in Xuanzang's seventh-century record of his travels to India, *Datang Xiyuji* (Great Tang Records of the Western Regions), and in the *Wang Och'ŏnjuguk chŏn* (Account of Travels to the Five Countries of India) by the eighth-century Korean Buddhist monk-traveler Hyech'o, both of whom refer to the Persians as those who practice incestuous marriages between mothers and sons. Nearly identical references occur in classical (Greek and Roman), non-Buddhist Indian, Arabic, and Chinese sources, all of which view Persians as those who engage in such immoral unions. The Indian Buddhist sources thus share in a judgment widespread among Persia's neighbors across the ancient world.

This stereotypical judgment of Persian behavior is not a groundless prejudice. The actual referent of such descriptions is clearly and obviously the Zoroastrian practice of *xwaētwadatha*, so-called next-of-kin marriage. In fact, in their doctrinal and theoretical rationalizations of the practice, some Persian texts advocate next-of-kin marriage with mother, daughter, or sister as superior in religious merit even to the ceremonial worship of Ahura Mazda, for it was through this type of marriage that the religious community could continue itself in purity.

Such references illustrate the thoroughgoing Indian Buddhist participation in a set of moral value judgments common to peoples from Greece to China, attitudes that see sexual relations between mother and son as wrong and indeed as the paradigm of depravity. What so exercises all these critics about the Persian case is, of course, not that some Persians engage in incest. Honest authors everywhere recognize that isolated cases of incest occur now and then. What stimulates such invective against the Persians is what these writers perceive to be Persian cultural acceptance, or even active encouragement, of such incestuous unions as a matter of policy. Isolated instances of incest can be understood as aberrations; they are, in almost a literal sense, the exceptions which prove the rule. But systemic patterns are a different thing, and present by their very existence a fundamental challenge to the universality and correctness of one's own system.[9] Whether ordinary Persians ever systematically engaged in what Indians and others would have judged to be forms of next-of-kin or even close-kin incestuous marriage is questionable; incestuous marriages in Persia appear to have been limited to a circle of elites. Nevertheless, as is so often the case, the perception here is more important than the reality, and the reputation of the Persians as a nation of incestuous sinners pervaded most of the known world throughout the first millennium of the common era. The Indian Buddhist sources, including the *Vibhāṣā*, in their acceptance of this reputation and employment of the trope as an illustration of moral turpitude, demonstrate that their authors viewed incest as the height of morally unacceptable behavior. Their presentation of the Mahādeva story demonstrates that these authors did imagine Indians capable of such acts, while their citation of the Persian example proves their disgust for such relations. The connection between the two scenarios is nowhere made more plain than in the *Dharmarucy-avadāna*.

What makes the rhetoric of the *Dharmarucy-avadāna* so effective is that this well-known cliché is turned upside-down. Indian Buddhists, as Indians in general, viewed the putative Persian practice of close-kin marriage as highly objectionable. The mother in the *Dharmarucy-avadāna* repeats nearly literally the words used to calumniate these Persian practices, pressing them into service as a justification and validation of her incestuous seduction of her son. An audience familiar with the stock expression and the common wisdom about such behaviors would have instantly seen the irony in her rhetoric.

This background, then, provides one piece of a puzzle, marks one step in our progress to demonstrate that the authors of the *Vibhāṣā* did not allude casually or in an offhand manner to Mahādeva's incest with his mother. This was not intended as, nor would it have been read as, an adventitious element of a story they might have borrowed for entirely other reasons. General cultural patterns confirm our own impressions, born of our own social morality, that the behavior attributed to Mahādeva was among the worst imaginable. The wider Indian cultural context makes increasingly probable the argument that this aspect of the characterization of the schismatic Mahādeva was central to the project of the *Vibhāṣā*'s authors.

We have already appreciated that to understand how these authors adapted the story of Dharmaruci to their needs, how they made Dharmaruci into Mahādeva, requires a careful examination of the tale of Dharmaruci, the account that either was itself, or must very closely represent, the original source of the Mahādeva tale. Further consideration of its dynamics is therefore in order.

10
The Bedtrick

At the outset of our discussion of the *Dharmarucy-avadāna*, we observed the central moral ambiguity of the portrayal of Dharmaruci himself. Another crucial element in this dynamic is the difference in knowledge between Dharmaruci and his mother, the disparity between their respective awarenesses and capacities playing a major role in our evaluation of their moral and ethical culpabilities. Since Dharmaruci is led into an incestuous sexual relationship with his mother entirely without his knowledge, he must be judged less culpable than his mother, not only for all the normal reasons regarding intentional and unintentional action, but also from the perspective that his actions could not constitute a violation of any barrier or taboo, of which he was entirely unaware. I will consider the possibility of relating such behaviors to a broader context of evolutionary biology and the development of incest taboos in the concluding sections of this study, but first it will be worth our while to explore the dynamics of the seductions in our stories.

The fashion in which Dharmaruci's mother seduces him is remarkable, but hardly unique in world literature, or even in Indian literature. This general type of deception has been traced in quite considerable detail in Wendy Doniger's fascinating cross-cultural study of the "bedtrick."[1] Most basically, the bedtrick consists in being led to have sex with a partner who is someone other than one expects or believes him or her to be. As Doniger puts it, the person you wake up with is not the person with whom you went to bed. Very clearly, in this sense, Dharmaruci did not go to bed with his own mother. How could he? He had been sleeping, rather, with a silent young woman so shy that she refused even to show herself to him—and he did this after he had received his mother's permission to go out and visit a friend. When Dharmaruci finally wakes up to the true situation, or rather when he is rudely awakened to it, he finds that the woman with whom he went to bed was entirely different from the one with whom he awoke—and in his case, more than most, quite shockingly so.

There is more than one way to understand the psychology of the bedtrick, how it works, and what it does to its victims. A strong feminist reading, for instance, sees the victimization of the bedtrick as equivalent to rape. Marliss Desens, a specialist in English literature, in which the trope of the bedtrick is quite common, writes as follows:[2]

> The bedtrick explicitly requires that at least one partner not have informed consent to the sexual contact. The absence of physical violence in most bedtricks should not become a pretext for ignoring the physical and emotional violation that occurs whether the deceived person is female or male. . . . At least one partner is always physically and emotionally violated in a bedtrick; while that partner has chosen sexual involvement, he or she has not chosen it with the person unwittingly embraced in the dark. . . .
>
> The legal system . . . denies that a man could be sexually assaulted—particularly that he could be assaulted by a woman. Recent feminist and psychological theory has pointed out the limitations of these societal beliefs and their harmful effects on both women and men. I follow the lead of these theorists in defining rape as any sexual contact to which a person, either male or female, does not have informed consent. Whether that assault takes the form of physical violence or manipulation and deceit is a difference only in means; for the victim, the violation is the same.

Legal theorist Jane Larson, who is concerned not with literature but with real world deceptions, takes an only slightly different view, arguing that the "purported distinction" between forcible rape and fraudulently induced sex "is one of degree rather than of kind. When sexual consent is coerced, whether by force or fraud, the result is nonconsensual sex, a moral *and* physical dispossession of one's sexual body."[3] We can understand her approach more fully when we take note of her motives. Her standpoint, she tells us, is avowedly one of advocacy:[4]

> In this Article, I seek to reinvigorate the debate over seduction and to redefine the boundaries of sexual coercion by reconceiving seduction as a viable tort. Sexual fraud, as I have named the tort for modern purposes, is an act of intentional, harmful misrepresentation made for the purpose of gaining another's consent to sexual relations. Throughout this Article I use the term "fraud" in this precise legal sense, not as the term is sometimes loosely used to refer to other, vaguely wrongful behavior. My purpose is to craft a legal vehicle that will address the physical and emotional injuries caused by deceptive inducement into sex. I begin from the premise that sexual fraud leads to nonconsensual sex because it deprives the victim of control over her body and denies her meaningful

> sexual choice. Like other sexual acts that are not fully consensual, sex induced by fraud has the potential to cause grave physical and emotional injury.

While the distinction that some legal theorists want to maintain is that between physical and mental violence, Desens and Larson emphasize that the mere absence of physical violence should not lead us to assume that no violence has taken place, that there has been no violation and, in that sense, no assault, or that such an assault is less serious than one which involves physical violence. As Doniger points out, "the reaction of people who discover that they have been the victims of a bedtrick include disbelief, fury, sadness, embarrassment, loss of self-esteem, and sometimes madness." And as she goes on, she seems to agree with the theorists she has cited:[5]

> Though it is less physically violent than a brutal physical rape, the bedtrick is a kind of delayed-action rape, a retroactive or retrospective rape, a rape with a time lag: first it fucks your body, and later it fucks your mind. Your body says yes and then, later, your mind says no. When you finally realize, ex post facto, that it was the wrong guy/gal, you reclassify the whole experience as rape. At the time of the act, the victim of rape experiences terror and the victim of the bedtrick experiences pleasure; later, the victim of rape experiences rage and shame, and when the truth of the act is revealed, the victim of the bedtrick experiences rage and a different kind of shame, tempered by mental remorse.

But despite having presented this apparently rather clear and unequivocal view, Doniger's subsequent discussion takes a somewhat different, and perhaps slightly less dogmatic, turn:[6]

> Is it worse to have your mind raped or to have your body raped? Different people will make different choices. The situation is more complex than Desens and the lawyers make it. We need different words; both rape and the bedtrick are forms of illegitimate sexual access, one by force and the other by guile; but English is a rich language, and "rape" should not be applied to both situations. The two phenomena can neither be conflated in a term like "rape-trick" nor be simply dichotomized. The anguish that a woman feels when, bound and gagged or at knife point, she is physically penetrated by someone she despises is different from the anguish that she feels when she realizes, after enjoying a night of passionate sex, that she had been with someone she did not love and could not distinguish from

> one she did love—or, worse, that she half knew the difference and could not stop her body from responding. The shock with which most victims of the bedtrick react to it is not unlike the reaction to a conventional rape, but the bedtrick violates the trickster as well as the victim. Both the bedtrickster and the victim suffer a kind of debasement, each in his or her own way, whereas in physical rape the rapist does not usually share the sense of debasement that is felt by the victim.

Inspired by these ideas to consider Dharmaruci's case, we can see at least two weighty elements at work: there is a dynamic of victimization in Dharmaruci's seduction by his mother, in which, at least in Doniger's reading, the mother, too, must be counted as in some sense a victim, albeit in a way radically different from the way in which Dharmaruci himself is victimized. And then there is the undeniable fist in the face of the incest: Dharmaruci's unwitting bed partner is not merely a woman different from the one he was led to expect—she is his own mother.

The authors of *Dharmarucy-avadāna* show themselves to be keenly aware of the dramatic and psychological necessities and possibilities of their plot. How could it ever be possible for young Dharmaruci to fail to recognize his mother in bed? There are many possible answers, chief among which we may want to consider one hinted at by Doniger: is it possible that Dharmaruci really did know, or that he suspected, but suppressed the knowledge? His violent reaction when confronted with the truth, in which he is said to have "dropped to the ground stunned and shaken," argues against such a reading. Rather, the authors of the text are at pains to point out, the young woman with whom Dharmaruci will be sleeping prefers to remain silent: there can be no voice to betray the deception. And the authors weave this into the plot with subtlety: "Gripped by timidity and bashfulness that girl won't say anything," Dharmaruci is told by the old procuress, in such a way that the silence is accounted for as a thoroughly natural aspect of the story. Of course, silence may also be a mark of subjugation: a feminist reading can hardly fail to notice that the woman is rendered voiceless, and thus, it could be argued, powerless, while nothing is said about the silence of the son. Yet such a reading too would be hard to defend in the context of the whole: here the mother's silence is voluntary, both a tactical and a strategic silence, the silence of the infiltrator rather than that of the helpless victim.[7]

A second sensual aspect of the bedtrick has to do with sight. Our text, like so many of its type, goes out of its way to emphasize the profound black of the night when the lovers meet, "at the time when forms are not recognizable," and again "in the evening when things are discerned indistinctly."[8] When Dharmaruci's partner departs after their sexual encounter, it is "at the end of the night, in the black, still hours of blind darkness, when the undiscerned shapes of forms do not appear," and so on, with other similar remarks, all emphasizing the utter impossibility that Dharmaruci might recognize his mother by sight. The dark and the silence, of course, are elements that appear in almost all stories of the bedtrick; without them, there can be no trick, for recognition is the enemy of deception.

A final aspect of Dharmaruci's inability or failure to recognize his own mother in the quiet dark hinges on a third sense, on his inability to compare her physically with any other woman, since the text makes a point of stressing his sexual inexperience. The potential problem of his refusing to recognize the other-than-expected physicality of his sexual partner therefore cannot arise.[9] There is an additional element of deception, which seems in an odd sort of way to double back upon itself. Dharmaruci, who is being deceived by his mother in the quiet, black dead of night, also "deceives" that same mother. "I'm going to a friend's house, and I'll sleep there," Dharmaruci tells his mother (and the word for friend is masculine, *vayasya*), as he leaves for the night—and she gives him permission to go. Dharmaruci thinks he is deceiving his mother, going off to a secret rendezvous with his anonymous young lover. And the mother allows herself to appear to be deceived because she is, in fact, rather the deceiver. To act like the mother of the matricide in the *Pravrajyāvastu* story, who suspects her son's intentions and thus prevents him from making a nocturnal assignation with a young girl, would be to subvert her own agenda. Her acquiescence to her son's imagined deception is nothing more than her acting to further her own deceptive machinations. Unlike what transpires in many other bedtrick stories, her deception is never seen through, but only revealed, and it is only the mother who can reveal it, since only she knows the true nature of this reality. Dharmaruci's victimhood here is obvious: he is the one without knowledge and thus without power. His actions are all directed and manipulated by another who does know and is thus powerful. The mother's control is so complete that even in his attempt to deceive her Dharmaruci is not actually pursuing his own agenda, but rather furthering hers. He has been so manipulated that he believes himself to be working against his mother for his own ends when in fact precisely the opposite is the case.

Dharmaruci's mother is also, to be sure, constrained by circumstances not entirely of her own making. This version of the story makes it clear that she does not necessarily wish from the very beginning to seduce her son; she merely wants to find some lover, any man who will be able to relieve her sexual tensions, but intercourse with whom will not subject her to public scandal. It is only when she realizes that social circumstances will prevent her from finding a lover that she turns, in desperation, to her own son. In this sense, although she has power over her son, she is also subordinate to larger forces within society—just as are all actors.

Within the frame of the family, however, it is clearly the mother who is in the dominant position with respect to the son, with all the attendant implications for the directionality of deception and manipulation that this entails.

In addition to this societal constraint, there is also an element of class involved in the indication that the wife cannot take a lover because of her reputation and because of the presence of her staff and servants. The first factor we may assume to have been generally very common in any ancient Indian community, regardless of social class. Although erotic texts like the *Kāmasūtra* or story collections like the *Śukasaptati* (Seventy Stories of the Parrot) portray a world in which adultery is almost a game, what we know about the structure of classical Indian society strongly suggests that sexual liberalism outside of marriage *on the part of women* was not much appreciated. Despite the subsequent turn the story takes with the mother's unusual solution to her problem, the depiction of the surrounding social environment rings true. While our story suggests some social status for Dharmaruci's family, they clearly do not belong to the very highest class or status. The family is depicted, as is frequent in Indian Buddhist literature, as one of merchants, and therefore is located in what we might today term the middle or upper middle class. The implication that it is perfectly acceptable for an unmarried young man to take a lover who is not a professional courtesan is also of interest. No blame is ever expressed over his conduct of taking a secret lover—only over the fact that she turns out to be his mother.

The chain of deception does not end when Dharmaruci learns of his lover's identity. Once mother and son are living together as lovers, they together deceive those among whom they live by concealing the nature of their relationship. And it is once again the mother who takes the initiative to replace this particular deception with another, by moving far away and establishing the pair in a foreign land, not as mother and son but as husband and wife. And once again we see the same pattern of deception unfold, at least partially and in a sort of inverted fashion: someone does "see through" this new deception only because of what he does not know—he sees truth because he does not see deception. An arhat from their hometown knows them, but only as mother and son, not as husband and wife. He penetrates their deception only because he is not at all aware that any deception exists. The mother has her final opportunity to deceive when, while still sleeping with her son, she also engages in a love affair with a merchant's son that she keeps secret from her own son and lover.

It is rather remarkable, and perhaps significant for my argument, that almost immediately after Dharmaruci eliminates his mother he loses all interest in deception, although not, it is true, his capacity to commit evil. He is depicted as repentant and as going to the monastic community for refuge as a means to expiate his sins. When he is asked, as part of the initiation procedure, whether he has committed any of the disqualifying acts—such as murder of his mother, father, or an arhat—each time he answers truthfully and without deception in the affirmative. Since it is his mother who initiated the chain of events that led not only to Dharmaruci's incest but to the subsequent series of murders, it is entirely convincing from a psychological point of view that he should cease to be interested in deception once his mother has been removed. It is true, however, that when he is refused ordination, he responds by burning the monastery to the ground, killing all the monks within, a pattern he repeats, the text says, countless times, until at last the future Buddha is able to contain him through a partial conversion.[10] This activity is, to say the least, antisocial, and indeed murderous and criminal, but it is not deceptive. In the modern idiom, one might suggest that while the motivations for Dharmaruci's deceptions have ceased, his damaged psyche remains.

The characterization of Dharmaruci in the *Divyāvadāna* as evil yet nondeceptive contrasts sharply with Mahādeva's intentionally duplicitous presentation of the Five Theses in the *Vibhāṣā* and elsewhere. The attribution to Mahādeva of these theses demands that he, as their author, be fully aware of their falsity. He is portrayed as offering them solely to rationalize his own failings, to explain how, while not truly an arhat, he should yet qualify and be recognized as such. A major thrust of the *Vibhāṣā*'s argument against Mahādeva's Five Theses is manifest in its attack on him personally. Not only are the theses themselves untrue, but they are known to their author to be untrue; he purposely authored them as deceptive untruths in order to conceal his failure to attain the state he claims for himself. The argument against the theses becomes an argument against their author, and the argument against their author comes to constitute proof of the falsity of those very theses. But the personality that would engage in such deception is not the personality of the incest victim, nor of the murderer who, without hesitation, acknowledges his guilt when interrogated, as does Dharmaruci. I believe that the authors who, in the *Vibhāṣā* and elsewhere, combined the Dharmaruci story with that of the initial sectarian schism fully appreciated this contradiction. In adopting and adapting to their needs the story of Dharmaruci, which they transformed into the story of Mahādeva, these authors excised, or tried to excise, any hint of moral ambiguity, any trace of complexity, and certainly any suggestion that their protagonist may not have been in total control of any of his actions. They cannot permit the doubt that Mahādeva might have been a victim, or the possibility that he did not intend to say what his Five Theses seem to imply. They must present their Mahādeva as a self-consciously evil figure in order to deny any ground for mediation between his ideas and theirs. Therefore, their Mahādeva is not the ignorant victim of a seductive bedtrick, but the conscious perpetrator of an incestuous sexual approach to his own mother.

In sharp contrast to Dharmaruci, Mahādeva knows precisely the nature of the sexual relationship in which he is involved. Moreover, and crucially, his deception does not cease with the removal of his mother, as did Dharmaruci's. His very promotion of the Five Theses, the purpose of which is portrayed as the concealment of his own failure to truly achieve arhathood, emphasizes his fundamentally duplicitous and untrustworthy nature. Mahādeva fits the role of heretical deceiver well, thanks to this thoroughgoing transformation from partial victim to nearly unqualified aggressor.

We should not overlook the difference these modalities of deception produce in light of otherwise similar examples. Doniger tells us:[11] "A paradigmatic bedtrick is the tale of the son whose mother mistakes him, at the very least, for someone who is not her son (as in Sophocles' *Oedipus the King*) or, at the very most, for his father." In the Dharmaruci story, of course, this is most emphatically not the case. There is a bedtrick, to be sure, but the mistaking of identity is not mutual (as it is in *Oedipus the King* and so many other such stories), nor that of the mother, but only that of the son. The mother is not the mistaker but the mistakee, as is the case so very often in examples from literatures from around the world.[12] Stories in which all parties to a deception are ignorant—and it can then hardly rightly be termed "deception"—differ fundamentally and typologically from those in which one party has knowledge, and therefore power and control, over another.

A startling example of a short story from an entirely different literature which, nevertheless, shares a great deal with the episode we are discussing occurs as the seventeenth chapter of the *Erotika Pathemata*, a collection of Greek "[unhappy] love stories" by the poet Parthenius, an author of the first century B.C.E. There we find the following story told of the vicious tyrant Periander:[13]

> It is also said that Periander of Corinth was, initially, reasonable and mild of disposition, but that he later became more bloodthirsty for the following reason. His mother was smitten with a violent passion for him when he was still a very young man, and for a while satisfied her desires by embracing the boy. But as time went on the passion got worse and she was no longer able to control her malady, so that she finally summoned up the courage to broach the subject with her son, telling him that a certain woman, a very beautiful one, was in love with him, and exhorted him not to look on while this woman was further tortured. At first he refused to corrupt a woman married according to all due laws and ordinances. But when his mother continued to press him, he consented. When the agreed-on night arrived, she pre-instructed her son that he must not show any light in the chamber and must place the woman under no constraint

> to speak, saying that she made this additional stipulation from modesty. When Periander agreed to do everything as his mother told him, she decked herself out as well as she could and went in to her son, leaving again secretly before the first glimmerings of dawn. Next day, she asked if everything had gone according to his taste, and whether she should tell the woman to come again, to which Periander replied that he was very keen, indeed that he had derived no little pleasure. After this she never stopped coming to her son and Periander even began to fall slightly in love. He began to consider it a matter of some urgency to find out who the woman was. For a while he begged his mother to ask the woman to speak to him, and, since she had brought him into a state of great desire, at some point to reveal herself: as it was, he was suffering an altogether senseless situation because he was not allowed to see the woman who had been his lover for so long. But when his mother forbade it, urging the woman's modesty, he told one of his servants to conceal a light. So, when she came in as usual and was about to lie down, Periander ran up and picked up the lamp; and when he saw his mother he rushed upon her as if to kill her. But he desisted, checked by a divine apparition; and after this he was stricken in mind and soul, plunging into savagery and murdering many of the citizens. Meanwhile, his mother, greatly bewailing her own fate, put an end to her own life.

The resemblance between this Greek story and our Indian tale of Dharmaruci may inspire us to wonder whether this very story, or one similar to it from Greek literature, might have been known in the Indian Northwest, the home of our Buddhist stories. For as we know, thanks to the incursions of Alexander in the fourth century B.C.E., Greek influence in this region was strong and persistent, a fact illustrated with great clarity for the earlier periods by the existence of the Bactrian Greek polis of Ai Khanum on the Oxus river. It is hard to know how much and what type of continued contact there was between the Greek world and once-Greek domains in the East, and while considerable attention has been given to the impact of Greek and later Roman models on the visual arts of Gandhāra in particular, not much investigation has been made into possible influences on narrative literature (despite famous examples of diffusion in the opposite direction).[14] Moreover, the period of composition of even the precursors of the Indian Buddhist literature in question can hardly go back to the period of Alexander, although just how far back their roots do lie is an open question. I am not suggesting that Parthenius's work in particular, the influence of which even on later Greek traditions is far from sure,[15] was known to Indian authors, something that seems unlikely. I only wish to mention the possibility of such cross-cultural transmission and to raise the question of whether in fact some such model may have been available to Indian writers, no matter how indirectly. As the ancient Buddhist literature of the Northwest becomes better known, some light may be thrown on these questions.[16]

Although there are differences between this episode in Parthenius's Greek work and our Indian stories, the similarities are so great as to allow us, or even compel us, to place the stories together from a typological or thematic point of view as representing a type or subtype, irrespective of any theoretically possible genetic connection. And in the context of our present discussion, it is not only the modalities of the deception, in which silence and darkness play such a big role, but what results from the revelation of the deception that draws our attention. For Periander becomes violent in response, the story tells us, to the deception practiced upon him, a similar but much more savage response than we see depicted in our Indian accounts.

Dharmaruci confesses himself, when he discovers the true identity of his sexual partner, to be depressed and bewildered. The Sanskrit words used here are *kheda*, which has the sense of exhaustion and pain, and *saṁmoha*, which has an implication of perplexity and stupefaction. This response falls well within the range of possible reactions of the victim of a bedtrick suggested by Doniger, and is not far from her "disbelief, fury, sadness, embarrassment, loss of self-esteem, and . . . madness," an enumeration that also well describes Periander's response. Perhaps Dharmaruci is not physically damaged by his experience, but his emotional damage is manifest. Yet, quite unlike Periander, he continues the relationship, even after he discovers the identity of his sexual partner. And this too should not entirely surprise us, for the seduction of Dharmaruci is not only sexual, but mental as well. All children are, in one way or another and some more than others, beholden to their parents, to whom they look up, from whom they seek guidance, and whom they seek to please. When the direction that guidance takes veers far from the conventional ethical standard, the observer, no matter how much he abhors ethical relativism, is hardly justified in blaming the child for conforming to the deviance of the parent. In this respect, it is not unreasonable to suggest that Dharmaruci was manipulated into continuing the sexual relationship with his mother, especially in the absence of his father. Indeed, the mother convinces him of the rectitude, or at least the general acceptability, of the course of action she asks of him and otherwise pressures him into continuing it by appealing to the aphoristic wisdom that "the female sex is like a road" and so on. Moral suasion and emotional blackmail, while surely not "the same" as other types of abuse, constitute abuse nevertheless, and it would be hard to deny that Dharmaruci's mother is engaging here (among other things) in psychological child abuse.

Incest becomes child abuse because of the inherent imbalance of power between child and parent. Any sexual approach from one in a relatively stronger position of power has the potential to be, even if it is not inherently, abusive, something that is widely recognized, for instance, in the prohibitions schools (even universities) set in place against relations between teachers and their (even adult) students. In the case of a child, moreover, the assumption is that the child has not little power, but none at all, and therefore the potential abuse is not just possible, but certain. Dharmaruci's case may be little different. The young man is manipulated, even raped perhaps, if we follow the interpretive approach of some feminist theorists. He would not be a victim of abuse only if his participation in the sexual affair were wholly voluntary—but his position vis-à-vis his mother makes such volition prima facie impossible.[17]

This conclusion, however, may be less evident than it seems. One could also make the opposite argument. The same set of circumstances that seem to make Dharmaruci into a rape victim may preclude characterizing him as a victim of abuse, as manipulated by another in a relatively superior position of power. Dharmaruci cannot be so manipulated since he has no idea of the identity of his sex partner; he cannot be victimized or manipulated by the power she holds over him, since he does not know who she is. Of course, after his mother reveals to him her identity, the equation changes completely. Now the son Dharmaruci is in the thrall of his mother and subject to her control. From that point on, it may be entirely fair to consider him as a victim of her manipulative devices.

What we do not see in this story may teach us as much as we learn from what is visible. There are a number of interesting tensions between presences and absences, several of which revolve around the issue of love. For Dharmaruci, there is a complete dissociation between sex and love. Although we have no specific evidence on this point, Dharmaruci probably loves his mother as a mother. Yet he has sex with an anonymous woman. The physical relationship of mother and son, even after the deception is rolled back and mutual recognition arises, even after the anonymous lover becomes his mother, is depicted as one of lust without love. The sexual bond is so powerful that after his mother reveals her identity to Dharmaruci, the sexual aspects of their relationship are able to overwhelm, or at least cohabit with, the normal mother-son dynamic. The anonymous lover-mother overpowers the nurturing mother, suppresses her, and represses her. Not unrelated here is the fact that later on Dharmaruci is clearly sexually jealous of his mother. But aside from the brief mention that he kills her in a jealous rage over her infidelity, and perhaps the earlier murder of his sexual competitor father, in which he is encouraged by his mother against his own inclination, the theme is not explored.

A contrast to the dynamic of Dharmaruci and his mother is presented by the case of Dharmaruci's father. His primary role is to be absent. Yet when he (re)appears, his love for and pride in his son are made clear through his comments to his fellow merchants and their subsequent actions after his death. We are led to the notion that in contrast to the present mother, who neither feels pride in her son nor particularly loves him, the long absent father does in fact feel affection for his son. To his absent loving father Dharmaruci is an individual, while to his present scheming mother he is an object, little more than a tool for her use.

Another issue (so to speak) that does not come up at all is procreation. As I have mentioned, and will explore further in Chapter 19, some of the greatest objections to incestuous relations revolve around the problem of offspring and what we now refer to as genetic damage. Although Dharmaruci and his mother are portrayed as having a long-term sexual relationship, never once does the issue of progeny arise.[18] Likewise, no attention is paid in the story of Dharmaruci, or elsewhere in the stories we have studied, to the mother's betrayal of her husband, although the theme of cuckolding is common in Indian story literature. The very pleasant collection of tales called *Śukasaptati* (Seventy Stories of the Parrot), which is better known in the West through its Persian version, the *Tutinama*, is framed by the conceit that a wife wishes to betray her husband and have a love affair in his absence. Night after night a clever parrot tells her stories to prevent her from venturing out to meet a lover.[19] Despite the existence of this text and others like it, we must certainly assume cuckolding to have been seen generally in ancient India as neither cute nor amusing, and the failure of the Dharmaruci story to pay any attention to the mother's sexual infidelity to her husband is, in this light, interesting.

Modern perspectives and questions are necessary and inevitable for us as modern readers. Without them, the ancient stories cannot yield meaning to us. But traditional readings do more than supplement modern problematics; they provide the essential grounding that keeps our readings honest. Parallels and contrasts allow us to frame our readings in authentic ways. A special kind of assistance can be found in traditional recastings of ancient stories, since these provide an exegetical or commentarial viewpoint and thus implicitly a check on our otherwise potentially unfettered modernism. We are therefore very fortunate to have access to a poetic retelling of the Dharmaruci story, to which we shall now turn.

11

Retelling Dharmaruci's Story

THE *DHARMARUCY-AVADĀNA* of the *Bodhisattvāvadānakalpalatā* (Wish-Granting Garland of Tales of the Bodhisattva), composed by the Kashmiri poet Kṣemendra in 1052 C.E., is a literary recasting of the *Divyāvadāna*'s story of Dharmaruci. While true to its model, this version presents some differences in emphasis and interpretation. Aside from its intrinsic interest and poetic value (lost, I am afraid, in my translation), this source may also be read as an interpretation of the *Divyāvadāna* story by an educated and knowledgeable Indian reader. Seen from this perspective, Kṣemendra's understanding of the *Divyāvadāna* story becomes for us an invaluable supplement to that earlier source. Kṣemendra's retelling reads as follows:[1]

> In the third aeon, long ago, there appeared in Jambudvīpa a Blessed One, Tathāgata, Krakucchanda, a treasury of unexcelled knowledge [120]. At that time in Ujjayinī there was an extremely wealthy man, a merchant named Candanadatta, famous for his commerce [121]. His wife was named Kāmabalā, (Embodying) the Army of the God of Love, and they had a son named Aśvadatta, whose beauty was like that of the God of Love, beloved to them as their own bodies [122]. Being desirous of gaining wealth, he went to sea, having entrusted the domestic affairs to his wife. For a rich man his thirst for wealth increases just like thirst increases when one drinks salt water [123].[2] His wife, with her husband gone abroad, deluded by the infatuations of youth, abandoned considerations of her household and could think of nothing but lust [124].
>
> After she set up the boy Aśvadatta in the money business, she would always stay in a turret of the palace and watch the main boulevard [125]. Being without any opportunity to do as she wished in a house of many servants and staff, she approached an old wet nurse and spoke with a deep sigh [126]: "Because I lack the freedom to wander where I will, mother, although I am here in a house of wealth, much property, and people subject to my orders, I am not truly happy [127]. When deprived of sexual union with a man, women are not pleased by status, honors, ornaments, or food

[128]. So I'll abandon this house and go away, behaving as I wish. Even this son of mine, having reached only his infancy, is not the abode of my love]129]. For fickle women addicted to physical pleasures do not tolerate the restraints of relatives connected with both families like rivers do not tolerate the restraints of an embankment built up on both banks [130]."

The wet nurse, upset because of her devotion (to her employer), spoke to the woman who was talking like this: "My dear, it's not right that you leave, abandoning such ample riches [131]. But here in this busy house, secret activity is not possible. In an instant news of one's confidential business will run around on the main boulevards [132]. How can you, inflamed by the heat of youth, protect your reputation? But how can you leave if it means kicking away the wealth of the house [133]? On one hand, an attack by the poison of lust, on the other a fall into an abyss in an instant—I don't know what you should do facing these two perils [134]. As long as she doesn't get rid of her clothing, philanderers eager with curiosity importune the wife of another even if it means staking their own lives [135]. Who does not desire the woman who, saying 'No! No! No!' while her quivering skirt and garments are being torn off, murmurs 'I'm leaving, let me go! Let me go! [136]' But having seen her unclad, the person who has thoroughly accomplished what he set out to do flees from the cage of her arms like a parrot freed from a cage [137]. The enjoyment of half an instant of blissful intercourse with a thief of love in the dark later on becomes a joining in the other world completely devoid of light (namely, hell) [138].[3] She walks with face downcast from the misery of her shame, as if searching for the lost jewel of her virtue on a rough road, miserable, her suffering fruitless [139].

"Once the scandal of her transgression is spread about, she weeps filling the whole earth with huge tears, seemingly incarnations of her deep depression, as if with pearls from the necklace of her unsullied virtue now snapped by the exertions of lovemaking [140]. Wanton women, gazing upon the smile of a child lovely as the cool-rayed moon, are suddenly saddened, their lotus-faces completely closed up like a flower when they hear their private domestic discussions being publicly bandied about, and their minds are filled with mistrust and suspicion when so much as a blade of grass is shaken [141].[4]

"Vain about their appearance, young women go out from their husbands' homes. But later, they are examined and abandoned by the judges in the market place [142]. Therefore, as long as you stay at home and engage in intercourse with men and no one learns of it, I'll tell you that it's okay [143].

"This boy of yours Aśvadatta is a youth who is relatively nearby. Because people will not suspect, he's the best choice for you to indulge in pleasure [144]. Where else can you find such a lovely and desirable lad? If this is how you handle things from the beginning, there won't be any problem [145]."

When she heard this speech of the wet nurse, she also considered it to be reasonable. Blind with her particular kind of severe passion, she did not perceive her descent into sin [146]. Then the wet nurse, gently praising to the boy the pleasures of sexual intercourse with a woman, directed his mind toward the sensual realm [147]. Leading him astray toward sensual pleasures, she spoke to him constantly, saying: "My dear, there is a certain woman whose husband has gone abroad who is just right for you [148]. At night in an empty house without any lamp, reclining in silence and extremely shy, she wants to have sex with you [149]."

Hearing these words of hers, the merchant's son, full of desire, continually partook of sexual pleasures with his mother in a hidden room [150]. But the increasingly swelling fire of lust of she who was constantly devoting herself to sexual intercourse at night in that secret chamber was not quenched [151]. She thought: "I cannot bear this permanent torment of concealment. For the enjoyment of pleasures of the flesh openness is essential, as they say [152]. There is no pleasure-feast at all in kissing or lovemaking without the savor of gazing upon each other's lotus-like faces [153]. So, having removed the toil of concealment, I will urge boldness in energetic enjoyment upon the youth [154]."

So thinking through the night, in the morning, when her body could be discerned, she disclosed herself to him by means of an exchange of clothes [155]. Seeing the mother who gave birth to him, he collapsed like a tree cut off at the roots, incapacitated by the poisonous attack of his sin [156]. As she sprinkled him with cold water, he gradually regained consciousness and let out a wail of distress, as if he had fallen into a vast chasm [157]. Embracing him in her arms, crazed with desire, a messenger rushing toward hell, she raised an eyebrow and spoke to him [158]:

"Why this unbearable despondency of yours, pointless and misplaced? Don't you know that it is not true that women are restrained by righteousness [159]? You haven't caused anyone to suffer or stolen anyone's wealth. Why do you imagine there is some sin in this common enjoyment of pleasure [160]? Women are like rivers, universally available, and constantly surging every which way without impediment. Why should not the son bathe without impediment in the very same river in which the father bathes [161]? The son walks down the very same path as the father. Women resemble roads, in that advances may be made upon them by everyone in common [162]. A woman is to be enjoyed by only one man; it is not right that one after another [have her]—this is merely an arbitrary rule invented by certain envious people [163]. In truth, there is no woman at all unsuitable to be approached for the sake of sexual pleasure. For women are to be enjoyed by father and son as a single vessel [164]."

Thus she energetically induced him toward a sexual liaison with her. And he, his lust aroused, constantly coupled with his mother like a beast [165].

Then, in the course of time, when his father came back from sea, secretly dispatched by his mother, he murdered him with poison [166]. Then, her lust ever increasing, a woman striving after unchecked pleasure, she openly and frankly spoke to her son, who was deluded by love [167]. "In order to obtain unrestrained pleasure, taking our goods and property, come! Let us go now to another country that will be free of obstacles [168]." Hearing those words he had sought for such a long time, he took their goods and property and went away with her [169].

Later, when they had settled in another country, the two of them concealing their sin declared that they were husband and wife and lived in complete bliss [170]. Some time after that a monk who was acquainted with them through having known them in their own country approached their house and affectionately spoke to the boy [171]. "Is your mother well? Does not your heart fall into painful regret when you think again and again of the native land you abandoned [172]?" Hearing the words spoken by the monk, he was as if struck by a stone. Alarmed by the recognition, he considered various strategies [173].

Having consulted with his mother and flustered by the fear that their secret might be betrayed, he invited the monk and without restraint killed him with a knife in the house [174]. Even killing a saint-monk, his mind did not quaver in the slightest. Cruel men become harder even than diamond through their sins [175].

For those who have fallen from the highest mountain peak of the Teaching headlong into precipitous caverns, pounded as they fall by many hundreds of outcroppings of error, there surely will be nothing but an uninterrupted series of falls [into unfortunate rebirths] [176].

Even though she was engaging in sexual intercourse with her son, she who was wholly devoted to sexual pleasures saw a merchant's son named Sundara and became filled with desire for him [177].

Sexual love increases through repeated practice of sexual enjoyment accumulated through experiencing sexual pleasure. Greed expands more and more when wealth becomes extensive. Thirst becomes intensely sharp by drinking salt water, and the tremendous torch of the submarine fire[5] blazes [ever more strongly] with the waters licked at by the tremendous torch [178].

Seeing her secretly meeting with that lustful new lover, Aśvadatta angrily killed that mother of his with a sword [179].

Weighed down by the mass of sin of three crimes of immediate retribution, he was quickly expelled from that town by the people, who had been incited by the local gods [180]. His remorse awakened, he quickly went to a large community of monks. Recognizing his own guilt, he begged for the going forth from suffering [181]. When no one offered ordination to that wicked man, he burned the community of monks to death as they slept at night [182].

But one monk, belonging to the lineage of the bodhisattvas, with a compassionate and warm mind then gave him ordination, not including the disciplinary rules [183]. When he energetically and persistently begged for the disciplinary rules, the monk said to him: "You are not worthy of assuming the disciplinary rules [184]. Just say this always: 'Homage to the Buddha! To the Buddha!' Just by hearing the name of the Victor, at the end of the aeon you will find release [185]."

Then at his death Aśvadatta fell into a dreadful hell, at the summit of which is the extremely violent cold fire of destruction [186].

Explaining "This is the Dharmaruci of long ago, whom I inquired about very long ago," the Blessed One, Tathāgata, concluded [188].

He fearlessly embraced his whirlwind of a mother, surging like a wave. Reaching maturity, he eliminated his father/obscured the sun, that treasury of radiance. One after another he violently assaulted those of the status and rank of saint and ordinary being. Polluted by the deep black smoke [of the monasteries he had set flame], is there no evil deed at all he did not commit [188]?[6]

This story in the *Bodhisattvāvadānakalpalatā* is not only broadly the same as that in the *Divyāvadāna*, but similar even in numerous details, a fact that highlights how very closely Kṣemendra hewed to his source. There are, nevertheless, several significant differences, and a study of both the correspondences and divergences will prove most interesting. We notice immediately that Kṣemendra has chosen to change the names of his characters; we cannot be certain whether he also changed the locale, since in the *Divyāvadāna* as transmitted in its manuscripts the expected reference to setting is absent. The names Kṣemendra gives the father and the protagonist, Candanadatta and Aśvadatta respectively, do not appear to be especially significant. But his name for the mother, Kāmabalā, surely is: it signifies something like "Embodying the Army of the God of Love (Kāma)" or "she who represents the Army of the God of Lust," a possessive compound with an extended meaning from a term with the basic meaning, "the power of lust." Thus already in his naming the poet sends a strong signal about the character of the mother, perhaps indicating his impression that it is her lustful nature that is the pivot of the story. In addition to many minor differences, Kṣemendra has also made some significant transformations in his presentation of the story, one of which is particularly important. In the *Divyāvadāna*, Dharmaruci's mother spontaneously sets out to seduce her own son and is initially opposed in these efforts by the go-between from whom she has requested help in finding a lover. That old woman, although she fairly quickly agrees, initially appears to be both surprised and perhaps even offended by the mother's suggestion that, in the absence of a suitable lover, she should make use of her son, saying: "How can you possibly engage in sex play with your son? It would [rather] be proper for you to enjoy sex play with another man." In Kṣemendra's recast version, it is the go-between herself who persuades the mother to seduce her son. Perhaps Kṣemendra is not, in fact, emphasizing the mother's lust as much as his source does. But I believe that Kṣemendra recasts things here for a different reason. In the *Divyāvadāna* we find either simply the word *vṛddhā*, "old woman," or one that has been taken to mean "procuress," *vṛddhayuvati*.[7] In the *Bodhisattvāvadānakalpalatā*, however, we find rather *dhātrī*, "wet nurse." In using this term, Kṣemendra appears to illustrate his familiarity with, and conformity to, the idiom of the Indian technical literature of erotics. In the famous *Kāmasūtra* of Vātsyāyana, for instance,[8] some discussion is given to the role of the go-between "foster-sister"[9] in arranging an assignation between a man and a young woman, although to be sure there are differences, since in Vātsyāyana's scenario the go-between attempts to persuade the young woman to pick a man of her choice and marry him, albeit secretly. Kṣemendra's wet nurse aggressively attempts to persuade the mother to action, an activity clearly related to the role assigned to this figure in the *Kāmasūtra* and allied literature.

The wet nurse's exhortation to Kāmabalā is long and elaborate, running to some fourteen verses. Since the entire story is told in only forty-seven verses, her proselytization consumes fully 30 percent of the poem. In contrast, although as a prose work with a slightly different narrative flow its correspondences are somewhat difficult to calculate, the entire episode of the seduction in the *Divyāvadāna*, from the mother's initial recognition of her passions to the arrangement of the place of assignation, covers no more than 17 percent of the text. This clearly demonstrates the relative weight Kṣemendra has given to this element of the story.[10] Since the wet nurse subsequently also persuades Aśvadatta to sleep with a woman who, she tells him, is married but whose husband is traveling (which is quite true, though misleading), she may be said to have seduced both parties, the mother and the son, although to be sure the mother knows from the beginning what is going on and does not object, while the son is kept in complete ignorance for a considerable time, an important imbalance with significant implications, as I have stressed above.

A major factor in the wet nurse's argument has to do with money. I earlier touched on the question of class and status and observed that one consideration is the need to preserve social reputation. In this text the argument is made more explicitly. Kāmabalā lives in a house of wealth, which she initially says she wants to abandon, leaving behind her son as well, in order to satisfy her sexual desires. Were she to attempt to carry on a love affair at home, the staff could not help but learn of it. The wet nurse's reaction is not to press the woman to control her urges, as would be "proper." The young woman has already proclaimed, in an elegant verse: "Fickle women addicted to physical pleasures do not tolerate the restraints of relatives connected with both families like rivers do not tolerate the restraints of an embankment built up on both banks." The attendant implication is that her lust is an out-of-control force of nature that cannot be artificially hemmed in. The nurse, however, appeals to an economic motive:[11] fleeing would mean giving up wealth, while to carry on an affair would destroy her reputation, as it would surely be revealed. The solution is to stay at home and make use of someone already available, namely, her very own son. Unlike in the *Divyāvadāna*, the mother is portrayed here as agreeing immediately: she thinks the suggestion is "reasonable." The word I have translated as "reasonable," *yukta*, is precisely the word that the go-between in the *Divyāvadāna* uses in her attempt to *dissuade* the mother from her suggested incest, saying, "It would [rather] be proper for you to enjoy sex play with another man," in which "proper" is the same *yukta*.[12] The correspondence is unlikely to be adventitious and provides an example of the clever way Kṣemendra has played with his source, not only on a more general thematic level but even with respect to particular vocabulary.[13]

The wet nurse's exhortation is worthy of attention, if only for the fact that she spends almost no time specifically advocating that Kāmabalā have a relationship with her son. Concentrating on the dangers of taking an unrelated lover, she accentuates the possible social, hence visible, dangers from one quarter, while quietly ignoring the moral, hence invisible, perils from the other. The first argument is that while an inaccessible woman is an attractive target, once her lover has gained his goal he is bound to reject her forthwith. And the reader need not adopt a radical feminist standpoint to cringe at the depiction: men love to rape women, especially if they resist: "Who does not desire the woman who, saying 'No! No! No!' while her quivering skirt and garments are being torn off, murmurs, 'I'm leaving, let me go! Let me go!'" Although, Kṣemendra implies that the woman should enjoy this, the aftermath will bring her only disappointment: "But having seen her unclad, the person who has thoroughly accomplished what he set out to do flees from the cage of her arms like a parrot freed from a cage." Given what seems to be the argument here, however, the verse immediately following is peculiar in the context: "The enjoyment of half an instant of blissful intercourse with a thief of love in the dark later on becomes a joining in the other world completely devoid of light." Kṣemendra seems to have the nurse say that adultery will lead to karmic retribution for both partners, such that the short instant of bliss in the dark night of the lovers' meeting entails a lengthy stay for both in the dark realms of hell. This threat can hardly be thought not to apply also in the case of an incestuous affair, which seems to make the warning somewhat inappropriate, and may suggest that the poet has slightly lost track of the overall context here or is borne along on the current of his poetic conceits.[14] Kṣemendra next offers a typically complex series of verses in which, after comparing the shamed woman's virtue to a jewel lost on the road, the tears of that betrayed lover are likened to pearls, in turn compared to her virtue.[15] A string of pearls snapped during lovemaking is a stock image for vigorous sex, but here the cascade of pearls onto the ground, rolling around everywhere, mirrors the tears a jilted woman sheds in her distress, just as it mirrors the scandal that spreads her tainted reputation far and wide. Not only is her reputation scattered about like the pearls from the broken string, it is further sullied, as are the pearls on the ground, by being trodden into the mire—as we would say, her name will be dragged through the mud.

Kṣemendra elaborates on his source in other ways as well, some having to do with the inner logic of the story. In the *Divyāvadāna*, the only reason for the mother's decision to reveal her true identity to her son seems to be her desire for convenience. But in the *Bodhisattvāvadānakalpalatā*, she thinks as follows: "For the enjoyment of pleasures of the flesh openness is essential, as they say. There is no pleasure-feast at all in kissing or lovemaking without the savor of gazing upon each other's lotus-like faces." This once again conforms to an idea from the erotic literature that all the senses must participate in the feast of lovemaking. At the same time, some things Kṣemendra has left almost as he found them in his source. The aphoristic presentation of a woman's promiscuity, in which she is likened to a road and so on, remains basically unchanged, just as there is not much modification of the arhat's murder, or of the contrite sinner's efforts to gain ordination in the Buddhist monastic community, although both are presented in less detail.

If some things such as the exhortation to incest are dramatically expanded, and some left almost unchanged, others are radically condensed. For instance, Aśvadatta's murder of his father is disposed of in a single verse, with no mention of the meeting between father and son, which in the *Divyāvadāna* allows us to glimpse the father's humanity and, as I have suggested, contrasts the father's love for his son with the mother's manipulative treatment. Another change in Kṣemendra's text has Aśvadatta agree to the proposed assignation with none of the hesitations he is made to express in the *Divyāvadāna*; on the contrary, the poet specifically notes that Aśvadatta is "full of desire," just as later he talks of "his lust aroused" as he "constantly coupled with his mother like a beast," a portrayal of the son that differs significantly from the somewhat reluctant portrait painted in the *Divyāvadāna*.[16] Of a piece with this revised portrait are the characterizations of Aśvadatta as "deluded by love," such that for a long time he himself wishes to hear his mother suggest that they flee together. Aśvadatta is much less a victim than the *Divyāvadāna*'s Dharmaruci; his seduction is so total that, perhaps like captives who fall prey to the Stockholm syndrome, he energetically and seemingly freely collaborates with the agenda of his seducer. For Kṣemendra, then, both mother *and* son are more overwhelmed by lust than are their archetypes in the *Divyāvadāna*. But there remains an imbalance.

While Aśvadatta is depicted as displaying both an untamed, animalistic sexuality and a compliant or even aggressive cooperation, Kṣemendra consistently emphasizes the overwhelming desire of his mother Kāmabalā: "the increasingly swelling fire of lust of she who was constantly devoting herself to sexual intercourse . . . was not quenched," and "her lust ever increasing . . . striving after unchecked pleasure," she later "was wholly devoted to sexual pleasures." Then Kṣemendra says:

> Sexual love increases through repeated practice of sexual enjoyment accumulated through experiencing sexual pleasure. Greed expands more and more when wealth becomes extensive. Thirst becomes intensely sharp by drinking salt water, and the tremendous torch of the submarine fire blazes [ever more strongly] with the waters licked at by the tremendous torch.

The poet has already told us, in describing Candanadatta's motivations for going to sea as a merchant, "For a rich man his thirst for wealth increases just like thirst increases when one drinks salt water." Now the steady increase in Kāmabalā's sexual passion is attributed to the same cause: the more you get, the more you want. Here too Kṣemendra is closely conforming to the *Divyāvadāna*, which introduced the idea of the mother's "infidelity" to her son and explained her desire to take another lover by saying: "and lusts are just like salt water—the more they are enjoyed, the more they are craved." Despite the fact that this image appears here and there in Indian Buddhist texts (as well as in modern Western contexts), and may in some sense be taken as obvious, I believe this to be another adoption of imagery and even wording from the *Divyāvadāna* version of his story, another example of Kṣemendra's direct reliance on and mirroring of his source.

Some things are made explicit in the *Bodhisattvāvadānakalpalatā* that are only implied in the *Divyāvadāna*. The final, summary verse, by saying "Reaching maturity, he eliminated his father," implies that Aśvadatta was still immature at the time he began the sexual liaison with his mother. This suggests that Kṣemendra, a careful student of the *Divyāvadāna*, understood Dharmaruci's mother to have been rather young at the time the story is taking place. In our discussion of the probability of mother-son incestuous unions being procreatively viable, we considered that a mother's youth would surely have a bearing on the psychological plausibility of a young man carrying on, much less initiating, a sexual relationship with his mother. The emphasis on the immaturity and inexperience of the son and the youth of the mother is no doubt intended to lend credibility to the scenario.[17]

Kṣemendra's retelling helps us understand how the *Dharmarucy-avadāna* has been traditionally read. As such, it assists us in tracing how the story of Dharmaruci was further adapted and transformed as the tale of Mahādeva. Although it is the only parallel version known now to exist in Sanskrit, the *Bodhisattvāvadānakalpalatā* does not contain the only parallel to the story of Dharmaruci in Indian Buddhist literature. Alongside this clearly derivative version, based directly on the *Divyāvadāna*, we find parallel and apparently independent redactions of the story as well. A survey of these sources will help us place the story of Dharmaruci in a broader context.

12
Dharmaruci in Other Sources

Kṣemendra's telling of the *Dharmarucy-avadāna* in his *Bodhisattvāvadānakalpalatā*, being based directly on the *Divyāvadāna*, cannot be considered independent of it, no matter how the poet may have modified the narrative. But while Kṣemendra's may be the only other known Sanskrit version of the story, this does not mean that Dharmaruci's tale is otherwise absent from Indian Buddhist literature, most of which survives, if at all, only in Tibetan and Chinese translations. In fact, stories quite similar to that in the *Dharmarucy-avadāna*—sometimes so close that we will have to say that they are the very same, although independently transmitted—appear more than once.[1] These parallel versions will, first of all, allow us to strengthen the argument that the *Vibhāṣā*'s Mahādeva story relies on some version of the Dharmaruci story. Second, they will complicate the notion that there is one and only one way to view the relation between the two traditions of the Mahādeva and Dharmaruci tales. Finally, these stories, each with its own variations, will enable us to broaden our perspectives on the meaning of the overall story within an Indian context.

Although we cannot be certain of its ultimate sources, the *Jifayue sheku tuoluoni jing* (Dhāraṇī-sūtra on Collecting the Joy of the Teachings and Getting Rid of Suffering), extant only in a Chinese version dating to the fifth century at the latest, undoubtedly presents a genuine Indian textual tradition of our story. Therein we find the following passage:[2]

> At that time the Buddha spoke to the members of the great assembly, saying: "When, during infinite aeons, I was still at the stage of being an ordinary person (**pṛthagjana*), my name was Zhetatuo. Living in the land of Jiatouluo I engaged in sales and peddling. I was dishonest and lied, and did all manner of evil deeds. It's impossible to recount my sexual perversity, and my immorality is impossible to fully detail. At that time, stupidly insensitive, I killed my father and made love to my mother. Over a number of years the people of the entire country all came to know of this, and loudly proclaimed: 'Now it's been a number of years since this Zhetatuo killed his father and made love to his mother.' At that time I

> pondered [the fact that I] was no different from the beasts; [what I did] wasn't the act of a human being. Then at night I jumped over the city wall at Jiatouluo, fled and hastened toward a deep marsh.
>
> "At that time the king of that country was called *Vija. He issued a proclamation to the people in his state: 'This fellow, Zhetatuo, has committed acts of sexual perversity, and his immorality extends to committing this offence. Whoever can lay hands on this person will be handsomely rewarded.' Then each and every person in this country responded to this appeal and was eager to get hold of me. Much alarmed, I left the state, and became a śramaṇa in another country. I cultivated the ten good [precepts], practiced seated meditation, and studied the Way. I wept day and night for thirty-seven years. Because of the obstacle of having committed the five sins of immediate retribution, my mind was never at rest, and I could not find peace. For thirty-seven years I lived in a cave in the mountains, always crying out 'Oh, how painful it is! Oh, how painful it is! With what mental [technique?] should I get rid of this pain?' When, sobbing with grief, I went down from the cave to beg for alms, on the road I found a large bowl. Within it there was a sūtra box, but only one sūtra inside: the 'Dhāraṇī on Collecting the Joy of the Teachings and Getting Rid of Suffering (*Jifayue sheku tuoluoni*).'
>
> "It is said that in the past Buddhas as many as the sands of the [Ganges] river, at the time of their nirvāṇa, always lived in the land of Piyueluo, preaching this dhāraṇī, bestowing it upon the great bodhisattvas. . . ."

The text goes on to explain that this *dhāraṇī*, or mystical spell, can save from the retributions of hell and so forth even those who sin severely. Zhetatuo abandons his search for alms and takes the *dhāraṇī*-sūtra back to his cave where he recites it for a year. He is, as we would expect, freed from the results of his evil actions.

The opening frame of this episode is itself similar enough to the stories of Mahādeva and Dharmaruci that we cannot be sure of its specific affiliations. But we find a further hint from the utterances attributed to Zhetatuo later in the passage: "Oh, how painful it is! Oh, how painful it is!" There is no mistaking here the connection with the fifth of the Five Theses in the *Vibhāṣā*. There Mahādeva is made to claim that the exclamation "Oh, how painful it is!" can be a means to motivate progress on the path of spiritual development, a view that the *Vibhāṣā* sees as heretical. We have seen that several thirteenth-century Tibetan presentations of the story of Mahādeva, including that of Sa skya Paṇḍita, also contained reference to this episode, and here something like six hundred years earlier we find the same in this *dhāraṇī* scripture. The authors of this text have very neatly integrated this element into the narrative context, and the story as a whole gives every indication of organic coherence and none of being a pastiche. Moreover, although we know this text only in its Chinese translation, we can be certain that it is unrelated to the story of Mahādeva as it was classically known in China, and thus it cannot depend on that tradition, since its appearance predates the translation of the *Vibhāṣā*, the locus classicus for the story, by some two centuries. Thus there are two possibilities for this remarkable parallelism with the story in the *Vibhāṣā*. It may be due to its reliance on some version of the *Vibhāṣā* circulating in India or Central Asia before it reached China. Or it may rely on a parallel transmission of the story more closely aligned with the version containing Mahādeva's fifth "thesis," that concerning the arhat's exclamation of pain, than with the Dharmaruci story, in which this episode plays no role. The implications of this discovery for any hypothesis concerning the sources of the *Vibhāṣā*'s account of Mahādeva remain unclear. Until and unless we can get some better picture of the history of the *Jifayue sheku tuoluoni jing* itself, and its relationship to other sources, we cannot be certain how to locate its evidence.

Regardless of its ultimate origins, this story containing a clear reference to what is elsewhere understood as one of Mahādeva's Five Theses appears here in Buddhist literature both in a context unrelated to accounts of sectarian schism, and in a genre far removed from the Avadāna narrative or Abhidharma polemical literature. This stands, if nothing else, as a measure of the evocative and provocative power of this tale of incest and murder. The same narrative that in another context is presented as the biography of the evil Mahādeva serves here to emphasize the power of the *dhāraṇī* text in which it is imbedded. Even sins as great as murder and incest, this text promises, can be overcome by the power of the Dharma, as conveyed in this specific instantiation, namely, the *dhāraṇī* to which the sūtra itself refers.

Another text with a difficult history is the *Mahāyāna Mahāparinirvāṇa-sūtra* (Mahāyāna Scripture on the Great Nirvāṇa of the Buddha). This scripture has come down to us in Sanskrit only in fragments, but in multiple complete Chinese translations, related to each other in diverse ways, and in two Tibetan translations, one from an Indic original and one made on the basis of one of the Chinese translations. For this reason, when attempting to make use of any material from the *Mahāparinirvāṇa-sūtra*, the greatest care must be exercised to control the exact source within the textual complex. The passages cited below belong to the longer recensions of the text, to the Chinese translations referred to as the Northern and Southern texts, both dating to the fourth century and in the present case identical with one another. The corresponding Tibetan version is based on just this Chinese tradition. Since the two Chinese translations are mutually dependent, and since the Tibetan translation is also dependent upon this same source, there is nowhere in this complex textual corpus any independent confirmation of the contents of the passages we are about to cite. Moreover, since the relation between this Chinese textual tradition of the expanded *Mahāparinirvāṇa-sūtra* and the putative state of the Indic text upon which these translations are ultimately based is not always known, we cannot firmly conclude that any particular passage in these Chinese translations goes back to an Indian *Mahāparinirvāṇa-sūtra*. In other words, the sorts of correspondences between independently translated Chinese versions of an Indic scripture, or between independent Chinese and Tibetan translations, which may in other cases suggest that certain contents, or even specific wording, might have stood in an Indic original lying behind those independent translations are not found here. This is all-important for us because we are primarily interested in what might have been said and thought about Mahādeva in India. With these reservations, then, and the attendant doubt regarding a possible Indian source acknowledged, we notice with interest the following passage from the *Mahāparinirvāṇa-sūtra*:[3]

> Great king, in Varanasi there was a merchant's son named *Ajita. He had secret sexual relations with his mother, and because of this he murdered his father. His mother then had an affair with another man, and when the son found out about it, he killed her too. There was an arhat who knew about this, and [the son] grew apprehensive about his knowledge, so he killed him too. After these three murders, he went to the Jetavana seeking to renounce the world. But the monks knew all about him, that he had committed three sins of immediate retribution, and refused him permission [to ordain]. Being refused, he grew angry, and that night he set a great fire which burned down the monastery, killing many innocents. Immediately thereafter he went to Rājagṛha, to wrere the Tathāgata was, seeking to renounce the world. The Tathāgata permitted him [to do so] by preaching to him the essentials of the teaching. He caused his heavy sin to be lightened and aroused in him the aspiration for unexcelled, perfect awakening. Therefore it is said that the Buddha is the world's best physician, not [the same as] the six [heretical] teachers.

Although it is true that the name is different, being given in Chinese in a form in which we can virtually certainly recognize the Indian name Ajita,[4] this episode clearly corresponds to the legend of Dharmaruci/Mahādeva. Some of the details are worth noting. Unlike most versions of the tale, though not without parallel, here the murder of the arhat takes place *after* the murder of the mother, a variant we know was transmitted in East Asian Mahādeva traditions since we observed it in the eleventh-century Japanese *Konjaku monogatarishū*, and in Tibet since this is the sequence followed by Dmar ston in his recounting.[5] Moreover, this version of the story contains the set of subsequent episodes, including the arson and final acceptance by the Buddha himself into the order, likewise attested, but not elsewhere in combination with the same inversion of narrative sequence. In addition, while the text is slightly ambiguous here, it appears to suggest that the Buddha permitted Ajita to ordain, in contrast to other versions in which his status is never fully regularized. Although we cannot name a direct source, it is possible that the authors of the *Mahāparinirvāṇa-sūtra* borrowed this episode from some version of the story of Dharmaruci or Mahādeva. While we must handle this episode with particular care, and not accept it as necessarily representative of an Indian tradition as such for the reasons stated above, it is hard to imagine upon what it might have been based if not on some version of the Dharmaruci/Mahādeva tale; the parallels are simply too close to convincingly explain otherwise. Despite the interest of this passage, then, and the great likelihood that it is directly related to the story of central concern to us, if this were the extent of what the *Mahāparinirvāṇa-sūtra* has to offer, we would have to remain very cautious. But there is more. In a completely different spot in this quite massive sūtra, likewise without certain Indic provenance for the same reasons cited above, we find explicit, if brief, mention of an evil monk named Dharmaruci:[6]

> Gentle sons, I have spoken the following for those beings who have committed the sins of immediate retribution: One who commits the five sins of immediate retribution will, upon death, go straight to the Avīci hell. And I said: The monk Dharmaruci upon death went straight to the Avīci hell, in which there is no place to rest.

This passage is truly remarkable. Dharmaruci's name is transcribed in its Indic form here, rather than translated into Chinese, and is therefore identifiable without question. Since his story as a sinful monk appears to be otherwise unknown in extant Buddhist literature in Chinese, we are virtually compelled to conclude that this reference in the *Mahāparinirvāṇa-sūtra* reflects some Indian source, although perhaps one now lost to us. The only Indian source we have met so far in which the name Dharmaruci is connected with the sins of immediate retribution is the *Divyāvadāna* (the eleventh-century *Bodhisattvāvadānakalpalatā* being clearly irrelevant here). Was there some relation between the traditions of the *Mahāparinirvāṇa-sūtra* and the (sources of the) *Divyāvadāna* within India?[7] Be that as it may, the significance of this passage for us lies most directly in its demonstration of the extent of circulation of the story of the serial sinner Dharmaruci; like the *Jifayue sheku tuoluoni jing*, the *Mahāparinirvāṇa-sūtra* also belongs to the genre of Mahāyāna scripture.

Once again, if this were the only source we knew, while interesting and potentially important in itself, there might be little more to say. But it is not, and our next source is also extraordinary, this time not for its genre but for its sectarian identity. For it does not belong to any tradition of the Sthaviras, the lineage associated with the opponents of the Mahāsāṁghikas, whose adoption of the story has been amply demonstrated. Rather, it belongs to a branch of the Mahāsāṁghika school itself. While once again the names of the central protagonists are not the same, the narrative correspondence can hardly be mistaken: there is no question but that the Dharmaruci story figures in a Mahāsāṁghika text.

The *Mahāvastu* (Great Events of the Buddha's Life), a text of the Lokottaravādin branch of the Mahāsāṁghikas, contains the story of Meghadatta, a friend of the bodhisattva, the Buddha-to-be, who is here styled Megha. In the very distant past Megha, the story tells us, hearing of the buddha Dīpaṅkara, traditionally listed as the very first buddha of our world, made an offering to him of flowers and received in return a prophecy of his future Buddhahood as Śākyamuni.[8] Megha became a monk under Dīpaṅkara, but his friend Meghadatta refused to join him and, it seems rather immediately, set out instead to commit as much evil as possible. The pertinent section of the text continues:[9]

> [Meghadatta] fell in love with another man's wife, whom he visited at every opportunity.[10] His mother, out of affection for her son, kept him away, lest [the husband] should take him for an adulterer and kill him.[11]
>
> —One infatuated knows not profit, one infatuated sees not morality. When lust overcomes a man, then he is in darkness—
>
> [Meghadatta] killed his mother and went to his mistress and in his infatuation laughingly told her what he had done. "I love you so much," said he, "that for your sake I killed my mother." The woman was horrified, and said, "Don't come to me any more."
>
> He fell in love with his stepmother, and so his stepmother told him, "Go and kill your father, and you shall become my husband." And so he killed his father.
>
> He came to be detested in the area, and his friends and relatives avoided him. And then he went from that area to another, saying, "No one will know me here." Now to that place there came, in the course of his wanderings through the provinces, a monk who was a spiritual advisor of

his parents and an arhat of great power. And the monk saw his [former] patrons' son in that place.

When [Meghadatta] in his turn saw that monk, he became apprehensive, and said, "This monk mustn't be allowed to cause me any trouble here in this area." Then he murdered that arhat-monk.

He then became ordained in the order of the one who was the perfect buddha of the time. When he was ordained in the order, he split the community, and drew the buddha's blood.

For committing the karmic acts of these five sins of immediate retribution, he was reborn in the great hells. In the course of a long period of time he passed through one life after another in the eight great hells and in the sixteen secondary ones. When the Blessed One Śākyamuni awakened to unexcelled, perfect awakening and set rolling the wheel of the Dharma, [Meghadatta became] a fish in the ocean, named Timitimiṁgila, with a body many hundreds of leagues in length.

When the householder Thapakarṇi, accompanied by five hundred companions, went down to the ocean in his ships, then there was a hungry sea monster, its mouth gaping wide in readiness for food. The ships of Sthapakarṇika[12] the householder set out to where the sea monster [waited with open] mouth. Lifting its mouth out of the water, it said: "Householder, these ships are doomed to the submarine depth. Do what you have to do, for your life is over."

They hail the gods and divinities, each invoking his own. Some invoke Śiva, others Vaiśravaṇa, others Skandha, others Varuṇa, others Yama, others Dhṛtarāṣṭra, others Virūḍhaka, others Virūpakṣa, others Indra, others Brahmā, and others the gods of the sea. At length the venerable Pūrṇaka observes and sees the householder Sthapakarṇika and his retinue of five hundred companions in their distress. He rose up from Mount Tuṇḍaturika and came flying through the air until he stood hovering in the air over the ship of Thapakarṇi on the sea. And all the five hundred merchants, joining their hands in supplication, stood up and cried: "Lord, lord! We take refuge in you!"

The Elder replied: "I am not the Blessed One. I am an auditor (*śrāvaka*). All of you with one voice cry out "Hail the Buddha!'" And all the five hundred merchants cried, "Hail the Buddha!" The sound of the Buddha's name reached the ears of Timitimiṁgila, and hearing this sound, [for the first time since] becoming the fish Timitimiṁgila in the great ocean, he realized [the name] that he had heard an immeasurable incalculable aeon before from the youth Megha, who had mentioned the name of the buddha Dīpaṁkara.

> The sound of the Buddha's name is unerring. And it occurred to [Meghadatta who had] become Timitimiṁgila: "A buddha has appeared in the world, whilst I am fallen into a state of woe." Deeply upset, he shut his mouth again, and he died of hunger, mindful of that sound "Buddha." Immediately upon his death, he was reborn in the great city of Śrāvastī, in a brahmin family, born at that time and upon that occasion as a boy.
>
> —As the Blessed One has said, "I say, monks, there is no [cause] other than karma."—
>
> That boy was named Dharmaruci, and when he grew up, he renounced the world into the Blessed One's community. By application, endeavor, and exertion, he directly realized the three knowledges, six superknowledges, and mastery of the [ten] powers.
>
> At the three times of the day he approached to bow at the feet of the Blessed One, and as often as he approached, every time the Blessed One inspired and reminded him, saying: "It's been a long time, Dharmaruci, it's been a very long time, Dharmaruci." And [Dharmaruci] replied: "Yes indeed, Blessed One, yes indeed, Sugata. It's been a long time, Blessed One, it's been a very long time, Sugata."
>
> The monks, in doubt, asked the Blessed One about this. "In the three times of the day Dharmaruci approaches the Blessed One, and the Blessed One says to him 'It's been a long time, Dharmaruci, it's been a very long time, Dharmaruci.' And he says to the Blessed One 'Yes indeed, Blessed One, yes indeed, Sugata. It's been a long time, Blessed One, it's been a very long time, Sugata.' Now, Blessed One, we do not understand the import of this exchange."
>
> The Blessed One explained the story to the monks in detail, beginning with [the story of] Dīpaṁkara. "I was the young man named Megha, and Dharmaruci was Meghadatta."

This is a story of sexual infidelities, murder of both parents and of an arhat, the ordination as a monk of the author of these actions, and his subsequent creation of a schism within the monastic community, a sin mentioned along with drawing the blood of a buddha seemingly as an afterthought and evidently merely to make up the full set of five sins of immediate retribution. It is true that there are differences between this story and the narrative tradition of the stories of Mahādeva and Dharmaruci, but these differences themselves are profoundly interesting and suggestive. In the first place, this episode begins with a nearly exact parallel to the story presented in the *Pravrajyāvastu* of the Mūlasarvāstivāda Vinaya in illustration of its rule barring the ordination of matricides. While in the *Pravrajyāvastu* the girl whom the matricide desires is a young maiden, here she is a married woman, and the mother's objection is framed as a desire to protect her son from the possible revenge of the cuckolded husband. The sequel, while highly abbreviated here, is the same: he kills his mother and brags about it to his potential mistress, who is horrified and rejects him. But then the Meghadatta story changes tracks: after Meghadatta, the Mahādeva/Dharmaruci character, kills his mother, the text replaces her with a stepmother, toward whom Meghadatta then directs his sexual desire. It is this displaced mother, as we hardly need the Freudians to identify her for us, who has him murder his father. Moreover, the pattern of culpability here, as in the *Dharmarucy-avadāna*, is not entirely simple. Meghadatta falls in love with his stepmother, but when she asks him to kill his father, she promises as a reward that he may become her husband. Promising payment in sex for the murder, she explicitly offers him fulfillment of the Freudian Oedipal wish—to kill the father and sexually possess the mother. While we have repeatedly seen the same general pattern in prior stories, here the quid pro quo is particularly directly expressed. In addition, it is crucial to notice here, as elsewhere in our materials, that the "Oedipal wish" is articulated not by the son but by the mother, a point to which I shall return. The text does not tell us whether the two, stepmother and stepson, then flee together, and the stepmother does not reappear in the story. After journeying abroad, however, Meghadatta does meet an arhat from his hometown and murders him for the same reasons that Dharmaruci did in the other stories. His ordination and subsequent crimes are then dismissed in a single sentence.

Now, if this were all that we could discover in this text, it alone would be remarkable, providing among other things a parallel from the Mahāsāṁghika tradition to a story (or better, two stories, one from the *Pravrajyāvastu*, the other from the *Divyāvadāna*) we have located otherwise only among Sarvāstivāda and Mūlasarvāstivāda materials. This certainly does not imply that the story necessarily predates the schism between the Mahāsāṁghikas and Sthaviras—it could just as easily represent a borrowing, either from one to the other, or by both from some third, even ultimately non-Buddhist, source. This text proceeds, however, to recount an extraordinary tale of a sea monster, who is none other than the karmically motivated rebirth of this criminal Meghadatta. The monster, although he has the opportunity to eat a boatload of delicious passengers, controls himself when he hears, recalls from his previous life, and is mindful of the name of the Buddha. And for this good deed of self-control and piety, he is reborn as a boy, named—Dharmaruci! The text then goes on to use precisely the words used in the *Dharmarucy-avadāna*, "It's been a long time, Dharmaruci," and so on. As astonishing as it may seem, we have here in a Mahāsāṁghika text a, perhaps slightly confused but nevertheless completely transparent,[13] parallel to the *Dharmarucy-avadāna*. But we are not done yet: the version of this story in the *Mahāvastu* is not the only one, nor does the sea monster belong to it alone.

What is clearly very much the same account, although radically simpler,[14] is also found in a relatively late, but still canonical, Pāli text, the Theravāda *Apadāna* (Stories). This was noted as long ago as 1895 by Éduard Müller,[15] who outlined the story of Dhammaruci (the Pāli equivalent of Dharmaruci) and pointed out its correspondence to the Dīpaṅkara story in the *Mahāvastu*.[16] Confusingly for us, in this version the Dharmaruci character is styled Megha, not the Meghadatta of the *Mahāvastu*, while the Megha of the *Mahāvastu* is here called Sumedha:[17]

> At that time I was a well-learned man by the name of Megha. Hearing the best of prophecies made to Sumedha the great sage, Sumedha, being completely put at ease,[18] was intent on compassion; and that hero having renounced the world, I renounced along with him. Restrained in the Pāṭimokkha and in the five senses, living purely the hero was mindful, acting according to the teachings of the Victor. Living thus I was incited by a certain bad friend into misconduct, and I lost the good path. Being under the influence of dubious reasoning, I left the order. Later, due to that bad friend I brought about the murder of my mother. I committed a sin of immediate retribution, and I carried out a murder with evil intentions. Having died, I went and was born in the great Avīci hell, where I stayed for a long while. And being fallen into evil destinies, I transmigrated in pain for a long time. I did not see the hero Sumedha again, that bull among men.
>
> In that aeon I was a fish in the sea, Timiṅgala. Seeing a boat on the ocean, I approached it in search of food. Seeing me, the merchants were fearful, and they mindfully called upon (*anu√smar*) the best of Buddhas. Hearing the great cry "Gotama!" they shouted, and remembering my former inclinations, I died. I was born as a brahmin in a wealthy household in Sāvatthī [=Śrāvastī]. I was called Dhammaruci and was one who hated all evil. Seeing the lamp of the world [the Buddha] at the age of seven, I went to the great Jetavana and renounced the world into the homeless state. I approached the Buddha during the three times of the day and of the night, and each time he saw me the Sage said to me: "It's been a long time, Dhammaruci."

While much shorter and considerably less detailed than the version in the *Mahāvastu*, there can be no doubt that at least the kernel of the same tale survives here, whether we judge this to be the result of simplification of an otherwise more elaborated version or, on the contrary, consider the other versions to have expanded on a terse core something like what we see here. On its own, but especially as seen through its partner in the *Mahāvastu*, we easily recognize the relation of this episode to the *Divyāvadāna*'s *Dharmarucy-avadāna*. There is, moreover, an additional element that needs to be brought into consideration.

We are actually not yet able to appreciate the full extent of the similarity between these *Mahāvastu* and the *Apadāna* episodes on the one hand and the *Dharmarucy-avadāna* on the other. One element I left aside in my initial presentation of the *Dharmarucy-avadāna* was the overall setting of the story. In the initial comparison, the context in which the story appears was irrelevant to my main point. But this is no longer true. As I noted at the time, I translated only the third and final portion of the *Dharmarucy-avadāna* from the *Divyāvadāna* (and the *Bodhisattvāvadānakalpalatā*), that which tells the story of incest and murder. Doing so, I ignored the frame within which the story sits. The *Dharmarucy-avadāna* as a whole (in both the *Divyāvadāna* and the *Bodhisattvāvadānakalpalatā*) begins with an introduction describing the present-day circumstances to be explained by the three stories of the past that follow.[19] The frame for the incestuous matricide's story is now important for us to notice, for it speaks of five hundred merchants who go to sea.[20] They are warned before their departure of the possible dangers that await them, catalogued in a list that begins with the sea monsters called Timi and Timiṅgala.[21] Returning from an island filled with jewels, the merchants indeed encounter an enormous Timiṅgala (here explicitly called a fish, *matsya*), whose gaping mouth is filled with sea creatures he is already eating. The *Divyāvadāna* then continues:[22]

> Then the helmsman said to the merchants: "Listen, gentlemen. There's no way we're going to survive now—no one will save us from this danger. For each and every one of us, the end is near. So, what should we do? Those of you who have a god to whom you offer devotion, pray to him! Maybe some divinity, so entreated, might save us from this great danger. There's no other way we can survive."
>
> So those merchants, scared of death, began to pray to Śiva, Varuṇa, Kubera, Mahendra, Upendra, and other gods to preserve their lives. But their prayers brought nothing in the way of protection of their lives from that deadly danger. And just in that fashion their vessel was quickly snatched by the rush of water toward the gaping mouth of Timiṅgala.
>
> Then a Buddhist lay follower got up and said: "Gentlemen, there is no escape from this deadly danger for us; we're all going to die. But let's all call out 'Hail to the Buddha!' with a single cry! If we're going to die, let's

> face the end mindful of our dependence on the Buddha, so that we may have a favorable rebirth." And thus each and every one of those merchants paid homage, saying in a single cry "Hail to the Buddha!"

The text goes on to say that, though far away, the Buddha heard their call, which he magically transmitted to Timiṅgala.[23] This creature was deeply affected as he realized that a buddha existed in the world at that time. Hearing the Buddha's name, the sea monster resolved not to open his mouth, and the boat escaped. It is at least not the explicit intention of the sea-faring lay follower (*upāsaka*) here to pray to the Buddha for salvation. Rather, the appeal is to an old and important idea, that of the decisive role of the state of mind immediately at the point of death. We have seen the importance of this notion elsewhere, in the *Mahāvastu*'s depiction of the death of the sea monster itself, and earlier in references to the moment of death of those suffering in hell for their crimes. The lay follower aboard the ship appears in the episode convinced of his imminent death; he is merely trying to assist his fellow travelers in orienting their own minds toward a positive karmic state that will benefit their future weal. The idea that prayer to a multitude of gods being unsuccessful, one may then more profitably turn to the Buddha is formulaic. Here, just as in the *Mahāvastu*, the text says that the merchants "began to pray to Śiva, Varuṇa, Kubera, Mahendra, Upendra, and other gods," but without effect.[24]

Although it can, by this time, hardly be doubted that the *Mahāvastu* and *Apadāna* transmit almost precisely the same tale of Dharmaruci as does the *Divyāvadāna*, stories of a great fish similar to that encountered at the beginning of the *Dharmarucy-avadāna* and at the end of the *Mahāvastu* and *Apadāna* versions are found elsewhere in Buddhist literature.[25] Given that we have now firmly established the connection between the story of Mahādeva and that of Dharmaruci, and having just recognized the important role played in the story of Dharmaruci by a great sea monster, it is of some interest to notice on a second-century B.C.E. medallion (see Figure 1) from the stūpa at Bhārhut—one of the very oldest, if not indeed the oldest extant Buddhist site in India—an illustration of a great fish attempting to swallow the passengers on a boat.[26] What makes this medallion particularly relevant for us is the astonishing coincidence—and it may be nothing more—that the illustration is accompanied by an intriguing inscription that adds yet another twist to the increasingly complex tapestry we are weaving. As is so often the case with such inscriptions, some matters remain unclear despite repeated suggestions of various scholars, but the overall meaning seems to be plain enough. The inscription labels the illustration thus:[27] "Vasugupta rescued by Mahādeva from the belly of Timitimiṁgila." Can this possibly be interpreted to provide us with any further connection, and moreover one comparatively quite old, between the story of Dharmaruci and that of Mahādeva?

FIGURE 1: Vasugupta rescued by Mahādeva from the belly of Timitimiṁgila. Second-century B.C.E. medallion from the stūpa at Bhārhut. Photo: John C. Huntington, courtesy of Huntington Archive.

One problem in understanding this inscription is of primary concern to us here:[28] Who are Vasugupta and Mahādeva? The question has been discussed before, although without any convincing conclusion being reached.[29] Lüders believed that the name Mahādeva must refer to the Buddha, an opinion shared by other scholars.[30] On the other hand, as Lüders did not fail to mention, "The designation of Buddha as 'the great god' does not occur . . . elsewhere in the Buddhist literature."[31] A possible exception to this was, once again, pointed out by Lüders himself. The same story of the dangerous sea creature about to devour a ship full of passengers until, at the last minute, he hears the utterance of the Buddha's name is found in the Chinese *Zapiyu jing* (Scripture of Miscellaneous Exemplary Stories).[32] There, when the sea monster *makara*—a creature very nearly if not precisely the same as a *timiṅgila*—is about to devour the vessel upon which he and the five hundred merchants are traveling, a merchant chief cries: "I've got a great god [*dàshén*= **mahādeva*] called Buddha. You should all stop the worship you were each doing, and single-mindedly call on him!" All five hundred then together cry out "Hail to the Buddha! [*nāmó fó*, **namo buddhāya*]." The fish hears this and thinks to himself "Now there's a Buddha in the world." He then decides to abstain from violence, and the merchants escape. "This fish in a previous life was a religious practitioner who committed (a) sin(s) and so obtained the body of a fish." Although the extremely close connection of this version with those we have examined from the *Divyāvadāna*, *Mahāvastu*, and *Apadāna* is obvious, it is something of a slender thread on which to suspend any theory that the Mahādeva in the Bhārhut inscription refers to the Buddha.[33] An additional problem is that in these stories the Buddha can be said to have saved the merchants only in a most general sense; he does not directly intervene, and it is rather a knowledge of his very existence that leads the sea monster to restrain himself. That the Vasugupta of the inscription may have been the name of the chief of merchants in the version of the story that the medallion illustrates is quite possible and itself provides little problem. But none of this allows us in any clear way to forge a sure connection through this Bhārhut inscription, in which the name (or epithet?) Mahādeva appears, with the story of Dharmaruci, and further onward to the Mahādeva of the schism account.

Does this old Indian inscription allow us to connect the name Mahādeva with a narrative episode similar to one presented elsewhere in which the central character is named Dharmaruci, or have we gone down a blind alley? We must conclude that the connection, if there is any at all, may be too obscure to dig out.[34] I introduced this material, however, not only because of its inherent interest, but also to emphasize that not all sources fit together as neatly as they seem to after the scholar has finished sewing up his airtight argument. Honesty demands that we pay fair attention even to evidence that may in the end land on the cutting room floor. It is, after all, patterns that provide the surest form of evidence, not individual pieces susceptible to varying interpretations.

To return to our texts and to greater certainty, an investigation of parallel versions of the extended tale of Dharmaruci, including his incarnation as a sea monster, has revealed to us the crucial fact that the core tale itself is preserved not only in Sthavira literature but in the literature of the Mahāsāṁghika sect as well. The implications of this may be profound. No longer may we rest content with the hypothesis that Sthavira opponents (if not enemies) of the Mahāsāṁghikas adopted and adapted a story from the literary traditions of their own sect and applied this to the calumnious tale of Mahādeva. Rather, it has become very clear in the course of our examination and juxtaposition of diverse sources—including the Sarvāstivāda *Vibhāṣā*, the Mūlasarvāstivāda *Dharmarucy-avadāna*, and the Theravāda *Apadāna*, all belonging to the Sthavira tradition, and the Mahāsāṁghika *Mahāvastu*, not to mention at least one Chinese source the sectarian identity of which is unclear, the *Jifayue sheku tuoluoni jing*, and probably the *Mahāyāna Mahāparinirvāṇa-sūtra* as well—that these texts transmit a story that cannot but have one common origin. The coincidence of shared elements great and small is just too thoroughgoing to imagine independent origins. This conclusion prepares the ground upon which we can begin to build a robust hypothesis regarding the ideological work the Mahādeva story was intended to accomplish. And that work could only be carried out in a certain context. It is to that context, then, that we now turn.

13
Incest in Indian Buddhist Culture

The ways we read and understand the stories we have studied are guided, to some extent, by our expectations, by the ways in which we choose to classify them, whether we undertake such classification explicitly or not. We will naturally tend to contextualize our stories among others of similar type, according to the genres to which we have decided they belong. In this respect, we have probably, from a naive and commonsensical point of view, implicitly assumed that many of our stories here can be categorized as "Oedipal."[1] But just how we define this category, and what we expect it to mean, are questions to which we must now devote some attention. There are, certainly, a number of episodes to be found in Indian Buddhist literature that might be, or in fact have already been, called Oedipal, for one reason or another.[2] The French Indologist and physician Jean Filliozat discusses one set of examples from Tantric literature, in which a person kills a deity equated with the father and has sexual intercourse with a deity equated with the mother. He cites a text in which the master yogin (*yogīndra*) is told to kill his father (*hanyāt . . . pitaraṁ*) and to have sex with his mother (*mātaraṁ saṁprakāmayet*), albeit the former is identified with the Buddha Akṣobhya, the latter with the goddess Māmakī.[3] In another only slightly less radical case, we are told that the Tantric practitioner (*sādhaka*) who has sexual relations with his mother, sister, or daughter will attain tremendous perfection in the supreme teachings of the Mahāyāna, and sexual relations with the mother of the Buddha will not stain him.[4] Such passages, which assume and play upon the intentional inversions and deliberate reversals typical of Tantric literature, are to be located within a conceptual and rhetorical world entirely different from that of the stories we have been studying, and thus cannot be evaluated on the same bases as those upon which we judge discussions of murder and incest in non-Tantric texts. In a sense, we may very well say that Tantric "culture" in its entirety is different enough from that of our mainstream non-Tantric sources to compel us to treat it as thoroughly foreign. For this reason I must bequeath an investigation of the Tantric Oedipal complex (or complexes, for they may well be multiple) to others.[5]

At the other end of the spectrum, as it were, we do encounter in the Pāli canon, often justifiably considered to be a rather conservative collection, a depiction not only of consummated incest, but of that between mother and son. The *Aṅguttara-Nikāya* contains the following:[6]

> Once, when the Exalted One was dwelling near Sāvatthī, at the Jeta Grove, in Anāthapiṇḍika's Park, a mother and son were both spending the rainy season in Sāvatthī, as monk and nun.
>
> They longed to see one another often; the mother often wished to see her son, the son often wished to see his mother. And from seeing each other often, companionship arose; from companionship, intimacy; from intimacy, opportunity for corruption;[7] and without giving up the training and making their weakness manifest, with infatuated hearts,[8] they gave themselves over to incestuous intercourse [*methunaṁ dhammaṁ paṭiseviṁsu*].
>
> And a company of monks went to the Exalted One, saluted him, and sat down at one side; and so seated they told the Exalted One all that had occurred. . . .[9]
>
> "What, monks, knows not this foolish man that a mother shall not be affectionately attached to her son, nor a son to his mother?"

Although not commented upon in the *Manorathapūraṇī*, Buddhaghosa's commentary to the *Aṅguttara-Nikāya*, the account is repeated in the almost certainly post-Buddhaghosa commentary to the *Sutta-Nipāta* (Group of Discourses), *Paramatthajotikā* (Illuminator of the Ultimate Meaning). Here, however, a further rationale is added:[10]

> Once when the Blessed One was dwelling in Sāvatthī in a village residence, a certain poor widow had her son initiated as a monk and herself initiated as a nun. Both of them longed to see one another often. When the mother obtained something, she took it to the son, and the son in his turn [shared things with his] mother. Thus they went to each other morning and evening, sharing what they had obtained [in alms], being happy together, asking after each other's health, without there being any suspicion. From their frequent meetings, companionship arose, from companionship intimacy, from intimacy opportunity for corruption, and through lust minds opened to corruption, [such that their] consciousness of their monastic initiation and their relationship as mother and son disappeared. Then having transgressed the boundaries, they indulged in illicit activities, and having given themselves up to infamy, sporting together

they dwelt amidst the cares of the household life.[11] The Blessed One asked the monks: "What, monks, knows not this foolish man that a mother shall not be affectionately attached to her son, nor a son to his mother?" And having censured them, he said "I see no other single form [so attractive as a woman]" and so on, thus in innumerable discourses inciting the monks, he said "Therefore, monks, here [I say]:[12]

As the poison called *halāhala*, as boiling hot oil,
As red-hot molten copper, so women are to be kept far away."

So in order to demonstrate the Teaching to the monks, [the Blessed One] spoke these four verses [*Sutta-Nipāta* 207–210] concerning himself, beginning with [*Sutta-Nipāta* 207] "From acquaintance arises fear."

The *sutta* upon which this is based is a rather peculiar text, made more interesting still by the fact that, immediately after the portion I have just cited, the scripture goes on to speak of the modes by which men may be captured and seduced by women in all the sensual dimensions, a section quoted in the commentary only by the beginning of a sentence "I see no other single form [so attractive as a woman]." Men are attracted, maddened, bound, and so on by the shape, sound, smell, taste, and touch of a woman. They are drawn to women by all their senses, and this leads the Buddha to proclaim rather emphatically near the end of the discourse that "one speaking truly should say of womankind, 'they are the all-encompassing snare of Māra,'"[13] Māra being the Buddhist incarnation of desire and evil. Such passages are, of course, far from rare in the often mysogynistic Buddhist literature.[14] But why should any author or editor choose a reference to mother-son incest to illustrate the dangers of women in general? Is the point intended to be that the allure of women is so very strong that, being careless, one may find oneself attracted even to one's own mother?[15] If this is indeed the message, it is presented very subtly.[16] On the other hand, the existence of a passage such as this certainly does not give us license to hypothesize that mother-son incest was a serious problem in the early Buddhist community, or even that it was a problem at all.[17] On the contrary, in light of what we know of this form of incest, this seems most unlikely. So why was this passage composed in the first place? Why was it considered significant enough to canonize (and to quote in a commentary), and what message was intended by attaching to it a screed against women in general? We receive precious little help from the *Paramatthajotikā*,[18] and the fact that this *sutta* appears never to have been translated into Chinese prevents us obtaining any help from that quarter either.[19] Nevertheless, it must set us thinking. If the psychoanalytical anthropologist Gananath

Obeyesekere is right in his claim that the Sinhalese find incestuous relations with the mother inconceivable,[20] how has this *Aṅguttara-Nikāya* passage and the version in the *Paramatthajotikā*—a text that was in fact composed in Ceylon—been managed in Ceylonese Theravāda exegesis? How might devout Buddhists within this tradition account for, if not understand, a canonical reference to a mother and son, nun and monk respectively, who were sexually involved with one another—or do they simply fail (or refuse) to acknowledge its existence?

In an effort to provide some context for the story of Mahādeva/Dharmaruci, I have so far concentrated on stories of mother-son incest and of a son's murder of his father or his mother. But there also exists in Indian Buddhist literature at least one very odd and potentially significant story of another type of incest, that between siblings. We must thus consider the advantages and disadvantages of grouping together with the other objects of our study a case which, from one point of view, may be thought to represent a significantly, if not entirely, different sociological phenomenon. From some perspectives there are certainly advantages to treating parent-child and sibling relations separately. With regard to social, and particularly psychological, concerns, one might well want to follow Twitchell in maintaining: "Parental incest is an act so different in motivation and consequence from sibling incest that it may deserve a separate name and category."[21] The question for the anthropologist, ethnographer, and indeed the student of literature and history, however, is whether within a given society or culture such a distinction is made. If it is not, the scholar is not necessarily justified in arbitrarily introducing it. As Leavitt reminds us:[22]

> As a result of cultural variation, "incest" as sexual activity is ambiguous and depends on what a culture means by "sexual" and "incest" behavior. Clearly, relatives in many cases do not avoid (all) sexual or incestuous contact, nor do they avoid the same kind of sexual contact from one culture to the next, nor is all sexual activity between relatives necessarily considered incestuous. Furthermore, sexual behavior (and incest) can certainly occur without intercourse or procreation.

There may well be good reasons why different types of "incest" should, at least initially, be treated differently from an abstract and theoretical perspective. Thus mother-son incest need not necessarily be placed within the same class as brother-sister incest. However, in the context of our investigations of ancient Indian materials, we should keep in mind that our normative Indian sources, be they Buddhist treatises or Brahmanical law codes, do make it quite clear that those authors who considered the issue explicitly did, in fact, place both kinds of behavior or both patterns of relations into one and the same category: sexual relations with one's mother, sister, and daughter are habitually forbidden conjointly.[23] In light of the indigenous Indian characterization, we may then legitimately expect to learn something of Indian Buddhist attitudes toward nuclear family incest by including a consideration of sibling relations.

What makes the story of sibling incest we are about to explore so very extraordinary, however, is not only the depiction of incest per se, but the fact that it plays a central role in the story of the origins of the Śākya clan itself.[24] For this is the story of the roots of Śākyamuni Buddha's family tree, a family which, while not a "Holy Family" in a Christian sense, nevertheless represents the origins of the Buddha of our age, and thus possesses a special symbolic, and perhaps even iconic, value. Versions of this legend are found in the Theravāda Pāli canon and commentaries, in texts of the Mahāsāṁghika and Mūlasarvāstivāda, and in literature of other sects as well. Whatever else we may say about this foundation myth—for it is hardly anything else—we must accept that it was widely transmitted throughout the Indian Buddhist world and beyond.[25]

According to the basic story, the sons of a certain king Okkāka (in Sanskrit Ikṣvāku) were banished and went into exile with their sisters. The version in the *Ambaṭṭha-sutta* of the Theravāda *Dīgha-Nikāya* (Long Discourses) says: "Out of fear of the mixing of castes they cohabited (*saṁvāsa*) together with their own sisters,"[26] using what is almost exactly the same euphemism we employ today in English and just as clearly pointing to a sexual relationship. The sons of Okkāka, according to this Pāli version, had sexual relations with their true, full sisters. The concern for "the mixing of castes" being expressed here is a fundamental one and displays an aspect of what we may even term an Indian obsession with marriage structures. This obsession makes itself known from a very ancient period through elaborate rules and byzantine regulations concerning caste and degrees of consanguinity within which marriages are permitted or restricted. Large sections of the Indian Dharma or legal literature are devoted to discussions of just this problem, and Indian Buddhist literature, too, displays a constant awareness of and concern for similar considerations. The clichéd stock phrases that begin Indian Buddhist avadāna tales, for instance, regularly include, in the notice of an initial marriage carried out between two families, the expression that a man "took a wife from a suitable family," signifying that the family of the bride had an appropriate caste relation to that of the groom, although our texts assume rather than specify the precise nature of the suitability.[27] In the present case, somewhat astonishingly, this concern for caste suitability seems to trump the otherwise nearly ubiquitous taboo against close-kin marriage. Buddhaghosa's commentary to the *Ambaṭṭha-sutta* expands somewhat the rationale for this union of siblings:[28]

> The princes thought: "We don't see any daughters of kṣatriyas who are appropriate (to our caste), nor young kṣatriyas who are appropriate for our sisters. Sons born through union with those who are unlike (in caste) are impure either on the mother's or the father's side, and will bring about mixing of castes. Therefore let us consent to cohabit together with just these our sisters." Out of fear at the mixing of castes, while treating their eldest sister as their mother (and not marrying her), they cohabited with the others.

The logic to which Buddhaghosa here appeals is interesting: the disability affects both the princes and their sisters, in that in their exile there are suitable mates for neither, and thus it is reasonable that they turn to each other. There is no attempt here to soften the reality of the incest, which, in the focus on caste purity, seems in fact to be entirely ignored.

In a version of the same sūtra preserved in the Chinese translation of the *Dīrghāgama*,[29] the story is cast somewhat differently. The mothers of the four exiled princes miss them and, upon receiving the king's permission, go to see them.

> Then the mothers said: "I will give my daughter to your son. You give your daughter to my son." And so they betrothed them to each other and they became husband and wife.[30]

The mothers of the four princes, consorts of the king who is the father of the princes, also each have at least one daughter, whose father is likewise the same king, of course. These mothers offer amongst themselves to have their sons marry their agnatic half-sisters, one mother's son to another mother's daughter. The king's co-wives marry their respective male and female offspring, half-siblings, to each other.[31] This reading is close in its core significance to the Pāli version, with the difference that the full siblings are here replaced with half-siblings. I understand this as a softening of the original, perhaps due to a desire to mitigate the ethical difficulties that would otherwise arise. The same modification is found in most of our sources.

The *Saṁghabhedavastu* (Section on Schism) of the Mūlasarvāstivāda Vinaya records such a softened version. In addition, this text provides an extended context for the episode. In order to reinforce the promise he has made to his new bride's father that any son of their marriage will succeed him, King Virūḍhaka Ikṣvāku banishes the four sons he has sired on his previous chief queen. Then:[32]

> Those princes took along their [true, full] sisters and, in due order, reached the bank of the river Bhagīrathī not far from the hermitage of the sage Kapila in the region of the Himalaya. There they built huts from leaves of the teak tree and dwelt there, surviving by continually killing animals [for food]. Thrice they approached the hermitage of the sage Kapila. Overwhelmed by the passions of youth, and being extremely severely afflicted by passions and lusts, they grew very pale and gaunt. Then at one point the sage Kapila noticed this state of affairs and asked them: "Why are you so very pale?"
>
> They replied: "Great sage, we are severely afflicted by passions and lusts."[33]
>
> He said: "Avoiding your full sisters, cohabit with your agnatic half sisters."[34]
>
> "Is it proper, Great sage, for us to do so?"
>
> "It is proper, sirs, since obviously you are disenthroned kṣatriyas."
>
> Accepting the words of the sage as authoritative, seeking after passions and lusts and giving rise to feelings of joy and delight, they had sex, made love with, and coupled with their agnatic half-sisters. And from that sex, lovemaking, and coupling sons and daughters were born and grew up.

Thanks to the resulting racket caused by the children, the sage Kapila is unable to engage in his meditative concentrations and tells the princes that he will depart. They insist that it is instead they who should go, and after they beg him to appoint a place for them, he does so. For this reason, they name the location Kapilavastu, meaning the place designated by Kapila. In time this town too becomes overcrowded, and they are then shown a new location by the gods, whence it is named Devadriśa, "shown by the gods."

> Then the [princes] met together and began a discussion, saying: "Sirs, since we were banished on account of [our father the king] taking a wife of appropriate (caste) [instead of a second wife whose child would not be eligible for the throne], none of us may take a second wife of appropriate (caste, who might compete with the legitimate sons for inheritance); he must be content with only the one." Thus they took just that single wife of appropriate (caste), and no second.
>
> Then on another occasion King Virūḍhaka, affectionately remembering his sons, said to his ministers: "Peasants, where are those princes now?" They explained the situation in detail: "Your Majesty banished them on account of some judicial decision. They took their own

> sisters and set out from here. . . . Avoiding their full sisters, they had sex with, played around with, and enjoyed sexual relations with their agnatic half-sisters, and as a result of that sex, playing around, and sexual relations were born sons and daughters.

The authors or redactors of this Vinaya seem to have been uncomfortable with the idea of a completely incestuous relation between the princes and their sisters. In regard to this scruple, however, and that which I believe also informed the Chinese parallel to the *Ambaṭṭha-sutta*, we cannot forget that according to widespread notions evident not only in the technical legal literature but in numerous considerably more popular sources as well, sexual relations with even an agnatic (or for that matter uterine) half-sister were strictly forbidden, a functional equivalence that leads me to wonder, from this perspective, why those who modified the story even bothered. What seems most probable is that, despite their legal equivalence, a relation between half-siblings was found affectively less objectionable than one between full brother and sister. The authors of the *Saṁghabhedavastu* have, incidentally, taken advantage of this story to introduce another, and probably completely unrelated, issue, namely, that concerning the rules for second marriages in the Śākya clan. The dramatic development of the tale has the four princes banished at the behest of the father of the king's second wife, who wishes her own son to become the heir apparent. To ensure her son's succession in preference to the four older princes of the king's first wife, the princes are banished. This plot is hardly unique, of course; in fact, it is almost a staple of Indian dramatic literature. Yet the Mūlasarvāstivāda Vinaya authors or redactors make this story into the logical reason for the promulgation of a ruling concerning marriage customs: since the second wife, by virtue of her being taken from an "acceptable" caste and family, is capable of bearing a child with full rights of inheritance, and since this has caused trouble for the princes, they declare that henceforth one must not take such a wife. In other words, the ruling does not bar remarriage or multiple marriages as such. It only prohibits remarriage with a woman whose status is such that a son of hers may compete with sons of the primary marriage for inheritance. The insertion of this legal stipulation here is interesting and deserves further study, but in the narrow context of the present story its significance seems obvious: a legal justification based on concerns of inheritance is appropriated for use in the context of a debate over close-kin marriage, perhaps because the widespread and seemingly constant consciousness of such fiduciary concerns lends an immediacy to the issue missing when the subject appears to be merely the rare possibility of close-kin marriages.[35]

If I am correct that the *Saṁghabhedavastu* story, like that in the *Dīrghāgama*, represents a modification of a more "original" version, in which the princes did wed their full sisters, the same modification appears to have taken place in other versions of the episode as well, such as that in the *Mahāvastu*. The framework here is the same as that in the Mūlasarvāstivāda account, the exiled sons alone in the wilderness with their sisters. The key passage reads as follows:[36]

> Those princes said: "There must be no corruption of our lineage." And out of fear of corruption of the lineage, they gave to each other in marriage their own agnatic half-sisters.

Another example of an attempt to mitigate the ethically questionable origins of the Śākya clan appears in the Chinese **Abhiniṣkramaṇa-sūtra*:[37]

> Then the princes settled there [in what became the city Kapilavastu] and, mindful of the words of their father the king that they seek to marry within their own clan, they were not able to find brides. Each accepted a maternal aunt and his sisters and took them as wife, according to the rites of marriage. In the first place they desired to follow the instructions of their father the king, and in the second place they feared introducing corruption into the lineage of the Śākyas.

Although it is repeatedly mentioned in the literature of diverse sects, this story and the resulting situation go almost unnoticed in other Buddhist literature. I know of only one exception. The origins of the Śākya clan are alluded to in Pāli literature in the commentaries to both the *Dhammapada* and *Jātaka*, when a people called the Koliyas are made to accuse the Sākiyas, with whom they share the same ultimate ancestry, of acting like dogs and jackals in sleeping with their sisters.[38] Here Buddhist texts themselves present an anecdote in which enemies of the clan of the Buddha bring up the calumny that that clan is of incestuous origin, a "historical fact" we know to have been accepted by the Buddhists themselves. But it is peculiar that these commentaries would invoke the episode in a clearly uncomplimentary light, and their reason for doing so remains unclear. As far as I know, this is the only secondary reference to this origin story in Indian Buddhist literature. Another peculiar fact is that while the literature of a number of Indian Buddhist sects knows the story of the brother-sister incest engaged in by the sons of King Ikṣvāku, sibling incest was demonstrably not approved of by Indian Buddhist authors in general. Indeed, we find in the works of authors who surely must have been familiar with this well-known legend vociferous criticism of the degenerate practices of incest engaged in by Persians, explicitly including sibling incest. What is all the more remarkable is that the Śākya legend itself explicitly appeals to the need to avoid introducing impurity into the Śākya family line as the rationale for this incest, and it is precisely this concern with the purity of lineage that the Persian Zoroastrians use to justify their own practices, although Indian Buddhist sources do not appear to mention this fact explicitly. This is a potentially interesting consentience, especially in light of the possibility of Iranian influences on the development of the life story of the Buddha.[39] It may in fact be that some similar concern motivated this legend to begin with, and that despite strong disapproval the story could not be excised; it could, however, be ignored, or (at least slightly) modified.

Buddhist authors, who have elsewhere demonstrated their abhorrence of incest, did preserve within their sacred scriptures a mythology of Śākya clan origins that involves brother-sister incest; all that these authors (or editors or redactors) could do was not dwell on the story and make efforts to mitigate the degree of such incest, despite the fact that from a normative legal perspective the mitigation would appear to have been toothless—marriage to one's half-sister or even aunt being every bit as objectionable as marriage to one's full sister.[40]

This story may lead us to wonder how other instances of incest appear in Indian Buddhist literature, or if they exist at all. They do exist, however, and consequently, if we wish to advert to Indian Buddhist attitudes to incest in our attempts to understand the possible impact of the story of Mahādeva—and this we must do in order to read the Mahādeva story in context—we should develop as complete a picture as possible of the range of depictions of incest in Indian Buddhist sources.

An example of the portrayals of incest to be discovered in this literature is located in a Jātaka tale preserved in Pāli. This recounts, as do all Jātakas, a former life story of the Buddha.[41] In this story the bodhisattva, the Buddha-to-be, is a son of the king of Benares named Udayabhadda; he has an agnatic half-sister named Udayabhaddā, the feminine form of the same name. Udayabhadda was, the story tells us, a born celibate (*jātabrahmacārī*), with no interest in sex, even in dreams.[42] His parents, wanting him to succeed to the throne, nevertheless pressure him to marry, entreaties he repeatedly refuses. Finally, he creates a golden image of a woman and tells his parents that when they find a woman who is as lovely as the image, he will accept the crown. They send this image throughout all of India, but without result. The text then continues, rather abruptly:[43]

> Adorning Udayabhaddā, they set her in his presence, and she stood there outshining that golden image. Then even against the couple's wishes they made his agnatic half-sister the princess Udayabhaddā his principal

> consort, and anointed the bodhisatta [that is, Prince Udayabhadda] in the rulership. But the two of them lived together in perfect celibacy. . . . Even though both were living in a single chamber, mastering their senses they did not look upon each other with desire.

The marriage described here differs, of course, from that described in the tale of the origins of the Śākya lineage, and the point is entirely different. Here there is not only no procreation but no sex at all, so while there is marriage (and thus endogamy), there is no incest per se. This crucial distinction between sex and marriage we shall revisit later. In addition to the endogamous marriage there is certainly also something reminiscent here of other stories we have seen, most especially with respect to the idea that, despite searching far and wide, the most desirable, most attractive, and best mate is to be found, after all, right at home, close beside one from the very beginning. The parallel to the situation in which Dharmaruci's mother found herself, and her solution to her problem, can hardly be missed.

The outline or frame of the Udayabhadda story is found repeatedly in such literature in virtually identical terms, save for the crucial difference that only in the *Udaya-Jātaka* is the bride a relative of the groom. One very well-known parallel appears in the life story of the great disciple Mahā-Kassapa, the man who went on to lead the Buddhist community after the Buddha's death.[44] This account is narrated not only in Theravāda but also in Mūlasarvāstivāda sources and those of other traditions as well.[45] The protagonist marries not his sister but a woman from another district, Bhaddakapalānī (and so the marriage is clearly exogamous). The marriage takes place only after a reluctantly executed search carried out by the very same means of a golden image. Since both Mahā-Kassapa and Bhaddakapalānī have hearts set on ascetic renunciation they, like Udayabhadda and Udayabhaddā, although wedded also live together in celibacy, both subsequently becoming renunciants.[46] The same theme of the golden image is also found in other Jātakas, the *Ananusociya-Jātaka* and the *Kusa-Jātaka*, and in the *Dhammapada* commentary as well, mostly repeated in almost the very same words.[47] Such parallels demonstrate once again the great adaptability of archetypal story lines. They are utilized in a variety of contexts, being altered slightly here and there, yet all the while retaining not only an overall structure but even considerable details in common. What is crucial for us to notice about the portrayal of the potentially incestuous match of Udayabhadda and Udayabhaddā is that the depicted refusal of a sexual relationship is not at all based on the consanguineous relation of the protagonists, something that is proved virtually beyond doubt by the existence of precisely parallel stories in which the protagonists are presented as unrelated. There is thus no explicit or even implicit criticism or disapproval of sibling incest in the *Udaya-Jātaka*.

The existence of such stories demonstrates that while incest is clearly condemned in Indian Buddhist literature, it is occasionally depicted, the objections to such relations being sometimes less weighty than other considerations. Further examples will help us better understand the range of depictions of the Oedipal in Indian Buddhist literature, and thus allow us to understand more globally the environment within which the Mahādeva story would have been read.

14
The Story of Utpalavarṇā

IT HAS now become clear that incest appears as an almost casual plot element in Indian Buddhist stories from time to time. There is, in addition, at least one relatively well-known story in which it appears as a central plot device.

The tale of Utpalavarṇā (Pāli Uppalavaṇṇā) is contained in the *Vinayavibhaṅga* (Vinaya Exegesis) of the Mūlasarvāstivāda Vinaya, with a significantly shorter parallel in the commentary to the Theravāda *Therīgāthā* (Verses of the Elder Nuns).[1] These two Buddhist versions differ from each other in some significant respects, not least of all in their relative degree of elaboration, but the story is also found in non-Buddhist sources, and some future full comparative analysis will have to take into account all of these materials.[2] In the meantime, we will direct our attention here to the Buddhist versions only. The Pāli tradition's presentation runs as follows:[3]

> The story is told that one morning an embryo was established in the womb of the wife of a certain merchant in the town of Sāvatthī, though she did not know it. At daybreak, the merchant loaded his wares in carts and set off in the direction of Rājagaha. As time went by, the embryo grew and reached maturity. Then her mother-in-law said to her, "My son has been away from home for a long time, and you are pregnant. You have done something wicked."
>
> She said, "I have known no man but your son."
>
> Even though she heard her say that, the mother-in-law, not believing her, threw her out of the house. She went in search of her husband, and in due course, she arrived [at the outskirts of] Rājagaha. Then as soon as her labor pains began, she went into a building close to the road and gave birth. She gave birth to a son who resembled a golden *bimba* fruit, and laying him down in the poorhouse,[4] she went outside for the obligatory [ritual] ablution [for purification after giving birth].
>
> Just then a caravan leader who had no son came along the road, and thinking, "This abandoned boy will be my son," he gave him into the hands of a wet nurse.[5]

> Then the boy's mother, having finished the obligatory ablution, returned bringing water [for the boy], but, not seeing her son, she was overwhelmed by grief, and wailing she did not go into Rājagaha, but simply continued on the road.
>
> A leader of a band of brigands saw her on the road and attracted to her made her his wife. Living in his house, she bore a daughter. Then one day, when she was standing holding her daughter, she quarreled with her husband and threw her daughter down on a couch. The girl's head was split open a little. After that she was afraid of her husband, and going back toward that very same Rājagaha [she had intended to visit to begin with], she wandered about, going where she pleased.
>
> Her son, when he was in the flower of his youth, ignorant that she was his mother, made her his wife. Afterwards, ignorant of the circumstance that the daughter of the band of thieves was his sister, he married her and brought her back to his home. In this way, he made his own mother and sister his wives and had them live with him. Therefore, both of them lived together as co-wives.
>
> Then one day, when the mother undid the daughter's hair net to look for lice, she saw the [scar of the] wound on her head. And asking herself, "Could she be my daughter?" being overcome with emotion, she went to a nunnery in Rājagaha and went forth into the homeless life.

In some particulars of special interest to us, this text is slightly ambiguous: it does not say that the mother recognized the truth that she was co-wife with her own daughter, nor is there any mention of the fact that she or anyone else recognizes that she has committed incest with her son. Seeing the scar on the girl's head reminds her of her own daughter, and of what she has lost, and this alone may be the motivation for the mother to leave the world and become a nun. The plot pivot is mother-son incest, coupled with brother-sister (or rather half-sister) incest. Two (separately) abandoned children of the same mother marry, after the son has unknowingly married his own mother, making mother and daughter, in addition to everything else, also co-wives. This arrangement is what scholars of European incest tales refer to as "double incest," a subtype of stories in which the incest doubles down through a generation. A key fact is revealed to the mother by a scar on the head of her daughter, whether or not either of them were aware of their true relationship. This cannot help but remind us of other instances of identification (by "token") in classical Oedipal stories in which the incest is committed unknowingly, perhaps most especially the scar on Oedipus himself as related in some central versions of the myth. While this is a valuable addition to our collection of Buddhist Oedipal materials, more detail is to be found in the other Buddhist recounting of this tale.

Although it is quite lengthy by any standard, and particularly so in comparison with its Pāli counterpart, the parallel version in the *Vinayavibhaṅga* of the Mūlasarvāstivāda Vinaya also motivates a number of quite different questions. The story begins as follows:[6]

> In the town of Taxila, there dwelt a householder, rich, with great wealth, many possessions, and much property, possessed of the wealth of Vaiśravaṇa, the god of wealth, rivaling Vaiśravaṇa in wealth. And he took a wife from a suitable family, and he had sex, made love, and coupled with his wife, and from that sex, lovemaking, and coupling, his wife at a certain time became pregnant. When eight or nine months had passed, she gave birth to a daughter, lovely, good-looking, and beautiful. Her eyes were like blue lotuses, she had the fragrance of the lotus, and the color [of her skin] was [golden] like that of the anther of a lotus. Her relatives gathered together, and after three weeks, that is, twenty-one days, they held a great birth celebration for the newborn. And they arranged to fix a name for her, saying "What name shall we fix for this girl?" The relatives said: "Since this girl's eyes are like blue lotuses (*utpala*), she has the fragrance of the lotus, and the color [of her skin] (*varṇa*) is like that of the anther of a lotus, we've decided that the name of this girl should be Utpalavarṇā," and so her name was fixed as Utpalavarṇā.
>
> She grew up into womanhood. Now her father had no son, and so he thought to himself: "I shall not give my daughter to just anyone because of his caste, nor shall I give her because he is wealthy, nor shall I give her because he is good-looking, but rather I will give her to one who will come to live here dwelling in my house as a son-in-law."[7]
>
> There was another householder of Taxila who had taken a wife from a suitable family, and had sex, made love, and coupled with her. And from that sex, lovemaking, and coupling, his wife at a certain time became pregnant. When eight or nine months had passed, she gave birth to a son. He was given a name appropriate to his caste, and he grew up into manhood. At a certain time, both his mother and his father having died, he was wandering about, and fate brought him to the house of that householder. The householder said to him: "Whose son are you?"
>
> "I am the son of the householder so-and-so."
>
> "Son, where is your father?"

> "He is dead."
>
> "Son, where is your mother?"
>
> "She is also dead."
>
> "Son, if that is the case, I will give my daughter to you, but you must become my son-in-law dwelling in my house."
>
> "Father, there is no objection. Since when I, indeed bereft of both my parents, was wandering and distressed, you said that, as it is without objection, let it be so."[8]
>
> The householder gave Utpalavarṇā to him, and when the appropriate solar and lunar day and time had arrived, he gave her as a bride, and that boy too for his part began to dwell in his house.
>
> Then, at a certain time, Utpalavarṇā's father having died, her mother, who had been used to sexual intercourse, began, for this reason, to be afflicted by passions (**kleśa*), although she was [otherwise] content with good food and clothing. And she thought: "If I were to summon another person here, my son-in-law would know of it, so I will have sex together with just him, make love, and couple." So she showed a sign (**nimitta*) to him. Because it is the way of women to captivate the senses, and to pursue their aims, she fantasized about him. And once again she showed a sign to him, and became intimate with him.[9]

Our story thus begins with a scenario in which a woman, the protagonist's mother, seduces her daughter's husband. This establishes the mise en scène through what, legally and affectively, is already an incestuous relation. Although her mother's seduction of her husband does not yet have any direct impact on Utpalavarṇā herself, it suggests that since her mother is an immoral libertine, she herself may have inherited something of that tendency. The story continues:

> At that time, Utpalavarṇā had become pregnant, and when the time arrived to give birth, she said to a servant girl: "Girl, call my mother to come to me."
>
> As soon as she had gone to do so, she saw her lying alone together with her son-in-law, and thinking for a moment, [the servant girl] waited there. As soon as they emerged, she said: "Since Utpalavarṇā has called you, please go."
>
> She went to her,[10] and she had just given birth to a girl. Utpalavarṇā said to the servant girl: "Girl, what kept you?"
>
> [The servant girl] replied: "May your mother and husband be healthy!"

[Utpalavarṇā] said: "What's the problem with them?"

So [the servant girl] told her just what had happened.

[Utpalavarṇā] said: "Girl, are you slandering my mother and husband?"

[The servant girl] replied: "Ma'am, if you don't believe me, I'll show you directly," and [the servant girl] waited intently looking for an opportunity to find the two of them. Then when the two of them went to be alone, she quickly went and said to Utpalavarṇā: "Come and look now!" [Utpalavarṇā] also quickly came along [with the servant girl] and looked, and when she saw those two embracing each other, Utpalavarṇā thought to herself: "Does this miserable woman not see any other man in Taxila, since she embraces her son-in-law? And does this miserable man too not see any other woman in Taxila, since he embraces his mother-in-law?" Having realized this, the situation became unbearable for her, and saying to her husband "You miserable man, from now on you can have sex with her!" she flung her daughter toward her father.[11] She tumbled down off her father's body and fell onto the threshold, where her head split open.

Thus ends the first act, as it were, of this drama. Neither Utpalavarṇā's mother nor her husband will reappear, but her daughter will play a central role in what follows.

Utpalavarṇā covered her own head and left the house,[12] and just then seeing a caravan on its way up to Mathurā, she went along together with it. The caravan leader saw her, and being enamored by her appearance and youthful good looks, he said: "Auntie, to whom do you belong?"

"Caravan leader, I belong to whomever gives me food and clothing."

The caravan leader made her his wife, and at the end of the journey when the caravan reached Mathurā, he left her there. Then the caravan leader delivered his merchandise and, picking up new merchandise, went back to Taxila. When the merchants there would invite one another to their respective houses and offer banquets, that caravan leader never offered dinner parties, and the merchants said: "Caravan leader, you never invite us over and offer us a meal."

He said: "You have women-folk at home, and they prepare the banquets, don't they? Since I have no one to serve, how can I offer hospitality?"

They said: "If that's the way it is, why don't you look for a girl?"

He said; "If there's any girl who's like my wife, I'll marry her."

They replied: "First, tell us what your wife looks like."

He described Utpalavarṇā's appearance and youthful good looks, and they said: "Caravan leader, she is a jewel of a woman! Still, we will search the land to see whether there may be another like her." And they began to search. Just then they saw that Utpalavarṇā's very own daughter resembled her, and they asked [her guardians, saying] "Has she [already] been asked [for her hand]?"

They said: "On whose behalf [are you asking]?"

"For a certain caravan leader."

"Sirs, what if we decide to give her, and then you have a problem, and after marrying her you forsake her and go away?"

"I will not abandon her."

"If so, then we will give her," and they gave her to him, and the caravan leader wed her. Then the merchants delivered their merchandise and, picking up new merchandise again, set out for Mathurā.

It is evident that quite a bit of time has passed here—some twelve or thirteen years, at a minimum. The omniscient narrator is aware of the identity of the young woman who resembles Utpalavarṇā, an identity that becomes clear to Utpalavarṇā too as time goes on.

Then in due course they arrived at a mountain village not very far away from Mathurā. The caravan leader left his merchandise and the girl in that mountain village and a little while later arrived in Mathurā. Utpalavarṇā greeted him by asking whether he had a good trip, saying: "Did your trip go well?"

"My dear, how could it have gone well? I was robbed."

"Sir, it is surely a joy that you survived the trip! There will be more wealth later on as well."

He stayed there a short while, and then said: "My dear, I will go to search for my stolen property."

She said: "Don't worry—go."

Immediately after he had left, an associate of his arrived. He asked Utpalavarṇā: "Where has the caravan leader gone?"

She said: "He went in search of his stolen property."

"Where was he robbed, and by whom?"

"I don't know; he told me he'd been robbed and was going to search for his stolen property."

He said: "Since it went more perfectly this time than ever before, he deceived you."

"Sir, tell me the story. What else went on?"

"He brought along a Gandhāran woman from Taxila, who is not fit to wash your feet."

"Sir, is this true?"

"It is true."

She told him "Wait," and he stayed without saying anything at all.

A short time later the caravan leader came back, and leaving aside the earlier humiliation, she said: "Sir, did you find your stolen property?"

"My dear, I found it."

"Sir, you deceived me. You were not robbed anywhere by anyone. I heard how you brought along a Gandhāran woman from Taxila. Bring her here, and give her to me. The wealth of one who is settled in two places becomes diluted, disappears, and is exhausted."

"My dear, even if it were to end up so, have not you heard that in a house in which there are two wives one drinks nothing other than cold porridge, and there will be fights, fault-finding, wrangling, and disputes?"

"Sir, relax! That won't happen. Go and bring her. If she is like a younger sister, I will take care of her with the idea that she is my younger sister. If she is like a daughter, I will take care of her with the idea that she is my daughter."

The text is being a bit ironic: the merchant's young bride is indeed Utpalavarṇā's daughter, as we, the audience, know. It is hard to decide if the authors intended poignance or humor here, but the text must, in any case, be read on at least two levels—simultaneously as a drama with its own internal dialogue, and as an aside, with a wink at the audience.

He said: "My dear, if so, there is no problem, and I will bring her." So he brought her, and when [Utpalavarṇā] saw her, she liked her very much.

Then on another occasion, Utpalavarṇā began to fix the hair of the girl, when on her head she saw that there was a scar. When she saw it she asked: "Girl, what befell you?"

She said: "I don't really quite know. According to my grandmother, my mother was angry with my father, and flung me such that I fell on the threshold, and that's how I got this scar.

"What is the name of your grandmother?"

"So-and-so."

> "What is your mother's name?"
>
> "Utpalavarṇā."
>
> Then she thought to herself: "There I was co-wife with my mother, while here I've become co-wife with my daughter. So in all events, I've got to go." Covering her head, she left the house and soon saw a caravan that was leaving for Vaiśālī. She once again joined that caravan, and having sex with its merchants [along the way] she arrived in Vaiśālī.

This transition marks another intermission, another segue between scenes. In the next sequence, Utpalavarṇā takes on the persona of a sexual professional. Having once been a conventional woman who married the man selected by her father, she became the wife of any man who would support her, even when he himself was not content with her alone. Now she continues her slide into sexual libertinism by offering herself freely to caravan merchants. Her next step is to regularize that activity.

> The courtesans living in Vaiśālī said:[13] "These merchants from Taxila don't have sex, make love, and couple with us." To that, one of the courtesans said: "Since they brought along a Gandhāran woman, whose feet we are not fit to wash, why should they have sex, make love, and couple with us?"
>
> The courtesans gathered and went to Utpalavarṇā, saying: "Woman of Gandhāra, since you have the same vocation as we do, why don't you join us?"
>
> She took off her head covering, and said: "From this moment, I shall join you," and she joined them.[14]
>
> Soon after, one day when those courtesans were gathered sitting around and drinking,[15] they chatted about the news, about how one of them had deprived a merchant of a certain amount of wealth, and then one said: "I took this much wealth from the merchant so-and-so," while another said: "We took this much wealth from the merchant so-and-so," and yet another said: "We took this much wealth from the merchant so-and-so."
>
> Now there lived in Vaiśālī the son of a perfumer, who was extremely ugly.[16] None of the courtesans had been able to seduce him, so the courtesans said: "That woman among us who is capable of seducing that particular perfumer's son we will call a woman of quality."
>
> Utpalavarṇā said: "Is he a man endowed with a male organ or not?"
>
> They said: "Yes, he's a man endowed with a male organ."
>
> "If I seduce him, will you make me your mistress?"
>
> "Yes, we will. If you are unable to seduce him, what will you do?"

"I will pay you sixty kārṣāpaṇas."

"Okay, let it be so."

Utpalavarṇā rented a house close by that of the son of the perfumer and instructed her servant girl, saying: "Girl, you are to purchase perfume every day from the perfumer's son so-and-so. If he asks to whom you take it, you are to say 'I take it to a certain young gentleman who has come to Utpalavarṇā.'"

The servant girl then purchased perfume every day from that perfumer's son. And he said to her: "Girl, to whom do you take the perfume every day?"

She said: "I take it to a young gentleman who has come to Utpalavarṇā."

Again, Utpalavarṇā said to the servant girl: "Girl, buy astringent, bitter, and pungent herbs from that perfumer's son. If he asks you to whom you take them, you are to say, 'Since the young gentleman is ill, they are for him.' If he asks you who is paying for them, you are to tell him, 'Utpalavarṇā is.'"

The servant girl took the money, and went to the perfumer's son's shop and said: "Please give me astringent, bitter, and pungent herbs."

He said: "To whom do you take them?"

She said: "Since the young gentleman is ill, they are for him."

He asked: "Who is paying for them?"

She said: "Utpalavarṇā is."

He thought to himself: "What a great woman she is! She takes care of him with her own medicines." And he became enamored with her. He said to the girl: "Girl, tell Utpalavarṇā: 'The perfumer's son said he would like to see you.'"

The girl told Utpalavarṇā, and she said: "Girl, go to him and say: 'The young gentleman is still not well.'"

She went and told him, and again and again he asked the girl on what day he should call. She told that to Utpalavarṇā, who thought to herself of what might be a good means to thoroughly attract him to her. Then she made a straw man and, sitting him in a chair, took him to the cemetery and burned him, after which mussing up her hair and pretending to weep, she began to walk not very far away from the shop of the perfumer's son, so that that perfumer's son saw her.

Since the Blessed One has said: "Women bind men in eight ways—by dance, song, music, laughter, crying, appearance, touch, and coquettishness,"[17] that perfumer's son became extremely enamored of her and said again to the girl: "Girl, I will go [to her] now." She told this to

Utpalavarṇā, who said to her: "Girl, go and say this to him: 'That young gentleman has died, but since my misery is now not yet over, how can I see you?'"

The more Utpalavarṇā resisted, the more the perfumer's son, full of desire, wanted to see her. Utpalavarṇā sent him a message saying, "Do not come to my house, but rather go to such-and-such a park," and the perfumer's son taking along much food and drink, and many garments and garlands, went to the park. He ate and drank together with Utpalavarṇā and soon became drunk.

Overpowered by the wine, he forgot who he was. Then Utpalavarṇā thought to herself: "Now he should be seen by many persons," and fastening a garland around his head and wrapping it around his neck, she led him to her house.[18] The courtesans saw that, were well and truly amazed, and said: "This Gandhāran woman seduced the extremely ugly perfumer's son—great job!" And they appointed her as their mistress.

Utpalavarṇā has now succeeded in turning her sexuality into a weapon and securing for herself social status. But naturally, the story cannot end there.

She had sex, made love, and coupled with that [perfumer's son],[19] and after some time she became pregnant. There are two warders in Vaiśālī, the eastern and the western. As the two were familiar with each other, one said: "Sir, I wonder if there is a way such that, even after the two of us die and are no more, our friendly relations might not be cut off."

The other said: "Sir, our children should be pledged in marriage to each other.[20] If I have a son, and you have a daughter, your daughter should be given to my son. And if you have a son and I have a daughter, I should give my daughter to your son. Then even after we are dead and gone, our friendly relations will not be cut off."

"Okay, let it be so."

When nine months had passed, Utpalavarṇā gave birth to a son, and thought to herself: "Men avoid a woman with a small child." So resolving to abandon it, she said to her servant girl: "Girl, take this boy and a lamp, go to a boulevard, and leave the boy someplace. Remain there off to one side until someone takes the lamp [that you have placed next to the baby] there in the public square."[21]

She took him, and placed him in a spot not very far away from [the house of] the eastern warder. She put down the lamp and waited off to one side. The eastern warder saw the lamp and, giving way to his curiosity, came over. As soon as he saw the boy, he took him and went to his wife, saying:

"Dear, here is a son for you." She took him joyfully. Then at daybreak, there was great happiness [in their household]. Their neighbors said to each other: "Sirs, what has happened to bring about such happiness in the house of this eastern warder?" One of them said: "A son has been born." Another said: "If his wife was not pregnant, from where did he get a son?" And another replied: "Sirs, some women may be pregnant without showing it."

The western warder heard the news and thought to himself: "He's had a son. If I were to have a daughter, he would become my son-in-law." So he presented him with clothing and ornaments.

When he had grown up and became a man, at one time he joined an association. Sometime thereafter, Utpalavarṇā once again became pregnant, and after nine months gave birth to a girl. She once again thought to herself: "Men avoid a woman with a small child." So resolving to abandon it, she said to her servant girl: "Girl, take this girl and lamp, go to a boulevard, and leave the girl someplace. Remain there off to one side until someone takes the lamp [and the child] there in the public square."

She took her and placed her in a spot not very far away from [the house of] the western warder. She put down the lamp and waited off to one side. The western warder saw the lamp and, giving way to his curiosity, came over. As soon as he saw the girl, he took her and went to his wife, saying: "Dear, here is a daughter for you." She took her joyfully. Then at daybreak, there was great happiness [in their household]. Their neighbors said to each other: "Sirs, what has happened to bring about such happiness in the house of this western warder?" One of them said: "A daughter has been born." Another said: "If his wife was not pregnant, from where did he get a daughter?" And another replied: "Sirs, some women may be pregnant without showing it."

The eastern warder heard the news and thought to himself: "Since he's had a daughter, she'll become my daughter-in-law." So he presented her with clothing and ornaments.

When she had grown up and became a woman, at one time she too joined an association.

The stage is now set with two new actors, another daughter and a son for Utpalavarṇā. What happens next should no longer surprise us.

Now at one time, five hundred association members went to a park, and they began to deliberate what would be an appropriate thing to do in the park in light of their age.

"Let's get a courtesan."

"Yes, let's."

"Whom should we get?"

"The Gandhāran woman."

"Okay, let's make a rule: any of us who does not have sexual relations with her will be fined five hundred kārṣāpaṇas by the association members."

Paying the Gandhāran woman Utpalavarṇā five hundred kārṣāpaṇas as a fee, they brought her to the park, and all of the association members had sexual relations with her in turns. The son of the eastern warder did not want to have sexual relations with her, but Utpalavarṇā said: "Young sir, have sex with me—otherwise they will fine you five hundred kārṣāpaṇas."

Fearful of this punishment, he had sex with her and, becoming enamored with Utpalavarṇā, he privately made her into his exclusive mistress. The Licchavīs got angry, and they said: "Since the son of the eastern warder privately made into his exclusive mistress a woman who is to be enjoyed by the group, let's go and kill him!"

Since everyone has friends, enemies, and those who are indifferent toward one,[22] one of the group went to the eastern warder and told him what had taken place. The eastern warder was terrified, and going to the Licchavīs, he prostrated himself at their feet and said: "I beg of you on behalf of my son!"

They said: "Oh, patriarch, what's wrong?"

He explained things to them in detail, and then one of them said: "Sirs, since this eastern warder has long been of use to us, if his son wants the courtesan, let's give her to him." The others said: "Okay, let it be so." And they gave Utpalavarṇā to him.

Since that son of the eastern warder had obtained her from the organization, he took Utpalavarṇā as his wife without any fear [about the previous death threats]. Then his father said to the western warder: "Sir, give your daughter as bride to my boy."

He responded: "Sir, your boy has taken a wife; what will he do with another bride?"

He said: "Sir, since we had an advance understanding, give her now! If I would have wealth, I would arrange servants for the wife of my son."

The western warder gave his daughter to the son of the eastern warder per their advance understanding. And the son of the eastern warder married her at an auspicious solar and lunar day and time.

At that time the Venerable Mahā-Maudgalyāyana walked to the house of the eastern warder, and said to his daughter: "Girl, your senior wife is your mother. Your husband is your brother. But don't feel resentment toward your mother, and don't let it occur to you that it will cause her to descend into hell."[23]

Utpalavarṇā is now married to her son, and once again co-wife with her own daughter. And things are about to get more complicated yet.

From having sex, making love, and coupling with Utpalavarṇā, a son was born, and the daughter [Utpalavarṇā's co-wife] was about to set him to play outside of the threshold, when just then a brahmin walking down the road saw him, and spoke the following verses:

Among people, the best of the best,
Incomparable, female auditor who defends the Victor,[24]
Superb like a mandāraka flower,
Sister, who is this boy to you?

She too spoke in verse:

Brahmin, he is my brother,
My brother's son, and my brother-in-law.
His father is my father[25]
Who was my brother and is now my husband.[26]

Utpalavarṇā heard this, and said to her servant girl: "Girl, what are these two saying?"

She replied: "These two are speaking the truth, not lies."

"What is the truth here?"

"Your son whom I left at the eastern gate is now this husband of yours. Your daughter whom I left at the western gate is now this junior wife of yours."

Utpalavarṇā thought to herself: "Previously, having been co-wife with my own mother, I also was co-wife with my daughter. In the present, again, being co-wife with my daughter, my son has become my husband. I must get completely out of here." So covering her head, she left the house, and very soon seeing a caravan headed for Rājagṛha she joined it and went to Rājagṛha.

We have here yet another transition between acts, motivated as before by Utpalavarṇā's learning of the circumstances into which fate has thrown her. But her luck is about to change.

There again she made her living as a courtesan. Once, an association of five hundred members went to a park and began to deliberate: "Sirs, what would be an appropriate thing to do in the park in light of our age?"

"Let's get a courtesan."

"Yes, let's."

"Whom should we get?"

"The Gandhāran woman."

"Okay." And paying the Gandhāran woman Utpalavarṇā five hundred kārṣāpaṇas, they brought her to the park. After eating and drinking, they had sex, made love, and coupled with her.

The Venerable Mahā-Maudgalyāyana knew that the appropriate time had come for him to convert Utpalavarṇā, so he walked around near the base of a tree not very far away from where they all were. Then one member of the association said: "This noble Mahā-Maudgalyāyana is in every respect free of the fetters of suffering, while we are sunk in the mire of lust."

Utpalavarṇā said: "In Vaiśālī I seduced an extremely ugly perfumer's son."

The association members said: "Why do you mention that? Do you want to seduce him too?"

She said: "Is he a man endowed with a male organ?"

"Yes, he is a man endowed with a male organ."

"If I seduce him, what will you do for me?"

"[We'll pay you] five hundred kārṣāpaṇas. If you're not able to seduce him, what will you do for us?"

"I'll be the concubine of one of you."

"Okay, let it be so."

Utpalavarṇā agreed and went to the place where the Venerable Mahā-Maudgalyāyana was and began to display her feminine cunning, feminine wiles, feminine craft, and feminine guile, but the Venerable Mahā-Maudgalyāyana remained with his senses fixed.

She thought to herself: "Since the touch of a woman is poison, if I embrace him, he will fall under my control," and so she began to embrace him. But the Venerable Mahā-Maudgalyāyana rose up into the sky like a goose king stretching out his wings and spoke the following verses:[27]

[You are] a hut which is a machine of bones
Wrapped in sinew,
With an impure rotten stench;
Reliant on others you take [their bodies] as your own.[28]

You are a leather bag full of shit,
Hollow, pox-ridden, and easily wearied,
With impurities always flowing out of
The nine orifices [of your body].[29]

If men knew you as I know you,
They would stay far away from you,
As from a cesspool in the rainy season.[30]

Since ignorant heretics
Obscured by darkness do not know,
Therefore they love you
Like aged elephants in the mud.[31]

Utpalavarṇā replied in verse:

Just so, very fortunate one,
Just as the Noble said:

[I am] a hut which is a machine of bones
Wrapped in sinew,
With an impure rotten stench;
Reliant on others [I] take [their bodies] as [my] own.

I am a leather bag full of shit,
Hollow, pox-ridden, and easily wearied,
With impurities always flowing out of
The nine orifices [of my body].

If men understood me as the Noble One discerns me,
They would stay far away from me,
As from a cesspool in the rainy season.

Since ignorant heretics
Obscured by darkness do not know,

Therefore they love me
Like aged elephants in the mud

I come humbly to the highly fortunate [master],
I ask for the Noble One to instruct me in the teaching.
I shall be your disciple in
The instruction in the highest wisdom.

Then the Venerable Mahā-Maudgalyāyana descended from the sky, and knowing her inclinations and tendencies, disposition and character, as Utpalavarṇā sat on a cushion, he instructed her in the teaching penetrating the Four Noble Truths such that with the cudgel of wisdom she smashed the twenty-peaked stone mountain of the mistaken philosophical view of belief in a real self, and attained the fruit of the Stream Winner.

Seeing the truth, she then said: "Noble One, I rely upon you as a spiritual guide. The Noble One has done for me what neither my father, nor my mother, nor the king, nor the gods, nor my ancestors, nor the ascetics or priests, nor my beloved or friends or relatives have done for me, namely, dried up the seas of blood and tears, leapt over the mountain of bones, barred shut the gateway to the undesirable destinies, opened wide the gateway to heaven and to liberation, pulled my feet out from the realms of hell, of demons, and of animals and established me in the realm of gods and humans. [Thanks to you] with the cudgel of wisdom I smashed the twenty-peaked stone mountain of the mistaken philosophical view of belief in a real self acquired from beginningless time and attained the fruit of the Stream Winner. Noble One, I am set out. Noble One, I am set out, so Noble One, I take refuge in the Buddha, the Dharma, and the Saṁgha, and I want to become a Buddhist laywoman. From now on as long as I live, I will be heartfelt and devout in my reliance on the refuges."

Then the gentlewoman[32] Utpalavarṇā prostrated herself at the feet of the Venerable Mahā-Maudgalyāyana, and said: "Reverend Mahā-Maudgalyāyana, I would take initiation and ordination in the well-spoken teaching and discipline and become a nun, practicing celibacy before the Blessed One."

He said: "Sister, come, let us ask your husbands."[33] She went to where they were, and said: "Sirs, will you allow me to take ordination?"

They said: "Gandhāran woman, why are you making fun of us?"

She said: "I'm really going to ordain; I'm not making fun of you."

They said: "If that's the case, then ordain!"

Having obtained their permission, she went to where the Venerable Mahā-Maudgalyāyana was, and he led her to where the Blessed One was. Arriving there, she prostrated with her head at the Blessed One's feet and sat down at one end of the line. When [he too] was seated at one end of the line, the Venerable Mahā-Maudgalyāyana spoke to the Blessed One, requesting: "Reverend, Utpalavarṇā requests to be initiated and ordained in the well-spoken teaching and discipline and become a nun."

The Blessed One said: "Yes, it's fine to ordain her." And he himself began to write a letter to Mahāprajāpatī.[34] When the Blessed One had composed the letter, King Bimbisāra came and asked him: "Blessed One, why is this courtesan here?"[35]

The Blessed One said: "Great king, don't speak so! She is your spiritual sister, who wishes to be initiated and ordained in the well-spoken teaching and discipline and become a nun."

"Blessed One, to whom do you write a letter?"

"Great king, to Mahāprajāpatī in Śrāvastī."

"Blessed One, let me be the messenger to convey it to her."

"Yes, Great king." And he appointed the king to convey it.

Utpalavarṇā received the letter and went to Śrāvastī. Mahāprajāpatī Gautamī initiated and ordained her and advised her, and alone, withdrawn, undistracted, and self-controlled, she understood that this five-fold wheel of transmigration is inherently unstable. She rid herself of all aspects of the conditioned realm, because they are characterized by decay, decline, destruction, and ruin. Ridding herself of all the defilements, she thoroughly understood through her own intuitive wisdom and in this very lifetime the unexcelled endpoint of the celibate life, that for the sake of which gentlewomen shave their heads and put on the ascetic's robes, and with complete faith go forth from the household life to the homeless life, [namely, she understood]: rebirth is exhausted for me; I have lived the celibate life; I have done what needs to be done; I will know nothing other than this [present] existence. Understanding this, she became an arhatī, free of the passions of the three realms. To her gold and a clump of dirt were the same, she looked upon the sky and the palm of her hand as no different, (cooling) sandalwood was to her like a (painfully cutting) sword, with wisdom she cracked open the eggshell [of ignorance],[36] she obtained knowledge and superpowers and penetrating insight, she turned her back on existence and possessions, desires and fame, she was honored, worshipped, and saluted by Indra and all the gods in his retinue.

Then the Blessed One said to the monks: "Monks, my female auditor has great magical powers, and among those of great power, this nun Utpalavarṇā is supreme."

The monks were curious about this, and in order to remove all their curiosity, they asked the Buddha, Blessed One, a question: "Reverend, what actions did Utpalavarṇā perform so that her eyes resemble a blue lotus, she has the fragrance of a lotus, and [her skin] resembles the color of the anther of a lotus? What actions did she perform such that she is not made by men to live in poverty, and such that she was ordained in the teaching of the Blessed One and, removing all her defilements, realized the state of an arhat? What actions did she perform such that you speak of her as a female auditor of great magical powers, supreme among those of great power?"

The Blessed One said: "Monks, since Utpalavarṇā herself performed and accumulated these actions, piled them up, actions that are about to ripen, advancing like a flood, and inescapable, who else than Utpalavarṇā herself would experience [the results of] the actions she herself performed and accumulated? Monks, actions which are performed and accumulated will not bear fruit [somewhere] outside [oneself] in the earth element, or in the water element, or in the fire element, or in the wind element. Rather, both positive and negative actions that are performed and accumulated will bear fruit in the aggregates, elements, and sense spheres of the clinging [to existence, that is to say, in the continuum that constitutes the individual].

> Deeds do not disappear even in one hundred aeons.
> [But] reaching completeness and the proper time, they produce results for beings.[37]

Monks, long ago in a certain mountain village there dwelt a householder, and he took a wife from a suitable family, and he had sex, made love, and coupled with her. At one time he took his merchandise and went to another country. Although she was content with good food and clothing, she was afflicted by sensual passions. Not far away [from where she lived] there was a bordello, and as she saw some men going in and other men going out of there, she thought to herself: "Since this woman [who runs the bordello] is kept from poverty, if she has been made rich by men, by what means might I too be kept from poverty by men?" And when she thought things over like that, she summoned a Digambara Jaina female devotee (**śrāvikā*)[38] to her, and said: "Sister, what means might there be to completely accomplish my ambitions and aspirations?"

She replied: "Sister, I have a brother who is a renunciant, an ascetic, a devotee (that is, a Digambara monk).[39] Undertake a vow to feed him. Then you will completely accomplish your ambitions and aspirations."

She said: "If that is so, go and invite that devotee to my house for a meal." And she fed him a meal. That householder's wife even prepared the food and presented it on leaves of the blue lotus. Since the ascetics [came there to] eat at all times, appropriate and inappropriate, she was delayed for a rather long time.

During a time when there are no buddhas, there appear in the world lone buddhas, who manifest their compassion for the poor and downtrodden, who delight in living in the outskirts, like a lone rhinoceros, who are the sole object of veneration for the world.

Just then a lone buddha was wandering around and came to that mountain village. In the morning he got dressed and taking his begging bowl and robes wandering for alms came to that house. The householder's wife saw his handsome appearance and good demeanor and thought to herself: "Since he's an ascetic and a devotee, I'll offer him a meal." She offered him a meal, and having satisfied him she did reverence to him again with leaves of the blue lotus. Since those devotees taught the teaching of the body, not the teaching of words, after that lone buddha ate the meal and rose up into the sky like a goose king stretching out his wings, he began to manifest the miracles which made the sky blaze and be radiant, rain fall, and lightning flash.[40]

Since magical powers quickly convert ordinary people, that wife of the householder paid respectful attention and prostrated herself at his feet, making the vow: "May the roots of merit I plant by paying reverence to this worthy lead me to be kept from poverty by men, and subsequently may I obtain those good qualities such that I may please the most outstanding noble teacher and not displease him."

"Monks, at that time and on that occasion the householder's wife was Utpalavarṇā. That she fed the lone buddha and made offerings to him on leaves of the blue lotus has resulted in her having eyes like a blue lotus, having the fragrance of a lotus, and having [skin] the color of the anther of the lotus. Thanks to the vow—'May the roots of merit I plant by paying reverence to this worthy lead me to be kept from poverty by men, and subsequently may I obtain those good qualities such that I may please the most outstanding noble teacher and not displease him'—she was kept from poverty by men, ordained in my teaching, ridding herself of all defilements

> and realizing the state of the arhat, and through this [vow] she pleases me, the most outstanding noble teacher, and does not displease me."[41]

Although telescoped in its own ways, as is its Pāli parallel,[42] this is a remarkable tale. Much if not most of its interest comes in the expansive narrative, but the connection between the two versions is both obvious and multivalent. The verses that Mahā-Maudgalyāyana speaks, and that Utpalavarṇā then repeats, are found also in the Theravāda *Theragāthā* (Verses of the Elders), there again ascribed to the same monk, and according to the commentary said to have been spoken to a prostitute, who is identified in the commentary to the *Therīgāthā* (Verses of the Elder Nuns) as the nun Vimalā.[43] This demonstrates that, beyond the broad correspondence of their respective versions of the Utpalavarṇā story, the narrative associated with this set of verses was also, in outline, even if independently, shared by the Mūlasarvāstivāda and Theravāda traditions. From the point of view of literary development, there can be no question that the Mūlasarvāstivāda version, whatever its ultimate historical relation to the story preserved in Pāli, must be seen as an elaboration on the same basic theme.[44] It is, moreover, remarkable not least of all for being included in a text belonging to the Buddhist monastic code—or rather we may say, it is remarkable among other things for what this may say to us about our image of what these codes were and what they contain. Still, Ralston, in the introduction to his extremely valuable collection of stories drawn from the Mūlasarvāstivāda Vinaya, may not have been entirely justified in saying that in this story:[45]

> [w]e are taken . . . into [the region] of such literary fictions as form a part of the "Thousand and One Nights." It, also, is not of a very edifying nature; but it is valuable as showing what utter nonsense many of the corrupted Buddhistic legends contain, and illustrating the custom prevalent among literary Buddhists (one in which they were perhaps surpassed by the Christian compilers of such works as the "Gesta Romanorum") of appending an unexceptional moral to a tale of an unsavory nature. The rapidity with which the narrator, at the close of the story of Utpalavarṇā, passes from the record of her dissoluteness to the account of her conversion is somewhat startling.

This is an important point worth pursing. Certainly Ralston is in part quite right here when he remarks on the abruptness of Utpalavarṇā's conversion. One of the most obvious features of the story from any point of view is Utpalavarṇā's complete lack of any sense of guilt or regret. Many of the actions she takes appear, from the perspective of a developed narrative, to be insufficiently motivated, and we are given relatively little psychological insight into her behaviors. She almost seems, from the point of view of the narration, to be along for the ride. But from a perspective that grants her some agency and assumes that she can indeed act intentionally, one might term her attitude thoroughly amoral, not only from a modern ethical perspective, but within the frame of ancient Indian society as well. Of course, the Victorian Englishman Ralston may have been upset by the image of Utpalavarṇā as a prostitute who offers herself to any and all, continually and repeatedly, mostly for money, but sometimes apparently for free (or for protection and other nonmonetary compensation). Yet this in itself would not have been seen as particularly problematic in ancient India. At least relatively high-ranking courtesans held an honored place in ancient Indian society, and, as proverbs and incidents such as the famous story of the "act of truth" of the prostitute Bindumatī in the *Milindapañha* (Questions of King Milinda) clearly demonstrate, their general accessibility may also have been seen in a positive light.[46] In that story, which is cited with approval, Bindumatī swears that she has never discriminated against any client, rich or poor, high or low, an avowal the veracity of which is verified by the river Ganges reversing its course.[47] Thus it is not likely that the characterization of Utpalavarṇā as a prostitute would in itself have bothered many in the tale's putative original audience, Buddhists or not; indeed, the opposite may be true, and it may well have been understood as ascribing to her an eminently respectable status. Nor is it likely that her actions in abandoning her children would have elicited much comment (although I should certainly like to think that flinging a newborn is never seen as acceptable in any society). Although there is as yet little evidence concerning the practice in ancient India in general, certainly in this story child abandonment is depicted as an accepted behavior, such that a man out walking in the evening does not find it remarkable to discover an infant, left together with a lamp to draw attention, in the vicinity of a busy intersection or town square.[48] In fact, the story as a whole is presented matter-of-factly, in an almost entirely nonjudgmental way, which makes the denouement, Utpalavarṇā's conversion, as Ralston noted, all the more peculiar.

One may gain the impression that the authors were at once fascinated with their subject, and yet unable to fully cope with their creation. One way of understanding this, from what might be close to a modern, feminist perspective, is to imagine that they found themselves unable to respond to the sexually liberated woman who acknowledges her sexual activities but is not herself scandalized by them—that authors who could imagine this woman and create her as a character in their tale nevertheless, when faced with the implications of her possibly revolutionary social autonomy, quailed and backtracked. At the end of their byzantine story of incest and guiltless sexuality, nothing is left to them but a total abrogation of the demands of narrative logic and the patterns of rational plot development—the only course is to invoke the deus ex machina. Such an interpretation is viable only up to a point. It is true that for no apparent logical reason at all, save her inability to seduce one individual man, Utpalavarṇā is made to repent her life choices and aspire to a vocation in almost every way the inverse of that she formerly led—ascetic where she was libertine, teleological where she was happy-go-lucky.

But there are alternatives to the speculation that the authors simply lost control of their story, or failed in their courage to carry through on its implications. We might, for instance, credit them with somewhat more psychological insight than we have assumed so far, and argue that the key point they wished to convey is that Utpalavarṇā's failure to seduce Mahā-Maudgalyāyana represented for her a repudiation of the one ability from which she derived her sense of self-worth, namely, her seductive powers. If she defined herself through her sexuality, its failure would mean a failure of her essential nature and trigger a consequent collapse of her very definition of herself. Buddhist literature is replete with examples of this type of logic, although it is usually presented in different forms, with an emphasis, for instance, on the inevitable aging of the body and the attendant loss of sexual attractiveness this implies. If this were indeed the authors' main point, they are rather subtle in their depiction of this aspect of Utpalavarṇā's conversion experience, to the point where they hardly refer to it at all. On the other hand, we can certainly read backwards and fill in gaps in the story, which, as I have suggested, is somewhat telescoped. When Utpalavarṇā says, "Is he a man with a male organ?" it is quite natural to understand her as saying, "If it's got a penis, I can seduce it." Such a reading would allow us to assume that when she encounters a man with a penis whom she cannot seduce, this failure challenges the central criterion through which she defines herself. It is, naturally, not easy to demonstrate the validity of such a suggestion. However, some support for this understanding of the episode may come from comparison with a similar exchange presented in a Hindu text, the *Mārkaṇḍeya Purāṇa*.[49]

In a passage from the very beginning of the *Mārkaṇḍeya Purāṇa*, the sage Nārada challenges the heavenly maidens, the Apsarases, as follows:[50] "I [will] deem she among you pre-eminent in good qualities (*guṇādhikā*) who by her power perturbs the supreme sage Durvāsas, who dwells in the Himālayas performing austerities." This must certainly remind us, not just vaguely but in its specific vocabulary, of the challenge of the courtesans that Utpalavarṇā takes up: "That woman among us who is capable of seducing that particular perfumer's son we will call a woman of quality (*bud med kyi yon tan dang ldan pa=*guṇavatī*)." The more important feature, however, comes not from the similarity of challenges or in comparison with Utpalavarṇā's subsequent seduction of the perfumer's son, but in her attempted seduction of Mahā-Maudgalyāyana, who may in this context be seen as a Buddhist equivalent of the Hindu sage Durvāsas. Mahā-Maudgalyāyana's response to Utpalavarṇā's attempt at seduction is to display his immunity to her charms, and thus convince her of the ultimate impotence of sexual desire and its powerlessness and meaninglessness in the face of the higher truths revealed in Buddhist teachings. But the Hindu sage's response is different, and this contrast serves to emphasize the program and narrative logic of the Buddhist story. The *Mārkaṇḍeya Purāṇa* passage continues:[51]

> Hearing that announcement of his, with trembling voices they all said "this is impossible for us!"
>
> Among them an Apsaras named Vapu (Beautiful), confident of [her ability to] perturb the sage, replied, "I will pursue the sage to where he dwells. Now will I make that coachman of his body, who has yoked the horses of his sense organs, into a poor charioteer whose reins drop before the weapons of love. Whether it be Brahmā, or Janārdana [Viṣṇu], or the Purple One [Śiva], even him I will now wound in the heart with the arrow of love."
>
> Having spoken thus, Vapu then departed for the Snowy mountain, to the hermitage where [even] the beasts of prey were quelled by the might of the sage's austerities. Stopping as far away from where the great sage was staying as a voice might travel, the lovely Apsaras, who had the sweetness (of voice) of the male cuckoo, sang. Hearing the sound of her song, the sage was astonished and went to where that radiant-faced maiden was. Seeing her, beautifully formed in every limb, the sage, composing his mind and knowing that she had come to perturb him, was filled with anger and indignation.
>
> Then the great master, the performer of mighty austerities, spoke to her as follows:
>
> "Since you, intoxicated with pride, came here in order to cause me suffering by obstructing my austerities, earned through suffering, O sky traveler, therefore censured by my wrath you will be [cursed to be] born, foolish woman, among the race of birds for the space of sixteen years, losing your own form and taking the form of a bird [as you pretended to be by singing in order to disturb me]. Four sons shall be born to you, O vilest of Apsarases, and without having gained affection among them, absolved from guilt by dying in the field of battle, you will regain your dwelling in the sky. There is nothing further for you to say [in appeal against this curse]!"

Despite their obvious similarities, there are strong contrasts between the Buddhist and Purāṇic episodes. In the Purāṇa the Apsaras's efforts to use her sexual attraction as a weapon against a holy man are rebuffed with disdain and recompensed with punishment. The Buddhist story takes an entirely different approach. The ultimate goal of the authors of the story of Utpalavarṇā is to demonstrate the salvific power of Buddhism. The Apsarases are by nature sexually seductive women, the heavenly wives of the divine musicians, the Gandharvas. Their power to attract human men, then, must be assumed to far surpass that of a mere mortal like Utpalavarṇā. The sage Durvāsas, like Mahā-Maudgalyāyana, is unmoved by this attempted seduction, of course, since his spiritual accomplishments have set him beyond such attractions. But he is interested in only one thing: himself. He does not view the Apsaras Vapu as anything other than an annoying distraction, and his response is one of "anger and indignation." He displays no interest in using the opportunity to teach or guide Vapu. This could hardly contrast more strongly with the response of the Buddhist sage Mahā-Maudgalyāyana, who meets Utpalavarṇā's attempts at seduction with equanimity, unconcern, and disinterest, in order to guide her past her mistaken attitudes. She does not annoy him, and, unlike Durvāsas, he does not become angry. And this I believe to be the key to understanding the story of Utpalavarṇā. While this independent "survivor" has her sense of self-definition, rooted in her sexually hegemonic power, shattered by the ascetic and unmoved Mahā-Maudgalyāyana, the destruction of that sense of self-worth is not the point of his response to her, and he has no wish to punish her. Mahā-Maudgalyāyana's goal is to persuade Utpalavarṇā not of the impotence of her sexuality, but of its meaninglessness. Her role in the story is to be converted, not, as is Vapu's, to be punished for her temerity or effrontery.

From this perspective, it would be wrong to see the tale of Utpalavarṇā as veering off from its logical course and crashing into an incoherent though morally uplifting finale. Surely the authors began with their ending—they knew that the tale must arrive at the salvation of its protagonist, and they knew that the more deeply mired she was in the world of sensuality, the more profound would be her liberation when she finally found her way to the world of Buddhist monasticism, defined as it is centrally as a life of celibacy. A cynical analysis might imagine that the authors' desire to present a tale of salvation led them to lavish their narrative efforts on an overly exaggerated background, with the result that they were not quite sure, in the end, how to connect their conclusion to their elaborately convincing background. But there is another much more charitable and contextually convincing reading, one which sees in the vision of the authors a faith in the salvific power of Buddhism so strong that for them there is nothing in the least unnatural or illogical in the very same sudden conversion that may strike us, as it struck Ralston, as jarringly discontinuous. In this reading, there is no failure of authorial nerve, but rather precisely the opposite: the very rapidity or suddenness of the narrative transition merely parallels the sudden, even instantaneous, conversion of the believer from indifference to faith. Utpalavarṇā sees the truth when Mahā-Maudgalyāyana displays it to her, and she immediately conforms herself to her new worldview. It is not that Utpalavarṇā's sense of self was shattered by her failure to seduce Mahā-Maudgalyāyana, and her conversion some sort of compensation. It is not, or not only, that she reacts defensively in self-preservation since she has lost that which theretofore had defined her both inwardly for herself and outwardly among her peers as an unconquerable seductress—although certainly this psychology cannot be ignored. Rather, the denouement portrays—is practically an advertisement for—the overwhelming power of the Buddhist truths to convince and to convert, since having confronted these truths head on one cannot help but immediately recognize their validity. From the perspective of the devout Buddhist authors of our tale, nothing could be more natural.

We may borrow an image from Gotthold Lessing and speak of an ugly ditch, the chasm which for him separates us from God and across which one leaps in the moment of faith. The jump is indeed discontinuous, and hence illogical, or rather alogical or translogical. The states are like quanta—discrete, without any points of contact: movement between them cannot happen gradually but only through a jump.[52] In this interpretation, our Buddhist narrative is a coherent whole up to *and through* Utpalavarṇā's conversion experience, since the very discontinuity of the conversion experience is coherently and realistically depicted, and highlights an integral part of the authors' message. Rather than signaling a failure of nerve, the trajectory of their narrative affirms the authors' faith and confidence in the salvific certainty of their tradition. Finally, within the broader external frame of Buddhist soteriology, this ultimate conclusion to the story is almost inevitable. Although Utpalavarṇā may be understood to have been motivated internally and psychologically by the collapse of her Ego—her conception of herself as defined by her ability to seduce—seen from a broader perspective, her subsequent conversion appears equally, if not more forcefully, motivated externally and religiously by the steamroller power of Buddhist truths to persuade, no matter how the ground has been prepared. In Buddhist literature no one is immune to the compelling force of the conversion experience, and Buddhist narrative literature has myriad examples of comparable sudden conversion experiences, in which no similar psychological groundwork has been laid. In this respect Utpalavarṇā's internal psychological state may be seen in the end to be nearly, if not entirely, irrelevant to the ultimate narrative consequences.[53]

There are aspects of this tale that allow us to discuss it in comparison with other similar Buddhist stories and in a broader comparative context as well. The complete ignorance of the true relationship between the protagonists here brings this story very much closer to one aspect of the classical Oedipal tale than are the other stories we have examined. For this reason, the story of Utpalavarṇā has the potential to evoke a sort of pathos, or sense of tragedy, that is entirely absent from the Dharmaruci/Mahādeva story, in which the mother is thoroughly aware of her actions from the start, and her son comes to be later. That the pathos in Utpalavarṇā's tale is not, in the end, made a significant element of the plot development is noteworthy and may even tell us something of how some aspects of the incest theme are seen in Indian Buddhist literature. Utpalavarṇā is a sexual libertine, and simultaneously a victim of mistaken identity, yet neither fact becomes grist for any morality-tale mill. From the perspective of classical Buddhist doctrine, the reasons for this are easy to understand: action, Buddhist texts constantly tell us, is defined as intention. Acts performed without conscious intention are, broadly speaking, not karmically potent, an idea familiar to us in our own legal system, which distinguishes, for example, between voluntary and involuntary manslaughter. Volition is central, and volition requires awareness. What light, then, does this shed on Mahādeva?

When we compare this story of Utpalavarṇā with that of Dharmaruci, we can detect similarities on a number of levels. We find, for instance, that they share very specific vocabulary, such as the terms *kleśa* in the sense of sexual frustration and *nimitta* as an invitation to sexual intimacy. At the opposite end of the spectrum, the overall scenario, with the substitution of son-in-law for son, resembles the Dharmaruci episode. Sociologically speaking, we are fully justified in seeing little difference between son and son-in-law with respect to their status within an Oedipal architecture, just as we noticed stepmother replacing mother in the *Mahāvastu* parallel to the Dharmaruci story. We will meet other examples of such substitutions shortly.

There is a larger contrast to be seen here as well, one I have labored to bring out earlier in a slightly different way. I have argued that, in the process of making the Dharmaruci story into the calumnious tale of Mahādeva, the adaptors, most crucially, adjusted the depictions of the protagonist's agency and intentionality. In the tale of Utpalavarṇā we have a mother who commits incest with her son, but unlike the otherwise similar depictions in the story of Dharmaruci, in Utpalavarṇā's tale there is no question of intention, since the act is carried out in mutual ignorance. The Mūlasarvāstivāda Vinaya tradition, which transmits the Utpalavarṇā story—the very same tradition which preserved the story of Dharmaruci—can thus be seen here in what are as close as we are likely to get to laboratory conditions: similar overall scenarios nevertheless evolve along significantly different narrative vectors, steered by differing intentional agencies in the commission of superficially kindred actions. Utpalavarṇā's story is told non-judgmentally, and her "sinful" actions are not karmically potent, since she lacked any intention to commit incest; Dharmaruci's mother, in contrast, is guilty of intentionally seducing her son. With this distinction as backdrop, the way in which Mahādeva's guilt with regard to his incestuous affair was carefully adapted to reflect a yet more direct level of intentionality and agency comes more clearly into focus. Needless to say, this applies only to the sexual dimension of Mahādeva's story, since it is by definition impossible to "murder" (although certainly not to kill) someone without intention. The point of my hypothesis, however, is that while the *Vibhāṣā* and allied literature most certainly attribute to Mahādeva a series of murders, characterized by their classification as three of the five sins of immediate retribution, the sexual dynamics of the tale are also central to their depiction and calumniation of Mahādeva. The gradations of moral culpability from Utpalavarṇā to Dharmaruci to Mahādeva illustrate, and indeed highlight, the specific intention of those responsible for the Mahādeva story to sculpt it in a fashion as calumnious as possible. Mere involvement in incestuous relations is inadequate to elicit sufficient censure in the cultural context of this literature: the compilers of the Mahādeva story felt it necessary to depict their protagonist as acting with a very specific intention, in order to ensure his guilt.

In Chapter 13 I asked a question about the scope of the Oedipal in Indian Buddhist literature. A further related issue is how Buddhist and more generally Indian Oedipal tales are related to a broader Oedipal archetype, if indeed such a generalized archetype exists at all. Scholars have addressed this question in the past, without however making use of Buddhist evidence. In Chapter 15, I will confront some earlier theories with the Buddhist evidence we have so far surveyed.

15
The "Indian Oedipus"

ONE OF this study's large-scale questions concerns the universality of the (or an) Oedipus complex, and whether and how Indian evidence might shed light on some debates of more general interest. In particular, how might such evidence suggest a modification of the architecture of any such complex? As one would imagine, the literature on the question of the universality of an Oedipus complex is huge.[1] Here I will pay special attention only to the case of ancient India, and in particular to its literary evidence, leaving aside psychoanalytic approaches to the question, including abstract studies of the Indian psyche and the like.

We are forced from the outset to acknowledge the formidable stumbling block placed in the way of clear and coherent dialogue by a rather radical disagreement over definitions. The classical Oedipal tale, as set forth by Sophocles, involves in outline a prophecy—the murder of a father by his son and the son's subsequent sexual union with his mother—followed by a revelation of what has transpired and pathos at the inevitably fulfilled prophecy. It is this which makes the tale a tragedy in the strict sense. The Freudian psychoanalytic conception, moreover, whatever its real relation to the myth as traditionally told, requires or assumes the protagonist's fundamental underlying fear of castration by his father. On the other hand, in general discourse and "psychobabble," almost any intergenerational and/or intergender conflict may be called "Oedipal." In what is to follow, I pursue a middle path, intending by the term "Oedipus complex" some combination of intergenerational sexual and aggressive relations, while remaining sensitive to the possibility of definitional ambiguity over the scope of the Oedipal when referring to other studies.

In one of the most important contributions to the question of whether we may fairly speak of an Oedipus complex in India, A. K. Ramanujan has offered the argument that although there are indeed Indian Oedipal tales, they are differently arranged than the classic Greek tale, the narrative point of view, among other things, being reversed.[2] Let us first consider the folk tale Ramanujan collected in North Karnataka. As he recounts:[3]

> A girl is born with a curse on her head that she would marry her own son and beget a son by him. As soon as she hears of the curse, she willfully vows she'd try and escape it: she secludes herself in a dense forest, eating only fruit, foreswearing all male company. But when she attains puberty, as fate would have it, she eats a mango from a tree under which a passing king has urinated. The mango impregnates her; bewildered, she gives birth to a male child; she wraps him in a piece of her sari and throws him in a nearby stream. The child is picked up by the king of the next kingdom, and he grows up to be a handsome young adventurous prince. He comes hunting in the self-same jungle, and the cursed woman falls in love with the stranger, telling herself she is not in danger any more as she has no son alive. She marries him and bears a child.
>
> According to custom, the father's swaddling clothes are preserved and brought out for the newborn son. The woman recognizes at once the piece of sari with which she had swaddled her first son, now her husband, and understands that her fate had really caught up with her. She waits till everyone is asleep, and sings a lullaby to her newborn baby: Sleep, O son, O grandson, O brother to my husband, sleep O sleep, sleep well, and hangs herself by the rafter with her sari twisted to a rope.

"The prize sought," says Ramanujan, "is not the older cross-sex member of the triangle but the younger."[4] That is, the son does not desire the mother, but rather the reverse. "It is the mother," Ramanujan says, "the Jocasta-figure, who is accursed, tries to escape her fate, and when finally trammeled in it, it is she who makes the discovery and punishes herself with death. The son is merely a passive actor, part of his mother's fate—unlike the Greek Oedipus."[5] This is a profound insight, and one that opens up entirely new windows into the examination of such material. Now Ramanujan's story may, in some respects, seem like a "soft" version of some of the Indian Buddhist tales we have examined. While there are surely structural similarities, there are also key differences, including the absence—important if we are comparing it with the classical Oedipus tale—of any prophecy in the Buddhist versions. Concerning the structural elements, Ramanujan plotted the fundamental differences he saw between the Greek Oedipus and his Indian Oedipus according to the directionalities of what he termed "aggression" and "desire," and he expressed the results of these plots graphically. While the distinction Ramanujan intends by the terms "aggression" and "desire" is certainly clear, it is worthwhile reiterating that the modalities of desire in this context are many, and some of them include a fair portion of aggression. Moreover, since it takes two to tango, it may be more precise to label the directionalities "vector of aggression" and "vector of expression of sexual interest," a practice I will adopt in the following. In Figures 2 and 3, which are Ramanujan's, arrows represent directionality, the minus sign (–) indicates the vector of aggression, and the plus sign (+) the vector of expression of sexual interest (Ramanujan's "desire").[6]

The contrast illustrated by these two plottings instantly becomes clear: instead of the Greek tradition's directionality from child to parent (Figure 2), with aggression expressed within one gender and sexual interest across genders, the Indian model (Figure 3) has the same modalities of expression, but with their directionalities reversed, from parent to child.

When, using this approach, we attempt to extend the paradigm and plot the story of Dharmaruci, we find something quite interesting. An appropriate representation of our story might look like Figure 4. In this depiction, the axis of desire—the vector of expression of sexual interest—is, just as Ramanujan has suggested for his "Indian Oedipus," from mother to son. In contrast, the father is not aggressive toward his son; if anything, the opposite is true. I have indicated this relation with only a dotted vector, however, since the more vital and insistent aggression is that directed by the mother herself toward the father, her husband. This is an element entirely missing in the types of stories plotted by Ramanujan, in which the relations between mother and father appear to be ignored. Both Dharmaruci and Mahādeva show aggression toward the father, but not exactly hostility. The distinction is interesting. These sons kill the father, but they do not hate him. He is simply in the way; as long as he is present—and until his return from a lengthy sea voyage, he is *not* present—he prevents continuation of the sexual relationship between mother and son. But that relationship is characterized predominantly as one of sexual convenience, not of affection. Therefore, in our diagram the minus sign represents aggression, not hostility, and the plus sign represents desire, not affection. Dharmaruci is raised in a home with an absent father and a distant mother, and the relational architecture that develops reflects this fact transparently. Another fact that our analysis has thus far ignored is the subsequent development of the story: the son ultimately kills his mother as well. Considering this, we may revise our plotting as in Figure 5.

While there is no question that the tales presented in the *Divyāvadāna* on the one hand and in the *Vibhāṣā* on the other are fundamentally one and the same, we do notice a startling difference, one to which we have become sensitized thanks to Ramanujan's analysis. In the *Divyāvadāna* story, as plotted in Figure 4, the instigation for both the incest and the patricide comes wholly from the mother (and the same is true in the *Bodhisattvāvadānakalpalatā*, although

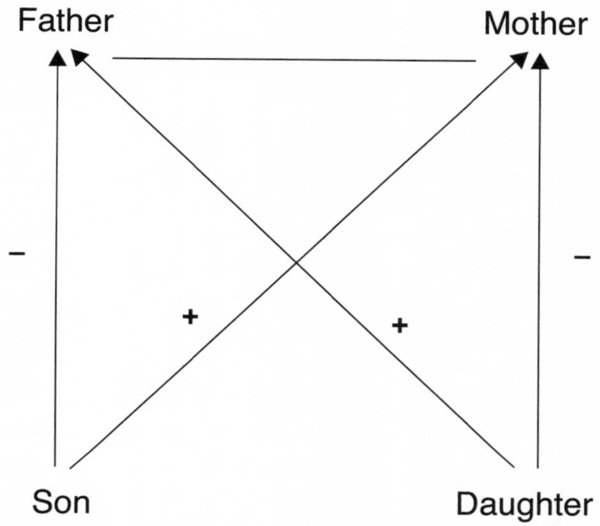

FIGURE 2: The Greek Model. *Source:* A. K. Ramanujan, "The Indian 'Oedipus,'" in *Indian Literature: Proceedings of a Seminar,* ed. Arabinda Poddar, 127–137 (Simla: Indian Institute of Advanced Study, 1972).

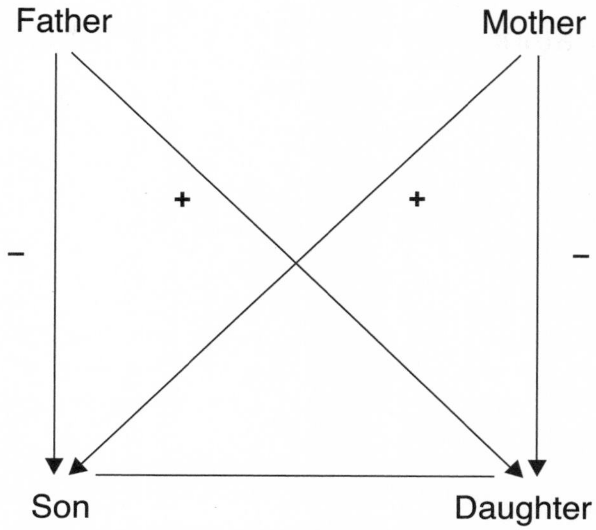

FIGURE 3: The Indian Model. *Source:* A. K. Ramanujan, "The Indian 'Oedipus,'" in *Indian Literature: Proceedings of a Seminar,* ed. Arabinda Poddar, 127–137 (Simla: Indian Institute of Advanced Study, 1972).

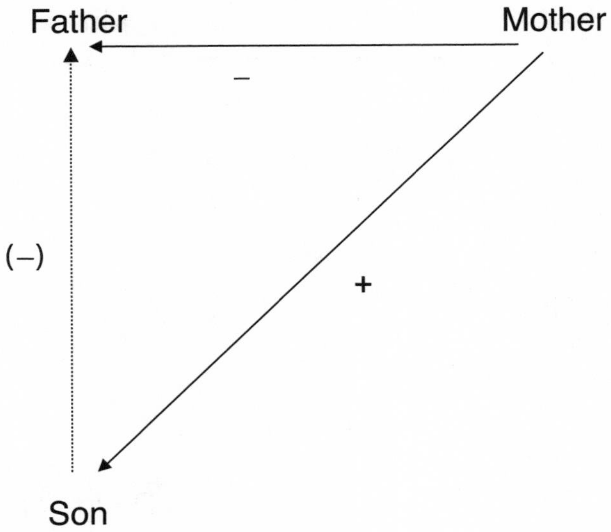

FIGURE 4: The Dharmaruci Story

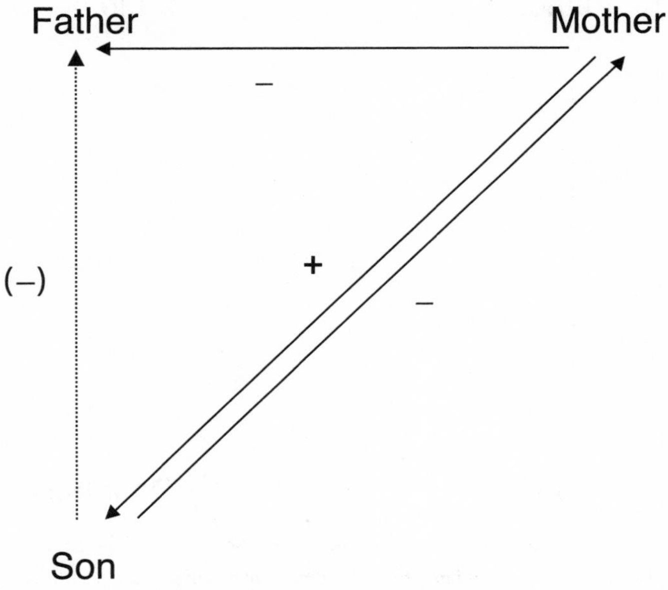

FIGURE 5: The Dharmaruci Story Revised

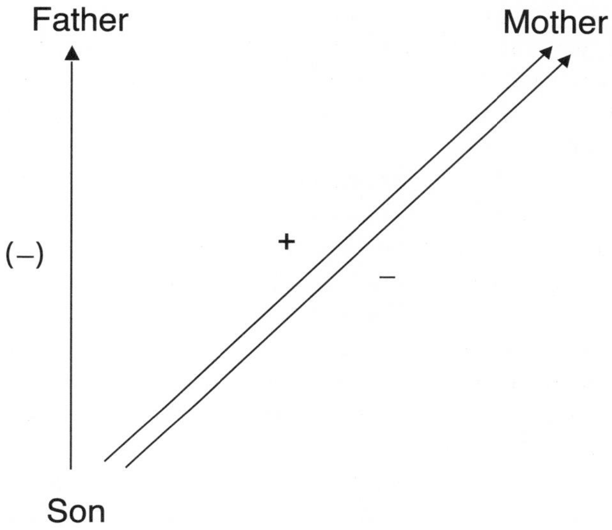

FIGURE 6: The Mahādeva Story

there she is pushed into the incest by the wet nurse). The directions of the vectors of both aggression and expression of sexual interest are from her and toward the father and son, respectively. In the *Vibhāṣā*, the case is quite different. The son "defiles his mother," which although laconic certainly conveys that the volition is that of the son. This same son plots the patricide together with his mother, motivated by his own fear, not that of his mother. This structure parallels the Greek model (Figure 2) nearly precisely, rather than either the arrangement of the Dharmaruci story or Ramanujan's Indian pattern. For the *Vibhāṣā*, then, we may suggest the architecture in Figure 6.

The accounts in subsequent and reworked versions of the story alter things yet again. In the *Konjaku monogatarishū*, Mahādeva searches for a wife and finally lights on the choice of his own mother. Subsequently, fearful of his father's return, he kills him immediately upon his arrival, the volitional directionality here once again conforming to that of the Greek model.[7] In the likewise Japanese *Hōbutsushū*, Mahādeva actually rapes his mother and kills his father to prevent any competition for possession of his mother. While these versions are then, in this respect, almost classically "Oedipal" in the Greek sense (without, of course, the prophecy and so on), other versions for which we have only later evidence more closely follow the *Divyāvadāna* in terms of Mahādeva's lack of volition, as for instance does the story quoted by Chōzen and attributed to the Indian Paramārtha. Additionally, in the *Mahāvastu* parallel, the Mahādeva character, Megha, lusts after his stepmother, but it is she who motivates him to kill his father, a constellation close to that in Dmar ston's Tibetan version, in which Mahādeva's murder of his father is the condition his mother places upon the consummation of his desire to possess her sexually.

There is something very important to be discerned in the way that the *Vibhāṣā* and allied texts have altered the directionality of the initial seduction that leads to the incest between Mahādeva and his mother. In the texts that wish to demonize Mahādeva, he is made the aggressor, whereas Dharmaruci is portrayed more as a passive victim. This distinction points directly to what I believe to be the key move of the *Vibhāṣā* polemicists. It is therefore only prudent to ask whether, despite the considerable weight of materials we have examined thus far, more evidence is available, before we are firmly convinced of the correctness of this hypothesis.

It is one thing for us to note that modern sociological and psychological studies demonstrate that in the real world, virtually all cases of mother-son incest are initiated by the mother (a pattern, we might note, also reflected in classical Greek and Latin literature).[8] It is another thing to suggest that this reality may somehow be mapped onto ancient Indian fiction. My claim rather is that in this particular respect the original form of our story conformed to the pattern recognized by Ramanujan, with the mother as aggressor. This case is dramatically strengthened, I believe, by the discovery that the pattern of mother-initiated, mother-aggressor incest is tolerably common in just that body of ancient Indian fiction, including Buddhist tale literature, while examples of such relations initiated by a son are extremely rare, though not nonexistent. It is to the evidence for this that we now turn.

16
Joseph and the Wife of Potiphar

IN CITING what he sees as displaced expressions of intergenerational aggression, and with the aim of demonstrating the ubiquity of an Oedipus complex in classical Indian literature, Robert Goldman has suggested that a young man's violence directed toward a superior figure is equivalent to the son's aggression toward his father. He argued for this by equating the father with the guru and showing that gurus and fathers are often functionally equivalent, an uncontroversial suggestion only strengthened by the fact that in traditional Brahmanical society one's primary teacher, one's guru, was ideally one's own father. Goldman, however, seems almost entirely concerned with intergenerational violence, and thus he devotes almost no attention to the complementary leg of the Oedipal triangle, the mother-son dynamic. This is based, apparently, on his belief that it is almost entirely nonexistent, at least in the Indian epic literature upon which he concentrated his attentions. But when we accept the same basic principle of substitution or displacement, we suddenly realize that, despite what is frequently said about the rarity of mother-son incestuous relations, both in reality and in lore, the store of materials at our disposal is not quite as impoverished as it might have initially seemed. In fact, contrary to what we have been led to expect, classical Indian fiction *does* depict mother-son incest, and not infrequently—it just does so (mostly, but not completely) indirectly. There is a well-recognized thematic element that includes precisely the pattern with which we are concerned, and for which there are ample examples from ancient India, although so far modern scholars do not appear to have categorized these examples as Oedipal. A familiarity with this typical, and perhaps even archetypal, pattern will allow us to further our understanding of the most likely original architecture of the sexual power relations between Mahādeva and his mother.

This common pattern is what is known to folklorists as stories of the "Joseph and the Wife of Potiphar" type. The key element in these stories is an attempted (though it is true, rarely consummated) sexual advance by an older woman to a younger boy, whose beauty is often explicitly emphasized. Here the displacements are from the mother to a woman in a relative position of power and from son to a young man in an appropriately subservient position. The vector of expression of sexual interest, we note, is from mother-figure to son-figure, and almost never the reverse, another important element to which Ramanujan has sensitized us. The classic example that gives the pattern its name comes from the story in the Hebrew Bible, Genesis 39, of Joseph, sold into slavery in Egypt and purchased by Potiphar, a high government official.[1] Thanks to God's help, Joseph rises in Potiphar's household, reaching a position of great trust. The text several times mentions Joseph's control over everything in Potiphar's house, and stresses his physical attractiveness.[2] When Potiphar's wife, the wife of the master and owner of the slave Joseph, invites him to sleep with her, he repeatedly refuses. This leads to her false accusation of rape and ultimately to Joseph's being sent to prison, whence he is extracted to interpret Pharaoh's dreams and so on. The portion of the paradigm of interest to us here is the very first part, the attempted seduction of a young man by an older woman in a relatively superior position.

Eighty years ago, Maurice Bloomfield published an article titled "Joseph and Potiphar in Hindu Fiction."[3] There he cited numerous examples of stories of this type, including tales of young royal chaplains and the queens of the kings they serve,[4] apprentices and the wives of their masters, and, most strikingly, sons and stepmothers. And what is so very convincing about the "displacements" in these stories is that quite frequently the sons themselves are made to identify the woman in question, who is always other than a biological mother, explicitly as "mother." In this regard Bloomfield cited (although without drawing attention to its broader implications) a verse of Indian proverbial wisdom:[5]

> The wife of a king, the wife of one's teacher, the wife of one's friend,
> The mother of one's wife, and one's own mother—these five are to be regarded as mothers.

It may be useful for us to focus on examples of this type of story in Indian Buddhist literature, while noting that they are quite as common in other varieties of Indian fiction. One such story is found in Pāli in the *Mahāpaduma Jātaka*.[6] In this story Prince Paduma's mother dies, and his father takes another woman as his chief consort. The king goes away to quell a provincial uprising, and upon his return Paduma goes forth to greet him. The new queen, his stepmother, sees his beauty (*rūpasampatti*) and sets her heart on him (*paṭibaddhacittā*). Returning to the city, the prince

> greets her, and asks her: "Mom, is there anything I can do for you?"
>
> "Did you call me 'Mom'?" And rising and seizing his hands, she said "Get in the bed!"

"Why?"

"As long as the king's away, let's the two of us enjoy ourselves in passionate bliss."

"Mom, you're my mother, *and* you're married.[7] I've never before heard of a propertied woman breaking the [moral] principles for the sake of passion. How can I do such a dirty deed with you?"

Two or three more times she asks, and he refuses, after which, just as with Joseph and Potiphar's wife, she pretends to have been raped by Paduma.[8] What is significant for us here is Paduma's explicit identification of his stepmother, who is never referred to in the story other than as the chief consort, as mother.[9] The stepmother's reaction to this appellation is also noteworthy: she recognizes that when Paduma calls her "mother" he precludes any possibility of sexual connection, as indeed he subsequently makes quite clear.[10]

Another equally vivid example is found in the *Divyāvadāna* in the famous story of Kuṇāla, the son of King Aśoka by his (junior) queen Padmāvatī.[11] Kuṇāla is also declared to be a very handsome lad, with especially lovely eyes. One day, spying him alone, Aśoka's chief (and therefore senior) queen, Tiṣyarakṣitā, entranced by his eyes, embraces him and says:[12]

> Looking at this splendidly beautiful body of yours, which gladdens my sight, and your pair of lovely eyes,
> My heart is thoroughly consumed by flames, like dry grass burned by a forest fire.[13]

When Kuṇāla heard this, he covered his ears with both hands and said:[14]

> It is not proper for you to speak such words in front of your son—[for] you are my mother.
> Turn away from this path of unrighteousness, for this is the cause of the path to hell.

Then Tiṣyarakṣitā, not obtaining the object of her desire,[15] was furious and said:

> I approached you charged with passion, yet here you don't want me.
> It won't be long at all, you idiot, before you'll be thoroughly through!

Although they may well be entirely unrelated historically, it is interesting to note a passage from a medieval Japanese text we encountered earlier, the *Sanron gengi kennyūshū*, which refers to a similar situation of sexual infidelity by a wife of Aśoka. This time, however, the man with whom Aśoka's wife is sexually involved is none other than Mahādeva. The passage immediately follows the mention that Mahādeva established a sizable monastic community of followers who claimed arhatship for themselves, an episode we studied earlier:[16]

> King Aśoka heard many things about him, invited him to the palace, and courteously made offerings to him. The royal consort then had a stealthy liaison with Mahādeva.

It is impossible to be sure, from this laconic reference, who seduced whom, or even if this is intended to refer to the same Queen Tiṣyarakṣitā whose story we have just seen, although it is the most economical interpretation to presume that "royal consort" here refers to Aśoka's chief queen, namely, Tiṣyarakṣitā, rather than to one of his many junior consorts. It is not difficult to imagine that, in their revision of an unsympathetic account of the schismatic Mahādeva, those who compiled the *Sanron gengi kennyūshū* or its source felt it was suitable to append a suggestion that he had an illicit sexual affair with the famous emperor's wife on top of all his other crimes. Nevertheless, although it is not absolutely clear, the text does suggest that it was the queen who seduced Mahādeva, rather than the other way around. This differs from most other examples only in the fact that here the seduction appears to have succeeded, something that reflects, once again, the low moral character of Mahādeva.

Bloomfield has cited a number of other passages, predominantly from Jaina literature, depicting superior women attempting to seduce relatively powerless men, occurrences which demonstrate that the pattern in question is far from restricted to Buddhist literature in India. One example is from Jinakīrti's *Pālagopālakathānakam* (Small Tale of Pāla and Gopāla), in which the wife of a merchant whose caravan the exiled Pāla has joined, spying his beauty, attempts to seduce him and when he declines, accuses him of rape.[17] In another passage from the same short text, the brothers Pāla and Gopāla are introduced as sons of the chief queen of King Mahāsena, whose second queen is Mahālakṣmī.[18] Once again, the story follows a now-familiar pattern. Mahālakṣmī sees the beauty of the boys and is smitten. She sends a deceptive message to Pāla via a sneaky slave woman (*śikṣayitvā nijāṁ ceṭīṁ śāṭhyapeṭīṁ*), who tells him:[19] "Lord, your mother (*tvaj-jananī*) Mahālakṣmī was bitten by a great snake." She instructs him to come with an antidote, which he does. He then directs Mahālakṣmī to drink the medicine, using to her the vocative "mother" (*mātar*). But she has other things in mind. She orders a slave to close the door, and speaks to Prince Pāla as follows:[20] "I have been bitten by the serpent of lust, and that bite has made me lose my mind. So shower me with the milky nectar of the embrace of your arms—by that I will quickly be restored to life!" The language here could hardly be more suggestive. The verb used with "nectar" (*pīyūṣa*, also "milk," the whiteness of which is not likely to be accidental here) is the imperative *niṣiñca*, literally, to "pour down or sprinkle," but also "to impregnate." Sexual imagery simply saturates the sentence. Can Pāla's response to this proposal from a woman whom he just addressed as mother be any surprise? "Hearing these words of hers, it was as if his ears were [smashed by] a cudgel. Pāla jumped out through the latticed window and went back to his own residence."[21] Another element of this story that requires notice is the stepmother's use of a go-between. This is a common element in the Dharmaruci/Mahādeva stories, and it is interesting confirmation of its generality to see it here as well.

Bloomfield also notices a number of related episodes in nonreligious Indian fictional literature, demonstrating its pervasive occurrence across subcultures, literary traditions, and genres. In the *Kathāsāritsāgara* (Ocean of Story), that vast compendium of Indian (mostly nonreligious) narrative, a young student, a stranger to the town and thus entirely under his teacher's protection, is sexually assaulted by his preceptor's wife. Although the text is not entirely clear on the point, it appears that the attack may have been successful, if not fully welcome. The student repairs to a different place and finds a new teacher—and, as the text makes explicit, this time he finds an old preceptor with an old wife![22] Another tale concerns three brothers. The wives of the elder two attempt to seduce the youngest brother, and although the episode is presented in skeletal fashion, the youngest brother does make it clear that to comply would be like sleeping with his mother.[23] Finally, in the story of the witch Kālarātri, the wife of a brahmin tries to seduce one of his students. She fails, but tricks her husband into believing that the student tried to rape her.[24] Later, in another episode, she meets that selfsame student by chance in a marketplace and boldly propositions him then and there.[25] His response fits our pattern:[26] "Don't talk like that—it's not right. You are my mother, the wife of my teacher." After she again suggests that he might save her life by agreeing, he says:[27] "Mother, do not set your heart on such a things as this. What righteousness will there be in incest?" And here the student uses one of the technical terms for incest, *gurutalpābhigamana* (going to the teacher's bed).[28] This combines the elements we have seen before: an approach by an older woman in a relative position of power, a woman whom the younger man considers as (or to be) a mother, and an explicit recognition that a sexual relationship under such circumstances constitutes incest.

A final, somewhat peculiar, case is found in the Pāli Jātaka of Hārita, but here the example seems to follow slightly different patterns.[29] In this story the bodhisatta, the Buddha-to-be in a former life, is an ascetic who has engaged in long years of extreme deprivation. Finally, he wanders down from his abode in the Himalayas to Benares, where he takes up residence in the royal park, a guest of the king. Then before the king goes away to quell a border disturbance (the usual excuse in such stories for the king's absence),[30]

> he gave the Great Being into the charge of the queen, saying, "Don't neglect our Field of Merit!"[31] and left. From then on she waited upon the Great Being with her own hands.
>
> Then one day, having procured food for him, while he was delayed she bathed in scented water, put on a robe of fine, smooth cloth, had the windows opened, and letting the wind strike her body she lay down on a small couch.[32]
>
> Later in the day, the Great Being, well dressed and well covered, holding his begging bowl, came flying through the sky and in the window. The queen heard the sound made by his robes of tree bark, and standing up in surprise she dropped her robe. The Great Being's eyes fell upon her private parts,[33] and the sexual passion (*kilesa*) he had dwelling within him for uncountable hundreds of thousands of millions of years sprang up like a sleeping poisonous snake in a box, erasing his meditative absorption. Being unable to fix himself in mindfulness, he went and grabbed the queen by the hands, and then they encircled themselves with a screen.[34] He engaged in worldly practices with her,[35] ate, and returned to the park (where he was staying), and thenceforth he daily behaved in just that same way.

This conduct becomes well known throughout the town, and the king is informed of it in a letter from his ministers. The king returns and asks both Hārita, the ascetic, and his wife about the matter. Both tell the truth, something that, the text emphasizes, is of the highest importance. In fact, it offers a remarkable judgment:[36] "While a bodhisatta may under certain circumstances take life, or steal, or engage in sexual activity, or drink liquor, he does not tell a lie that involves deception that injures anyone's welfare." Rather than being upset at this adultery, in what seems almost like a New Age ending, the king exchanges verses with Hārita until the latter regains his composure, returns to his asceticism, preaches to the king, and eventually is reborn in the heavenly realm of the Brahma world.

Despite their mutual act of drawing the screen around themselves and the queen's deshabille, the queen does not actively seduce the ascetic. Indeed, it is almost as if he attacks her, save that her acquiescence is made clear by the use of the plural verb to describe the act of drawing the screen, an act they therefore explicitly perform together.[37] This vector of expression of sexual interest from the ascetic to the queen provides a nuanced contrast to the other examples we have examined. It may be significant, however, that there are two close parallels to this story within the same Pāli Jātaka collection, and in both of these the bodhisatta, though strongly sexually attracted to the queen, manages to restrain himself.[38]

As if to prove that for every rule there are at least one or two clear exceptions, it is possible to cite one Indian Buddhist story, albeit in Chinese translation, in which a son *does* sexually approach his own, biological mother. Even this story, however, is not without ambiguities, as its conclusion shows. The story is found in the *Zabaozang jing* (Storehouse of Sundry Treasures), a collection of stories translated into Chinese in the fifth century. In it we read the following:[39]

> Long ago, there was a young woman, gorgeous and beautiful. She renounced the world to practice the way among the non-Buddhists. Once, people asked her: "With a face like yours, it would have been fitting for you to remain a laywoman. Why did you renounce the world?"
>
> The woman answered them, saying: "The reason that I have renounced the world is not that [I feel myself to be] unattractive these days, but rather that for several years I have been repelled by sexuality. When I was still living with my family, thanks to my beauty I was pushed into [married] status while young. Early on I gave birth to a son. As he grew up, he became an unequalled beauty. Gradually I realized that he had grown emaciated, as if he were ill. I immediately asked him the cause of his illness, but he refused to say. When I persisted in asking him, my son did not trust me, but spoke to me, his mother, saying: 'If I do not speak frankly, I fear my life will not be safe. If I do tell everything frankly, my shame will be enormous.' Then he told me, his mother: 'I want you, mother, with an intimate sexual desire! Because I can't have you, I am ill.' I, his mother, said: 'From ancient times, has there ever been such a thing as this?' But then I thought to myself: 'If I do not comply, my son could even die. Now, it would be better to violate propriety in order to save my son's life.' Then I hailed my son, saying I wanted to do as he wished. As my son was about to get up on the bed, the earth suddenly split apart, and my son just then fell in alive. I was terrified and reached out my hands to grab my son, but I grabbed hold [only] of my son's hair. So today since all I have is my son's hair, I cherish it close to me. Because I experienced this event so keenly, I renounced the world."

There are a number of features of this small tale that link it to others we have looked at, including the physical ill-effects of unrequited sexual energy, this time in the son rather than the mother, as happened in the story of Dharmaruci. What is remarkable here, however, is the explicit directionality of the sexual desire, from son to mother. This is hardly tempered by the authors' drastic solution to their moral dilemma, of having the earth swallow the son moments before his incest is realized. I would argue, in light of the many parallel examples, that it is precisely the direction of desire from son to mother that makes the realization of this incest so very difficult for this story's authors to countenance.

Another story also tells of a narrowly averted incestuous relation between mother and son. In the Jaina *Kathākośa* (Treasury of Stories), a work of perhaps the fifteenth century although relating much older contents, we find the story of Madanakumāra, who is taken with, abducts, and plans to marry a woman, Jayasundarī, who is also strongly attracted to him. At the last minute, their true relationship as mother and son is revealed (by a pair of talking parrots, one of whom was Madanakumāra's brother in a previous life), the marriage is cancelled, and both become Jaina renunciants.[40] In this example, too, we have an averted incestuous relation, but one in which, crucially, the son's approach to his mother is not intentional, for he is ignorant of the nature of their relationship. This provides a sharp contrast to the Buddhist story in the *Zabaozang jing.*

These few examples are exceptional. All the other instances we have noticed, drawn from a wide variety of classical Indian literary sources, suffice to demonstrate that the standard pattern of such tales agrees with what we find in the *Dharmarucy-avadāna*, namely, that the direction of expression of sexual interest is from mother to son. This pattern is clearly the predominant and very much preferred one, not only in a select group of Buddhist texts but in ancient Indian literature generally. On this basis, and taking into account the other evidence we have seen for the priority of the Dharmaruci tales over those of Mahādeva, we are well justified in surmising that the authors or adaptors of the Mahādeva story intentionally modified the mode of sexual aggression, the direction of desire. They took an original mother-to-son configuration—in Ramanujan's view typical of the Indian variant of the Oedipus tale—and transformed it into the son-to-mother orientation they could better use, more typical of the Greek Oedipal architecture, but in an Indian context rare, especially aberrant, and demonstrative of a particularly perverse and objectionable character.

By taking note of this "Potiphar's Wife" type of relationship, and recognizing in it a displaced incestuous mother-son configuration, we greatly increase our appreciation of the scope of the Oedipal in classical Indian literature generally. In fact, the evidence suggests that the pattern characterized by a mother-to-son vector of sexual interest rivals or even surpasses in frequency of occurrence the pattern characterized by father-to-son aggression, the pattern that Goldman recognized as almost the unique representative of Oedipal aggression in Sanskrit, as typified by the epic corpus upon which he concentrated his attention.[41]

Given the Buddhist materials we have studied, and in light of our newly gained appreciation of some long-known but heretofore underutilized non-Buddhist Indian stories, what may we then conclude about the idea of an "Indian Oedipus"—or are we even ready to attempt this yet? In fact, there remains some Indian evidence, this time from Hindu sources, that will allow us to modify some of what has been said even about Hindu attitudes toward the Oedipal.

17
Further Dimensions of the Oedipal in India

Ramanujan's proposals for mapping an "Indian Oedipus" certainly provide powerful tools for the analysis of this story type. And yet, pinning down a single type of Indian Oedipus, or even strictly delimiting the subcultural preference for a certain type of presentation, is a more complex proposition than the examples presented so far may suggest. Several peculiar cases, while not typical, demonstrate that rare patterns may exist, as we have seen in the preceding chapters. I have noted the absence of any prophecy from the Buddhist stories we have studied, a feature that significantly differentiates them from not only the Greek Oedipus model, but from other Oedipal stories in which a prophecy and its fulfillment play a central dramatic role, especially in the creation of true tragedy. But there is at least one Indian Buddhist example of just such an Oedipal prophecy, or at least half a prophecy, since it concerns the foretelling of only a patricide, not of mother-son incest. This example comes in a version of a story of King Ajātaśatru, as found in the *Cīvaravastu* (Section on Robes) of the Mūlasarvāstivāda Vinaya.

When a woman named Celā is born, "a semiologist saw her and predicted 'She will give birth to a son. He will kill his father, and will rule taking the crown for himself alone.'"[1] The king whom Ajātaśatru will kill, Bimbisāra, in fact knows of this prophecy, but when he sees Celā he is so taken with her fantastic beauty and youth that he immediately falls in love, and says:[2] "Sir, a son who kills his father does so for the sake of the throne. If I have a son, I will confer the crown [of succession] upon him right at his birth." And indeed he does have a son, who ultimately does kill Bimbisāra, his father. We thus have here a prophecy of patricide and its fulfillment. The tragic element is missing from this story, however, since all along the king knows the true identity of his son as the one foretold to be his killer. There is, therefore, no suspense and no pathos upon the revelation of secret identities of the type that underlies the classical Oedipal dramatic pattern.

I have already referred several times to Goldman's suggestion, implicit or explicit, that classical Indian literature, or at least Hindu literature, lacks real mother-son incest. This absence, however, may not be quite so complete as Goldman apparently imagined. Setting aside the central Buddhist examples we have studied at length, we have already seen that there is no shortage of examples of *displaced* mother-son incest in a wide variety of genres of Indian fiction, non-Buddhist as well as Buddhist. But further and even more direct evidence of the existence of the Oedipal in Hindu literature is also available.

Goldman points out the fact, from which he draws important conclusions, that there is no explicit mother-son incest in either of the two Indian epics, the Hindu scriptures par excellence. When we turn to the closely related Hindu Purāṇic literature, however, we find at least two explicit depictions of actual—neither displaced nor symbolic—mother-son incest. This literature, while arguably somewhat less culturally significant than either of the epics overall, has nevertheless been highly influential throughout the Hindu world since the medieval period (let us say, for the sake of argument, from the tenth century onwards).[3] As such, it must certainly be taken into account in any evaluation of classical Hindu ideology and imagination.

Our first example is found in the *Brahma-Purāṇa*, in a section of the text called the *Gautamī-māhātmya* devoted to praise of the sacred spots on the Godāvarī river:[4]

> The sacred spot called "The Destruction of Evil" wards off evil and danger. I shall explain its name. Listen carefully, Nārada!
>
> It is told that there was a famous brahmin known as Dhṛtavrata. His wife was a young woman named Mahī, admired by everyone, and he had a son named Sanājjāta, [radiant] like the sun. Dhṛtavrata then died, O Sage. After that the beautiful young widow with a young son, seeing no one to watch over her, went to the retreat of Gālava. Delivering her son up to him, the wanton woman, deluded by sin, wandered through many lands, desiring a lover, indulging her lust. Her son was born to mastery of the Vedas and supplementary studies in the house of Gālava, but thanks to his mother's fault, his mind was drawn to prostitutes.
>
> There was [a forest] known as Janasthāna, inhabited by all varieties of peoples, and Mahī settled down there making a living through prostitution. Her son likewise wandered through many lands, full of desire, and he too in time settled down there in the Janasthāna forest. The brahmin son of Dhṛtavrata longed for prostitutes, and in her turn Mahī, too, was looking all around for men who would give her money [for sex]. She did not imagine he was her own son, nor did he imagine she was his mother, but, as fate would have it, the two of them, mother and son, engaged in sexual intercourse. Thus mother and son passed many days,

neither of them knowing their relation as mother and son. Although [the son] was behaving like that, his actions wicked, still he was well-intentioned thanks to the character he inherited from his father. Listen, Nārada, to the strange tale.

While acting with reckless abandon, he did not give up this [basic religious principle]: having performed the morning's ritual bath, afterwards [a brahmin should work] to acquire wealth. Earning much wealth through his learning, he donates it.

In this way, getting up in the morning [Sanājjāta] went to the [Southern] Ganges river [the Godāvarī] as is proper. Performing all the rites in the appropriate order, beginning with purification and bathing, and honoring the brahmins, he turned his attention to his own affairs.

In the early morning when he went to the lovely [river] Gautamī, he was unenergetic as if all his limbs were leprous, oozing purulent blood. But having bathed in the Ganges, he became lovely and peaceful, like Sūrya and Agni, as if the sun personified. That brahmin did not see this dual form of himself at all.[5]

The Lord Gālava was wholly devoted to his asceticism and knowledge, and taking refuge in the goddess Gautamī, he was surrounded by sages. That brahmin [Sanājjāta] was constantly there too, attending at the sacred spot. Doing honor to Gālava, he then went to his own dwelling. Before doing his oblations at the Ganges Sanājjāta's appearance was one way, while after his bathing and morning prayer it was another. Having seen his dual appearance, Gālava was constantly surprised and thought that there must be some reason for it. And being surprised like this, Gālava addressed that brahmin. The teacher then greeted Sanājjāta, who was going to his home, enthusiastically calling the wise one, with compassion and uncertainty.

Gālava said to him: "Who are you? Where are you going? What do you do for a living? Where do you take your meals? What is your name? Where do you sleep? Who is your wife? Tell me!"

Hearing Gālava's words, the brahmin in turn spoke to the Sage, saying: "Tomorrow I will tell you everything, after I have understood all the facts."

Having spoken thus to Gālava, Sanājjāta went home. Having eaten at night together with her, he lay down to sleep, and spoke to that loose woman, trembling as he recalled what Gālava had said.

The brahmin said: "You are endowed with all the virtues, and even though a loose woman, you are loyal to your man. A love such as ours must last as long as life itself! But let me ask you something: What is your name? Where is your family? What is your hometown? Where are your relations? Tell me everything!"

The loose woman said: "I was the wife of a well-known brahmin named Dhṛtavrata, a pure ritual priest. My name is Mahī, and I left my clever young son named Sanājjāta in Gālava's retreat. But through my earlier transgression I gave up the behaviors natural to my (brahmin) family. And though now I am a wanton woman here, brahmin, understand that I am a brahmin (too)!"

Hearing what she said, it was if his vital organs had been pierced, and he immediately plunged to the ground. [Then] the prostitute spoke to him.

The prostitute said: "What happened, noble brahmin? What happened to your love for me? What did I say that made you so change your mind about me?"

Calming himself, the brahmin spoke to her: "Dhṛtavrata was my wise father. I am his son, Sanādyata.[6] My mother is Mahī—and you are she, who by fate has come to me [as a prostitute seeking a patron]!"

Hearing this, she, too, was extremely distressed. They were both aggrieved, and when the sun had risen, the brahmin went to that tiger-like sage Gālava and informed him.

The brahmin said: "I am the brahmin son of Dhṛtavrata whom you previously looked after and initiated, when I was left by her, and she is my mother, Mahī, Lord. What can I do, and what might lead to an expiation for what I have done?"

Hearing what the brahmin said, Gālava proclaimed: "Don't worry! I've noticed this unprecedented dual appearance you have. Then I inquired of you, heard the report, and knew that whatever that you would have to do [as expiation] all disappears in the Ganges. Because of the greatness of that sacred spot, by the grace of that goddess [the river] you were purified daily, my dear. You should have no doubt about this. At daybreak day after day your body [appears] full of sin, [but] I see that time and again your body [comes to be] filled with the highest virtue. Coming, you are filled with sin, but going, you are blameless. I always see that, and therefore [I know] you are now purified by the goddess. Therefore nothing more remains that you need do. As for this mother of yours, brahmin, who is known as a loose woman, she has felt much repentance and has turned round from her sinfulness now. Since love is a natural thing in the realm of living beings, great merit is fated to come about through contact with the good. She was exceedingly filled with regret due to the merit she had practiced formerly, and having bathed here in this sacred spot, she will become purified."

> Both of them, mother and son, Nārada, did so, and after bathing, both without doubt became free of sin. From then on, that sacred spot has been known as Dhautapāpa (Where Sin Was Washed Off), Pāpapraṇāśana (Destruction of Evil), and Gālava. Whether the sin be a major or a minor one, or a simple one, the sacred spot Dhautapāpa, which bestows excellent merit, will destroy them all.

The pattern here cannot help but remind us of other examples we have seen, including the story of Utpalavarṇā, in which a son inadvertently has sex with his mother who is working as a prostitute. The aim of this text clearly is to glorify the salvific power of a particular sacred spot on the Godāvarī river, and this too bears a similarity to other instances in which the incest motif is employed as a backdrop to emphasize the extraordinary potency of a proffered cure. In Buddhist cases the cure may be the power of a particular Buddhist text, or part of a text, such as the *Jifayue sheku tuoluoni jing*, while in this Hindu case it is the power of a particular pilgrimage spot, a *tīrtha*.[7] The conceit of the story, however, remains the same: a son and mother are drawn or thrown together and commence a love affair in complete ignorance of their true relationship. That the *Brahma-Purāṇa* considers sexual relations with the mother abhorrent, or even unthinkable, in ordinary terms is clear from another episode in the same text, an account of the lust of Śiva's son Skanda.[8] He attempts to seduce the wives of the gods, and in order to stop him his mother Pārvatī makes herself appear before him each time, so that any wife of a god upon whom Skanda looks appears to him as his mother.[9] This neuters him (*vairāgyam agamat*),[10] as is confirmed by Skanda's promise to the river/goddess Gautamī that he will always look upon women as the same as his mother.[11] A bit later, being pressed to accept a reward, he wishes that merely bathing in that particular spot in the river will cause anyone who has committed the great sin of incest to be washed clean of that sin.[12] This presentation confirms our earlier conclusion that incest is seen as among the very greatest of sins. At the same time, it suggests that the authors imagined it as common enough to necessitate a special spot for its expiation and purification,[13] a potentially very interesting fact about the Indian Oedipal imagination.

A second example from the Hindu Purāṇic literature is found in the *Setu-māhātmya* of the *Skanda-Purāṇa* and concerns the story of a brahmin named Durvinīta (Mr. Badly Brought-up), who, while staying for a long time with his widowed mother Ruci, becomes deluded and rapes her. In contrast to the story in the *Brahma-Purāṇa* in which the protagonists are unaware of their biological relation, Durvinīta of course realizes the nature of the crime and repents and expiates his sin almost immediately.[14]

Long ago, in the Pāṇḍya region (of the Deccan) there was a very learned brahmin named Idhmavāha. He had a wife named Ruci and a twice-born child named Durvinīta. In his youth the boy's father died, and Durvinīta performed his father's funeral. He dwelt for some time in the house with his widowed mother. There were then twelve years of famine, due to drought. So the brahmin went to another region together with his mother, and when he reached Gokarṇa, there was an abundance of food thanks to the accumulations of grain there. He spent a long time together with his widowed mother. Then, when many days had gone by, the criminal Durvinīta, his mind deluded by the ripening of his previous negative karma, alas, his body pierced by the arrows of the god of love, his mind deformed by lust, forcefully drawing himself toward his mother who was repeating, "No! no!" with mind deluded by passion had sexual relations with her, O Brahmin. That Durvinīta, exhausted, immediately after ejaculating thought of his sin and howled in his enormous suffering. And thinking: "Oh, what a sinner I am, the worst of those who commit the great crimes. For under the influence of the arrows of the god of love, I went to [my own] mother," [he went to] where sages were, and spoke to those sages with a mind filled with disgust: "Twice-born ones, with compassion for me tell me the expiation for the sin of incest, you who know the wisdom of the sacred lore. If death will bring expiation, I will die—of this there is no doubt. Now, whatever you venerables declare to be my penance, I will do that, brahmins, truly, be it dying or something else."

Having heard that speech of his, some of those supreme sages, having made up their minds that to talk with him would lead to sin [for themselves], were silent, while some sages quite vehemently said repeatedly: "You are an evil-minded person who committed incest with your mother, the worst of those who commit the great crimes. Go! Go!" the brahmins said. But restraining them, the omniscient Vyāsa, storehouse of empathy, accustomed to compassion, spoke then to Durvinīta: "Go quickly. At Rāma's bridge, at the 'Bow's tip,' together with your mother, when the sun is in Capricorn, in the month Māgha for a whole month without respite, with senses controlled, with anger controlled, without doing injury to anyone, for one month fast and ritually bathe, along with your mother. You will surely become cleansed of the sin of incest. For there is no sin that is not driven away by bathing at a holy spot. The 'Bow's tip' is oft praised in the sacred lore, treatises, and ancient legends as that which destroys the five great crimes.[15] Therefore, go to the 'Bow's tip' in haste, along with your mother. Take my advice as gospel, just like the statements of the Vedas, O Brahmin."

The text then narrates how the boy follows the advice of the sage and is indeed cleansed of his sin and so on. This *Skanda-Purāṇa* story and that in the *Brahma-Purāṇa* illustrate with clarity that stories of actual mother-son incest exist in ancient Indian literature, not only in that of the Buddhists and Jains, the heterodox outsiders, but within the core Brahmanical/Hindu tradition as well. Both texts I have cited recognize mother-son incest as among the very worst of the most serious crimes. But it is quite clear from these examples that such relations are not *entirely* tabooed within even Hindu Indian literature, despite the extremely negative light in which they are seen. Moreover, aphoristic literature provides us further evidence that incestuous relations were well within the range of the classical Indian imagination, as exemplified by the following verse of common wisdom:[16]

> One should not stay in a secluded place together with one's mother, sister, or daughter—[for] the sense faculties forcefully overcome even a wise man.

Such examples prove that whatever taboos may have existed against the direct depiction of incestuous behaviors in Hindu literature, exceptions may also be found, and that consequently whatever culturally defined distance may be posited between Hindu patterns on the one hand and Buddhist (and perhaps Jaina) patterns on the other cannot be seen as an entirely unmediated gap. There are no doubt differences between the Hindu and Buddhist subcultures, but certainly no impenetrable seal separates them.

By exploring the ways incest themes are developed in both Buddhist and Hindu literatures, I have been attempting to solidify the groundwork for a defensible contextual reading of the *Vibhāṣā*'s story of Mahādeva. Our discussions thus far have succeeded in forging a good basis upon which to build a picture of the "internal meaning" of the Indian Buddhist stories of Dharmaruci, and hence of Mahādeva. It is natural now to try to construct a comparable picture of the "external significances" of these stories. Having given careful attention to the ways in which our Indian stories might, from the point of view of their internal structure, be considered "Oedipal," and having explored some of the complications attendant on this approach, it may be helpful now to look at our stories from another perspective entirely.

In a certain sense, we can think of stories like words: sounds do not become words in isolation, but take on meaning only within the context of an utterance. If stories seem to be different, it is because we usually encounter them in context; sometimes, if need be, we automatically invent or assume a context for them. Just as we usually hear words within a conversation or narrative flow, we usually meet stories within a larger cultural "conversation." When we find the same, or very much the same, story imbedded in more than one context, however, this difference of framing may highlight the otherwise backgrounded context, and we may begin to appreciate the role that context plays in our appreciation and interpretation of the story.[17] Of course, it is the patterns of this context that have already allowed me to argue for some of the internal meaning of our stories: I have argued on the basis of just such contextual patterns for the importance of the *Vibhāṣā*'s shift in direction from a mother's seduction of her son to a son's sexual approach to his mother. I have also suggested that several of the Indian stories we have studied, both Buddhist and Hindu, take as their contrasting external significance the advocacy of particular religious practices, whether devotion to a *dhāraṇī* scripture or pilgrimage to specific sacred sites. And we must also presume that for some of our sources any apprehension of an original contextual significance will remain forever beyond us. This indeed appears to be the case with the *Dharmarucy-avadāna* from the *Divyāvadāna*; while we may reasonably postulate the original and ultimate source of the story preserved in this collection to have been somehow related to the Mūlasarvāstivāda Vinaya, I have not as yet found it in any Mūlasarvāstivāda source, and am thus prevented from even speculating on some hypothetical original meaning. In trying to comprehend the "external significance" of the Mahādeva story, however, we may also find it helpful to look somewhat farther afield.

The most basic question this study seeks to address is the meaning of the story of Mahādeva. If the conclusions I have drawn so far are correct and the developed story of Mahādeva has its roots in the story of Dharmaruci (or in its source), the original context of which was apparently entirely independent, then one central question must be what those who adopted and adapted the Dharmaruci story accomplished, or tried to accomplish, by reframing it. That we can say little or nothing of the contextual significance of the Dharmaruci story itself is a handicap, but it is not fatal. For we can make our case about the transformation of Dharmaruci into Mahādeva even if we must take a decontextualized Dharmaruci as a starting point. I have already suggested some possible goals sought by those who effected this transformation, which focused in the first place on a limited internecine struggle between two divisions of the Buddhist monastic community.

In order to further frame the significance of the Buddhist transformation of the story of Dharmaruci and its re-presentation as the tale of Mahādeva, and in order to imagine some of the potential, but apparently unrealized, ramifications of the story, it will be very useful to highlight what the authors or editors of this tradition have *not* done, and what those later in the tradition who inherited and subsequently further modified and retold the tale likewise did *not* do with it. Such an approach may backlight, as it were, what the Buddhist tradition *did* do with its own tale, by illustrating what others have done with similar materials and by contrasting this with what the Buddhists did, and more importantly did not do, with theirs.

18
The Medieval European Oedipal Judas

FOLKLORE IS often spoken of as if it were universal. While any claim to genetic universality (of a Jungian variety, for example) is demonstrably untrue, there are nevertheless intriguing commonalities and striking parallels discoverable between traditions of widely disparate societies. Sometimes, of course, we can prove that similar stories from distant places are interdependent, that one relies on the other, or that they share an origin, and sometimes we may suspect a filiation even when we are not able to demonstrate it. But it is equally interesting when we can be certain that such parallel tales are historically entirely independent, despite their shared features. In this context, and for an even more important reason I will explore in a moment, it is with no little interest that we notice a remarkable and undoubtedly totally independent parallel to the tale of the Oedipal Mahādeva in the medieval European story of Judas Iscariot. This is a tale the earliest known versions of which may be securely dated to the twelfth century, although they very likely had appeared sometime earlier.[1] The best-known version of the story is preserved in the *Legenda Aurea* (Golden Legend) of Jacopo da Voragine, composed around 1265 or slightly thereafter and the most widely known text in Europe during the Middle Ages after the Bible. P. F. Baum, whose massive study of these materials remains the standard, summarizes the usual version of the story as follows:[2]

> Judas was the son of Jewish parents living at Jerusalem: his father's name was Reuben, his mother's Cyborea. One night Cyborea dreamed that she was about to conceive and that her child was destined to become the destruction of the whole Jewish race. In great anxiety she related her dream to Reuben, who advised her to pay no attention to such matters—they came from the evil spirit. In due time, however, a son was born; the memory of the dream returned, and in fear lest possibly it might come true, the infant, Judas, was set adrift on the sea in a small chest. Wind and waves brought him to the island of Scariot—whence his name. Here the Queen of the island, who had no children and was eager for a young prince to succeed to the throne, discovered the babe, which was very

> handsome, and sending word throughout the land that she was with child, had Judas secretly nursed until she could proclaim him as her own. Thus Judas was brought up in royal fashion, as heir to the kingdom. But it came about before very long that the Queen had a son by the King. The two children grew up together, but after a time the wickedness that was in Judas' nature began to come to the surface, and he frequently beat and otherwise abused his putative brother. In spite of the Queen's remonstrances he continued to maltreat the true prince, until finally in a fit of anger the Queen made known to him his irregular origin. In wrath at learning this Judas seized the first opportunity to kill his brother, then for fear of the consequences took ship and fled to Jerusalem. There his courtly manners and evil instincts secured him a place in Pilate's retinue. One day Pilate, looking into his neighbor's garden, was seized with an irresistible desire for some fruit which he saw there; and Judas agreed to procure it for him. Now, although Judas was ignorant of the fact, the garden and the fruit were the possession of his own father, Reuben. Before he succeeded in gathering this fruit, Reuben appeared; an altercation followed, which developed into a fight; and finally Reuben was slain. Since there were no witnesses to the murder, Reuben was reported to have died suddenly, and Judas, with Pilate's connivance, took in marriage the widowed Cyborea, together with the house and property. The bride was extremely unhappy and sighed frequently. Being asked one day by her husband the cause of her grief, she related enough of her story to enable Judas to recognize his double crime of patricide and incest. Both were afflicted with great remorse, but on Cyborea's suggestion Judas resolved to go to Jesus and seek pardon and forgiveness. He soon became a favorite disciple, and was made steward of the Twelve. But again his evil nature asserted itself, and he betrayed his Master to the Jews for thirty pieces of silver: thereafter he again suffered remorse and, having returned the money, hanged himself.

The basic rationale for the development of this story is not obscure. As Lowell Edmunds puts it, "Since neither the New Testament nor the apocryphal tradition knew anything of the early life of Judas, it was convenient to tell it in terms of the Oedipus story, so that Judas' betrayal of Christ proved to be the recrudescence of the inveterate evil already displayed in heinous crimes."[3] There was naturally considerable interest in the evil figure who betrayed Jesus, who not only turned his back on, but actively worked for the destruction of, God. But since the Gospel sources—which among themselves are far from uniform in their treatment of this figure—lacked the desired details, and most particularly a prior history, as did other post-canonical literature, it proved possible to adopt and adapt an existing story to fill this lacuna. It is, in one sense, not at all hard to imagine very much the same thing being said about the tale of Mahādeva: since the anti-Mahāsāṁghika traditions knew little or nothing of the origins of the Five Theses they despised—not even, apparently, that they were actually unrelated to the Sthavira-Mahāsāṁghika schism with which they were only later associated—it was convenient to attach to the accounts of those pernicious theses a tale of the most rude, and in fact evil, man, casting that criminal as their propagator.

The structural similarities between the medieval European tale of Judas and the Indian Buddhist story of Mahādeva are remarkable and provide us a comparative point of reference from which to examine the fusion of an Oedipal background with the story of a known miscreant. But the contrast in the contextual significance of the two tales is even more remarkable and revealing.[4] While it is true that we actually know very little about how the story of Mahādeva was used in India (or elsewhere, for that matter)—although to set this ignorance in its context, we know very little about how any Indian Buddhist literature was used in India—our sources suggest that in the polemical and dogmatic context into which it is placed by texts like the *Vibhāṣā* and its allied literature, it was anything but a popular tale. The thrust of the story, its raison d'être in both the *Vibhāṣā* and the later historical literature, is to attack a particular set of doctrinal positions, probably crucial to a certain group of theoreticians, including later doxographers and historians of Buddhism whose interests include plotting the evolution of Buddhist institutional structures. But these doctrinal and (quasi-)historical concerns are hardly likely to have been of interest to, or even understandable by, a popular audience in any time or place, and it is noteworthy that such considerations play no part in most later Tibetan and Japanese retellings of the tale.

This question of audience may be extended to the text of the *Vibhāṣā* as a whole, and even further to the entire Abhidharma literature of which it is a part, as well as to the historical literature. The *Vibhāṣā* is the very antithesis of a popular text; it is a scholastic compendium which, even had copies of it been widely available—which they almost certainly were not—would have remained a closed book to any reader without a rather massive amount of prior knowledge and training. In this sense, the Abhidharma literature is every bit as "esoteric" as the more famous (or notorious) Tantric corpus, and both in the same sense that we might term a modern book on advanced particle physics "esoteric." Even if such a book were freely available to anyone and everyone, in the absence of the requisite training its contents remain unknowable even to the individual who opens the book before him and reads the words. A book on advanced particle physics written in English is not a closed book to me in precisely the same sense as one on

American history written in Russian, but both are, for me, almost equally unintelligible.[5] The same thing may be said of the Buddhist Vinaya literature, the texts devoted to the rules and regulations of the monastic institution. They almost certainly would have been of no interest to anyone who was not a monastic. Moreover, mere access to such literature was meant to be restricted to monastics. And even then, there is probably no good reason to believe that ordinary monks would have been broadly familiar with the technical literature of Indian Buddhist monasticism. Of course, the narrative story literature that makes up the bulk of many of the known Vinaya texts may be understood to have provided (among other things?) an accessible means of conveying the necessary basic lessons in proper monastic behavior and procedures, without which monastics could not have functioned in the monastery. Whether or not this is the case, and what it would imply were it true, it suffices to say that what these stories were plainly *not* designed to do, at least as pieces of Vinaya, is provide an accessible and understandable store of tale or story literature for the common people. Both the Abhidharma and the Vinaya are technical literatures, composed by an educated elite for an in-house audience, and even the narrative materials contained within these textual corpora are, or contain, arcana that place them thoroughly beyond the ken of nonspecialists. It is a further question what gradation of accessibility there may have been between, for example, some probable original Vinaya context for the story of Dharmaruci and its revalorized incarnation in the Abhidharma as the story of Mahādeva, but again, this is a question we cannot answer.

In light of the question of the general accessibility of Indian Buddhist narrative literature, and even if only as a comparison and no more, it may help to devote some attention to the contextual meaning of the story of the Oedipal Judas in medieval Europe, structurally so very similar to the Mahādeva story. And here, in contrast to the case with our Indian Buddhist stories, we do know something about how this story was used, how it was composed, and the results which, while surely not directly attributable to the story itself alone, can hardly be unrelated to it either. For while we may accept, as has been suggested above, that "[s]ince neither the New Testament nor the apocryphal tradition knew anything of the early life of Judas, it was convenient to tell it in terms of the Oedipus story, so that Judas' betrayal of Christ proved to be the recrudescence of the inveterate evil already displayed in heinous crimes," this answers only the question of why the abbreviated story of Judas was supplemented by the story of Oedipus, and even this only in part. It does not speak at all to the question of why this happened at a specific time, nor does it address the issue of the impact the story may have had.

Several intriguing proposals have been made with respect to these issues. "Why," asks Thomas Hahn, "did medieval stories endow Judas with the attributes of Oedipus?" And he attempts to answer his own question as follows:[6]

> The motive perhaps lies in the treason of Oedipus—his betrayal of King Laius, his father; of the Queen, his mother; and of the city of Thebes, which he ruled as king. To the Middle Ages, Judas was the supreme traitor: he betrayed Jesus, who was not only his own master but also the king of all the earth and the spiritual spouse of every faithful soul. The ideals and realities of feudal ties made treason the most hateful of crimes, whether capital treason toward the king, his queen (sexual intimacy was treasonous since it threatened proper succession by blood), or the immediate lord; or petty treason toward one's spouse. Judas, by selling out, breaks all the most sacred ties and shows himself a traitor over and over. For this perfect treachery, Dante places him at the nadir of hell, in Satan's mouth.

This is surely suggestive, and the characterization revealed here must have played an important role in the interpretation of the legend. Yet another factor is undoubtedly the context of the debates, beginning in the mid-eleventh century, over the definition of incestuous marriage. Medieval Church laws regarding incest were extremely complex and in an almost constant state of flux. The motivations for these rules has occasioned much debate, and it is quite clear that incest was a matter of considerable importance to the medieval imagination,[7] a fact which Baum himself already noted as relevant to the case of the Judas legend.[8] More generally, Baum proposed a scenario for what he cautiously called "a theoretical early history for the legend":[9]

> Judas Iscariot betrayed to death our Blessed Lord and Savior. No act could have been more villainous. The man who could do that would be guilty of the most horrible crimes. But we know nothing of the early deeds of this Judas. He was a thief. He sold Jesus Christ to the Jews. He even took his own life. He may even have committed incest, that crime which Holy Church has just condemned so violently and punished with excommunication. If incest, probably parricide, too, equally horrible and wicked; for the mediæval mind, which invented gargoyles, knew no limits of horribleness to which it could not go.—And so perhaps (or if not so, then in some analogous fashion) the legend of Judas may have been born.

As interesting and suggestive as they are, what these ideas of the association of Judas with betrayal and incest (and the overall hypothetical scenario for the creation of the legend) overlook is a brute chronological fact. The time of the creation, and especially the rapid popularization, of this Judas-Oedipus legend corresponds precisely to the period of the rise of violent antisemitism in Europe.[10]

While it is not easy to track the earliest versions of the fused Judas-Oedipus story, at least one tradition of which was almost certainly oral, it had already been committed to writing at the latest in the early twelfth century and had clearly circulated somewhat before that time. Let us remember, then, that the First Crusade, with its accompanying mass murder of Jews in Germany, dates to the end of the eleventh century (strictly speaking, the crusade was declared by Pope Urban II on 27 November 1095), although hatred of Jews simply on the basis of their faith goes back far beyond this date. The period of the almost sudden popularization of the Judas legend, exemplified by the *Legenda Aurea*, is the thirteenth century—with multiple vernacular versions found from Wales to Bohemia, and somewhat later even beyond[11]—precisely the time in which the historian Alain Boureau sees the beginnings of antisemitic hatred, which he distinguishes from an earlier anti-Judaism. The earlier attitudes were prejudicial, to be sure, but radically distinct from the hatred that led to accusations of well poisonings, ritual murder of Christian children, and so on.[12] It is a matter of scholarly controversy precisely how the evolution of violent antisemitism in medieval Europe should be understood, and how, when, and why certain factors came into play. But what is beyond dispute is that the attacks and mass murders typified if not initiated by the First Crusade—or the massacre in Blois in 1171 or those accompanying the plague of 1349 and one could, sadly, go on and on—continued against Jewish communities throughout Germany and much of Europe for centuries and, despite some happy years, saw their resurgence, although tragically not their conclusion, in the unspeakable horrors of the Holocaust. Can it really be solely coincidental that this very legend of the Jew Judas, betrayer of Jesus, made through fusion with the story of Oedipus not only a traitor but an incestuous patricide, continued to circulate, down through the middle of the twentieth century—collected in Russia in 1917, in Cyprus and Crete in the 1930s, and in Ireland as late as 1959?[13] We need not follow the entire argument of the psychoanalyst Norman Reider to share his insight that "[t]he Judas legend arose in this setting of the Crusades and mass anti-Semitism," nor need we be Freudians to agree with his subsequent implication: "What more criminal act could be posited on Judas than incest and parricide? If, for political and economic reasons, it was necessary to make scapegoats, then the Jews became such in reality and Judas in myth and legend."[14]

Here Reider has put his finger on the key equivalence: Judas is a historical figure of legend, but real-life Jews were everywhere, and no doubt thanks in part to this very legend they, present in the flesh before their Christian tormentors, were imputed to share in the guilt of the absent Judas of history. Judas is the archetypal traitor, a feature that would have made him especially anathema to medieval people, for whom feudal ties made loyalty an especial virtue. But Judas is historically distant, and no matter the postulated identity between Judas the betrayer and contemporary Jews, this fact alone would not necessarily have allowed real Jews themselves to be tarred with the brush of betrayal. However, thanks to centuries of law and practice that systematically excluded Jews from economic and social intercourse with Christians—even if in some cases this isolation was intended to protect rather than punish, and if informal contacts such as those required for money lending were never really cut off—Jews were in most cases already outside of and excluded from the interlocking webs of loyalty and trust that defined Christian feudal society. Judas the traitor looks like the medieval Jew because the medieval Jew, too, is not loyal, not to his feudal lord nor to God—not to the feudal lord, because he is forbidden that status, and not to God since the Jew, of course, repudiates Jesus as the Christ, the messiah.

It is one of the remarkable facts about most of the scholarship on the Judas-Oedipus legend that it overlooks this crucial connection with the Jews. The scholar most responsible for the elucidation of the relevant sources, Paull Franklin Baum, appears himself to have been entirely blind to the dark side of these tales. He wrote:[15]

> Either the mediæval legend of Judas enjoyed a greater posthumous popularity in England than elsewhere, or fortune has been more generous in preserving us English specimens of its later development. At any rate, *lives* of Judas, based on the legend, were printed in Great Britain down to the year of Grace 1828, in five separate versions, some of which went through several editions. This is a record of which the legend—and England!—may well be proud.

The England that Baum praises for the preservation of these legends is the same England that for centuries produced virulent antisemitic literature—even through the centuries during which Jews had been expelled from England.[16] How far the Judas legend may be implicated in the history of English antisemitism is a subject that, to the best of my knowledge, has yet to be studied. Nevertheless, since it can hardly be doubted that the overall environment in which the legend was able to persist so aggressively was one of an equally persistent antipathy for Jews, some connection or feedback between the two, the legend and the ethos, is not unlikely.[17]

Despite the apparent blindness of many scholars to the crucial issue hidden here just beneath the surface, there are a number of elements in the Judas story itself that allow us to peek inside and discover the inherent antisemitism of its portrayals and the ways in which the story could not help but have been understood by medieval people. An example, already pointed out by Rand, is that while some manuscript traditions of the story locate the origins of Judas in the Hebrew tribe of Judah, an obvious identification with his name but one which only reinforces the sense that he is the paradigmatic Jew, other sources may be more subtle in seeing Judas as from the tribe of Dan. Rand and others see this as a possible allusion to the idea that the Antichrist would belong to this very same tribe,[18] an identification that is accepted by Baum, who concludes: "Judas assumes the rôle of Antichrist; and it is but natural and logical that he should be accredited with incest."[19] This almost literal "demonization" of Judas works in other ways as well.

Perhaps the most vivid contribution to our appreciation of the impact of the Judas legend comes from its contrast to a very similar legend, the oldest known version of which is preserved in Old French from the mid-twelfth century. This is the story of Pope Gregory, a wholly imaginary figure, to be sure. In the *Legenda Aurea*, in fact, the juxtaposition of Judas and Gregory could not have been missed: Jacobus places the story of Pope Gregory directly after his account of Saint Mathias, within which is related the story of Judas, the connection between these two being that Mathias is said in some traditions to have taken the place of Judas to reconstitute the group of twelve disciples of Jesus. An outline of the story as recounted in German by Hartmann von Aue in his poem *Gregorius*, composed in 1200, runs as follows:[20]

> On his deathbed the widowed Duke of Aquitania commends his young daughter to the care of her brother. The unmarried siblings are devoted to each other, and sleep in the same room. Tempted by the devil, the brother rapes his sister; at first she is upset, but then they enjoy an incestuous affair which is halted only by the discovery that she is pregnant. On the advice of a faithful steward, their baby is born in secret and exposed in a chest in a tiny boat with money, fine fabrics, and a tablet indicating his rank and the circumstances of his birth; the brother sets off on pilgrimage to the Holy Land, where he soon dies. The sister, distraught at the loss of both brother and baby, becomes a duchess and devotes herself to good works.
>
> The baby's boat is found by fishermen; their lord, an abbot, makes himself responsible for the child, and baptizes him with his own name. Gregorius is raised by the fishermen; when he enters the monastery school, he excels in his studies. His jealous foster-mother knows that he is a foundling; when Gregorius hits her own son in a quarrel, she maliciously taunts him about his origins. The abbot shows Gregorius the tablet, and gives him the money that was in his little boat, and clothes made from the rich fabrics. Elated by the discovery that he is of noble birth, but horrified by his conception in such sin, Gregorius sets off to seek his unfortunate

> parents. Arriving by chance at his mother's city, he finds it under siege by a duke who wishes to marry the duchess. Gregorius defeats the unwelcome suitor in single combat; the barons advise the lady to marry her new young champion, to whom she is strangely attracted. They are very happy, but every day Gregorius emerges weeping from a secret perusal of the tablet which describes his parents' sin. A prying maid brings this to the lady's attention; she finds the tablet, and realizes that she has married her long-lost son. Both are horrified by this revelation. Warning his mother not to abandon herself to despair, as Judas did, Gregorius rules that both must devote themselves to penance, and leave the country at once.
>
> He arrives after some days at a lonely fisherman's house by a lonely lake, and asks about a suitably remote place to do penance. The fisherman rows him out to a rock, shackles him to it, and throws away the key. In his haste, Gregorius loses his precious tablet. He spends seventeen years on the rock in very harsh conditions. At the end of this time, the Pope dies in Rome, and two eminent churchmen dream that his successor is to be a holy man named Gregorius, currently living on a rock in a lonely lake. They eventually come to the fisherman's house; the key to Gregorius' shackles appears miraculously in the fish caught for their dinner, he is freed, and the tablet miraculously found. On the way to Rome his healing powers are demonstrated, and he becomes an admirable Pope. Gregorius' mother, hearing of his fame but unaware of his identity, decides to go to Rome to seek absolution for her sins. Gregorius recognizes her from her confession; after an enjoyably ambiguous conversation he identifies himself. She enters a convent, and they both live piously in Rome till they die.

While there is no patricide in this story, the father (himself an incestuous sinner) having conveniently died on his own, the parallelism, and more particularly the contrast, to the Judas story is nevertheless evident. As Ohly has emphasized at length, Judas and Gregorius are characterized by their respective despair and penitence, rhymed in the Old French version as *désespérance* and *pénitence*, and theologized in Latin as *desperatio* and *poenitentia*.[21] The key to the latter notion is the idea of the "good sinner," the man who commits evil but repents and through faith finds salvation. The contrast is not merely implicit: Gregorius and his mother despair when they realize what they have done, and as Hartmann remarks: "I know well that Judas, when he hanged himself for sorrow, was no sorrier than these two are here and now."[22] But the fundamental distinction between the sorry Judas and the "good sinner" Gregorius is that Gregorius repents. "Against Judas, who despaired, [the Gregorius story] sets the portrait of a sinner who passes through the same trials, but repents: the elect as against the damned."[23]

In what does this despair consist? "Judas fell far away from God because he did not trust in the grace that follows on repentance."[24] Despair means lack of faith, and repentance means acceptance of the absolution that only Christian faith, and thus the Christian Church, can provide. In a medieval context, there is one obvious way to read this:[25] Judas' rejection of the absolution Jesus offers is nothing other than the model for Jewish rejections of the Church's offers of conversion. Present, living Jewish people are represented in the Christian imagination as Judases not only because Judas was a Jew, not only because of their feudal "disloyalty," but because they continually and constantly recapitulate his greatest crime—not the betrayal of Jesus, evil as that was (though they *do* recapitulate it, in that by their usury they copy Judas' acceptance of the thirty pieces of silver), but rejection of salvation, rejection of Christian truth itself. Christians and Jews begin from the same point, but they respond to their situations differently. And the two stories, of Judas and Gregorius, illustrate the results of those different choices. As Boureau says, "Incest functions as an origin myth: the incestuous person without repentance engenders the Jew, the repentant incestuous person the good Christian."[26] There are, of course, other aspects to the complex that suggest different imbedded agendas—for instance, the idea that Gregorius' papacy is meant to recall Peter, another traitor, but one whose repentance likewise saves him.[27] But for our purposes more interesting still is yet another story, this one very clearly produced through a further fusion of the legends of Judas and of Gregorius, resulting in the story of Saint Andreas of Crete. In summary, this story reads as follows:[28]

> A merchant receives a prophecy that his wife will bear a son who will kill his father, marry his mother, and rape three hundred nuns. When their son is born they mutilate his body and expose him in a little boat. He is found and raised by a community of nuns; one day, in a fit of lust inspired by the devil, he rapes three hundred of them. He is driven out and arrives in the town of Crete, where he is employed as a watchman by his natural father; neither knows of their true relationship. At night, his father comes disguised to the vineyard as a test, and is killed by Andreas. Andreas then marries his mother, who subsequently recognizes him because of his scars.
>
> She sends Andreas to a priest, who refuses to absolve him. Andreas kills him, and then two more equally obstinate priests. The Bishop of Crete eventually absolves him, but imposes a severe penance on both mother and son. Andreas is chained at the bottom of a deep cellar; when it is filled with earth to the top, his sins will be forgiven. His mother has a padlock put through her nose; the key is thrown away, and she is ordered to wander through the world praising God until it is found again. After thirty years the key is miraculously found in a fish, and she goes into a

> convent. Andreas is found sitting on top of his cellar, which has filled up with earth. On the death of the Bishop of Crete Andreas succeeds him, and lives a most holy life.

Here we have an incestuous patricide who, through repentance and faith, like Gregorius gains absolution and high Church office. This demonstrates that, in this genre of literature, it is not Judas' patricide that differentiates him from Gregorius. This is a claim that the texts themselves never make, but one that in our comparative context we might have wondered about, particularly in light of our earlier observation that for the *Vibhāṣā* it is explicitly Mahādeva's murders that are his greatest crimes, not his incest. In the medieval world, what differentiates Judas from Gregorius is their respective faiths in God or, we may say directly, that one character is a Jew and the other a Christian.[29]

I have introduced this comparative material because, although so similar to them in many ways, it also reveals a number of contrasts with our Indian Buddhist stories. First among these is the polemical contexts in which the respective traditions transmit, and therefore give meaning to, their respective legends. The story of Judas-Oedipus contrasts with our tale of Mahādeva-Dharmaruci in that the Buddhist story did not, as far as I know, ever appear in India in anything that could remotely be considered a popular form. This contrasts sharply with the Hindu materials studied by Goldman, who has pointed to the importance of the epics in the inculturation of Indian children, and thus of what he recognizes as the Oedipal elements therein in the development of the Indian psyche.[30] It is true that by the thirteenth century in Tibet, and somewhat earlier in Japan, the story is presented in contexts that may be seen as roughly equivalent to European popular or vernacular literatures; it has been extracted from an original polemical context and reinvented as something closer to pure entertainment fiction. One could argue that equivalents to such literature once existed in Buddhist India, but have simply been lost to us, perhaps because almost all our extant Indian Buddhist literature in Indic languages or in translation is precisely that which has been preserved by the monastic institutional organization itself. Moreover, there may well have been oral traditions different from or parallel to the written traditions of which we are aware, just as there certainly once existed many visual sources, now irrevocably vanished. There is nothing to be said to such suggestions, for we cannot speak of something for which we have no evidence at all. Whatever the reason, extant Indian Buddhist literature knows the Mahādeva story only from specialized, technical texts and not in any more popular form.

The Judas story, in contrast, appears to have originated and been transmitted largely or even entirely as a popular or semipopular story, and it was meant to do its work among common people as well as among the elite. The development of the legend was not, of course, unrelated to the scholarly tradition—how could it have been recorded in writing if it were? As Baum tells us:[31]

> That portion of the development of the legend for which we have documentary evidence, and which we can follow with some feeling that we are really close to the facts, took place after the legend had come into the hands of clerks or monks, after it had penetrated into the Scriptoria of the monasteries and taken a humble station among the vitae sanctorum to be read in the church service; and under such conditions, however the legend may have maintained itself among the people, affecting and affected by the new forms it assumed through clerical influence, we cannot expect to follow the work of the people as distinct from the monks, or even to separate the two at all.

On the other hand if, as seems almost sure, the story that was grafted onto the legend of Judas was related to the classical Oedipus, then if "we argue that the life of Judas is derived from the myth of Œdipus, we absolutely exclude the theory of a popular origin for the legend, and commit ourselves to the theory of a clerical or ecclesiastical origin. There is no difficulty, however, in the theory that the life of Judas was invented by some early monk on the basis of the Œdipus story."[32] Despite this evident clerical role in the transmission and evolution of the Judas-Oedipus story, it remains the case that in the very well-studied European ecclesiastical literature, the official literature of the Church, which is to say in the European Christian functional equivalents of texts like the *Vibhāṣā*, we do not find the story,[33] and it appears to be virtually certain that it did not originate in that milieu. This contrast may be sufficient to suggest, if not indeed to demonstrate beyond question, that the contexts and environments out of which the respective tales of the Oedipal Judas and Mahādeva grew, and within which they were transmitted, are quite different, even radically so.

By taking cognizance of this contrast between the medieval European story and our Indian Buddhist story, we are able to better appreciate the place of Mahādeva's story within its tradition, and to further appreciate what it was intended to accomplish, and what effects it did not have. This is what I proposed earlier to call its "external significance." There can be little doubt—I would dare say none—that our Buddhist tale had anything other than a learned origin. But this is not to say that the story we know now as the tale of Dharmaruci was similarly an elite product, which seems considerably less likely. And when we come to a story such as that of Utpalavarṇā, although it is recorded in a Vinaya text we cannot escape the strong impression that we have entered the world of Indian fiction occupied by creative works like the *Kathāsāritsāgara*.[34]

The contrast with the European material also allows us to ask questions of our sources that we otherwise might have overlooked. To what extent is the Sthavira telling of the story of Mahādeva intended to demonize him and, more importantly, his followers, the Mahāsāṁghikas? For all the rhetoric of sins of immediate retribution and implications of schismatic instigation, the available sources do not seem to demonize those who are identified as followers of Mahādeva. Modern preachers sometimes speak of hating the sin but not the sinner, and indeed, this very much seems to be the attitude of our Buddhist sources, at least in this case. I noted earlier the absence from Buddhist thought of any real notion of damnation, an idea we saw illustrated time and time again in stories that portray terrible crimes, but follow these accounts with depictions of redemption. In this respect, our stories are much closer to the *Gregorius* legend than they are to the Judas story, with its inherent demonization of the Jew. The sinner is redeemed through his repentance and his acquisition of insight, and his misled followers, as mere pawns of his deceit, are not themselves held to be liable. Of course, there is a great deal we do not know about the social history and context of the Mahādeva story and its applications, and thus I cannot claim a categorical distinction between the impact of the European tale and that of our Indian story. We know next to nothing about most aspects of intersectarian relations in ancient Indian Buddhism, about whether and how, for instance, sects may have struggled one against another for patronage or material support. If we knew more about such things, we might be able to say whether one group might have offered public criticisms of another in the fashion that the Mahādeva story suggests would have been possible. Although arguments from silence are extremely dangerous, it is worthwhile noting that we have no evidence that any such internecine struggles took place—but of course we equally have no evidence that they did not. In the end, everything we know of the overall worldview of Indian Buddhist thought and rhetoric argues for a vast divide between that tradition and the European context of the Judas tales, a fact that only highlights the structural similarities of the Judas and Mahādeva stories and their radically different significances.

Each story we have studied in comparison with our central Mahādeva/Dharmaruci narrative, Buddhist and non-Buddhist, Indian and non-Indian, has served, in its own way, as a laboratory, a controlled experiment through which we could observe how changing certain parameters might alter an outcome. I believe that the accumulation of evidence has made clear how the story of Mahādeva would have been expected to function, and what the authors of the Mahādeva account were trying to do. This leaves us with the very basic question of why incest in particular was chosen as the central tool. Just what is it about this theme that so affects us?

19
Why Incest Taboos?

There are, naturally, many more comparative approaches to the incest themes in our texts than those I have been able to explore here. In world literatures, incest themes are well known and have been accorded considerable attention by scholars, at least since the time of the psychoanalyst Otto Rank early in the twentieth century.[1] The meaning and significance of these themes is not only occasionally unclear, but without exception always dependent on context. For instance, considering just the case of European literatures, after appearing in a number of ways in medieval literature,[2] most often in the service of dogmatic religious agendas, the trope comes into its own especially in Gothic and Romantic literature, but virtually always in entirely secular contexts. As Peter Thorslev says, "It is probably safe to say that in no period has there been so widespread and intense an interest in the theme of incest as in the late eighteenth and early nineteenth centuries, particularly in Germany and England." And he goes on:[3]

> Incest as a popular theme was first revived in England in Gothic novels and dramas and in Germany in *Schauerromane*. It has a rather obvious surface significance here, of course, for its shock appeal and for an additional source of sensationalism. These were largely novels and dramas of female sensibility and therefore of persecuted heroines; incest was one more, perhaps the ultimate, horror to be visited upon a sensitive and long-suffering young woman—especially after the Gothic appetite had become jaded with murders and tortures and uncomplicated rapes. . . .
>
> The marvels and horrors of the Gothic—particularly the unexplained supernatural marvels—preparing as they did for the rise of Romanticism, signify an irruption of the irrational into the well-ordered eighteenth-century literary universe; they are the poet's or the novelist's way of expressing the possibility that there is not only moral evil (a result of the misdeeds of man) but also ultimate and metaphysical evil in the universe around us—evils never satisfactorily accounted for in optimistic eighteenth-century theodicies.

The meaning of incest in the literature of the Romantics has been further nuanced by Alan Richardson, who sees it at the very heart of that movement. Whereas, he tells us, in Gothic literature the common portrayal of incest is that between parent and child, for the Romantics it is sibling incest which holds center stage. And the reason for this has precisely to do with the overall context and background of this literature as a whole:[4]

> When the Romantics portray an erotic relationship (and it is not a common theme), the ideal they look towards is a total sympathetic fusion. Such sympathy cannot come about spontaneously, through an intuitive recognition of spiritual harmony, but must be developed through experience and shared associations. Since the happiest and most intense associations are those of childhood, a relationship modeled on that of siblings becomes the best foundation for a powerful sympathetic love. But as erotic love blurs with sibling love, or vice versa . . . , an odd reaction takes place, and the relation is shattered by death. The Romantic poet is drawn to mingle the two kinds of love by a fascination with the power of sympathy, but that power is broken by the unconscious horror of incest, and the fascination turns to guilt or revulsion shortly before or shortly after the union is consummated. While quickening the sibling bond of childhood associations with the power of erotic passion seems to promise the most perfect sympathy, the resulting union cannot last. The combined attraction and untenability of this program may help account for the odd infrequency of erotic happiness (as opposed to erotic tragedy) as a theme in English Romantic poetry.

According to these hypotheses, then—only two examples from a quite considerable literature—the uses of incest themes in Gothic and Romantic literature respond to particular circumstances and backgrounds and are intended to evoke particular, highly contextualized meanings. The lesson to be taken from this is not that comparison across cultural or chronological boundaries is pointless, but only that we cannot import an explanatory model from one literary context into another and expect it to necessarily yield significant results. Given this fact of the multivalent contextuality of the meaning of incest, is there nothing at all we can say about it cross-culturally, as a literary theme or otherwise?

To address this challenge on its most basic level, we must turn to the fundamental question of why humans everywhere feel an abhorrence of incest. We may frame the question narrowly within the central focus of our investigations as follows: if the significance of incest (indeed even its definition, as we shall see in a moment) is thoroughly contextual, how and why does the portrayal of Mahādeva, not merely as a patricide and matricide but equally if not more powerfully as a practitioner of incest, so very forcefully serve to stigmatize him and by extension facilitate dismissal of the views he is reputed to have propounded? To attempt a comprehensive answer leads us straight into the deep, though hardly still and quiet, waters of general social and anthropological theories of incest.

Part of the motivation for the substantial scholarly attention given to incest may be the underlying notion that one can best grasp the essence of a system by looking carefully at its boundaries, the regions in which the system begins to break down.[5] Anthropology is most fundamentally a study of the human, and, for humans, kinship systems lie at the very heart of what it means to be a social being. Incest, therefore, as one region in which kinship systems begin to break down, is a natural target of attention. But of course, there is more to it than this. There is also very much the element of an attraction to what repels. "Incest prohibitions," William Miller suggests, "which in some form are as close to a cross-cultural universal as there might be, are generally maintained by disgust."[6] Whether this is always entirely true,[7] there is no question that we are drawn, in some way, to what disgusts us, and there can be little question that one of the things that disgusts us, or disgusts most of us, is incest.[8] People must have told and retold the stories of Dharmaruci and Mahādeva not because they were repelled by them, but because they found them fascinating, perhaps in much the same way that we are frequently fascinated by traffic accidents or natural disasters.[9]

In order to more deeply understand why the authors of the story of Mahādeva chose to employ a tale of incest as their polemical tool, we should try to come to grips with a number of fundamental problems to which I have alluded above, but whose consideration I have deferred. Just what is incest, why is it considered to be so bad, and what reactions do we have to it?

I have already suggested a simple answer to the second and third of these questions: people react badly to incest because they are disgusted by it. And what is disgust? According to Miller,[10] "Above all, it is a moral and social sentiment." And why do we feel disgust? Other students of what are sometimes called the "moral emotions" maintain that "anything that reminds us that we are animals elicits disgust. . . . Insofar as humans behave like animals, the distinction between humans and animals is blurred, and we see ourselves as lowered, debased and (perhaps most critically) mortal."[11] If this is true, it may be less than coincidental that so many stories of incest include some reference to such acts being bestial, the act of animals, and correspondingly, the existence of these examples may well stand as one piece of evidence for the correctness of the suggestion.

The idea that animals naturally engage in incestuous relations appears to have been (and may well still be) almost universally held, appearing in sources as diverse and unrelated to our Indian materials as the Chinese *Liji* (The *Rites*), Plato's *Republic*, Ovid's *Metamorphoses*, and Chaucer's *Canterbury Tales*,[12] not to mention in innumerable idiomatic expressions, folk beliefs, and the like.[13] However, interestingly, this view of animal behavior is almost certainly a misconception. In a natural environment animals very rarely engage in close-kin inbreeding activity (I will come to "incest" in a moment). Older scientific studies appeared to confirm folk wisdom in seeing close-kin inbreeding in some animals, but such studies were concentrated on zoo and domestic animals, whose behaviors are far from natural.[14] Given a limited number of possible sexual partners, the urge to reproduce can indeed lead to close-kin breeding, but this situation does not represent the instincts expressed in a natural environment of choice. Of course, we might expect that premodern people would have had a hard time recognizing and appreciating the details of the social structures of wild animal communities, no matter how closely they lived in contact with them, and would have tended to base their ideas on the domestic animals with which they were familiar, whether these were farm animals or pets. Under such circumstances, they concluded that animals inbreed, since among the limited communities they would have been able to observe, this may well have been the case. Modern scientific studies have had a hard time determining that this is *not* true, in some cases resorting to genetic matching for clarification.[15] However, while maintaining a due sense of humility concerning the possible ethological knowledge of premodern peoples, we should keep in mind that they might also have simply extrapolated from certain sets of facts to others that we may see as quite distinct. Animals engage in open copulation—without shame, it would appear. One who speaks ill of other humans saying that they "have sex like animals, indiscriminately" need not believe that animals engage in close-kin sexual relations; the slur is applicable to a variety of unwelcome human sexual behaviors. This explanation, in the end, may be closer to the true origins of the common associations of human incest with animalistic sexual practices than is the assumption that premodern people drew protoscientific conclusions from observations of animal communities that behaved, as we now know, in a constrained and unnatural fashion (in the literal, rather than the moral, sense).

In this light, it is entirely beside the point that animals in the wild rarely engage in behaviors we might classify as incestuous. What is crucial is that human beings believe these unacceptable actions to be of a kind with the—by definition uncivilized and uncultured—behaviors of beasts. Since humans are also animals, according to this view it is this reminder of our own animalism that so evokes our disgust. For Miller,[16] on the other hand: "Disgust must be accompanied by ideas of a particular kind of danger, the danger inherent in pollution and contamination, the danger of defilement." We need not investigate here the broad range of cross-culturally stable features of disgust, including that reactions to it appear to be widely if not universally recognizable,[17] to agree that humans react with disgust to things they find polluting and contaminating in a defiling sort of way. Whether it is the animalism of incest that motivates this feeling of defilement, much less the ultimate confrontation with mortality, is a question we cannot definitively answer. We can affirm, however, that whatever is judged incestuous in some cultural context does, in that context, indeed motivate reactions of disgust. But it nearly goes without saying that the particular configurations of relations that are classifiable as incestuous are themselves not always cross-culturally stable.

Incest taboos of some type are found throughout most, if not all, societies of the world.[18] Just why incest, in general, however defined, is tabooed, nevertheless remains an extremely contentious question. Despite its apparently wholly theoretical nature, this problem is of interest to us here since it may help us more globally to understand what is so very horrible about incest, and why most perceive it as disgusting. In turn, insight into this question will allow us to appreciate more fully the choices of the authors of the Mahādeva story.

Group behaviors and behaviors of individuals within a group are widely held to survive if they confer evolutionary benefit on the group. This has led a number of scholars to approach the question of incest taboos from just this point of view. But what evolutionary benefit could be conferred by an avoidance of incest? And here is where just the first of a series of fundamental confusions has arisen for so many who have addressed this problem. The answer frequently given to this question is that incest leads to birth defects; this association was then noticed by primitive peoples, who developed rules to avoid this negative result, thus conferring the evolutionary benefit of increased overall or "inclusive" fitness onto their offspring. But incest does not lead to birth defects. Inbreeding may, but inbreeding and incest are far from the same thing.[19] A failure to appreciate this crucial distinction has permeated a great deal of literature on the subject. Inbreeding is a biological concept, incest a social or moral one.[20] Nonreproductive sexual relations between a stepmother and stepson, for instance, may well be considered incestuous, but even procreative sex between two such individuals would not (normally, all other things being equal) be classifiable as inbreeding. Of course, nonreproductive sexual relations can, in the very first place, neither be classed as nor result in inbreeding, which by definition involves breeding. So the very first crucial point we must recognize is that incest and inbreeding are two entirely different things.[21]

The second point is that restrictions on marriage are not the same thing as restrictions on sexual relations.[22] Therefore, discussions of permitted and impermissible marriage patterns need have nothing necessarily to do with discussions of the limits of incest. As Robin Fox wryly noted,[23] "All teenagers understand the difference between sex and marriage, but academics, perhaps understandably, are not so well informed." Therefore, understanding marriage systems does not necessarily help us to understand systems of incest taboos.[24] The technical terms endogamy and exogamy refer, roughly, to marrying in and marrying out of a somehow specified social unit. How such a unit is defined is obviously crucial, but for our purposes what is even more important is that such sets of restrictions on marriage are distinct from restrictions on sexual behavior, at least in principle, even if not articulated as such.[25] In fact, in many social contexts they are so distinct that a man, while expected to produce an heir, would not necessarily be expected to maintain sexual relations with his wife beyond that required to achieve reproduction. Nor would he, correspondingly, be expected to refrain from other sexual relations, most particularly so long as they are nonprocreative. Such guidelines do not typically sanction close-kin sexual contact, but by the same token they serve to emphasize that the considerable cultural attention devoted to questions of marriage should not be confused with questions of sexual relations as such. It is for this reason, if no other, that the famous tag line "marry out or die out," intended to convey that inbreeding will bring about loss of fitness, a decline in genetic viability, misses the mark. From the genetic point of view, whom one marries is irrelevant; with whom one procreates is everything.

A third point concerns just what it is about incest taboos or restrictions that we wish to understand. Most scholars seem to have assumed that understanding the source of such restrictions confers an understanding of their present logic. As Arens, among others, has pointed out, however, origin and function are not necessarily the same thing.[26] The reasons, that is, that some practice or idea came about and the reasons it persists need not correspond. Therefore, understanding the possible origins of certain types of restrictive behaviors is not at all necessarily the same thing as understanding why they continue to exist. This is particularly relevant for the sorts of historical studies in which we are engaged, since the posited evolutionary origins of incest taboos and barriers under consideration all lie in the remote, prehistorical past of the human race (or even in our prehuman evolution). Evolutionary biologists and anthropologists are, in fact, hardly interested in the history of humanity at all, only in its prehistory, for that is the time in which the basic patterns of human behavior were forged. If, therefore, the origins of certain types of restrictions on sexual behaviors in, one may say, "primitive society" and the function of those restrictions in later societies differ, an investigation of their origins alone may be of little direct use.[27] Nevertheless, we must start with hypotheses about the origins of "incest avoidance," keeping in mind that an answer to this question may not, in the end, be precisely what we are after.

Nancy Thornhill states the basic evolutionary hypothesis as follows:[28]

> The theory of evolution by selection suggests that individuals will not exhibit systematic inclinations to behave in ways contrary to their own reproductive advantages, for example, by preferentially engaging in sexual liaisons with close relatives that would end in the production of defective offspring. Selection for close-kin mating avoidance seems to have produced the psychological mechanism that promotes voluntary incest avoidance in humans.

According to this view, humans avoid close-kin mating for evolutionarily evolved biological reasons, and the mechanism for the maintenance of this avoidance is psychological. This formulation points to the tip of a rather large iceberg. While there are a number of possible approaches to the question of the source and/or function of incest taboos,[29] there are really only two significant schools of thought, one aligned more or less closely with the ideas of the Finnish thinker Edward Westermarck (1862–1939) and another faithful to the theories of Sigmund Freud. Westermarck's basic idea is that childhood propinquity breeds a positive aversion and that this aversion leads to the development of prohibitions. For Freud, children invariably have incestuous feelings, and it is to combat these that incest taboos and prohibitions were introduced. Since the ideas of Westermarck are likely to be less familiar to most readers than are Freud's, it may be helpful to spend a few moments introducing his approach.

Westermarck, in a frequently quoted passage, wrote as follows:[30]

> Generally speaking, there is a remarkable absence of erotic feelings between persons living very closely together from childhood. Nay more, in this, as in many other cases, sexual indifference is combined with a positive feeling of aversion when the act is thought of. This I take to be the fundamental cause of the exogamous prohibitions. Persons who have been living closely together from childhood are as a rule near relatives. Hence their aversion to sexual relations with one another displays itself in custom and in law as a prohibition of intercourse between near kin.

Although one might think that there is no real way to test such a hypothesis, since controlled experiments are clearly impossible, not to mention unethical, in fact some scholars believe that ways have been found to work around this constraint. By looking at children raised on Israeli kibbutzim, at girls placed into arranged childhood marriages in Taiwan (*sim pua* marriages), and at first-cousin marriages in Lebanon,[31] scholars who follow Westermarck believe they can confirm his hypothesis that early childhood propinquity leads to later life aversion to physical sexual intimacy. Why should this be the case? This question gets to the heart of the problem. While Freudians believe that certain forms of sexual activity between close kin are attractive but forbidden, tabooed, for those who follow biosocial theory the fact is rather that such relations simply hold no attraction: children do not want to have sex with their parents, parents do not want to have sex with their children, and siblings do not want to have sex with each other. But why not? Westermarck's answer is that early sustained contact produces sexual disinterest, a position that has been refined by more recent scholarship.[32] And although Westermarck himself did not follow the question in this direction, his answer, as is natural from the point of view of evolutionary biology and sociobiology, has led later investigators to hypothesize an original motivation for this aversion, namely, that close-kin sexual contact is avoided in order to avoid inbreeding, which in turn is avoided in order to avert possible genetic damage. There are, however, complications with this view, at least as it is naively formulated.

"[I]nbreeding is the mating of relatives more frequently than expected by chance, and outbreeding is the opposite."[33] Such a definition is perfectly acceptable, especially when we keep in mind that mating is never completely random, and rarely even partially so.[34] However:[35]

> Inbreeding is clearly a continuous variable and it is not possible to adequately describe the continuum using the dichotomy "inbred" versus "noninbred." Since all members of a species have common ancestors and are therefore related, the question becomes, how close should the relatedness between mates be for their offspring to qualify as inbred? Different authors dichotomize the continuum at different (and often unspecified) points, which results in considerable confusion in the literature.

Inbreeding as a technical concept in biology refers to circumstances that may be mathematically defined. Although such calculations rapidly become complex, we may simplify matters by introducing only the calculations on relatedness. If we assign the subject (what anthropologists call "ego") the value one, his or her relation to an individual entirely unrelated to ego has a value of zero. The relation between a full brother and sister, those who share both parents' genetic material, has a value of 0.5. This is referred to as an *r* value.[36] The degree of biological relation between individuals may, in this way, be objectively calculated, and it is possible to estimate the probability of cumulative genetic abnormality between specifically related breeding pairs.

The usual or typical view is that inbreeding is deleterious because it increases overall genetic homozygosity, promoting the likelihood of an increase in the expression of recessive deleterious alleles, hence mutations, and correspondingly vitiating any heterozygote advantages that otherwise would accrue through outbreeding.[37] Such overall loss of fitness is referred to as inbreeding depression. On the other hand, the counterpart to this is outbreeding depression, "a reduction of fitness when individuals from normally noninterbreeding populations are crossed, [which] results from the disruption of coadapted gene complexes,"[38] meaning that the offspring of those genetically too far apart lose the adaptive advantages enjoyed by progeny of genetically more similar parents. The evolutionary aim is to maximize fitness, which is achieved by a balance between inbreeding and outbreeding. Interestingly, although it is hard to know to what to attribute this fact, this balance may conceivably have been somehow understood or adapted to in higher order social systems, such as that of the Brahmanical lawgivers of ancient India, who set strict rules establishing essentially concentric circles of forbidden and permitted marriage patterns (with an obvious presumption of equivalence between marriage and mating), only those matches falling within a middle zone between close family and total outsiders being allowed.[39]

In order to clarify the kinds of relations under consideration, we may advert to a scheme proposed by Thornhill. She suggests we think of three types of "incest," which she terms incestuous inbreeding, nonincestuous inbreeding, and relations between those related only by marriage. She defines the first as "sexual relations (mating) between closely related individuals: Individuals whose relatedness by descent r is $\geq 1/4$ (e.g., parents and offspring, siblings and half-siblings)." The second is constituted by "marriage between genetic relatives related by $r \leq 1/4$ (e.g., various degrees of cousins)."[40] Setting aside the evident conflation here of the entirely distinct categories of sexual relations, mating, and marriage, we may simply note the widely shared distinction between relations within and without the nuclear family (extended to include half siblings), indicated by the key pivot point of $r=0.25$.

From the point of view of theory it may help to visualize some of what we are discussing by presenting it graphically. In Figure 7, all of the parameters should be understood to be flexible and contextual, since the definitions of concepts such as "relatives" are themselves inevitably contextually determined. Figure 7 allows us to quickly understand that not all sexual relations between relatives,

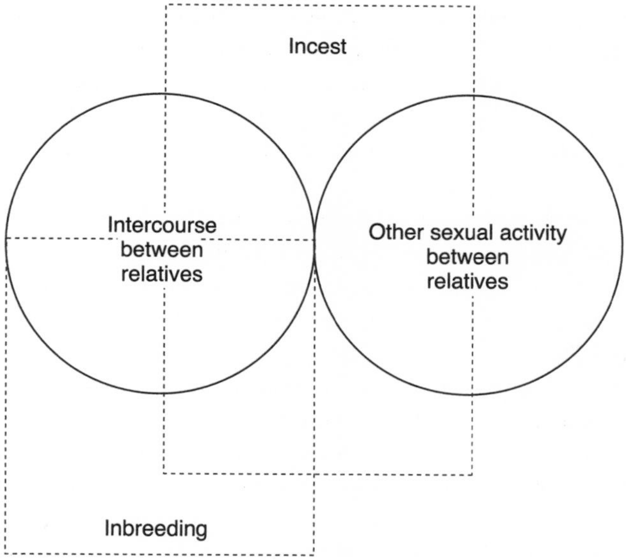

FIGURE 7: The Relationship between Incest and Inbreeding. *Source:* William H. Durham, *Coevolution: Genes, Culture and Human Diversity.* Copyright © by the Board of Trustees of the Leland Stanford Jr. University.

even if incestuous, constitute inbreeding, and not all inbreeding need be conceptualized as incest.

Accepting, at least provisionally, that incest taboos, themselves culturally conditioned, owe their genesis to a primitive recognition of the dangers of inbreeding depression,[41] we are still left with the question of the function of, and motivation for, the continuing taboo structures. The effect Westermarck predicted seems to have been well established: early childhood proximity leads to later sexual disinterest. How precisely this works is a complex problem, probably related to the major histocompatibility complex, but the result seems unquestionable.[42] The central significance of this fact is that human beings avoid sexual relations with those with whom they were in close residential contact in the early years of life, not those to whom they are biologically, which is to say genetically, related. The mechanism through which one recognizes such individuals may be similar to that which would permit the recognition of biological kin, but it does not appear to function in the same way. The connection between mechanisms to avoid inbreeding and those to avoid sexual relations with those together with whom one resided in childhood may well be that the normal pattern of dwelling in the formative periods of human development was co-residence of family groups, that as a rule those who lived together were, in fact, genetically related.[43] Why this did not lead to the evolution of mechanisms for avoidances based on genetic affinity, but rather generated others based on co-residence, is a question for evolutionary biologists. For our present purposes we must move instead in the opposite direction, toward questions of incest, and most particularly extended incest taboos.

Why are certain classes of relations so radically tabooed? Given that there are evolutionary reasons to avoid mating with members of one's extended nuclear family, or with slightly more distant relations, what is the rationale or justification for extending such incest taboos or prohibitions beyond these individuals?[44] This is a very difficult question to answer, and there is no guarantee that the answer will be the same for every social or cultural setting, and some very good reasons why it would not be. For extensions of prohibitions on sexual relations almost certainly belong exclusively to the domain of the cultural. There is probably no other way to explain the extension of restrictions on sexual contact—paradigmatically, potentially reproductive intercourse—between those closely related genetically to a ban or restrictions on such relations between those belonging to larger kinship groupings (not only affinal, those created by marriage, but even fictive or putative kinship groupings, such as those created by godparenthood or adoption). The basic reason is this: while there are genetic and evolutionary advantages to the avoidance of inbreeding, there are no comparable disadvantages to reproductive intercourse with genetically unrelated individuals—sex with a foster parent or stepparent, for instance. The mechanisms of this extension remain unexplained. It does, however, seem safe to assume that, given the enormity of the basic transgression, any behaviors that might be (mis)understood to resemble, lead to, or otherwise cause association with the core offense were also prohibited, just to be on the safe side, as it were. I do not, therefore, necessarily see the need to invoke systemic motivations for such extensions.[45]

Before considering how all of this may fit into the general pattern we see in our Indian materials, we are obliged, by tradition if nothing else, to note that Freud, and most Freudians, reject much or most of these biosocial hypotheses regarding the origins of incest taboos.[46] For Freud, in a well-known assertion:[47]

> The most preposterous attempts have been made to account for this horror of incest: some people have assumed that it is a provision of nature for the preservation of the species, manifesting itself in the mind by these prohibitions because inbreeding would result in racial degeneration; others have asserted that propinquity from early childhood has deflected sexual desire from the persons concerned. In both cases, however, the

> avoidance of incest would have been automatically secured and we should be at a loss to understand the necessity for stern prohibitions, which would seem rather to point to a strong desire. Psychoanalytic investigations have shown beyond the possibility of doubt that an *incestuous love-choice* is in fact the first and the regular one, and that it is only later that any opposition is manifested towards it, the causes of which are not to be sought in the psychology of the individual.

For Freud and his followers, at their most basic incest taboos are motivated by a recognition of the social unacceptability of the expression of natural urges that are within every child (especially every male child). In complete agreement with James Frazer, Freud felt that the only reason for a prohibition was a natural propensity for men to engage in the prohibited act. He wrote:[48]

> The law forbids men to do what their instincts incline them to do; what nature itself prohibits and punishes, it would be superfluous for the law to prohibit and punish. Accordingly we may always safely assume that crimes forbidden by law are crimes which many men have a natural propensity to commit.

As Westermarck himself pointed out in response to this suggestion, it is unlikely that Frazer would maintain that the existence of laws against bestiality proves a corresponding propensity for men to wish to engage in sex with animals.[49] A truly prodigious amount of mental effort over the years has gone into debating Freud's ideas, some of which are no doubt of great utility. But with regard to his notions about infantile sexuality, from an evidentiary point of view or an approach that is even remotely scientific, there is very little, or perhaps nothing at all, to be said for his position.[50] But why, then, if people do not "really" wish to engage in it, the fascination, the concern, with incest? The short answer is one presented to us by Miller above: we are fascinated precisely because we are disgusted, precisely because we cannot imagine ourselves doing it—this is what draws us to contemplate incest and to dwell on it. It is not because we want to do it, but because we cannot imagine ourselves doing it. And neither could the ancient Indians.

Our general acceptance of Westermarck's ideas leads us to wonder whether there may be any direct applicability of the so-called biosocial theory of incest to our literary and historical investigations. But here a certain note of caution is called for. If we wish to apply theoretical models, of incest in this case, not to social facts but to literary presentations and depictions, we face serious problems. On the one hand, as I have maintained as one fundamental base of this entire inquiry, fiction is a window into the mind, and people cannot speak or write what they cannot think. On the other hand, while literary depictions may pretend, in some way, to portray reality, they are not reality. Therefore, the question of the applicability of a social theory to a literary depiction cannot become a test of the theory itself, which makes no claims to describe a world of the imagination, but only a world of fact and reality. A theory may convince us that a literary depiction of the world conforms to reality, but that same literary depiction cannot then be invoked in its turn as evidence for the correctness of a theory of the world. Richardson reminds us of this when he questions the application of certain psychobiological readings to Romantic sibling incest themes:[51]

> By taking the evolutionary theory of incest avoidance seriously, and working from the assumption that something like the Westermarck effect does hold over time and across cultures, one can make sense of the two features of Romantic incest that critics have had most trouble accounting for: that incestuous desire, though idealized, nearly always ends tragically; and that this pattern holds equally for biological siblings, foster or adopted siblings, and various other co-socialized pairs. But the significant parallels between the Westermarck hypothesis and the recurrent narrative pattern of Romantic incest exist for historically contingent reasons. British Romantic writers just happened to have represented sibling incest in a manner consistent with the evolutionary approach currently back in favor, though in other times and places writers could—and did—come up with alternative representations of incest having little or nothing to do with cultural universals or biopsychological mechanisms.

In a similar fashion, some of our Indian stories may be read as "supporting" a Westermarckian approach. Utpalavarṇā does not raise her own children, who are, moreover, raised apart from one another. None of the conditioning predicted by the propinquity hypothesis could apply to their relations. But these individuals are entirely ignorant of their mutual relationships at the time they engage in sexual relations, and when they learn the truth, they cut off their relations. Whatever aversion they feel is not ameliorated by their lack of childhood propinquity, since insofar as any reaction is depicted at all, what is portrayed is exactly a disinclination to sexual contact. In Dharmaruci's case, the situation is quite different. We may presume that he was raised by his mother, or in close proximity to her. But he, too, is not aware of her identity when they first begin their sexual relations, although his mother is. Still, even after Dharmaruci discovers the identity of his sex partner, he continues their relations. It would, in the first place, be rather difficult to argue that patterns such as these conform in any way to the aversions predicted by the biosocial theory. Moreover, many vivid stories of aversion take place precisely between individuals who are neither related biologically nor shared any close childhood residence, stories of the Joseph and the wife of Potiphar type. All of these examples, then, clearly belong to a domain of the culturally motivated extension of incest taboos or aversions and cannot be explained as resulting directly from evolutionary adaptations.

In evaluating fictional incest scenarios, we are not free to employ anthropological or biosocial theory as if the object of our theorization were constituted by real individuals, any more than we are free to directly psychologize about fictional characters or those concerning whom we have no real information (and we might think here of equally illegitimate cases like Erik Erikson's *Young Man Luther* or attempts to make psychological claims about the Buddha). We *can* talk about the ideas of the authors of such stories, but this is an entirely different thing. Hence, for example, we may be tempted to speculate that since, in all likelihood, the sons of King Ikṣvāku and their sisters, or half-sisters, were reared separately, we should not expect them to have developed the natural aversion to sexual contact predicted by the Westermarck hypothesis. But this is to assume that there really were sons of King Ikṣvāku, and daughters of the same, and that they really did marry and procreate. Or equally unconvincingly, it is to assume that the authors of these tales were so aware of the Westermarck effect, *avant la lettre*, that they were able to craft their narratives to take advantage of it. This does not seem a fruitful approach. I would suggest, rather, that since we are dealing with undoubtedly fictional stories, we should instead ask what it is that allowed the authors of these tales, within an Indian cultural context clearly hostile to such relations, to nevertheless depict these configurations without disapproval.

Writing about medieval literature, Elizabeth Archibald says:[52] "There are . . . many stories which assume that incestuous desire is not an incredible perversion found only among barbarians, pagans, heretics, or power-mad tyrants (as well as among animals), but rather an overwhelming emotion that may strike quite normal and respectable Christians, even some previously notable for their heroism and virtue." There are examples in Indian Buddhist literature of the attribution of incestuous desires to foreign barbarians, such as the Persians, examples fully shared with classical Greek and Roman literature, from which they are repeated by medieval writers as well. So, too, there are good Indian Buddhist examples of incest stories that, if not portraying the behavior entirely positively, at least do not criticize it, such as the story of the sibling incest that spawned the Śākya clan, a parallel to the medieval portrayals of "normal and respectable Christians," with one important difference. The medieval stories are tales of desire and redemption, or in some cases stories of desire alone, but almost without exception these stories participate in a discourse of fundamental importance to medieval Christianity, that on desire and the body. There are Buddhist examples of such accounts, to be sure, such as the *Aṅguttara-Nikāya*'s isolated episode of a mother and son, monk and nun, and their incestuous relations, and, of course, the stories of Mahādeva and Dharmaruci and their respective mothers may fall into this category as well. But the Buddhist stories are sometimes about something else, something either more deeply embedded in Indian culture, like the dynamic of caste which motivates the sibling incest of the progenitors of the Śākyas, or about a kind of fate and salvation such as we see in the story of Utpalavarṇā. In this sense, the medieval European Christian stories and the Indian Buddhist stories work, in the end, in rather different ways. For the Indian Buddhist authors of such tales, concerns other than those of sexual morality trumped their interest in depicting preferred social arrangements. Sometimes we cannot well understand the choices of these authors, as in the case of the mother-son incest episode in the *Aṅguttara-Nikāya*, the motivations for which remain mysterious. But more frequently we can offer hypotheses about the intentions of ancient Buddhist authors, speculations that place the level of their concern with sexuality far below the attention they lavish on issues of direct concern to the practice of the Buddhist path. If in our reading of these Buddhist stories we insist on understanding them through our own modern questions about sexuality, power, and the like, we will blind ourselves to the true agendas of their authors. This is not to say that such literature cannot also be read in light of contemporary questions, but only to insist that the two types of reading be kept separate and distinct.

20
Forging Mahādeva

IN THE end, we return to two basic questions with which we began. The first is the question of what contribution our Indian Buddhist evidence makes to broader evaluations of Oedipal mythology and its patterns; the second is what we have learned about the process through which Indian Buddhist authors forged—in a dual sense—their story of the Oedipal criminal Mahādeva, and the results of that creation.

In speaking of the contribution our Indian materials may make to comparative studies, I have argued most fundamentally for finer and more contextually sensitive subcultural distinctions than have heretofore usually been made in the localization of Indian materials. While it is tempting to speak comparatively of cultural patterns of Greece and of India, painting both in bold brushstrokes, some of these generalizations inevitably show themselves to be overly broad. Although I am equipped to speak only of the Indian half of this pair, the materials we have been able to assemble from both Indian Buddhist and non-Buddhist literatures have obliged us to reconsider some earlier suggestions of Ramanujan concerning the Indian Oedipus—not necessarily to reject them, but to rethink what they may really mean, and how they may best be understood. Ramanujan wrote: "There are very, very few stories of actual patricide in Hindu myth, literature, and folklore," and, "There are no Laius-figures killed in the Indian tales where mother marries son."[1] The examples we have studied may, under one interpretation, be seen as vivid exceptions to these nearly categorical claims. Still, we must be careful. The second of Ramanujan's claims is not contradicted by our materials in the strict sense, since in none of our stories does the murdered father have a major, Laius-type role, thus rendering any parallel to the Laius of the Greek story only very partial. Likewise, none of our Buddhist tales contains any prophecy comparable to that in the Greek story. Still, we have located ancient Indian Buddhist stories in which sons do kill their real, biological, and socially recognized fathers, even, as in the case of the Dharmaruci/Mahādeva tale, implicitly or explicitly in order to sexually possess a real, biological mother. Do not these examples challenge Ramanujan's assertions? Here some nuance is required. Ramanujan, as always, worded his claim carefully. And when we pay as much attention to what he wrote as he no doubt paid in writing it, a potentially deeply significant fact emerges: our stories, while Indian, are not "Hindu" as such, which is to say they are not Brahmanical, but belong to quite another (sub)culture coexisting contemporaneously within the same geographical region. In this light, our core materials do not, after all, represent what Ramanujan characterized as "Hindu myth, literature, and folklore." What they embody instead is Indian Buddhist myth, literature, and (in some senses) folklore. This is a distinction with profound and far-reaching consequences. What initially appeared to be a disagreement with Ramanujan's claims seems now to point to a more fundamental agreement, even if heading off in a direction that Ramanujan himself may not have foreseen.

There are further possible dimensions to this issue. The other scholar who has devoted significant attention to the issue of the Indian Oedipus, especially in the premodern period, is Robert Goldman. The key to Goldman's approach to Oedipal conflict in the Sanskrit epics is his claim that "it is possible, if we are willing to abandon a fixation on the actual father, mother, son triangle of the famous Greek story, to demonstrate that the oedipal struggle is to be found represented in and is in fact the central issue in a fairly large number of the most widely known, often retold, and most popular of Indian's traditional legends."[2] Goldman goes on to explain that he refers to "the substitution of various male figures, notably the guru or aged brahmin sage, and to a much lesser extent the elder brother, for the father and female figures such as the guru's wife, the sister-in-law, and often a cow, for the mother." He thinks of these as "displaced versions of the oedipal triangle."[3] Several pages later, Goldman continues:[4]

> If the scope of inquiry in this matter [of Oedipal conflict in the Sanskrit epics] is restricted to materials that conform closely to the classical legend of Oedipus, i.e., a legend in which a son actually kills his own father and marries his mother, then indeed one is hard put to find any such episodes in all of the Sanskrit literature. Even if one allows for the extraordinarily strongly expressed taboo on maternal incest that is characteristic of Indo-Aryan culture and excludes or represses this part of the story, it is still difficult to find Indian myths or legends in which a son kills or even shows any significant aggressive behavior towards his actual father.

The scope of Goldman's claims here, like that of Ramanujan's, needs to be carefully noted. A few sentences later, Goldman uses the expressions "Indian mythological texts" and "Sanskrit epic and puranic lore." If he intended to limit the applicability of his remarks to this corpus, his earlier use of the expression "Sanskrit literature" was incautious. Indeed, as Goldman himself points out in some detail,[5] the sixteenth-century Tamil Śaiva devotional text Parañcōtimuṉivar's *Tiruviḷaiyāṭaṟpurāṇam* has "the story of a brahman who, filled with lust, makes love to his desirable and willing mother. His father is aware of this but chooses to ignore the matter for fear of a scandal until one day he comes upon the couple actually making love. The older brahman reviles his son, who then proceeds to hack him to pieces."[6] Goldman goes on to explain that the central point of the story becomes the fact that "the grace of Śiva can save even the most depraved of men. An acting-out of the oedipal fantasy is taken here to be the very worst conceivable sin and can thus serve more dramatically to demonstrate the compassion and power of the god. . . . The thrust of the tale is devotional and it is for this reason that it can use the otherwise generally tabooed topic of actual oedipal incest and murder as a test case of divine grace."[7] Similar episodes, understandable in much the same terms, may be located elsewhere in Indian literature. They appear in the Buddhist *Jifayue sheku tuoluoni jing*, which likewise uses its tale of Oedipal crime to showcase the superior power of the text's *dhāraṇī* (which is to say, the text itself) to save even such criminals from hell. But they also appear in Hindu Purāṇic texts, the *Brahma-Purāṇa* and *Skanda-Purāṇa* episodes we studied, which employ the motif of mother-son incest to emphasize the purificatory power of pilgrimage to sacred spots. As is clear from his remarks, Goldman himself is aware of a certain diversity in the classical Indian traditions and is willing to make a bit of room for such oddities. Yet his conclusion appears to revert to a more dogmatic and less nuanced stance:[8]

> [I]n traditional India's strictly hierarchical and rigidly repressive family, representation of a son actually attacking his own father or entertaining sexual thoughts about his own mother is subject to the strictest sort of taboo. . . . the rule is that active oedipal aggression must, in general, whether in the law books, the epics or the conscious mind, be displaced onto father and mother surrogates.

Considerable evidence argues against the full version of this proposition, even observing the more nuanced and thus stricter bounds of the purely Hindu literature Goldman considers to lie within the scope of his survey. Moreover, despite his concluding formulation, which refers to both aggression and expression of sexual desire, Goldman's study consistently emphasizes the former, perhaps because he considers examples of the latter to have been so tabooed as to have been (almost?) completely nonexistent. The materials we have studied, however, demonstrate this to be partially untrue: Classical Indian literature, including some central Hindu Purāṇic texts in Sanskrit, does contain explicit examples of mother-son incest. Goldman's claims about the rarity of intergenerational violence, on the other hand, appear to be more firmly grounded. Still, Sanskrit words for matricide and patricide are well attested, even in very old sources, some of which are not at all obscure outliers on the fringes of normative culture but formative works of the most orthodox traditions. The grammatical construction of the terms for matricide, patricide, and the murder of a brother is, for instance, explicitly described in Patañjali's second-century B.C.E. commentary to the grammar of Pāṇini, in the context of preclassical Vedic language, and at least the first two terms appear in the later second millennium B.C.E. *Atharva Veda*.[9] Later, the sins of matricide and patricide and the means of their expiation are both mentioned in the *Kauṣītaki Upaniṣad*, when the god Indra promises that, if they "perceive" him, even those who commit such crimes will not suffer for them.[10] While this does not show that the crimes themselves were common, or even commonly thought about, it does demonstrate that Hindu Indians were quite capable of contemplating not only the sexual aspects of Oedipal behavior, but its murderous aspects as well, enshrining direct reference to them in some of the tradition's core texts. Whatever form the taboos against such acts may have taken, they were neither, in any literal sense, "unthinkable," nor were they so thoroughly tabooed as to be totally absent even from culturally central religious or scholarly works. But this, of course, is not precisely what Goldman claims. His position is not that such acts are inconceivable, but rather that the drive to commit them is displaced onto surrogates, and in this regard, despite the contrary examples I have cited, it is reasonable to maintain that Hindu literature in general does go out of its way to avoid portrayals of direct and unmediated Oedipal situations as such.

Contrasting the evidence and assertions of Ramanujan and Goldman with the Buddhist tales we have studied, it becomes clear that Buddhist literatures in India sometimes (although certainly not always) followed radically different taboo structures, partook of different sets of cultural stereotypes, and otherwise significantly distinguished themselves from Brahmanical literatures. This should not surprise us. As Obeyesekere warned:[11] "[T]he Oedipus complex is not only culturally variable but . . . even within a single culture there might be several Oedipal models with one form dominant insofar as it is the most frequent form or reflective of the ideal cultural value configuration." In this light, Ramanujan and Goldman are perfectly correct when they speak of Hindu Oedipal patterns, insofar as they are speaking of a certain specifically delimited realm or realms of Indian culture. At the same time, one may also just as properly consider classical Indian Buddhism, although thoroughly Indian in many fundamental respects, to be in other respects located in or constituted by (sub)cultures significantly at variance with those of the always dominant Hinduism. Indian Buddhist expressions of social mores, while often clearly conforming to broader generalized patterns, may also on occasion represent radically different attitudes, at odds with the majority view.[12]

We are left with the question of the Indian Oedipus. Is it even possible to speak of such a classification, distinct from and in some respects an inversion of the canonical Greek model? The tools Ramanujan has given us, when applied to the sources we have been able to bring forward, suggest that we are better off thinking not of "the" Indian Oedipus in the singular but of Indian Oedipuses in the plural. Certain patterns distinguish these Indian arrangements from the architecture of the Greek story, while others are much more closely allied to it. We know that our Buddhist stories are Indian because we discover them in Indian texts, but the lesson we learn from the differences between the story of Dharmaruci in the *Divyāvadāna* and the tale of Meghadatta in the *Mahāvastu*, for instance, is that to speak of a single Indian pattern of Oedipal architecture, even a single Buddhist pattern, is to drastically oversimplify the full range of Indian evidence. There are two major consequences of this realization. On the one hand, the richness and variety of this evidence compels us to look within India itself, at the necessity of further and more nuanced delineations of subcultural divisions, toward the local contexts within which this diversity arises. Classical India was populated by a variety of communities, not all of which shared in the dominant Hindu cultural archetypes (which are themselves, of course, also plural). On the other hand, this very same evidence also drives us to recognize that simple binary distinctions between Greek and Indian models likewise fail to do justice to the diversity of our Indian evidence within an outward-looking comparative framework.[13]

Given this plea for the autonomy of the local and the necessity of recognizing variants, not only externally between distinct traditions but even internally within single traditions, we may turn our attentions back to the Oedipal calumnies of the *Vibhāṣā*, and ask: how did Indian Buddhists, and in particular the authors of the *Vibhāṣā*, think about the patterns of sexual behaviors we have been discussing? And further: how did they manipulate their understandings for rhetorical or polemical ends? We are now surely justified in concluding that, within the world of the Indian Buddhist imagination, there were multiple models of sexual relations. We may therefore hypothesize with considerable confidence that the choices that the authors of the *Vibhāṣā* made when they transformed Dharmaruci into Mahādeva were quite purposeful choices, intentional decisions articulated within an environment of multiple and conflicting models of incestuous and Oedipal relations.

The presentation of Mahādeva found in the *Vibhāṣā* cannot be properly appreciated in isolation. The forging of the Oedipal Mahādeva may be understood only in light of parallel but crucially different formulations, in contrast to which its own calumnious character appears. The Dharmaruci story, representatively related in the *Divyāvadāna*, by its existence and its presentation alone comes close to proving that the *Vibhāṣā*'s story of Mahādeva represents an intentional adoption and, most importantly, a selective adaptation of earlier materials. Moreover, the Dharmaruci story is far from our only piece of evidence suggesting that classical Indian literature in general, and Indian Buddhist literature in particular, contains regular patterns of depictions of incestuous relations, in contrast to which the irregular formulation of the *Vibhāṣā* cannot help but be seen as of the result of intentional manipulation. Most crucially, the evidence demonstrates that Indian Buddhist literature does not maintain strict taboos against depictions of incestuous relations, even those between mother and son. In these, however, nearly without exception, it is mothers who are depicted as sexually aggressive toward sons. The *Vibhāṣā*'s reversal of this directionality is a significant and vital element in its campaign to vilify Mahādeva.

Does not this suggestion place a particularly heavy burden on a single expression in the *Vibhāṣā*, that Mahādeva "defiled his mother"? The argument I offer here does not assume or demand that no other Indian text accuse Dharmaruci/Mahādeva of initiating a sexual relationship with his mother. Such a source may exist, waiting to be discovered.[14] Rather, my argument appeals to the large-scale and widely found *patterns* of depictions of such relations in classical Indian literature in proposing that the *Vibhāṣā*'s inversions of normal patterns convey, and were intended to convey, a particular significance of immorality and depravity, of an especially calumnious accusation of intentional Oedipal criminality. According to Buddhist ideas of karmic responsibility, the key to all such responsibility, in terms of blame but also in terms of merit, lies in intention. That Dharmaruci is unaware of his transgression exempts him from almost all responsibility for his sin (until, learning the facts of the matter, he elects to continue the incestuous intercourse). Mahādeva, as a conscious and intentional actor, bears full responsibility for his own misdeeds throughout.

As Victor Mair has categorically pointed out, the account of Mahādeva in the *Vibhāṣā* is "the purest of polemics" and "was clearly written with a vindictive and well-defined purpose."[15] But Mair is, at the same time, careful not to suggest that the story was fabricated for use in this particular polemical context.[16] In fact, although he seems to have known none of the parallels adduced in the present study, other than those he himself translated, of course, he states that it appears "that what we are dealing with is a folktale of long standing and broad circulation that has been intentionally adapted for sectarian aims." Our evidence supports Mair's assessment.[17] I believe it to be a virtually certain conclusion that the authors of the *Vibhāṣā* (or some otherwise unknown text or tradition upon which they relied) intentionally adopted from some pan-sectarian pool of narrative, a pool reflected in texts belonging both to the Sthavira and Mahāsāṁghika lineages, the preexisting calumnious story of an Oedipal anti-hero, and they did so in order to attribute to this villain the propagation of doctrinal stances they found unacceptable.

The authors of the *Vibhāṣā* took the pre-existing story of an Oedipal criminal, the story of Dharmaruci, and further criminalized its already morally problematic protagonist, inverting the direction of sexual interest to attribute to him an even worse character, while giving him a name likely to evoke images of danger and destruction. The Dharmaruci tale itself, however, is neither monolithic nor subject to only one type of reading.

An observation of Wendy Doniger, offered, it is true, in a significantly different context, suggests a different perspective on the Dharmaruci story. Doniger writes:[18]

> The weak have to lie and trick because they lack the power to win in a direct confrontation. Women lack the physical power to overcome their male enemies and usually lack the political power to overcome them as well. Thus . . . women trick men, outmaneuver them, a fact that may be interpreted from a woman's point of view ("We are forced to trick them, and we can do it") but also from a man's point of view ("Women are dishonest, and always manage to get their way through secret manipulations").

Doniger's suggestions offer a fruitful point of comparison. For it is not only the point of view that differs in the various formulations of our tale, but the depicted power relations as well. Indian Buddhist literature in general, including the stories studied here, is deeply and profoundly misogynistic. In this respect, it may be possible to read most of the Buddhist stories we have studied as promoting, even if only tacitly, the idea that women by nature set out to trick men. The feminist critique Doniger suggests seems to demand that we see the mother in our stories as victim, whether she is deceptive by nature or by force of circumstances; she is a victim, according to this reading, not only in the *Vibhāṣā*'s reorganized telling, but even in those stories where she acts as deceiver. She is driven to these acts of seduction and incitement to murder by, for example, the social pressures that, perhaps most explicitly in the *Divyāvadāna*'s telling, expect of her complete celibacy and suppression of her own desires and her right of self-determination, even in the face of the lengthy absence of her husband or any other means to self-fulfillment.

There is something to learn here. But whether this modern reading is felt to be compelling or suggestive in its own right, drawing attention as it does to aspects of intergender dynamics that are frequently ignored, it most certainly does not represent the way any ancient Indian audience would or could have understood these stories. For all of Dharmaruci's transgressions, his mother is also portrayed in an extremely bad light. It is only when we come to the story of Mahādeva that we reach a complete demonization of the son and a corresponding characterization of his mother as victim. We may believe that patriarchal structures impute to women responsibility for assaults upon them. But this does not empower us to view the subsequent reorientation of the axis of aggression in the recast Mahādeva story, from mother to son, as representing some re-evaluative viewpoint. It is not that the mother's victimhood is now recognized for what it is, no longer concealed behind a screen of denial that instead plotted her as complicit in, if not wholly responsible for, the assault upon her. Rather, this reorientation, a result of a conscious alteration, is designed to lay responsibility for an unacceptable action more squarely and unequivocally on Mahādeva's shoulders. It is not a change that had any interest in the mother's role. The change in the status of the mother, from plotting aggressor to passive victim, is only a side effect of the intended transformation, that of the characterization of Mahādeva—the intention is to move only one piece on the board, although that move has an impact on other pieces as well.

Naturally, not each and every aspect of the story of Mahādeva in the *Vibhāṣā* represents a calculated rhetorical strategy of Oedipal calumny. The *Vibhāṣā* never explicitly includes Mahādeva's sexual transgression of defiling his mother among his serious crimes, which are enumerated as three murders. It is further implied by the overall context that he is complicit in, if not technically guilty of, the creation of the schism that produced the first two sects, this being the most serious possible crime catalogued in Buddhist doctrine. In this light, one can hardly avoid asking how important Mahādeva's incest is to this story. Perhaps it is only we today who are fascinated and disgusted by incest; perhaps it was something that ancient Indian Buddhists did not consider terribly serious. We learn from Indian sources, however, both Buddhist and non-Buddhist, that this is exceedingly unlikely to have been the case. Indian Buddhists quite clearly *were* concerned about incest, as their frequently expressed attitude toward alleged Persian practices and other evidence demonstrates. They were also concerned about sexual matters in general, as evidenced, among other things, by the almost obsessive attention given to sex in monastic codes. One can hardly argue, then, that the *Vibhāṣā*'s failure to draw explicit attention to Mahādeva's incest signifies its unimportance; everything we have been able to learn about what Indian Buddhists thought of such behaviors suggests that they would have viewed Mahādeva's sexual behavior, like his violent actions, as despicable and repellent.[19]

As Bernard Faure tells us,[20] "there has never been in Buddhism a full-fledged discourse on sexuality." Moreover, at least as far as Indian Buddhist sources are concerned, the extensive attention given to the dangers of sexuality, and the restrictions placed on possible activities, apply primarily, if not exclusively, to those who formally and voluntarily placed themselves within the purview of Buddhist monastic regulation. This applied paradigmatically to monks and nuns, but also to laymen and laywomen, *upāsakas* and *upāsikās*, who undertook to uphold many fewer regulations and restrictions than monks or nuns, but who nevertheless through their voluntary assumption of this smaller set of guidelines agreed to maintain certain restrictions on their freedom, including restrictions on sexual activity. Buddhist monastic literature clearly considered unchastity to be the most dangerous threat to the monastic state, a status borne out by its paradigmatic placement as the first among the most serious violations of the monastic code (*pārājika*). But even the restrictions applicable to laymen and laywomen had no applicability to the general public, the populace at large. We do occasionally see some indications of a generally expected morality of sexual conduct in some Buddhist sources, as, for instance, in the *Abhidharmakośa*'s idea that there are four kinds of perverted sexual activity (*kāmamithyācāra*), namely, sex with certain women (a class comprising the wife of another, one's mother, sister, or female maternal or paternal relatives),[21] sex other than vaginal sex even with one's own wife (that is, anal or oral sex), sex in certain places such as shrines or monasteries, and finally sex at certain inappropriate times, such as when the woman is pregnant, when she is breastfeeding, or when she has taken a vow.[22] It is true, then, that for the author of the *Abhidharmakośa*, who codified, of course, the thoughts of a whole tradition, certain types of sexual activity were generally inappropriate, even for those who had in no way voluntarily restricted their behaviors through any formal process. Other than references such as this, however, Buddhist morality had little to say about sexual mores for people in general, and such discussions as there are certainly never approached "a full-fledged discourse on sexuality." Here in connection with the story of Mahādeva we are not speaking of any formally articulated discourse but of an almost entirely unconscious assumption of propriety and decency. For the Indian Buddhist authors of our texts, and for their Indian audiences, incest was objectionable, mother-son incest particularly objectionable, and mother-son incest initiated by the son thoroughly beyond the pale. The *Vibhāṣā*'s authors made use of this common, if implicit, morality, crafting their revision of the tale of Mahādeva around it. In its turn this tale sheds light on one aspect of the discourse on sexuality in ancient India by highlighting a transgressive dimension, a behavior that simply could not be countenanced by anyone under any circumstances. It does not represent a complete discourse on sexuality, nor even a partial systematic discourse. Rather, it stands as a cairn, marking a border beyond which no civilized person may pass.

There is a tendency in some scholarly writing to present every conclusion as if it will revolutionize the understanding of a given field. My results here do not demand the wholesale rewriting of histories of Indian Buddhism, or call for profound revisions to accepted ideas of the meaning of Buddhist philosophy or spiritual practice. But they have other significance. At the outset I offered some reflections on the balance between merely echoing what our sources say to us and creating, based on these sources, entirely new meanings unknown to the worlds of those sources themselves. One thing that has become clear through our investigations of the construction, or forging, of the story of Mahādeva is that this balancing act is not ours alone. Buddhist historians and polemicists of ancient India also engaged in efforts to make sense of a tradition that had been passed down to them, not as a matter of abstract academic interest but out of a need to validate their identity and locate themselves within a sacred continuity of lineage. The historians and polemicists of the Sthavira tradition—and chief among them the authors of the *Vibhāṣā*—understood their place within the institutional structure of Buddhist monasticism in terms of a story of the schism that rent the once unified holy community of the Buddha. It is one thing for us to determine that almost certainly the Five Theses attributed to Mahādeva were historically unrelated to that fundamental schism, belonging instead to a distinct and later division into subsects within the Mahāsāṁghika lineage. It is quite another thing to understand that Sthavira historians, doxographers, and polemicists thought both that these Theses were the cause of the fracture and that one particularly evil individual was responsible for their propagation. For in suggesting that the authors of the *Vibhāṣā* "forged" the story of Mahādeva, I do not mean to suggest that they were aware of any historical inaccuracy in their presentation. Rather, their notion of the balance point between what a source says and what may be legitimately drawn from that source differs in some respects from that of the modern historian.

The authors of the *Vibhāṣā* forged the story of Mahādeva from their point of view in the sense of giving it form, shaping it, as one forges metal into an object. And to be sure, there is a creativity involved in this process, for they brought out and emphasized what they understood to be the true meaning of the sources from which they worked. We, on the other hand, in light of what we have learned of their sources, may be more inclined to understand that those authors forged the story of Mahādeva as one forges a document or a counterfeit banknote. Having studied both the "unrevised" story of Dharmaruci and the recast story of Mahādeva, it seems to us quite clear that the latter is a recreation of the former with its protagonist suitably demonized. But it is not that we are right and they are wrong. It is not that what the authors of the *Vibhāṣā* did was illegitimately modify the story of Dharmaruci, turning it into an Oedipal calumny. It is rather that history is not only one thing at a time: it is not a mere sequence of events. If it were, then the task of the historian, the ancient or the modern, would indeed be merely to line up the facts, hoping and expecting that out of this array some order, and thus some significance, would emerge. But as Alain Boureau reminds us, facts on their own are silent, and placing them in a sequence does not, in and of itself, suffice to extract from them meaning. The authors of the *Vibhāṣā* told the story of Mahādeva as they felt proper. Our job as modern historians is to understand what they did, and why they did it. The plural, complex, and multivalent picture that emerges from such an investigation is what we mean by "history." When the object of this study is religious, the result is a history of religion, but that fact does not remove it from the domain of rational inquiry. Historical investigations of religious phenomena abide by the same rules of evidence and the same expectations of coherence as all other historical endeavors. Perhaps, in the end, one of the most solid results of the present study is the conclusion that careful sifting and analysis of even polemical, ideologically charged, and emotionally and morally sensitive materials can uncover human motivations and thought processes that demonstrate just how much we do share even with authors whose world was so distant from our own.

Notes

Chapter 1: Incest and Schism

1. While many authors appear to employ the term "parricide" as equivalent to "patricide," parricide is a more general term denoting one who murders either parent, a close relative, or even some distinguished person, while patricide refers specifically to the murder of a father. I distinguish these terms accordingly.

2. Boureau 1986: 30.

3. This challenge exists for others as well: a political historian, for instance, who imagines Hegalian forces of history to have the same reality as facts on the ground falls into the same fallacy.

4. An example of such an absurdity is Freud's fantasy about primal hords murdering fathers, plain nonsense through and through, both historically and in terms of the Lamarckian "collective mentality" he claims it reveals. In his 1913 *Totem and Taboo* Freud laid out this scenario of the primal, prehistoric event in which a group of brothers slay their father in order to possess his women, reacting to their transgression with the creation of the incest taboo and rules against patricide (which becomes totemism). Since this event marks the de facto creation of human culture, the transition from tribe to society, the Oedipus complex, characterized by the incest taboo, must perforce be found in every society. How the same primal event could have occurred everywhere in the world is one of the more basic questions Freud apparently had no interest in considering, although the problem, along with others, was noted early on, for instance by the great anthropologist A. L. Kroeber (1920, 1939). For attempts to defend some version of Freud's ideas in this regard, see, for instance, Paul (1976), Fox (1980), and Spain (1987). A helpful if quite unsympathetic survey may be found in Wolf (1995: 476–496).

5. This vocabulary should not be taken to imply that the Greek pattern is the core, original, and true form, of which others are incomplete reflections, although from an orthodox Freudian perspective this is almost certainly the only way to see things.

6. Goldman 1978: 329.

7. Ibid.: 364.

8. Doniger 1993: 83. Compare the assertion of the psychoanalyst Rank (1992: 272, published in 1912) who, while noting the possibility that tales may diffuse from one culture to another, nevertheless maintained the existence of "a psychological identity . . . superseding any original ethnographic relationship."

9. More technically speaking, it would make good sense to distinguish "Brahmanism" from a subsequently developed "Hinduism." In order not to complicate matters here, however, I use the term "Hinduism" without further distinction to encompass the totality of the brahmanical and Hindu tradition (including even Vedism, where relevant).

10. For premodern India, absolute dating is a virtually unachievable goal; even placing a text within a span of several centuries is often impossible.

11. In his critique of Marcel Hofinger's deep concern with the historicity of accounts of the so-called Council of Vaiśālī, Paul Demiéville (1951, 240) wrote: "In general, the historical value of Indian Buddhist texts seems to me to lie, as often as not, in what one can deduce from them concerning the authors who have redacted them, their mentality, their doctrines, their milieu and their age, when this can be determined." We may also note the interesting and suggestive remarks of Ruegg (1999), particularly regarding the relation of narrative and theory-building.

Chapter 2: The Creation of Sects in Early Buddhism

1. A distinction is sometimes made between "sect," as a rendering of Indic *nikāya*, and "school," as a rendering of *vāda*. While potentially important, this distinction is often less than entirely clear in our sources, and I will freely use the terms "school" and "sect" as synonyms.

2. Strictly speaking, a view that sees schism as close to heresy, although distinguished by the notion that while "heresy is opposed to faith, schism is opposed to charity" (Cross and Livingstone 1997: 1463a), is closer to the Roman Catholic stance than that of Protestant thinkers.

3. Such debates (whether or not any actual face-to-face meetings in the form of "councils" ever took place) could have been of interest only to an educated, almost certainly monastic and scholastic, elite. The issues which shaped Buddhism and Buddhist history in nonelite contexts were naturally much different.

4. The idea of the entirety of Buddhist scripture being contained in a Tripiṭaka, "Three Baskets," comprising discourses (*sūtra*), monastic code (*vinaya*), and doctrinal systematics (*abhidharma*), whatever its true historicity, assumes a slightly later stage of the tradition.

5. Many books on Indian Buddhist history are equipped with diagrams illustrating this structure; see, for instance, the charts in Lamotte (1958: 585–594).

6. See Nattier and Prebish 1977: 246–247 (and on the context of controversies concerning the arhat, Bareau [1957]). Cousins (1991: 40), however, disagrees, saying, "At most it is only arahats without higher attainments and higher knowledges who are being (slightly) depreciated." The overall structure suggests that the Sthaviras, though fewer, maintained the old ways, while the Mahāsāṁghikas, though in the majority, were laxist. This seems at least in part to be an ex post facto rationalization for the respective names of the two sides.

It is sometimes maintained that Mahāsāṁghika ideas ultimately led to the "heretical" doctrine of the Mahāyāna bodhisattva replacing the arhat as the goal of Buddhist practice. They are therefore sometimes made responsible not only for the primal schism, but for the putatively unorthodox evolution that grew ultimately to dominate the Buddhism of Central and East Asia, if not of India itself. The problem of the origins of the Mahāyāna is too complex to enter into here, but suffice it to say that any simple derivation from the Mahāsāṁghikas seems now unlikely. For some discussion, see Silk (2002b).

The connection of Mahādeva's "heresy" with the Mahāsāṁghika and the Mahāyāna is made explicit by the medieval Chinese scholar Jizang in his *Sanlun xuanyi* (T. 1852 [XLV] 8b19–22, translated in Demiéville 1932: 30–31), in which it is said that Mahādeva inserted Mahāyāna sūtras into the Tripiṭaka. Although rejected by the Sthaviras, these were accepted by the Mahāsāṁghikas, a fact that led to the sectarian split. Jizang himself is a Mahāyāna author, which makes his assertion curious; see Silk (2006).

7. The best discussion of all the issues is Tsukamoto (1980, especially 229–246, 262–266, and also see his index); for a short early version, see Tsukamoto (1965). For a careful study of the Mahāsāṁghika–Sthavira schism, the Five Theses, and the role of Mahādeva, see Kanakura (1962: 265–311); for the Five Theses themselves (266–267)—I thank Sasaki Shizuka for first directing me to this study. See also, among others, La Vallée Poussin (1910); Demiéville (1932); Bareau (1955a: 88–111); Lamotte (1956) and his somewhat more detailed discussion (1958: 297–312); Prebish (1974); Nattier and Prebish (1977); Sasaki (1991); Cousins (1991, although I cannot follow much of his reasoning); and Ja-rang Lee (1998, 2000, 2001). As early as 1857 Vassilief discussed the question; see the French translation of his work (1865: 58). Compare also Kabata (1959), an attempt to conceptually relate the Five Theses to the roots of Pure Land thought in India.

8. See Lamotte 1956: 148–149; 1958: 300–301.

9. Mair 1986: 23–24, which I have modified, translating *Apidamo dapiposha lun* T. 1545 (XXVII) 511b20–28 (*juan* 99). See Nattier and Prebish 1977: 262, with reference to Bareau (1955b). The same account is found in Kuiji's *Yuqieshidilun lüezuan* T. 1829 (XLIII) 1b23–27 (*juan* 1), in abbreviated fashion, and cited in several other texts, some of which we will notice below.

10. Cousins (1991: 41) suggests that Mahādeva is having a dream—a nightmare—and that because arhats do not dream, this is another clue that Mahādeva is not, in fact, an arhat. This is not wholly impossible, but the text in no way indicates that Mahādeva is either asleep or dreaming; rather, it seems to suggest that in the quiet of the night he is sitting and contemplating his condition.

11. On "official" evaluations of authenticity, see Lamotte (1947). I have discussed the idea of an authoritative teacher from a different point of view in Silk (2002a).

Chapter 3: The Story of Mahādeva

1. Kanakura 1962: 269; see Watanabe 1954: 330. The theses are found in both translations of the *Jñānaprasthāna*, T. 1543 (translated by Saṁghadeva and *Buddhasmṛti in 383), and T. 1544 (translated by Xuanzang between 657–660), although this is not necessarily the first place they are recorded.

2. An interesting investigation would be to compare the biography of Mahādeva with that of another enemy of Buddhism, Devadatta, who expounds his own set of Five Theses, on which see, for instance, Satō (1963: 786–797); Mukherjee (1966: 74–86); Nakada (1995); Matsumoto (2001). On Devadatta's crimes, see Lamotte (1944–1980: ii.873–877), with his usual detailed notes. A further related question would then be whether and in what way Devadatta's conflict with the Buddha is an Oedipal conflict, in

accord with the insight of Goldman (1978) that gurus are, Oedipally speaking, father-figures. On this theme, see Obeyesekere (1990: 149–156). With regard to gurus as fathers, notice too the provocative dimension that, at least for the *Rāmāyaṇa*, as Hara (2002: 7) has pointed out, a woman's guru is her husband (in the critical edition 2.110.2cd: *viditaṁ tu mamāpi etad yathā nāryāḥ patir guruḥ*).

3. For example, Lamotte (1958: 305) discusses the version of Paramārtha (discussed in Chapter 5) under the heading "Mahāyānist authors inspired by the Vibhāṣā." Nattier and Prebish (1977: 247) write of the *Vibhāṣā*: "Since this account has been embellished with narrative details not found in our other sources, it should be read with some caution; still, there are no grounds that would warrant ignoring it altogether." The former portion of this notice is mistaken, since as we shall see the other sources referred to are either dependent on the *Vibhāṣā* or totally independent of it; either way, there is no "embellishment."

4. The translation is that of Mair (1986: 20–21 = 1994: 109–111), which I have modified. The full account is in Xuanzang's translation of the **Abhidharma-Mahāvibhāṣā*, T. 1545 (XXVII) 510c24–512a19 (*juan* 99), with the portion quoted found at 510c24–511a16. Translations or close paraphrases prior to Mair's are found in Lamotte (1956: 151–152; and 1958: 304); Watters (1904–1905: I.267–268); Demiéville (1932: 33–34); Mizuno (1967: 88); references outside of Japanese scholarship, which refers directly to the Chinese, usually quote one of the above. While Sasaki (1998: 12–13) is a very slight revision of Mair's translation, his Japanese translation (2000: 250–251) is made directly from Chinese. In the preceding pages he also translates the passages that provide the polemical context for this story, including, inter alia, the relevant material from the *Jñānaprasthāna*. It is important to note that the entire chapter in which this passage occurs is absent in the version translated two centuries before Xuanzang by Buddhavarman (T. 1546, translated in 427; Demiéville 1951: 263, n. 1), as noted already by Ui (1924: 89–90). Watanabe (1954: 330–345) contains a comparative study of the two translations of the *Vibhāṣā*, especially in light of their common basis in the *Jñānaprasthāna*.

5. As was noted already by Demiéville (1951: 264), the verse is found in numerous other texts, among which see, for example, *Dhammapada* 173, equivalent to *Udānavarga* 16.9. A table of the parallel occurrences of this verse can be found in Mizuno (1991: 26). We will find it recurring in the sources studied here as well. I translate the verse here from the Chinese text, and slightly differently below, depending on the version in question.

6. Sasaki (1998: 46–47, n. 14) suggests that Mair's rendering of *dùchūjiā* with "to ordain him as a novice" is wrong, since technically a śrāmaṇera would be able neither to learn the Vinaya nor to have disciples. Sasaki apparently comes to this conclusion because the sentence immediately following the excerpt cited here says that almost immediately after renouncing the world (*chūjiā*), Mahādeva, being intelligent, was able to memorize the Tripiṭaka and grasp its meaning, the Tripiṭaka, of course, including the Vinaya. Sasaki therefore suggests "ordain him as a monk" as the proper rendering of *dùchūjiā*. However, in light of Sasaki's own observation on page 23 concerning the irregularity of Mahādeva's ordination (see note 7 below), and the fact that the Chinese text makes no explicit statement, this seems less than obvious.

7. As Sasaki (1998: 23) points out, such an ordination is illegal. In the first place, those who commit any of the five sins of immediate retribution are disqualified from

ordination, a point developed further below. Moreover, it is the duty of the monk performing the ordination to question the applicant concerning his qualifications; failure to carry out the ordination rite correctly also invalidates the subsequent ordination. Sasaki is clearly correct that the author of our text knew these facts well, and composed the story with this in mind; as we will see, authors of other versions likewise demonstrate their awareness of this irregularity. I am much less comfortable with Sasaki's apparent willingness to attribute some historicity to the account, as when he says "we can learn from the legend that a quack *bhikṣu* called Mahādeva led the Buddhist order at Pāṭaliputra, cooperating with the king" (1998: 24).

8. The story continues as follows (T. 1545 [XXVII] 511a16–c19 [*juan* 99]; this translation is a much modified version of Mair [1986: 21–25], and also in light of Sasaki [1998: 13–17; 2000: 251–253]):

> Now Mahādeva was quite brilliant and so, not long after he had renounced the world he was able to recite the text and grasp the significance of the Tripiṭaka. His words were clear and precise and he was skillful at conversion. In the city of Pāṭaliputra, there were none who did not turn to Mahādeva in reverence. The king heard of this and repeatedly invited him into the inner precincts of the palace. There he would respectfully make offerings to Mahādeva and entreat him to lecture on the teachings.
>
> Later, [Mahādeva] left [the capital] and went to dwell in a monastery where, because of impure thoughts, he had wet dreams. Now he had previously declared himself an arhat, but when he ordered a disciple to wash his soiled robes, the disciples spoke to him saying: "An arhat is one in whom all the outflows have been exhausted (**kṣīṇāsrava*). How then, Master, is it possible that you still have such a thing?"
>
> Mahādeva spoke to him, saying: "I was afflicted by Devaputramāra. You should not think this strange. Now the outflows may broadly be classified into two categories: one due to defilements (**kleśa*) and the other due to impurities. The arhat has no outflows due to defilements, but he is yet unable to avoid those due to impurities. Why? Although the defilements of arhats are extinguished, how can they be without urine, feces, tears, spittle, and the like? Now, the Devaputramāras always hate the Buddha's teachings. Whenever they see someone who is cultivating goodness, they invariably attempt to ruin him. Even an arhat is afflicted by them, and therefore I had an outflow. They caused it. You should not be skeptical about this." This is termed "the origin of the first false view."
>
> Again, Mahādeva wished to make his disciples like him and be closely attached to him. He deceptively arranged a strategy by which he sequentially recognized [the monks' attainment of] the four fruits of the śramaṇa [**śramaṇaphala*]. At that time a disciple bowed to him and said: "Arhats and others [Stream Winners, Once Returners, and Never Returners] ought to have true knowledge [of their own liberation]. How is it that none of us have this sort of self-awareness?"

> [Mahādeva] then spoke to him, saying: "Arhats also have ignorance. You should not, then, disbelieve in yourselves. I tell you that the forms of ignorance fall broadly in two types. One defiles, and the arhat lacks this. The other does not defile, and the arhat still has this. On account of this, you are unable to have full awareness of yourselves." This is termed "the origin of the second false view."
>
> At another time, his disciples once again spoke to him, saying: "We have heard that a sage has transcended all doubts. How is it that we still harbor doubts in regard to the Truth [**satya*]?"
>
> And again, Mahādeva spoke to them, saying: "Arhats also have doubts. There are two types of doubts. One is dispositional doubt, and the arhat has thoroughly cut this off. The other is doubt regarding what is and is not the case, and the arhat has not yet cut this off. Lone buddhas are still accomplished [although they have this doubt]. How could it be that you [as mere] auditors would be without doubt about the truths and thereby deprecate yourselves?" This is termed "the origin of the third false view."
>
> Later, when the disciples opened and read the sūtras, they saw [explained that] the arhat has the eye of wisdom. He is able by himself to recognize his own liberation. And for this reason they spoke to their master, saying: "If we are arhats, we ought to recognize it ourselves. How is it, then, that we must be initiated by our master into that fact and are without the direct insights which would enable us to recognize it ourselves?"
>
> To this, [Mahādeva] replied: "There are arhats who are only able to know this through another, and not able to recognize it themselves, for example Śāriputra, foremost in wisdom, and Mahā-Maudgalyāyana, foremost in supernatural powers. If the Buddha had not informed them, they would not have recognized this themselves. How can it be then that those who are initiated by others into that fact recognize it themselves? Therefore you should not endlessly inquire in regard to this." This is termed "the origin of the fourth false view."

Then follows the section on the fifth false view, translated in Chapter 2, after which the text continues:

> Mahādeva later compiled the aforementioned five evil views, and composed a verse:
>
> Enticement by others, ignorance,
> Doubts, initiation by another,
> Manifestation of the Path through a shout:
> These are termed the Buddha's True Teaching.
>
> With the passage of time, all of the senior monks in the Kukkuṭārāma monastery gradually died off. Once, on occasion of the Uposatha rite on the night of the fifteenth of the month, it was Mahādeva's turn to ascend the pulpit and recite the

monastic rules. He then on his own accord recited the verse which he had composed. At that time there were in the assembly [monks who] were still practicing and those who had achieved the goal (**śaikṣāśaikṣa*), those who were very learned (**bahuśruta*), those who strictly upheld the precepts (**śīlavat*), and meditators (**dhyāyin*). When they heard what [Mahādeva] had said, there was no one who refrained from reproving him: "For shame! Stupid man! How could you say such a thing? This is unheard of in the Tripiṭaka." Thereupon they countered his verse, saying:

> Enticement by others, ignorance,
> Doubts, initiation by another,
> Manifestation of the Path through a shout:
> What you say is not the Buddha's teaching.

Upon this, an unruly controversy erupted that lasted the whole night long. By the next morning, the factions had become even larger. People of the capital from the commoners up to important ministers came one after another to mediate, but none of them could bring a halt to the argument.

The king heard of it and himself went to the monastery. At this point, the two factions each stated their obstinate positions. Then, when the king had heard what they had to say, he too became filled with doubt. He inquired of Mahādeva: "Who is wrong and who is right? With which faction should we now align ourselves?"

Mahādeva said to the king: "In the Prātimokṣa it is said that if one wishes to terminate controversy, he should go along with the voice of the majority."

The king proceeded to order the two factions of monks to separate themselves. In the faction of the saints and sages, although there were many who were elders, the total number of monks was small. In Mahādeva's faction, although there were few who were elders, the total number was large. So the king followed the majority and allied himself with Mahādeva's assembly. He criticized and suppressed the members of the other assembly and, the matter concluded, returned to his palace.

9. However, in the case of the Mahādeva story, this implausibility among other more technical reasons seems to have persuaded Ui (1924: 88–89) of the impossibility of the tale being historically true.

10. The text reads "*qí zǐ zhǎngdà rǎnhuì yú mǔ.*" The word *rǎnhuì* (to defile) has mother (*mǔ*) as its direct object, a relation that is clearly marked by *yú*. On *rǎnhuì*, see Silk 2007a. While it is theoretically true that in classical Chinese grammar *yú* can mark a passive, I do not believe that is its significance here. If it ever functions this way in Buddhist translations, it is exceedingly rare. If, however, we were to read the sentence with this grammar, it would mean: "He grew up, and was defiled by his mother." The likelihood of this being correct is, in my opinion, virtually nil.

Chapter 4: The Buddhist Context of Sin

1. See for example the quasi-etymological definition of *ānantarya* in the *Abhidharmakośabhāṣya ad* IV.96 (Pradhan 1975: 259.21–24, translated in La Vallée Poussin 1923–1931: iii.204). By saying that the scholastic tradition speaks of this category I do not intend to imply that it is an innovation not found in the scriptural corpus. The technical term itself is found in the Pāli Vinaya, and the items are listed, for instance, in the *Aṅguttara-Nikāya*. The same is true for the canonical corpora of other sects as well.

2. According to the *Abhidharmakośabhāṣya ad* IV.99c (Pradhan 1975: 261.2, translated in La Vallée Poussin 1923–1931: iv.207), sins other than the creation of a schism in the monastic community do not necessarily result in rebirth in the worst of the hells, Avīci (*anantarakalpam avīcau mahānarake vipacyate* | *anyais tu nāvaśyam avīcau*), although they may (*ad* IV.80d, Pradhan 1975: 251.4: *ānantaryakāriṇāṁ tu tatra vānyatra vā narake*, where *tatra* refers to *avīcau* in the previous sentence). Precisely the same is found in the *Vibhāṣā* (T. 1545 [XXVII] 185a4–7 [*juan* 35]).

3. See Silk 2007b.

4. Such ideas should, in principle, always be found elsewhere, namely, in the canonical corpus (the Sūtra and Vinaya, the discourses of the Buddha, and his monastic code), since the avowed aim of the Abhidharma is no more than to systematize the unsystematically presented preaching of the Buddha. In order for an idea to be acceptable, to be orthodox, it must conform to the teaching of the Buddha; hence, from a normative point of view there can be no source for Abhidharmic categories other than the canonical scriptures. Nevertheless, of course, the Abhidharma literature did introduce innovations. This is a process common to every religious tradition, in which innovation is concealed as restatement and representation of the original revelation. In the Buddhist context, while many lists and categories in the Abhidharma literature reproduce what already stood in the existing canonical Sūtras and Vinaya, this is not always the case.

5. We may note also the set of six *abhiṭhāna* in Pāli, so called in the commentary to the *Khuddakapāṭha* in *Paramatthajotikā* I (I.189, 21–22; quoted by K. R. Norman 1992: 192–193; and in the *Critical Pāli Dictionary* of Trenckner et al. 1924–: I. 348b): matricide, patricide, murder of an arhat, drawing the blood of a buddha, creating a schism, and adopting another teacher (=heresy). The items are listed together with others in the *Aṅguttara-Nikāya* (Morris and Hardy 1885–1900: i.27 [I.xv]). A number of the references here and in the following were already noted by La Vallée Poussin (1923–1931: iv.201–202) in the notes, where there are also other examples of lists of the five sins of immediate retribution "plus alpha."

6. In the case of Devadatta, it is made quite clear that the murder of a female arhat, an arhatī, is included in this category; see Lamotte (1944–1980: ii.875). The murder in question is that of the nun Utpalavarṇā, whom we shall meet later.

7. *Aṅguttara-Nikāya* (Morris and Hardy 1885–1900: iii.146, 28–30 §V.13.9 [129]; iii.436, 20–22 §VI.9.3 [87], etc.). The order of listing is unlikely to have been motivated by the rules for compounding in Sanskrit or Pāli; both orderings, mother-father and father-mother, are found in both languages.

8. *Abhidharmakośabhāṣya ad* 105ab. This is the order of presentation in the *Dharmasaṁgraha* §60 (Nishiwaki 1962: 16). The *Vibhāṣā* (T. 1545 [XXVII] 620c9–11 [*juan* 119]) agrees that the murder of one's mother is more severe than that of one's father. A number of other texts share this evaluation, such as the **Saṁyuktābhidharmahṛdaya* (T. 1552 [XXVIII] 898b24–25 [*juan* 4]). Elsewhere the *Abhidharmakośabhāṣya* (*ad* IV.96) gives the list with the last two items in reverse order. See also *Mahāvyutpatti* §§8760–8764, apparently based on the *Ekaśatakarma* (but cf. T. 1453 [XXIV] 461c25–27 [*juan* 2]); the Mūlasarvāstivāda *Upasaṁpadājñapti* (Jinananda 1961: 14.16–20), *Bhikṣukarmavākya* (Banerjee 1977: 63.2–3), and *Vinaya-sūtra* (Bapat and Gokhale 1982: 23.20–21), and the Mahāsāṁghika Lokottaravādin *Bhikṣuṇī-Vinaya* (Roth 1970 §35, 43).

9. *Abhidharmakośa* (Pradhan 1975: 264.4, 10) 105ab: *saṁghabhede mṛṣāvādo mahāvadyatamo mataḥ*, and then in the commentary *sarvalaghuḥ pitṛvadhaḥ*.

10. Walleser and Kopp (1924–1957: ii.8,24–9,1) = DPG 41: 342.18–21: *sace pitā sīlavā hoti mātā dussīlā no vā tathā sīlavatī pitughāto paṭisandhivasena vipaccati* I *sace mātā sīlavatī mātughāto** I *dvīsu pi sīlena vā dussīlena vā samānesu mātughāto va paṭisandhivasena vipaccati* I *mātā hi dukkarakārinī bahūpakārā ca puttānan ti* I. The variants are significant, especially in the phrase marked *, but I follow the Burmese text.

11. A passage in the *Divyāvadāna* credits both father and mother with such generosity (Cowell and Neil 1886: 51.20–22): *duṣkarakārakau hi bhikṣavaḥ putrasya mātāpitarau āpyāyakau poṣakau saṁvardhakau stanyasya dātārau citrasya jaṁbudvīpasya darśayitārau* (Mother and father do what is difficult for a son, they are nurturers, nourishers, fosterers, givers of milk, teachers of multifarious ways of the world). In the *Abhidharmakośabhāṣya* (Pradhan 1975: 263.9, *ad* IV.103d) only the mother is so characterized (although at 262.22–23 both parents are called *upakārin*, benefactors, since they are the source of one's bodily existence, *ātmabhāvasya tatprabhavatvāt*). Such notions are not limited to the Buddhists. A passage from the *Mahābhārata*, partially cited by Meyer (1930: 199, n. 1) says: "Neither mother nor father is to be blamed, since they are both one's former benefactors. But, since she has endured suffering in carrying [one during pregnancy], of the two the mother is the more venerable" *(na dūṣyau mātāpitarau tathā pūrvopakāriṇau* I *dhāraṇād duḥkhasahanāt tayor mātā garīyasī).* Meyer refers to a southern text, the so-called Kumbakonam version; I am grateful to Reinhold Gruenendahl (email 22 July 2004) for locating the passage in the Critical Edition (Sukthankar, Belvalkar, and Vaidya 1933–1966: vol. 1, app. 37, lines 14–15, appended after 1,57.69f.).

12. *Śatapatha-Brāhmaṇa* XI.4.3.2; I cite the translation of Eggeling (1882–1900). Nevertheless, in some Jaina stories thieves actually discuss this question, cited in Bloomfield (1926: 216).

13. Passages like this make absolutely clear the pervasive Brahmanical influence on the fundamentally *kṣatriya*, or warrior-class, epics. Of course, this influence is seen in a multitude of other dimensions as well, not least the fact that they were transmitted in Sanskrit, rather than in a vernacular language.

14. See Meyer (1930: 487–489), who makes copious references to the epic and legal literature, as well as Kane (1968–1977: II.593–594) for additional references. See also Hara

2003: 23–27. It is true that, as Meyer (1930: 488, n. 1) details, not all legal texts treat such murders with the same seriousness. Among the differences the most particular and obvious are caste-wise differentiations in severity and, as Kane points out, some law books do authorize kings to punish women by death. See also Jamison 1991: 216; 1996: 261, n. 21.

15. I thank Gregory Schopen for reminding me of the story in this context. See most centrally among the secondary literature Feer (1878), Brough (1957), and Klaus (1983).

16. Whether this is part of the larger pattern that Schopen (2001 and elsewhere) has detected between Buddhist canon law and the Dharmaśāstra is a question that must await further research.

17. T. 1545 (XXVII) 511c18–20 (*juan* 99).

18. I adopt this rather cumbersome circumlocution for *pakatatta*, which indicates a monk who is not subject to any disciplinary restrictions on his monastic status and is thus not only a monk, but in good standing vis-à-vis the rules of monastic conduct; see Nolot (1996, nn. 18, 19, 27, 50).

19. Oldenberg (1879–1883: ii.204,8–9 [VII.5.1]): *bhikkhu kho upāli pakatatto samānasaṁvāsako samānasīmāya ṭhito saṁghaṁ bhindatī ti.* Translated also in Horner (1938–1966: 5.286).

20. Pradhan (1975: 261.7–11 [IV.100ab, with commentary]): *kaḥ punar eṣa saṁghaṁ bhinatti* | *bhikṣur dṛkcarito vṛttī bhinatti bhikṣur bhinatti na gṛhī na bhikṣuṇyādayaḥ* | *sa ca dṛṣṭicarita eva na tṛṣṇācaritaḥ* | *vṛttastho na bhinnavṛttas tasyānādeyavākyatvāt* |. See the translation in La Vallée Poussin (1923–1931: iv.208); and note Yaśomitra's commentary in Wogihara (1936: 427.17–22).

21. See the *Vibhāṣā* (T. 1545 [XXVII] 602c20–603a3 [*juan* 116]), but note that it speaks here of a person, **pudgala*, not a monk. However, both the **Saṁyuktābhidharma-hṛdaya* (T. 1552 [XXVIII] 899a3–14 [*juan* 3]) and Saṁghabhadra's *Apidamozang xianzong lun* (T. 1563 [XXIX] 886b25–c8 [?] [*juan* 23]) also specify that the offender must be a monk.

22. We may contrast this with the case of Devadatta, who clearly was a regularly ordained monk and thus liable to the technical accusation of instigation of a schism. See the note in Lamotte 1944–1980: ii.873–874, n. 1.

23. In the Mahāsāṁghika *Bhikṣuṇī-Vinaya* (Roth 1970 §35, 43), following the listing of this item as one that restricts access to ordination, is added: *ciraparinivṛto kho puna so bhagavāṁs tathāgato 'rhan samyaksambuddho* (although that Blessed One, Tathāgata, Arhat, Complete and Perfect Buddha is already long in nirvāṇā). Nolot (1991: 20, n. 48) draws attention in this context to the fact that in modern ordination rituals, the ordinand, in taking refuge in the Buddha (in the formula: "I take refuge in the Buddha; I take refuge in the Dharma; I take refuge in the Saṁgha"), adds "although he is long in nirvāṇa." As far as I know, the texts that discuss this question do not raise the possibility of one doing harm to a (living) buddha in another world-realm.

24. Possible objectors could include those who uphold views such as those espoused by Mahāsāṁghika Lokottaravādins, the authors of the Lotus Sūtra or the *Upāyakauśalya*, and so on. For a brief discussion of some parallel issues, see Silk 2003b.

We find elsewhere the idea that it is impossible to harm a buddha. As Peter Skilling tells us (2003: 288, n. 3): "According to the Pāli commentaries, the blood of a Tathāgata cannot literally be shed, because his body cannot be wounded (*abhejjakāyatā*). 'Lohituppāda' means a congealing of blood within the body, where it comes together in one spot, under unbroken skin. In other words, it is a bruise." Skilling does not cite references, but according to Trenckner et al. (1924–, s.v. abhejjakāyatā), the passage is found in the *Manorathapūraṇī* (ii.6,11), *Papañcasūdanī* (iv.110,27), and *Vibhaṅgaṭṭhakathā* (*Sammohavinodanī*) (427,4).

25. This issue has recently been discussed by Skilling 2003.

26. See a number of the papers collected in Schopen 1997.

27. Two inscriptions from Sāñcī are mentioned by Skilling (2003: 292–293), namely, those numbered by John Marshall 396 and 404.

28. *Abhidharmakośa* and *bhāṣya ad* IV.106–107ab, in Pradhan (1975: 264.22–265.4); Tibetan in Derge Tanjur 4090, *mngon pa*, *ku* 219a1–4. The passage was translated in La Vallée Poussin (1923–1931: iii.219–220). The same list of five is given in the *Mahāvyutpatti* §§2330–2334, where, however, the classification (§2329) is termed *upānatarīya*, a term I have not seen elsewhere—but see my remarks in Silk 2007b.

29. Pradhan prints *sukha°*; Hirakawa et al. (1973: 432) suggest emending to *mukha°*. The Tibetan translatation has *zhal du 'du ba'i sgo*, demonstrating that *mukha°* was the reading before the Tibetan translators. The *Vyākhyā* (Wogihara 1936: 430.27) is printed as *sukha°*, but see La Vallée Poussin's citation (1923–1931: iv.219, n. 2).

30. *Sphuṭārthā Abhidharmakośavyākhyā* of Yaśomitra, in Wogihara (1936: 430.21–28); Tibetan in Derge Tanjur 4092, *mngon pa*, *ngu* 78b6–79a2. The text goes on to explain that according to the opinion of Vasumitra, theft of the wealth of the monastic community means forcible confiscation of permanent endowments. Yaśomitra agrees and explains that what is meant by the expression "removal of the wealth of the monastic community" is the forcible confiscation of that upon which the monastic community depends for its continued existence.

31. The appositional reading of this item is clearly confirmed by both the Tibetan and Chinese translations of the *Abhidharmakośa*, as well as the Tibetan translation of Yaśomitra's commentary; see Silk 2007b.

32. The list of forbidden women in the *Abhidharmakośabhāṣya* (*ad* IV.74ab, Pradhan 1975: 244.14–15) comprises the wife of another, one's mother, one's daughter, and maternal or paternal kinswomen. The passage is translated in La Vallée Poussin (1923–1931: iv.157). See also Silk 2008a.

33. Pradhan (1975: 263.15): *yaḥ pitaram arhantaṁ hiṁsyāt tasyāpy ekam eva syād ānantaryam āśrayaikatvāt*. See La Vallée Poussin 1923–1931: iv.215.

34. Bhattacharya (1957: 185.20–186.1); Chinese in T. 1579 (XXX) 318b21–22 (*juan* 9); Tibetan Derge Tanjur 4035, *sems tsam*, *tshi* 93b7. See Silk 2007b.

35. The concept is also entirely different from the Christian notion of original sin.

36. There are sources that appear to exclude from salvation those who perpetrate the five sins of immediate retribution. A famous example (although how important it may have

been in India is itself questionable) is found in the nineteenth vow of Dharmākara, the bodhisattva who became the buddha Amitābha, in the foundational scripture of Pure Land Buddhism, the *Sukhāvatīvyūha*. Dharmākara vows to save all who believe in him (Kagawa 1984: 120, §8–g, vow 19): *sthāpayitvānantaryakāriṇaḥ saddharmapratikṣepāvaraṇāvṛtāṁś ca sattvān* (except those who commit the sins of immediate retribution, and those beings who are obstructed by their hostility to the true teaching). There appears to be some conflation of what other texts treat quite separately, namely, sinful actions on the one hand and apostasy or disbelief on the other. In this light, I have some doubts about Gómez's interpretation of this exception clause (1996: 232), since he appears to take notice of the first of the pair of disqualified individuals only.

37. H. C. Norman (1906–1914: iii.68,1–69,10)=DPG 51: 39.8–26; cf. the translation in Burlingame (1921: ii.306–307). The story was noticed by both Malalasekera (1938: II.546–547) and Hecker in Nyanaponika and Hecker (1997: 102–103).

38. *Jātaka* 522 (Sarabhaṅga). Fausbøll (1877–1896: v.126, 11–20)=DPG 74: 122.22–123.2; cf. the translation in Cowell et al. (1895–1907: v.65).

39. Conversely, at least from the point of view of systematic theory, the same applies to the fruits of positive actions, which likewise can never have more than a temporary, hence limited, effect. Theoretically speaking, one cannot escape the circle of transmigration, *saṁsāra*, and attain nirvāṇa, the summum bonum, through karmic action, since karmic action functions only within the limited and endless flux of birth and rebirth. How this putatively original "pure" idea may have been adapted and modified in practice, if this is indeed what happened, is a question requiring separate treatment.

40. It is striking that the Chinese Buddhist tradition preserves a complex of popular stories about the very same (Mahā-)Maudgalyāyana (Mulian in Chinese), in which he is depicted, in this respect at least, in a diametrically opposed way: as the epitome of the filial and devoted son. See Teiser (1988: 113–167) and Cole (1998 passim), as well as the sources cited in both. A survey of Chinese and, particularly, Japanese sources is given in Iwamoto (1968). Similar stories are found in Indian materials, such as the *Pūrṇāvadāna* (Story of Pūrṇa) of the *Divyāvadāna*; see Cowell and Neil (1886: 51.18–52.26). The text was translated by Burnouf (1844: 270–271); cf. also Tatelman (2000: 77–79). The Chinese translation was translated into Japanese by Iwamoto (1968: 172–174).

41. Individuals lack a "self" in the sense of a permanent, unchanging essence. What the "person" is, what provides the identity of the individual, is his karmic stream (*santāna*), the flow of his karmic energy. The individual, then, is the sum of his accumulated actions, from the beginningless past, and the forms he takes in each incarnation in the world are merely one result of the momentum of that karmic stream. Any factor expressed in that flow persists as a facet or characteristic of the individual only until the latent karmic energy that motivates that factor is exhausted. Thus all characteristics of any individual are, by definition, only temporary.

42. These lists, however, require further study. For instance, the treatment of debtors is considerably more complicated than it may at first seem, as discussed by Schopen (2001).

43. A long list of physical deformities that debar one from ordination is given at Oldenberg (1879–1883: i.91,7–22 [Mahāvagga I.71]). For a study of the list in the Pāli Vinaya and its commentary, see Sasaki (1996).

44. More accurately, the story illustrates what will become the offense. The first "offender" cannot be an offender, since the rule to be promulgated does not yet exist, and there is no retrospective imposition of the new rule.

45. A connection between the *Vibhāṣā* account of Mahādeva and this Vinaya text was already noticed by Demiéville (1951: 263, n. 2). I translate here from the Sanskrit text established by Näther (1975: 46.19–48.24=2003: 30.12–31.33). Näther's text improves upon the readings given by Lévi (1932: 27.23–29.7) and Dutt (1939–1959: iii.4.53.18–56.16); the Tibetan translation is edited in Eimer (1983: 309.6–312.13); the Chinese is found in T. 1444 (XXIII) 1038c27–1039b18 (*juan* 4)—this translation appears to be rather free, or perhaps based on a somewhat different original. Translations from the Sanskrit are found in Näther in German (1975: 90–93), now in English (2003: 45–48 due to Claus Vogel and Klaus Wille); and in French in Lévi (1932: 37–39); and in French from Tibetan in Feer (1883: 94–96).

Precisely this same story is found in the fourth-century *Dharmapada* commentary in Chinese, the *Chuyao jing* (T. 212 [IV] 627a29–c4 [*juan* 4]), quoted from there in the sixth-century compendium *Jinglü yixing* (T. 2121 [LIII] 237c29–238a22 [*juan* 45]), the latter translated by Chavannes (1910–1911: iii.269–270, §478), and again (almost certainly independently) in the eleventh-century *Nārakapūrvikāvadāna* of Kṣemendra's *Bodhisattvāvadānakalpalatā* (§82, Das and Vidyābhūṣaṇa 1888–1918: II.680–691). See also the summary version in Tucci (1949: 517); and the translation of Padma Chos 'phel's *Ston pa'i skyes rabs dpag bsam 'khri shing* in Black (1997: 371–373); and probably upon this basis subsequently in the *Bhavaśarmāvadāna* of the *Aśokāvadānamālā*. edited in Iwamoto (1978: 217–230); see Mejor (1992: 108, note d).

In the Mūlasarvāstivāda Vinaya the prohibition of patricides from ordination, which immediately follows the prohibition of matricides—though when first introduced (Eimer 1983: 142.7–8) they are in the opposite order—is illustrated with precisely the same story, mutatis mutandis, translated in Näther (2003: 52ff.) from Tibetan, since the Sanskrit manuscript does not bother to repeat the story, saying only *yathā mātṛghātaka evaṁ pitṛghātako vistareṇa vaktavyaḥ*; Näther (1975: 52.13–14=2003: 34.13–14).

46. On the significance of the garland, see Silk 2007c.

47. Added after the Chinese translation.

48. These are, of course, for the use to which we put toilet paper.

49. This sentence has the look of a narrative interjection, common in this literature.

50. The transition from this sentence to the next (or internally in this sentence itself) is very abrupt, which suggests that some text may be missing. While the Tibetan translation agrees with the Sanskrit (Näther 1975: 47.25, 2003: 31.3; Eimer 1983: 310.22; translated in Feer 1883: 95), the Chinese (1039a19–20) adds: "Then he went to the wealthy man's house. After he arrived there, he saw that young woman, and his body trembled." There seem to be two basic possibilities: (1) Yijing's text contained material missing from the extant Sanskrit text and from the source of the Tibetan translation (because it was

lost in those traditions or because Yijing had a different recension), or (2) Yijing sensed the discontinuity and patched the text. As noted above, there are other cases in which the same question might arise. Further careful comparative studies of Yijing's translation, which here as elsewhere often appears to be rather free, will shed light on this question.

51. The relation between *dhātrī* and *janitrī* deserves to be explored. Notice that in *Nāradasmṛti*, for instance, to have sexual relations even with a wet nurse qualifies as incest (*gurutalpaga*) (Lariviere 1989: 184; Strīpuṁsayoga 72–74; trans. 157). The treatment in the *Viṣṇusmṛti* (36.4–7), while similar, does not mention the *dhātrī*.

52. It is not entirely clear who is being designated with *ayaṁ sa* here. The sequel, in which the son and true murderer is free to perform his mother's funeral and simply depart, suggests that he is not confessing his own guilt here (in which case we might expect **so 'haṁ* instead). Rather, he may be reporting his friend who tried to prevent him from meeting the girl as guilty of the crime, or he may simply be implicating some (nonexistent) thief in the murder he has in reality committed. Feer (1883: 96) understood the Tibetan text differently: "Lui, effrayé, épouvanté, prit la fuite et s'en retourna chez lui. (En trouvant) le glaive qu'il avait placé prés de la porte, il dit: Ce voleur, le voici, (c'est moi qui), aprés avoir tué ma mère, me suis enfui."

53. Here only Tibetan adds: another said "eat poison" (*dug zo shig*).

54. As printed, the Sanskrit text actually reads: "He thought, 'It is possible to cover over one's evil actions, but not to destroy them. I will renounce the world in this [community] and destroy [my evil karma].'" Vogel and Wille, in Näther (2003: 47, n. 82), suggest that the expressions "but not to destroy them" (*no tu kṣapayituṁ*) and "and destroy [my evil karma]" (*kṣapayiṣyāmi*) are interpolations. It is true that they lack a Tibetan equivalent (and Chinese differs here), and from one point of view hardly make sense. I provisionally accept their emendation. I nevertheless wonder whether it may be possible to understand *no tu kṣapayituṁ* as "without destroying them," so that the thought of the sinner is: I can hide these sins, without destroying them, that is, make them appear to be nonexistent, without actually erasing them. Then only the subsequent *kṣapayiṣyāmi*, which is, in any case, uncomfortable without connective *ca* directly after the likewise finite verb form *pravajāmi*, would be an intrusion.

55. Since this story is offered in illustration of the prohibition of matricides from ordination, the narrative conceit assumes that the postulant is not questioned about this matter prior to being granted ordination. It is only as a result of the problems occasioned by the ordination that such an inquiry is made a requisite part of granting entry into the monastic community. The stories mentioned earlier, in which the illegitimacy of ordaining a matricide plays an important part, assume the prior existence of this prohibition, which is common to all known traditions of monastic Buddhism.

56. On the stock phrase here, see La Vallée Poussin 1923–1931: vii.91, n. 2.

57. Näther 1975: 48.26–27=2003: 3134–35: *nāśayata yūyaṁ bhikṣavo mātṛghātakaṁ pudga(la)ṁ asmād dharmavinayāt*, with the subsequent stipulation being that one must inquire of an individual seeking ordination, *māsi mātṛghātaka* (You're not a matricide, are you?).

58. Näther 1975: 49.2–3=2003: 31.39–40: *sa saṁlakṣayati kim idānīm avapravrajiṣyāmi pratyantaṁ gacchāmīti.*

59. Näther 1975: 49.6=2003: 32.2: *tasya cāvavādena prabhūtair arhatvaṁ sākṣātkṛtam.*

60. The particular mental state of an individual at the moment of death is held to be of the gravest significance even among many non-Buddhist and non-Indian traditions, including those that have no notion of rebirth as such.

61. Näther 1975: 50.15=2003: 33.4: *satkāyadṛṣṭiśailaṁ jñānavajrena bhi(t)tvā.*

62. Ibid.: 51.26–29=2003: 33.34–36: *aho Buddha* | *aho dharma aho saṁgha : aho dharmasya svākhyātatā yatredānīm evaṁvidhā api pāpakāriṇo vinipātaṁ gatāḥ evaṁvidhaṁ guṇagaṇam adhigacchantīti.* It is not clear to me why the evildoers are referred to here in the plural. Is it possible it is a plural of respect (see Renou 1975: 276 §207) that the arhat uses in deference to his preceptor?

63. See Nolot 1999: 64–65=SVTT §VI.3, and 59=SVTT §VI.1a, citing the Pāli Vinaya (Oldenberg 1879–1883: i.88,20–21 [Mahāvagga I.64.2]) and the *Samantapāsādikā* commentary (Takakusu and Nagai 1924–1947: 1016,15–16).

64. See the detailed studies of Clarke 1999, 2000.

65. Oldenberg (1879–1883: i.90,1 [Mahāvagga I.69.4]).

66. Oldenberg (1879–1883: i.45,27 [Mahāvagga I.25.6]), and following for the services due the preceptor by his pupil. On the role of the *upajjhāya*, and the connected role of the *ācariya*, see Sasaki (1997). These terms designate the two supervisory roles older and more senior monks take with respect to a new ordinand, in which they make themselves responsible for his education, as it were; they are required of every monk.

67. My translation includes in brackets the commentary's gloss. *Abhidharmakośabhāṣya ad* IV.80d, Pradhan (1975: 250.20–22): *abhavyo 'yaṁ pudgalo dṛṣṭa eva dharme kuśalamūlāni pratisaṁdhātuṁ niyatam ayaṁ narakebhyaś cyavamāno vā upapadyamāno vā kuśalamūlāni pratisaṁdhāsyatīti.* Saeki (1887: 711 [17a4,9]) identified the quotation as from *Madhyamāgama juan* 37, in which I cannot locate an equivalent passage. However, Pāsādika (1986: 89, §342) cites—with "?"—the suggestion of Fujita Kōtatsu that the sentence corresponds to T. 26 (I) 601a25 (*juan* 27—suggesting that Saeki's reference is misprinted), but I confess that I cannot see the putative connection there either. However, as Saeki already pointed out, precisely the same point is made in the *Vibhāṣā* as well (T. 1545 [XXVII] 184b89 [*juan* 35], with the larger discussion beginning at 184a1 and continuing).

68. I do not know whether traditional sources take note of this dynamic, and if so what they have made of it. Of a quite different nature is the idea behind passages such as the following from the *Guhyasamājatantra* V.3 (Matsunaga 1978: 15, and see the translation in Snellgrove 1987: 170): "Even those who commit great evils such as the sins of immediate retribution and so on attain success in this Buddha vehicle, the great ocean of the Mahāyāna" (*ānantaryaprabhṛtayo mahāpāpakṛto 'pi ca* | *sidhyante buddhayāne 'smin mahāyānamahodadhau* ||). Likewise, some Buddhist theologians have discussed the salvation of those who commit the five sins of immediate retribution—on the case of Hōnen, see Maeda (2003).

69. T. 2043 (L) 162a1–9 (*juan* 9). Compare the translation in Li 1993: 149. The version in the **Aśokarājāvadāna*: T. 2042 (L) 120c10–18 (*juan* 5), which was earlier rendered into French by Przyluski (1923: 366), reads as follows:

> In South India there was a man who had sexual relations with the wife of another.
>
> His mother said to him: "To have sexual relations with [the wife of] another is a very evil practice. There is no evil to which the path of sexual desire does not lead."
>
> Hearing this, he killed his mother, and then he went to the other's home in pursuit of that woman. But in the end he did not get her. His mind was filled with loathing, and he then renounced the world.
>
> Not long afterwards he memorized and could recite the sūtras of the Tripiṭaka, and he taught many pupils. The disciples [of Upagupta] followed [him and his] group of students to the place where the Venerable [Upa]gupta was, but the Venerable knew the crimes of which the man was guilty, and he did not speak a word to him, but only thought to himself: "One who has committed such transgressions cannot obtain the fruit of the path."
>
> Since the Venerable [Upa]gupta did not speak, [the man] led the members of his group back to the place whence they had come.

This episode has, in fact, been associated with the Mahādeva story before. Lamotte (1956) remarked: "This anecdote referred to in the *Aśokāvadāna* bears remarkable resemblance to the version of the *Vibhāṣā*" (150–151), an observation repeated by Tsukamoto (1980: 237), while Strong suggested (1992): "It may be that here the text wishes to distance Upagupta from another reputed matricidal fornicator, the great heretic Mahādeva, who is sometimes said to have been from Mathurā [as is Upagupta]" (320, n. 11). Why, if this were a concern, the text includes the story at all is a question Strong does not address. Is the whole account constructed (or borrowed) only so that Upagupta can refuse to see the evil monk?

70. The attribution in this Northwestern Indian literature of serious immorality to a man from the South is worth noting, although it may be nothing more than yet another example of vilification of the Other. An interesting possibility, however, which takes into account the specifically sexual nature of the objectionable behavior, is that the northern authors of these stories were aware of South Indian patterns of consanguineous marriages (even though these are never sanctioned between relatives more closely related than uncle and niece or first cousins).

71. The Chinese here is *jiāotōng*.

72. The text here says *gèng hào tārén*.

73. The Chinese here is *chānghuì*. This word appears twice in the *Yogācārabhūmi* (T. 1579 [XXX] 360a6 [*juan* 15], 368b1 [*juan* 17]), another text translated by Xuanzang. In the second instance, it is compounded with *jiā*; we are fortunate to have the Sanskrit original of this latter passage in the *Ābhiprāyikārthagāthānirdeśa* (Maeda 1991: 77.1), which provides us the equivalent *veṣa* (more normally written *veśa*), confirming the mean-

ing as "prostitute." In both spots the meaning is the same in the Tibetan translation, Derge Tanjur 4035, *sems tsam, tshi* 197a5 *smad 'tshong ma*, 216a1 *smad 'tshong gi gnas.*

Chapter 5: Mahādeva in Other Sources

1. Paramārtha's translation is T. 2033 (*Buzhiyi lun*), Xuanzang's T. 2031 (*Yibu zonglun lun*), and that of an unknown translator T. 2032 (*Shibabu lun*). For details, see Silk 2006: 172–173, n. 14.

2. T. 2031 (XLIX) 15a17–23; Teramoto and Hiramatsu 1935: 4–5 (Chinese). See Lamotte 1956: 149–153 = 1958: 301–305. An English translation of Xuanzang's translation is found in Masuda (1925: 14–15), French in Bareau (1954: 235–236). Xuanzang also refers to Mahādeva in his *Datang Xiyuji*, for which see Silk 2006.

3. The text continues: "What are the four communities? (1) *Nāga community. (2) Border community. (3) Bahuśrutīya community. (4) Sthavira community. The Five Theses are . . . ."

4. T. 2033 (XLIX) 20a22.

5. In Chinese he is once again called *wàidào*, in Tibetan *kun tu rgyu* = **parivrājaka*. Although the usual implication of these terms is "non-Buddhist sectary," here the context makes clear that one should understand something like "unorthodox Buddhist, not a real Buddhist," and so on.

6. The Tibetan is in Miyasaka in Takai (1928/1978: 2.15–20); and see Teramoto and Hiramatsu (1935: 3.1–5): *lo nyis brgya pa la gnas pa'i tshe kun tu rgyu lha chen po zhes bya ba rab tu byung ste mchod rten gyi ri la gnas pas dge 'dun phal chen po'i lugs lnga po de dag yang dag par rjes su brjod cing | yang dag par rjes su bsgrags nas mchod rten pa'i sde dang | nub kyi ri bo'i sde dang | byang gi ri bo'i sde zhes bya ba sde pa gsum rnam par bkod do ||*. The Tibetan was long ago translated by Vassilief (1865: 229).

7. T. 2031 (XLIX) 15b1–4. See also T. 2032 (XLIX) 18a17–20; T. 2033 (XLIX) 20b2–4. These texts are also found in Teramoto and Hiramatsu (1935: 14). All three Chinese versions are translated side by side in Lamotte (1958: 309–310); T. 2031 is translated by Bareau (1954: 237); and Masuda (1925: 15). Note that in Paramārtha's version, only two sects are mentioned, the Caityaśailas and Uttaraśailas.

Much the same can be found also in the closely related *Nikāyabhedavibhaṅgavyākhyāna* (Commentary on the Classification of the Divisions of Buddhist Monastic Communities) of Bhāviveka (or Bhavya). This text also knows a Mahādeva and his theses (their number not mentioned), connected with a branch of the Mahāsāṁghikas (Miyasaka in Takai 1928/1978: 21.4–8; Teramoto and Hiramatsu 1935: 25.18–26.3 = *Tarkajvālā* in Derge Tanjur 3856, *dbu ma, dza* 150b7–151a1; earlier translated in Rockhill 1907: 189; Bareau 1956: 176–177; Walleser 1927: 84): "Again, as a division of the *Gokulikas, there are the Sthaviras called *Caityaka. A wandering ascetic named Mahādeva renounced the world and dwelt at *Caityaśaila. Again, when he proclaimed the Theses of the Mahāsāṁghikas, the *Caityaka order was created."

8. The first point is made explicitly by Kuiji (in his *Yibuzonglunlun shuji*, Zokuzōkyō I.83.3,218d10–12), who says: "Previously in the first century [after the Buddha's nirvāṇa]

there was a Mahādeva who was the instigator of a dispute among the monks. This [Mahādeva] now has the same name as the former [Mahādeva], and thus [the text] says 'again.'" See also the note to much the same effect cited in the *Sanron gengi kennyūshū* (T. 2300 [LXX] 461c23–25 [*juan* 5]), apparently from the *Sifenlü xingshichao pi* compiled by the fifth patriarch of the Nanshan Vinaya school, Dajue. I owe this latter identification to the kindness of Dr. Yao Zhihua (Centre of Buddhist Studies, The University of Hong Kong). Demiéville (1951: 268, n.), without reference to this passage, remarks: "In other words, the recension translated by Xuanzang reduplicates the character, following a procedure which, it seems to me, may be considered absolutely normal among Indian historians of ancient Buddhism, when they find themselves having difficulty resolving contradictions posed by diverse traditions or opposing legends." He then cites as an example the *Samantapāsādikā*'s conclusion that the Theras of the third council were reincarnations of those of the second.

9. Of course, the name Mahādeva itself exists in the Pāli tradition, applied to at least nine separate persons, none of whom, however, can be connected with this issue; see Malalasekera (1938: ii.505–506).

10. The *Vibhāṣā* was published between 656 and 659, and Vasumitra's text in 662. See the *Kaiyuan shijiao lu* T. 2154 (LV) 557a18 and 557b5 (*juan* 8).

11. Kanakura (1962: 278, 281 n. 9, and again 282) states that the reference to Mahādeva was later added to the original text from which Xuanzang translated. Demiéville (1951: 268, n.) appears to agree, at least in part, saying that "without doubt this name was extracted from the *Mahāvibhāṣā* in order to be interpolated into the recension brought back from India by Xuanzang." It is not, however, absolutely clear when or by whom Demiéville considers the interpolation to have taken place, while Kanakura is clear in stating his opinion that the addition was made to the original text (*genbun*) from which the translation was made, not at the time of its translation (281, n. 9), yet adding (278) "here we can recognize the influence of the *Vibhāṣā*." Frauwallner (1952: 244, n. 2) clearly states his opinion that the addition is due to Xuanzang. Lamotte (1956: 150=1958: 302) states the borrowing as a fact: "Among the translators, Hiuan-tsang [Xuanzang] alone precisely states that the originator of the Five Propositions was Mahādeva, the information being taken from the Vibhāṣā." There may be no way to finally decide the issue, but it should be noted that there is ample evidence elsewhere of Xuanzang's willingness to add explanatory glosses to his translations. I am not aware of any systematic study of such additions, which would, however, be likely to produce interesting results.

12. Nattier and Prebish 1977: 261, 264. It is worth noting that essentially the same case was already made with, if anything, more vigor and greater control of the relevant sources by Ui Hakuju (1924: 84–88, 91); and see also the observations in Shāstrī (1931: 838–839); as well as by others afterwards, such as Frauwallner (1952: 248); Kabata (1959: 168); Mizuno (1967: 91); see also Tsukamoto (1980: 246—I do not know if the same was found in the first edition of his study in 1965). Katō (1950: 42–43), on the other hand, accepts the historical existence of two Mahādevas, one of whom was, for him, a great bodhisattva.

13. The proper name of this individual, that by which he referred to himself, is simply Ji; for a detailed discussion of this issue, see Weinstein (1959: 129–136), who prefers

the appellation Cien. For the sake of convenience, however, I maintain the name by which he is generally known in scholarship, Kuiji.

14. Zokuzōkyō I.83.3. For information on this and the points that follow, see Demiéville (1932: 15–18).

15. Paramārtha's work is the *Buzhiyilun shu* (Commentary on the Treatise on the Diversity of Sects), which was lost by the eleventh century and is thus not available to us as an integral unit; Demiéville (1932: 16, and 17, note c, citing T. 2300 [LXX] 455a22–23 [*juan* 5]). Demiéville notices that Kuiji states that he will avoid pointing out differences between Xuanzang and Paramārtha; it therefore makes sense that he would quote the *Vibhāṣā* version in Xuanzang's translation, rather than the different version transmitted by Paramārtha, on which see below.

16. *Yibuzonglunlun shuji* I.83.3: 215d8–216a7; also found in Koyama (1891: 1.27b7–29a5), who carefully notes the variants. See Demiéville (1932: 33, note c); for another approach to Mahādeva by Kuiji, however; see Silk (2006). It is true, of course, that the verbatim presentation of Xuanzang's account in Kuiji's text may be of some different independent significance—for a study of the latter's working methods, for instance.

17. Demiéville (1932) refers to this monk by the name Chūkan, which may also be read Chūgan. I refer to him by his monastic name, Chōzen.

18. T. 1852 (XLV) 8b17–19. See Demiéville (1932: 30); and Saigusa (1970: 162ff.). According to Demiéville (1932: 18), the content of Jizang's work itself is, with a few minor exceptions, "borrowed from one end to the other from Paramārtha's commentary on the Treatise of Vasumitra," referring to Paramārtha's now-lost *Buzhiyilun shu*.

19. Chōzen's note T. 2300 (LXX) 455b4–6 (*juan* 5) reads: "As for the controversy over the Five Points, [*juan*] 99 of the *Vibhāṣā* has this introductory account, which differs somewhat from that given by Paramārtha in the *Buzhi shu* [=*Buzhiyilun shu*]. I cannot recount it in full, so now I will just summarize the discussion." See Demiéville (1932: 33). Later Demiéville (1951: 267, n. 2) suggested that Paramārtha summarized and "on many points modified" the version in the *Vibhāṣā*.

20. T. 2300 (LXX) 455b6–21 (*juan* 5). I have gained materially in making my translation by studying that of Demiéville (1932: 33–34).

21. The text contains a gloss here; it begins by using the name Datian, which it then clarifies by explaining that Mohetipo (Mahādeva) is translated as Datian.

22. The term here is *sītōng*.

23. At 455b20, the first character in the line, *suì*, is a misprint for *zàng*.

24. Sasaki (1998: 23).

25. T. 1852 (XLV) 9a21–b6; my translation is heavily indebted to that in Demiéville (1932: 50–51).

26. That is, those who pretend to be legitimate monks in order to profit materially from the monastic life.

27. The same story of the later Mahādeva is found in Kuiji's *Yibuzonglunlun shuji* (Zokuzōkyō I.83.3,218d15–219a10); and in Chōzen's *Sanron gengi kennyūshū* (T. 2300 [LXX] 461c26–462a19 [*juan* 5]), translated in Demiéville (1932: 51–53), clearly based on

the commentary of Paramārtha, which reinforces the picture we have acquired of a tradition that is broadly aware of certain discrepancies in its own foundational legends.

28. Yamada et al. (1959: I.306, *kan* IV.33, "Tenjiku no Daiten no koto,"), translated by Mair (1986: 26–27), which I have modified. A headnote in Yamada's edition notes the source as *Vibhāṣā juan* 99 and also cites the parallel in the *Sangoku Denki, kan* 3.28.

29. The text breaks off at this point. Yamada's note finishes out the story from the *Vibhāṣā*.

30. For the dates of the author (whose name may also be read, following convention, as Taira no Yasuyori), I follow Koizumi et al. (1993: 523–525), with the proviso that there is considerable uncertainty over their precise accuracy.

31. I translate the text edited by Koizumi in Koizumi et al. (1993: 316–317), which has been dated to around 1183. There are a number of recensions of the same basic collection (see the detailed study in Koizumi 1971: 186–286). Our story is told in the same words in at least two, the so-called seven-scroll (*nanakan*) and nine-fascicle (*kyūsatsu*) versions. The version in the Minobusan manuscript (Uryū 1973: 177–178) has slightly different wording in some places and omits the portion given in my translation as the last paragraph, that is, the identification of the brahmin in question with Mahādeva and so on. A somewhat different version, which does include the last paragraph but contains interesting variant readings (and is presented in considerably more sinified orthography than other versions), is printed in the *Dainihon Bukkyō Zensho*, vol. 147: 138ab=440ab (Tokyo: Bussho Kankōkai, 1913). Although there is significant Japanese scholarship on this collection—one listing is found in Koizumi et al. (1993: 536–541)—I know of no published Western language studies. My gratitude is due my wife, my colleague Michael Bourdaughs, and most especially Stanford graduate student Lorinda Kiyama (email Feb. 29, 2004) for their helpful comments on, and corrections of, my translation.

32. As Lorinda Kiyama has pointed out to me, the word *imaimashii* here and below in reference to the monks' response to Mahādeva carries a sense of abhorrence arising from a perceived superstitious inauspiciousness. The actions of Mahādeva and his mother are abnormal, and thus have negative effects on others in the community, to which they respond.

33. Yamada Shōzen (the author of the notes, based on Koizumi's materials—see p. xiii) in Koizumi et al. (1993: 317, n. 8) identifies this with the *Vibhāṣā* (T. 1545 [XXVII] 512a14–18 [*juan* 99]). I find slightly odd that what I would expect to be classified as a treatise (*ron*) is referred to here as scripture (*kyō*); in the few other cases in the same text in which Yasuyori uses the term *kyō*, he either refers to a scripture or the source of the attribution remains unidentified. My unfamiliarity with the conventions of this medieval Japanese literature prevents me from saying whether the usage is unusual or my sense is simply the result of different expectations.

34. There may, nevertheless, be some reason to see some connection between this version and a short vignette in the Mahāyāna *Mahāparinirvāṇa-sūtra*, for which see below in Chapter 12.

35. The exact dating of the work is problematic. For a detailed discussion, see Ikegami (1976: 16–19). He concludes that it probably belongs between 1427 and 1443, but he

notes that a date as early as 1407 has been proposed (and is often found in reference works).

36. In *Dainihon Bukkyō Zensho* (Tokyo: Bussho Kankōkai, 1913): 148: 84a4–16 (266–267), *kan* III.28, "Makadaiba akugyōji," translated by Mair (1986: 27–28), which I have modified. The text is also edited in Ikegami (1976: 195–197).

37. Note the remarkable error: Magadha is the eastern area of the Gangetic plain, southern Bihar state, while Mathurā is almost directly south of Delhi, far to the west. The geographical relation between the two is precisely opposite of what the *Sangoku Denki* states. This has also been remarked by Ikegami (1976: 195, n. 3).

38. This is, of course, the same verse as that found in the *Vibhāṣā*, although the wording is not quite identical.

39. *Tsuini shukke wo motomu sō soku yurusu.*

40. The text continues, but this is the portion relevant to our investigations.

41. According to a personal communication from Lorinda Kiyama, "The *Hōbutsushū* is structured as a guidebook for the Buddhist practitioner, first through the six paths of rebirth and then onto practices for enlightenment. Each section begins with quotations from sūtra passages and Confucian texts or Chinese histories in Chinese, followed by stories (often abbreviated) in vernacular Japanese, followed by a series of illustrative *waka* poems. These three types of texts are interspersed with terse commentary. The order of presentation of texts suggests that the *Hōbutsushū* might have been used as a prompt book or source book for sermonizing. From its creation all the way to the end of the Edo period, it was used as a reference book for *waka* poetry—it contains over 400 poems." It is therefore, she emphasizes, not quite right to call it a *setsuwa* collection, at least in the same sense as one may refer to the *Konjaku* as such an anthology.

42. For a fuller account of the Tibetan sources, see Silk 2008c.

43. Van der Kuijp 1996: 398.

44. The Sanskritist Sa skya Paṇḍita gave his text an Indic title; its Tibetan title is *Legs par bshad pa rin po che'i gter*, usually called *Sa skya legs bshad*, or simply *Legs bshad*. The cited verse is numbered 151 in the edition of Bosson (1969).

45. The text is printed in Rhoton 2002: 325–326. Rhoton has divided the entire verse work into three sections, and these into paragraph units; those translated here are numbered (somewhat arbitrarily) §586–597 of the third section. On the divisions, see David Jackson's note on p. 277. According to p. 28 of Rhoton's book (prepared for the most part by Jackson), this text follows that in *Sa skya pa'i bka' 'bum* (Collected Works of the Sakya Founding Masters) (Tokyo: Tōyō Bunko, 1968–1969): 5:297.1.1–320.4.5 (*na* 1a–48b5). My translation is indebted that in Rhoton (2002: 172–174), and I owe my knowledge of this passage to the kindness of my friend David Jackson.

46. That is, he is (or claims to be) a monk, but since he lacks both an *upādhyāya* and an *ācārya*, he cannot legally be a real monk.

47. See Martin 1997: 43–44, §54. However, Martin states that much of this work undoubtedly belongs to a somewhat earlier period.

48. Chab spel tshe brtan phun tshogs (1987: 98.20–101.3).

49. Literally "dharma and vinaya."

50. For a discussion of the possible sources of Mkhas pa lde'u's version, see Silk 2008c.

51. According to Roesler 2002a: 432.

52. The best discussion I know of this figure is found in Stearns (2001: 69–78). As noted by Roesler (2002a: 433) and by Stearns (2001: 197, n. 298), according to the colophon of the transmitted text, the commentary was originally composed by another disciple of Sa skya Paṇḍita, Lho pa kun mkhyen Rin chen dpal. Since this version was unclear and in part mistaken, Dmar ston corrected and rewrote the work under the direction of Sa skya Paṇḍita. Whatever may be the reality of this account, the commentary, without doubt, came from the atelier of Sa skya Paṇḍita.

53. See Silk 2008c. Almost precisely the same story is recounted in a number of similar later commentaries on the same text, all obviously dependent on Dmar ston's work. One may thus see the translation in Davenport (2000: 115–117) of the *Legs bshad pa rin po che'i gter gyi don 'grel blo gsal bung ba 'du ba'i bsti gnas* of Sa skya mkhan po Sangs rgyas bstan 'dzin (1904–1990) for a version with only minimal differences from that translated here. I am grateful for the help I have gained from this translation in making my own of Dmar ston's text.

54. I am not certain how to identify this place.

55. That is, by being a dishonest receiver of alms, he renders the charity of the givers void of the religious merit they would have gained by donating to a worthy recipient.

56. An interesting idea! The allusion appears to be to the fact that certain disciples of the Buddha, while transmitting his ideas, did not understand them. This claim is commonly made about Ānanda, who is a perfect transmitter of the Buddha's preaching because, not understanding the content, he is compelled to recite it word for word, and not paraphrase; see Silk (2002a). But it is an unusual suggestion to make about Śāriputra.

57. Again, Mahādeva is being disingenuous: the destruction that is a quality of arhats is the destruction of their ignorance and other impediments to their awakening, not destruction in general, and certainly not the destruction of the very powers characteristic of the arhat.

58. For these sources, see Silk 2008c.

59. See the remarks of Roesler (2002b: 161) and (2002a: 435), as well as these two papers of hers passim. I am grateful to Dr. Roesler for her kind suggestions and assistance with this material and for sharing with me the pages of Ëndon (1989: 129–130) relevant to our story. I regret that my ignorance of Russian prevents me from making full use of the contribution of this Mongolian scholar. I am, however, very grateful for the kindness Andrey Fesyun (Moscow) showed me in obtaining a copy of this book (from Siberia!) and translating for me into English several relevant passages.

60. I am not sure whether the explicit distinction into thematic sections should be attributed to the author or to his commentators, but the internal structure is, in any case, quite clear.

61. This understanding follows the outline of Go rams pa; see Rhoton (2002: 276).

Chapter 6: Schism Accounts in Buddhist Doxographies

1. On the difficult question of the identity and date (sixth/seventh/eighth century?) of the author of the *Tarkajvālā*, see Ruegg (1990). Whether the name of this author is properly to be Bhavya, or Bhāviveka (the form Bhāvaviveka appears to almost certainly be an error), and whether these refer to the same individual, we cannot decide here.

2. Derge Tanjur 3856, *dbu ma*, *dza*, 149b5–150a2, corresponding to *Nikāyabheda-vibhaṅgavyākhyāna* (Teramoto and Hiramatsu 1935: 22.9–23.10; Miyasaka Yūshō in Takai 1928/1978: 18.17–19.8). *Tarkajvālā* IV.8 and following constitutes the *Nikāya-bhedavibhaṅgavyākhyāna*. Kanakura (1962: 285) recognizes that the content of the *Nikāyabheda*° and the *Tarkajvālā* is identical, but seems unaware that the former is in fact an extract from the latter, a fact which also seems to have been unknown to Bareau (1954: 232), who says that it is "possible" that the great sixth-century Madhyamaka master Bhāvaviveka (as he knows him) is also the author of the *Nikāyabheda*°. (Bareau clearly assumes that it is the sixth-century Bhāvaviveka who wrote the *Madhyamaka-hṛdayakārikā* and its commentary, the *Tarkajvālā*.) The passage has been translated in Rockhill (1907: 186–187); Walleser (1927: 81–82); Bareau (1956: 172–173); and Kanakura (1962: 286–287).

3. As discussed in Silk (2008c), there is good reason to believe that there were not two kings, one named Nanda and another Mahāpadma, but that Mahāpadma was the ruler of the Nanda dynasty. If so, we may emend our text by removing a *dang* and read **rgyal po dga' bo pa dma chen po zhes bya ba*. The problem was noted by Rockhill (1907: 186, n. 2); and La Vallée Poussin (1909: 183, n. 3); and later, for instance, by Bareau (1955a: 91). The wider chronological problems of dynasties and reigns have also attracted the attention of scholars—see, for example, the detailed studies of Tsukamoto (1980, esp. 62ff.).

4. The sentence *de ltar bzhugs pa na bdud sdig can bzang po thams cad kyi mi mthun pa'i phyogs su gyur pa* is difficult to construe, and may be corrupt. It has been understood differently by Bareau (1956: 172): "Pendant qu'ils demeuraient ainsi, Māra, le vicieux, se transforma de façon à être semblable à un homme ayant toutes les qualités (*bhadra*)"; and Kanakura (1962: 286, and 289–290, n. 6): "kono yō ni karera ga jūshita toki, akuma badora ga subete ni hantai suru mono to natta." Kanakura understands *mi mthun pa'i* (*ba'i*) *phyogs* as *vipakṣa* or *pratipakṣa*, while Bareau takes this *mi* as "person." It is also possible that *bzang po thams cad* should be taken as a unit, in which case may the expression may mean that Māra "set himself in opposition to all the good"? But other sources attest to the existence of the name *Bhadra. Although no resolution is possible, I received helpful suggestions from Ulrike Roesler and Akira Saito.

5. The expression *dge slong gi cha byad* (*du*) may be restored with almost total confidence as **bhikṣuveṣeṇa*. It occurs, for instance, in the *Aṣṭasāhasrikā* (Wogihara 1932–1935: 513.22 [Mitra 242], 679.20 [331], 775.10 [388], 776.14 [389]), where it appears in an expression identical to what we find here: *māraḥ pāpīyān bhikṣuveṣeṇa*.

6. For reasons I do not fully understand, and which are never stated, Lamotte consistently reconstructs this name as Sāramati (1956; 1958: 308). Tsukamoto (1980: 237) offers Sthitamati or Sthiramati.

7. As there is considerable difficulty over the exact way to take these five items, I omit a translation here.

8. For details, see Silk 2008c.

9. Dorji (1974: 27a3–4 [53]); Schiefner (1868: 43.22–44.4); Tāranātha (1985: 40b5–41a2). The translation is modified from that found in Chimpa and Chattopadhyaya (1980: 85).

10. Dorji (1974: 25b1–2, 5 [50]); Schiefner (1868: 41,6–11, 18–20); Tāranātha (1985: 38a4–b1, 5–6). The translation is that of Chimpa and Chattopadhyaya (1980: 79–80).

11. The translation, slightly modified, is that of Chimpa and Chattopadhyaya (1980: 80).

12. Kanakura (1962: 291, n. 15) has opined that the various versions recorded in later Tibetan sources are based on Kashmiri (by which he means Sarvāstivādin) and Sammatīya sources, with some authors such as Tāranātha conflating the traditions.

13. See de Jong (1997: 29ff.). In this particular case, La Vallée Poussin (1910: 415) seems at least willing to profess polite agnosticism: "Whether, as pointed out by Watters, our schismatic has something to do with the Mahādeva of Buddhaghosa, a saint and a missionary . . . [or] whether he is merely an incarnation of Śiva, as suspected by Professor Kern—we confess we do not know. It is safer to believe that there was a schismatic Mahādeva."

14. See Silk (forthcoming c) for some discussion of this figure.

15. Kern (1903: II.318–320). I do not think Demiéville's criticism (1932: 33, note e) of Kern is altogether to the point. Noting that Kuiji gives Mahādeva's family name as Kauśika, Demiéville remarks that this is a nickname or the surname of Indra. Then he adds, "This is not quite Śiva, with whom Kern wants to identify our Mahādeva!" It seems to me to be rather Demiéville who, quite uncharacteristically for him, has gone off the track here. Although I believe that the whole line of reasoning is invalid, just for the record note that Kauśika is also an epithet of Śiva; see Böhtlingk and Roth (1855–1875: II.468).

16. Neither the published biography of Régamey (Loutan-Charbon [1978]) nor the memoir published on the occasion of the dedication of his bust at the University of Lausanne (Anonymous [1984]) appear to so much as mention the word "Buddhism," much less offer any account of his career as a Buddhist scholar. More recently, however, Jacques May (2001) has provided an appreciation and bibliography of Régamey's academic side.

17. Régamey 1938: 8–9. Some of what Régamey says here was anticipated by Kern (1903: 253, with n. 2).

18. Régamey's parenthetical note: "in the *Mahāparinibbānsutta*, *Dīgha-Nik.* II, p. 162 and in the *Cullavagga* p. 284, 285."

19. The reference here is to the first council, held after the death of the Buddha to codify his genuine teachings.

20. For the Pāli sources, see Malalasekera (1938: II. 1231–1232 [Subhadda 6]); for additional sources in Chinese, see Akanuma (1931: 637); and for convenience Lamotte (1944–1980: i.205ff., in the notes).

21. It is not significant that the same name is associated with the episode in the fifth-century Chinese version of the *Samantapāsādikā*, T. 1462 (XXIV) 673c2 (*juan* 1) (translated in Bapat and Hirakawa 1970: 2), since this text should almost certainly be considered as belonging to, or intimately related to, the Theravāda as well. For references, translations, and discussions of the relevant passages bearing on the episode of the "subversive" reaction to Śākyamuni's death, see Waldschmidt (1944, 1948: 289–293); Bareau (1971: 223–230); and Durt (1980). The problem is complicated, but neither of the names, Subhadra or Bhadra, is in any way connected with this legend in any tradition other than that of the Theravāda.

22. See, for instance, Gonda (1977: 269, n. 255) for a *Śiva-sahasranāma-stotra*, a collection and praise of a thousand names of Śiva.

23. I am indebted to my friend Harunaga Isaacson for bringing this and other relevant points to my notice.

Chapter 7: The Story of Dharmaruci

1. Mair 1986: 19.

2. Mair probably followed Japanese scholars like Yamada (1959: I.306), the editor of the *Konjaku monogatarishū*. On the second point, see, however, Enomoto (1993), who discovered a small fragment of the (or rather, a) *Vibhāṣā* in Sanskrit, published in Enomoto (1996).

3. See, however, Silk forthcoming b.

4. The accounts have now been presented together by my good friend Hiraoka Satoshi (2000); whether it was he or I who first made the connection during his stay in Ann Arbor in the late 1980s, during which he was intensively studying the *Divyāvadāna*, neither of us now recall.

5. The basic text translated here is that found in Cowell and Neil (1886: 254.3–262.6). However, I have treated both the *Divyāvadāna* version and that of Kṣemendra in Silk (forthcoming b), which contains reedited texts of both versions, along with detailed notes. The story has been translated before, by Heinrich Zimmer into German (1925: 60–79), and now by Hiraoka Satoshi (2000: 24–29; 2007: I.451–459) into Japanese. In addition, an extremely quick and not entirely accurate précis was given by La Vallée Poussin (1929: 208–209). See also the summary and notes in Hiraoka (2002: 55–57).

6. Conjectural restitution suggested by the parallels noted by Speyer (1902: 125) in the *Avadānaśataka* at Speyer (1906–1909: I.285,17–286,2, and II.29,7–9).

7. Although not so unusual in this literature, the use of the imperfect *āsīt* here may imply that the father *used to* engage in trade and so on, but is now out of the picture.

8. The preceding paragraph is basically formulaic, the outline being found in more or less this form throughout Buddhist narrative literature.

9. Or "troubles" (*kleśa*), but certainly the reference here is sexual. We will find precisely the same vocabulary in a passage from the Utpalavarṇā story quoted below. (The use of *kilesa* in Pāli in a sexual sense is well known.)

10. With the implication that he is already married? In the *Kāmasūtra*'s discussion of the role of the go-between (*dūtī*), she is instructed to praise the (already married) woman's good qualities (5.4.4 [and 47]); see the translations in Daniélou (1994: 346); and Doniger and Kakar (2002: 116).

11. This, too, is a trope in the *Kāmasūtra*, in which in parallel we find the same persuasion directed at a woman (5.4.12; Sharma [1997]): *śr̥ṇu vicitram idaṁ subhage tvāṁ kila dr̥ṣṭvāmutrāsāv itthaṁ gotraputro nāyakaś cittonmādam anubhavati* I *prakr̥tyā sukumāraḥ kadācid anyatrāparikliṣṭapūrvas tapasvī* I *tato 'dhunā śakyam anena maraṇam apy anubhavitum iti varṇayet.* I am indebted to the translations of Daniélou (1994: 348) and Doniger and Kakar (2002: 116), but would nevertheless suggest the following: "Listen, lucky woman! This is something wonderful. That young lover over there, of good social position, went out of his mind as soon as he saw you. Since the miserable fellow is by nature a delicate boy and has never before suffered like this on account of anyone else, it is possible now that he may even end up dying of it."

12. As Zimmer understands, of upper garment and head covering.

13. Note that, as we would expect in ancient India, the merchant's wife is portrayed as illiterate. Almost the same scene is played out in a passage from the *Cīvaravastu* of the Mūlasarvāstivāda Vinaya (Dutt 1939–1959: iii.2.23,19–24,1; Raghu Vira and Lokesh Chandra 1974a: folio 801=244b10), in which a merchant sends word to his wife that he will shortly be home; see Ralston (1882: 91): *tena patnyādi saṁdiṣṭaṁ bhadre prāmodyam utpādaya : svastinā saṁpannārtho ham āgataḥ kitama..air divasair āgata eveti sā śrutvā vyathitā* . . . . The Tibetan translation reads (Derge Kanjur 1, *'dul ba, ga* 59a6–7): *des chung ma la bzang mo dga' ba skyed cig* I *kho bo don grub nas bde bar 'ongs te* I *zhag 'di tsam kho na phyin par 'ong ngo* II *spring ba des thos nas . . . snyam du phongs par.* Two points may be made here: First, what is perhaps implicit in the Sanskrit is made explicit in Tibetan, namely, the wife is said to "listen to the letter" (*spring ba=*lekha*; see Tshe ring dbang rgyal's dictionary in Bacot 1930: 105a1). Second, although Dutt read the last word in our quotation as *kathayati*, the manuscript and the Tibetan translation of *phongs pa* make clear that the correct reading is *vyathitā*, namely, that she was alarmed or distressed, and she did not speak but thought what follows.

14. This looks like a narrative interjection, since it is not quite clear who the "I" could be otherwise. The reading in Gilgit is: "Given over to lust as I am, there is no evil act which is forbidden, I say."

15. Literally, "learners and those without anything left to learn" (*śaikṣas* and *aśaikṣas*).

16. See Edgerton (1953 s.v. -jātīya [2]). The actual implication of the term *bodhisattvajātīyo bhikṣu* is not entirely clear to me, and my translation is little more than an evasion. Zimmer (1925: 77) translates: "ein Mönch, der war von der Art der Werdenden Buddhas." What is difficult to understand is that, as the text explicitly says just a few lines below, this monk *is* the bodhisattva, that is, a previous incarnation of the individual who will later become Śākyamuni. This suggests that *bodhisattvajātīyo bhikṣu* may indicate something like "a monk whose lineage is that of being a/the bodhisattva," "a monk who

stands in the birth-line, *jāti*, of Śākyamuni and is, perforce, a/the bodhisattva," or even "a bodhisattva by birth," which I believe amounts to precisely the same thing. In the *Bodhisattvāvadānakalpalatā*, studied below, the equivalent expression is *bodhisattvāṁśa bhikṣu*, with apparently an identical meaning.

17. Rules of training=*śikṣāpada*.

18. La Vallée Poussin (1929: 209–210) observes rather unsympathetically: "The story of Dharmaruci, not later than the second century A.D. at the latest, is one of the first testimonies of the Buddhist religion where it suffices to say 'Lord, Lord,' the religion, philosophically impoverished and in which works are useless, which consists in the incessant repetition of the name of Amitābha." In this I cannot agree with the great Belgian master. What the future Buddha advocates for the sinner Dharmaruci is not salvation through the repetition of the name of the Lord (much less that of Amitābha), but merely concentration on the three refuges. This does not strike me as innovative or in any way particularly noteworthy. To prevent further trouble, he seems willing to "ordain" Dharmaruci, but the Buddhist practice appropriate for the latter is the most basic and introductory available. In refusing to teach Dharmaruci the rules of training, it may be that he is in essence denying him true access to the monastic state and thus not ordaining him at all.

19. This is what he says at the beginning of the story. Being questioned about the meaning of this cryptic utterance, the Buddha narrates the three past stories that constitute the *Dharamarucy-avadāna*.

20. There do exist two recently discovered, very small manuscript fragments (in the Schøyen collection) that prove the existence of some elaborated version of the Mahādeva story in Sanskrit. However, the available text is so limited that little can be said at this time. I plan to publish an initial edition and preliminary study of these fragments in volume 4 of the series Buddhist Manuscripts in the Schøyen Collection.

21. Whether they have named him or renamed him depends, of course, on the relationship between the versions of the story in the *Vibhāṣā* and the *Divyāvadāna*, and on whether the source version known to the authors of the *Vibhāṣā* assigned a name to the protagonist. Thus, while this question is likely to remain unsolved and insoluble with certainty, I believe that the name "Mahādeva" was chosen specifically for the impressions it would be likely to evoke.

22. This conclusion will stand even should intermediate versions be discovered, in which, for instance, Mahādeva is presented in a more nuanced light. Such a discovery would not change the fact that the *Vibhāṣā* and other important sources have erased nuance.

23. This stance is not universal in all related versions of the basic story: the narration of Upagupta's reactions to the matricide monk in the **Aśokarājāvadāna* and **Aśokarājasūtra*, for instance, parallels the *Divyāvadāna*'s picture of the monastic community's rejection of the penitent criminal Dharmaruci.

24. As a comparative note, we may recall that *teshuvah* (repentance) is one of the central cornerstones of Jewish religious ideology; some, in fact, consider it the most basic religious attitude.

Chapter 8: Abuse and Victimhood

1. Schlesinger 1982: 22. For the older literature, see the survey in de Young (1985: 97–100, §§270–279).

2. I have omitted the fourth and final item, "(4) loss of control in one or more family members," since I have no idea what this means.

3. These and other ideas are suggested by Finkelhor (1979), summarized in de Young (1985: 91–92, §256). The conclusion in Frances and Frances (1976: 243)—"Because the male and female differ in how they participate in the processes of separation-individuation and Oedipal resolution, the incest taboo operates asymmetrically within the family and operates with greater strength in the mother-son than in father-daughter dyad"—seems to me dangerously close to being circular.

4. Frances and Frances 1976: 239.

5. Cited in Shepher 1983: 45.

6. Frances and Frances 1976: 240.

7. See Silk forthcoming a.

8. Although there is a vast gap between the formative periods of human cultures during which such patterns would have evolved and historical periods, it is nevertheless of interest to note that normative Indian texts stipulate that a girl should be married between three months to three years after her menarche. The rationale is that otherwise the father of an unmarried, and thus not pregnant although menstruating, girl would be guilty of the murder of her (unproduced) embryo. See Jamison 1996: 237–240.

9. There is a growing body of scholarship on the question of so-called royal incest, which may be an exception to this idea. The basic outlines of the logic of the problem have been sketched by van den Berghe and Mesher (1980: 304–305) as follows:

> In developing this argument [about royal incest as an attractive strategy for kings only under the condition of polygyny], we did not even mention the possibility of mother-son royal incest. The probability of such a strategy is extraordinarily low for four reasons. First, the odds against success are high, since the king's mother would be well along in her reproductive career by the time she could mate with her son. Obviously, a younger kinswoman is a far better bet for the king. Second, from the mother's viewpoint, the incentive to try for incestuous offspring is much less than for a king's sister or daughter. The king's mother has already hit the fitness jackpot by producing a son who is king, and who will, under a patrilineal system, produce a kingly grandson. By contrast, under patriliny the king's sister's or daughter's *only* chance of producing a king is by marrying her royal brother or father. Under patriliny, the king's mother's incentive to mate incestuously is thus no greater than is the king's sister's in a matrilineal system. With the near guarantee of her son producing a kingly grandson ($r=\frac{1}{4}$) on his own, the problematic production of a son-grandson with an $r=\frac{3}{4}$ is not an attractive bet. Should she still want to adopt the incestuous strategy, she would be better advised

to do it by proxy through a daughter who has a longer reproductive career ahead of her, and for whom the game has far better odds.

Two other reasons have been advanced for the lower probability of mother-son incest compared to father-daughter and sibling matings. One is the greater closeness of the mother-son bond in infancy and early childhood, a bond which more reliably produces sexual aversion. Fathers and daughters and siblings, especially if separated by several years of age, are typically in more distant contact. The other explanation of the differential frequency has to do with male dominance in initiating sexual (including incestuous) relationships. Where age dominance clearly reverses gender dominance, as in the mother-son relationship, the male is much less likely to assert himself sexually.

10. Lawson 1993: 264. For the points that follow, in addition to Lawson's study, see Banning (1989); Krug (1989); and Hetherton (1999).

11. Krug 1989: 117–118.

12. Hetherton 1999: 163.

13. It should be obvious that we can say absolutely nothing of actual social circumstances regarding issues such as child abuse—assuming we can clearly define it at all—in ancient India. Our sources simply do not permit it, no matter the hermeneutical tools we may choose to apply to the problem. Furthermore, we must approach with great caution and suspicion any suggestion that we may directly apply cross-culturally, much less to an ancient period, the results of recent research in North America or Europe.

14. We may notice that in one study of female sexual offenders (Matthews, Mathews, and Speltz 1991) the victims (most of whom are not the sons of the offenders, it should be emphasized) ranged from infants to late adolescents. This selection, however, may be an artifact of the scope of the reported research. I do not know of any relevant studies that break out the range of data we might like to compare.

15. De Young 1985: 92.

16. See Hetherton 1999: 168. Such studies also generally introduce serious class biases, since those wealthy and powerful enough to escape the social work, judicial, and public health networks remain invisible to researchers.

17. If we were pressed to locate in Buddhist thought a systematic rationale that might be brought to bear as an explanation for the evil character of a sinner, we would probably turn not to simple ideas of karma, but rather to particular notions regarding the individual who cuts off his "roots of goodness" (*kuśalamūla*), an act that some schools believe dooms one entirely, while others see it as a temporary but nevertheless delaying setback to spiritual progress.

18. See Tables 2 and 3 in Wisdom (1989); she does not address the correlation in the text of her article.

19. In a Canadian study by Dutton and Hart (1992), the isomorphic pattern was found to be dramatic: "physical abuse increased the odds for physical abuse in the family fivefold and abuse of strangers and non-family members twofold. Being a victim of sexual abuse increased the odds of committing sexual abuse against strangers fivefold and

within the family eightfold" (135). Wisdom (1989) and Dutton and Hart (1992) are also summarized in Raine (1993: 246–249). These studies, at least, make clear that sexual victims overall react less strongly than other victims The correlation between sexual abuse and violence toward strangers is 0.79, and toward family 2.47, while the correlation between any abuse suffered and any later violence is 2.99.

20. Boublil 2002. Some research on father absence during early childhood and the characteristics developed by boys later on suggests that one or more of the following may occur (Draper and Harpending [1982: 257]):

> rejection of authority, particularly when it is imposed by adult females; exaggerated masculinity (often regarded by psychologists as "overcompensation" for insecure masculine sex-role identification); rejection and denigration of femininity; greater interpersonal aggressiveness; increased risk of arrest and incarceration; and a relatively exploitative attitude toward females, with sexual contact appearing important as conquest and as a means of validating masculinity.

I have not reviewed the studies upon which this claim is based, but I expect that it would be extremely difficult to control for the multitude of factors that probably contribute to the characteristics listed, even if one could develop an objective typology by which to recognize them.

21. Nevertheless, it is worth noting that the absence of the father means that the mother's legitimate sexual outlet is absent and that the son's protector and role model is absent.

22. Even the fact that modern scholars and our ancient authors appear to agree in not recognizing a link between sexual abuse and later criminality should, especially since the evidence from the Indian side is the completely negative one of silence, not be judged probative in any way.

Chapter 9: Persian Perversities

1. The verse is found in Jātaka 65 (Fausbøll 1877–1896: i.302,3–4=Cowell et al. 1895–1907: i.161), Jātaka 536 (Fausbøll 1877–1896: v.446,1–2, and see 447,7–9=Cowell et al. 1895–1907: v.241), and in the *Dhammapada* commentary to XVIII.5 (H. C. Norman 1906–1914: iii.349,8–9=Burlingame 1921: iii.124). A variant of the last quarter reads: "They know no limits."

2. Fausbøll (1877–1896: i.302,5–16); DPG 70: 289.20–290.5.

3. Cowell and Neil 1886: 257.13–20.

4. I have discussed these materials in much greater detail in Silk (forthcoming a).

5. Derge Tanjur 4088, *mngon pa, i,* 192b7–193a6; Peking Tanjur 5589, *mdo 'grel, khu* 233a5–b5; sTog Kanjur 286, *mdo sde, ci* 302b4–303a5. I learned of the passage from Kasugai (1954), who quotes and translates most of it. Kasugai (1960) translates the passage into English, but with many errors.

6. *Vibhāṣā* T. 1545 (XXVII) 606a16–21 (*juan* 116). Translated in Kasugai (1960: 113); Kawasaki (1975: 1099); and Lindtner (1988: 440). The passage is quoted by Saeki

(1887: 685) and on this basis is referred to by La Vallée Poussin (1923–1931: iii.148, n. 1). This and several other relevant passages are quoted in Saitō (1998: 119–121).

7. Cited and translated in Lindtner 1988: 439, n. 18; and Kawasaki 1975: 1102, n. 2=Derge Tanjur 3856, *dbu ma*, *dza*, 281b3.

8. *Abhidharmakośabhāṣya* ad IV.68d (Pradhan 1975: 241.9–11); see La Vallée Poussin (1923–1931: iii.147–148).

9. Leavitt (1990: 973) looks at the issue from another perspective: "Institutional cases of incest are theoretically and evidentially more important to the question of incest avoidance because, unlike individual cases (which are reported in statistical rates or case studies), institutional cases are culturally legitimated behaviors. As such, they would appear to more readily challenge the notion that genotype structures for incest avoidance are violated only by rare individuals and deviant cases."

Chapter 10: The Bedtrick

1. Doniger 2000.
2. Desens 1994: 17, 142, 153 n. 21, cited by Doniger 2000: 76.
3. Larson 1993: 420; also cited in Doniger 2000: 77.
4. Larson 1993: 379–380.
5. Doniger 2000: 78–79.
6. Ibid.: 84.
7. Much feminist theory of incest, such as Bell (1993), appears to assume that the only, or at least the predominant, mode of incest is father-daughter. It then proceeds immediately to investigate this in terms of asymmetrical power relations: men are predatory, women victims. Without wishing to comment on the general applicability of such a critique, I may nevertheless remark that at least in fiction, which after all represents nothing other than imagination, other configurations do occur, and those might profitably be brought into the conversation. This can happen constructively only if prejudicial political agendas are set aside at the outset.
8. Doniger (2000: 173) reminds us of Shakespeare's "pitchy night" in *All's Well That Ends Well* IV.4. And as she says elsewhere (191): "Since, for humans, vision is the king of the senses, it is vision that must be stymied when a human is to be sexually flummoxed." See also her p. 441.
9. The question of the sense of smell is never alluded to anywhere in this story or in any other version I know. Although the human sense of smell is less acute than that of many other animals, it can nevertheless accurately distinguish between even close family members, and there is good evidence that sons of Dharmaruci's presumed age are able, other things being equal, to recognize mothers on the basis of odor, at least under experimental conditions; see Weisfeld et al. (2003); for a discussion of a possible mechanism through which such recognition takes place, see Penn and Potts (1998, 1999) and the literature cited there. Needless to say, use of perfumes or unguents makes olfactory identification impossible, and the circumstances of our story, while silent on this point, would certainly allow us to imagine that the mother perfumed herself.

10. This process follows a common pattern: the Buddha is frequently able to do what other monks cannot, to break the very rules he has established for others to follow. As one example, see the discussion of the Buddha's use of robes forbidden to other monks in Silk (2003a). On the perhaps unexpectedly complex question of whether the Buddha is to be considered a monk, see Silk (2002c).

11. Doniger 2000: 385. She has also offered (p. 469) a survey of what she, following Lévi-Strauss, calls the "mythemes" of the bedtrick, in the context of attempting a structural analysis. The defining mytheme, she suggests, is that "[t]he victim does not know the identity of the trickster during the sexual act." In the context of the well-known structuralist fascination with +/− dyads, she suggests, among a number of other possibilities, "[t]he trickster is incestuously related to the victim." Although I am not convinced of the utility of such structural analyses, our examples may be accommodated by Doniger's scheme.

12. Ibid.: 16: "One might think that this double-edged sword of a bedtrick played on one's spouse would be equally dangerous for husbands and for wives, but in the literature at large, far more bedtricks are engineered by wives than by husbands. In part, this is an example of the broader fictional bias that assumes that women fool men more often than they are fooled. In part, it results from the male authorship of our texts."

13. I quote the translation of Lightfoot (1999: 341–343, with critical edition); another translation is found in Stern (1992: 37–38). The story is repeated by other authors, for instance by Diogenes Laertius in his "Life of Periander" (*Lives of Philosophers* I.96), in considerably less detail. For more, see in addition to the mostly philological commentary by Lightfoot (1999: 482–489), the study (with French translation) in Puiggali (1983), and earlier, Radermacher (1942).

14. A few very cautious notes are given by Karttunen (1997: 285). For an introduction to some ideas about Greek and Roman influences on Indian arts, see the papers in Allchin et al. (1997). For a sketch of the evidence for diffusion of story westward from India, see Sedlar (1980: 99–106).

15. Lightfoot 1999: 297.

16. A survey of recent discoveries of Buddhist literature from the Northwest, including local compositions, appears in Salomon (1999).

17. The power-relations aspect of the definition of incest can be derived from reversing one of the Sanskrit technical terms for incest, *gurutalpagamana*; it is the violation of the domain of the guru that is objectionable. Other categories—for example, brother-sister—are subordinated to the primary one, as we will see later. It would seem that at least in the normative Indian legal tradition, the prime and paradigmatic violation is not parent-child, but student-teacher, although Goldman (1978) would argue that the reason for this is the strong taboo against even mention of familial incest relations.

18. Other Indian Buddhist stories of incest do mention children, but never, as far as I know, the problem of defective offspring. I owe thanks to Dominik Wujastyk for reference in this context to the Indian medical category of *kulajaroga*. He also draws attention to the discussion in *Carakasamhitā*, Śarīrasthāna III, on the formation of the fetus and on hereditary diseases.

19. It is one charm of the text that the parrot pretends to wholeheartedly approve of her intention to cheat on her husband, wishing only to educate her so that she may not be caught. His lessons in the end take such a long time each night that she is ever unable to actually carry out her intentions—precisely the parrot's aim all along.

Chapter 11: Retelling Dharmaruci's Story

1. See Silk (forthcoming b) for a re-edition and detailed treatment of this text, originally published in Das and Vidyābhūṣaṇa (1888–1918: II.802–821; the verse numbers are in brackets). Much remains to be done on this interesting and important work, not least in the area of the influence of the work's Tibetan translation and subsequent recastings on later Tibetan literature, on which see the short note by van der Kuijp (1996: 401–402). For a study of the Indian text and its history, see Mejor (1992); earlier Tucci (1949: 437–441), particularly regarding the influence of the work on Tibetan pictorial art; on this see also Rani (1977); note the recent bibliography, Kirde (2002). A prose version of our story is translated in Black (1997: 399–401); see Mejor (1992: 29–31). The relation between Kṣemendra's version of the *Dharmarucy-avadāna* and that in the *Divyāvadāna* was noted by Tucci (1949: 438), who provides a summary of the *avadāna* on pp. 522–524. For valuable suggestions, I am grateful to Martin Straube.

2. That is, the more wealth he has, the more he wants, just as one who drinks salt water craves more as he attempts to slake his thirst. This image is discussed below.

3. The sentiment has a remarkably suggestive cross-cultural parallel. In his study of the rabbinic interpretations of the story of Joseph and Potiphar, a topic I will examine in Chapter 16, James Kugel (1990: 44, translating *Genesis Rabbah* 87:6) mentions a remark found in the fifth- to sixth-century compendium of commentaries, *Genesis Rabbah*, which says of Joseph's reaction to the suggestions of Potiphar's wife that they have a sexual liaison: "He would not listen to her, to lie with her in this world, so that he not be with her in hell in the world to come."

4. Two images are joined here. The wanton woman engages in nonprocreative sex and thus rues her lack of children, but she is also saddened and made slightly paranoid by fear of rumors circulating about her.

5. A legendary fire created by the wrath of the sage Aurva; had it not been cast into the ocean it would have consumed the earth. A whirlpool constantly feeds it, yet it remains unextinguished. An example of the proverbial use of this undersea fire in a similar context is found in the *Nāradapañcarātra* 1.14.100, cited by Sternbach (1953: 82, §417): "The mind is not satisfied with [all that is] best, the undersea fire not with [all] the waters, the earth not with [all] the dirt, so a promiscuous woman (*kulaṭā*) is not satisfied with [all] men," *na śreyasāṁ manas tṛptaṁ vāḍavāgnir na pāthasām* । *vasuṁdharā na rajasāṁ na puṁsāṁ kulaṭā tathā* ॥.

6. The text then adds a colophon: "So runs the 89th sprig in the *Wish-granting Garland of Tales of the Bodhisattva* (*Bodhisattvāvadānakalpalatā*), the *Dharmarucy-avadāna*, composed by Kṣemendra."

7. On the word *vṛddhayuvati*, see the remarks in Silk (forthcoming b).

8. *Kāmasūtra* III.5.1–10.

9. The foster-sister is specifically said here to be acting as a go-between (*dūtī*); see *Kāmasūtra* III.5.10: *dūtīkalpaṁ ca sakalam ācaret.*

10. I calculate the length of the entire story as 230 lines in the edition of Cowell and Neil (1886), of which the seduction is covered in 40 lines (254.18–256.2).

11. Subversively reading between the lines, we may also detect the nurse's self-interest in retaining her own position.

12. Cowell and Neil 1886: 255.8: *yuktaṁ syād anyena manuṣyeṇa sārdhaṁ ratikrīḍām anubhavitum.*

13. The extremely close correspondence between the text of the *Dharmarucy-avadāna* transmitted in the perhaps fifth-century Gilgit manuscripts and the probably nineteenth-century Nepalese *Divyāvadāna* manuscripts demonstrates the stability of the text over time, and thus the likelihood that the version of the *Divyāvadāna Dharmarucy-avadāna* known to Kṣemendra in the eleventh century and upon which he based his retelling closely approximated that known to us today.

14. We note another apparent incoherence in verse 156, in which the mother both changes clothes with the boy *and* stays with him until morning in order to reveal herself. Unless the poem is acutely abbreviated here, with the whole scene of the son's discovery of his mother wearing his clothes elided (in which case we could hardy follow it, if we did not already know the story from the *Divyāvadāna*), the change of clothes makes no sense if the mother stays until dawn when her son can see her in the flesh.

15. In both cases the word for "virtue" is *śīla*, which quite clearly has nothing of its Buddhist technical sense here.

16. On the equation of promiscuity with animal behavior, see Chapter 19.

17. One final point we might make about these versions of the story is that the sexual relationship between mother and son is, although certainly not condoned, also not characterized in either text by noticeably obscene or lewd vocabulary. Such vocabulary is, however, very rare in the Sanskrit literature that has come down to us, so its absence may be of no special significance. On the notion of obscenity in Sanskrit poetics, see Masson-Moussaieff (1971).

Chapter 12: Dharmaruci in Other Sources

1. Other materials are potentially but less obviously related. For example, there is a peculiar pair of famous and controversial verses found in the *Dharmapada* corpus that refer to patricide and matricide, though not to incest; see Pāli *Dhammapada* 294–295, Patna *Dharmapada* 47, *Udānavarga* 33.61 [=29.24] and 33.62, and Gāndhārī *Dharmapada* 12. An extensive list of parallels is found in Mizuno (1991: 38). See Bernhard (1967). The verses might be rendered: "Having killed mother and father, and two warrior kings, having destroyed the kingdom along with its followers, a brahmin courses unconcerned. Having killed mother and father, and two kings learned in the Veda, and having killed a tiger as the fifth, a brahmin courses unconcerned." Regarding this, see Prajñāvarman's *Udānavargavivaraṇa* commentary (*ad Udānavarga* 29.24, Derge Tanjur 4100, edited in

Balk 1984: ii.824–825); a translation, somewhat modified from Rockhill (1892: 210), says: "There lived in a certain mountainous district a very daring man who desired to become king. He lovelessly put to death his father and mother, the king, two pure Brahmans, and a great many inhabitants of the country, and then made himself king. Then he thought, 'I will go before the Blessed One and question him; if he approves of my conduct, I will be glad, and will not destroy monasteries and the like, but on the contrary I will do him many good services.' And this [verse in question] was thus spoken. He heard it and deeply believed, and became a great householder." Intriguing, if nothing else, is that the criminal here makes a threat to destroy monasteries after committing both patricide and matricide, which cannot help but remind us of Mahādeva's monastery arsons.

2. The text is contained in the *Guan Xukongzang pusa jing*, T. 409 (XIII) 680a10–27 and elsewhere. See Silk (forthcoming d) for a detailed study of this text.

3. T. 374 (XII) 479a21–b2 (*juan* 19)=T. 375 (XII) 722a24–b5 (*juan* 17). The only reference I have seen to this story in the context of the Mahādeva story is in Katō (1950: 39). For the Tibetan translation of this passage, from Chinese and agreeing very closely with it, see Derge Kanjur 119: *mdo sde, nya*, 309b6–10a3. My translation is from the Chinese.

4. The reading may be reconstructed following Pulleyblank (1991) ? ajitta, modern reading *āyìduō.*

5. There are also some interesting parallels with the story cited from the *Hōbutsu-shū*, the author of which could have known the Mahāyāna *Mahāparinirvāṇa-sūtra* and certainly did know the *Konjaku.*

6. T. 374 (XII) 566c6–9 (*juan* 34)=T. 375 (XII) 813a28–b2 (*juan* 31). For the Tibetan translation, see Derge Kanjur 119: *mdo sde, ta*, 203a5–7.

7. This is an interesting hypothesis, since in light of the well-established Mūlasarvāstivāda identification of the *Divyāvadāna* it might suggest Mūlasarvāstivāda influence on the *Mahāparinirvāṇa-sūtra* in the fourth century, either in India or in the course of transmission of the scripture eastward toward China.

8. For notes on the legend, see Lamotte (1944–1980: i.248–249, n. 2). Placing Śākyamuni's aspiration to awakening in the time of Dīpaṅkara acknowledges that Śākyamuni himself did not reign as buddha in our world at the beginning of this great cycle of time, while still grounding him in that mythical time of origins. This solves an unexpressed problem for the tradition: our Buddha must be the best of all buddhas, but he is not the first individual to become a buddha in our world, nor will he be the last (since the future buddha Maitreya will succeed him). But since he is *our* buddha, he must be the *best* buddha, and if he is the best, he must also be the first. Different traditions deal with this problem in different ways, but one of the strategies, seen here, is to place Śākyamuni at the beginning as a bodhisattva, a buddha-to-be, thus preserving both his universally acknowledged place as the buddha of our time and also his presence at the founding moment of the Buddhist tradition in the paradigmatic mythical past.

9. Senart (1882–1897: I.243.18–246.12); Yuyama (2001: 35–36, folios 70a5–71a6). I have largely followed the rendering of Jones (1949: I.199–202), but with a number of modifications. The resemblance of this story to Mahādeva's is so striking that it is difficult

to understand why it has not previously been adduced in discussions of the Mahāsāṁghika-Sthavira schism. While its similarity to the story of Dharmaruci in the *Divyāvadāna* was mentioned by Lamotte (1944–1980: i.410, n. 1), and much earlier, although very briefly, by Serge D'Oldenburg (see Wenzel 1893: 335), Lamotte was nevertheless less interested in this episode than in the subsequent story of Dharmaruci. Lamotte also quoted a portion of the *Apadāna* account cited below. Considering Lamotte's interest in both the Mahādeva stories and the Dharmaruci cycle, his failure to make a connection between the two here is puzzling.

10. *kāle vā vikāle vā*. Perhaps Edgerton (1953 s.v. *vikāla*) is right to take the word *vikāla* in the sense of "wrong time," or "out of season," rather than in the classical Sanskrit sense of "evening." Jones renders "early and late," and this too may be acceptable if we understand it as equivalent to "at any old time." Another possibility is that it refers to times appropriate and inappropriate for intercourse, meaning that Meghadatta had intercourse with the woman even at impermissible times.

11. The syntax here is still not entirely clear to me, but I owe thanks to Lance Cousins (email communication, Nov. 9, 1994) for a helpful observation on this passage; see also Senart's note (1882–1897: I.563).

12. The fluctuation in the spelling of this name is not significant; I follow the printed edition.

13. I mean "confused" only from the point of view of the parallel tale, not objectively speaking.

14. Here as elsewhere I do not intend to imply that shorter versions are "simplified" in the sense that they are the result of pruning an originally longer version. I use such expressions merely to indicate relative complexity and detail, without any implication of logical or chronological priority.

15. Müller (1895: 169), and in detail in (1896).

16. See also Barth (1899: 625 = 36 of the reprint), and cf. Bechert (1958: 19, with n. 56).

17. The Dhammaruci story is found in the *Apadāna* as number 486 in the Pali Text Society (henceforth PTS) edition, in Kashyap's (1959) edition 489 = 49.9 = verses 164–189 (pp. 66–67). The printed texts of the *Apadāna* are famously bad. I have consulted the PTS edition (Lilley 1927: 429–431); Kashyap (1959); Müller (1896: 55–56); and DPG 58. I translate what I consider to be a reliable text, but have not taken into account the multiple variants, which may or may not actually reflect real manuscript traditions. A partial translation of this episode is found in Lamotte (1944–1980: i.411–412). The later *Apadāna* commentary *Visuddhajanavilāsinī* also refers to the tale; see Godakumbura (1954: 489.1–14), and the slightly different readings in DPG 65: 209–210.

18. I am not sure about *saṁvissaṭṭho*, but probably it is related to Sanskrit *saṁviśvasta*, on which see Edgerton (1953 s.v.).

19. Since what may well have been the ultimate source of the Dharmaruci story complex, perhaps in a Vinaya tradition, has so far not been identified, we can say nothing of any putative "original" context.

20. Cowell and Neil (1886: 228.22–233.20).

21. Although the editors print *timiṅgila*, the edition reports (229, n. 4) the manuscripts as reading *timiṅgala*, which is also the reading found in the Gilgit manuscript (or *timiṅgāla*; Raghu Vira and Lokesh Chandra (1974b, folio 1375.3); at 1456.1 we have *timiṁgilagila*, and in l. 8 *///mitimiṁgala*).

22. Cowell and Neil 1886: 231.21–232.9; translated in Zimmer (1925: 7–9).

23. Cowell and Neil 1886: 233.11–12: *punar bhagavatā sa nādas tathādhiṣṭhito yathā tena timiṅgilena śrutam.*

24. A similar, although interestingly different, example occurs in the *Cīvaravastu* of the Mūlasarvāstivāda Vinaya, in the story of a childless man (importantly, although he has no children at all, the text emphasizes that he has no son, which is to say, no heir). In search of a son the man entreats a host of gods, beginning with Śiva, Varuṇa, Kubera, Śakra, and Brahmā, and going on to various minor gods, such as gods of parks, forests, crossroads, and so on. Being unable, despite these prayers, to sire any children at all, the man "repudiating all gods, placed his faith in the Blessed One"; Dutt (1939–1959: iii.2.136, 9–10, 20), the last *sarvadevatāḥ pratyākhyāya bhagavaty abhiprasannaḥ*. The text is translated in Schopen (1995: 498).

25. See Lamotte (1944–1980: i.410–414), translating *Da Zhidu lun* T. 1508 (XXV) 109a13–25 (*juan* 7), with as usual copious references in the notes. For examples, see the stories in the *Ekottarikāgama* T. 125 (II) (20.3) 597a22–599c4 (*juan* 11), and the *Fenbie gongde lun* (T. 1507 [XXV] 45b9–c9 [*juan* 4]), parallel to the version in the *Divyāvadāna* (Cowell and Neil 1886: 246.5–254.2). See also the **Mahākaruṇāpuṇḍarīka*, T. 380 (XII) 957b11–c16 (*juan* 3) = Derge Kanjur 111 (*mdo sde, cha* 89b4–90b3). There *mójié(dà)yú*, a standard transcription + classifier of *makara*, is equivalent to Tibetan *chu srin*. Reference to the story found here appears elsewhere. Vasubandhu's *Vyākhyāyukti* (whence quoted in Bu ston's *Chos 'byung*) mentions the story of Dharmaruci who, when he was reborn as a sea monster, upon hearing the mere name of the Buddha kept his mouth closed (and did not eat the shipwrecked sailors cast into the sea), because he was formerly accustomed to reverence the Buddha. The text reads (Jong Cheol Lee 2001: 279 = Derge Tanjur 4061, *sems tsam, shi* 123b4–5; quoted by Bu ston, see Lokesh Chandra 1971: 31b2–3 [694]): *chos dga' chu srin du gyur pa na* | *sangs rgyas kyi sgra tsam zhig thos pa las sngon* phyag 'tshal ba** tsam la goms pa'i phyir kha btsums te 'dug pa yin no* || (* B *mngon*, ** B omits *ba*). This passage was translated in Obermiller (1931–1932: I.81–82), who restored the name Chos dga' as Dharmananda, but in light of the parallels, this is almost certainly to be corrected to *Dharmaruci.

26. The medallion in question (with a total height of 51 cm) is now kept in Varanasi (Benares) in the Bharat Kala Bhavan. Apparently the first published photograph is that found in Sircar (1961); earlier only a drawing was available, in Cunningham (1879: plate XXXIV.2). While the inscription informs us that the depicted sea creature is a *timitimiṅgila*, it is fair to say that it is indistinguishable from the *makara* seen in other Bhārhut medallions; see those illustrated in Ghosh (1978, plates XIXa, b, c). As Ghosh has written (1978: 74–75, concerning his illustration a; more or less similar are b and c):

> The mythical creature is represented as having an elephant's scalp to which a crocodile's snout with parted jaws set with peg-like crocodile teeth has been engrafted. Its body resembles that of a fish and is covered with scales, but the tail is coiled like that of a serpent. It has elephantine forelegs and fish-like pectoral and tail fins. The upper jaw is curbed [*sic*] upwards to form an incipient proboscis, but not the long trunk of the elephant.

The *timitimiṅgila* has also been discussed by Hora (1955: 10–12), although his suggestion of an identification with the whale shark, *Rhineodon typus*, is to be disregarded. Whatever the origins of the creature, most likely the crocodile (and according to Gail Maxwell of the Los Angeles County Museum of Art, originally the *Gavialis gangeticus*), after a time it is merely understood as a generic ferocious sea creature; cf. also Hora and Saraswati (1955). As pointed out already long ago (Barua and Sinha 1926: 62), *timi*, *timiṅgila*, and *timitimiṅgila* are said to be creatures of progressively increasing size, each of which is capable of consuming the former.

27. The inscription reads: *timitimi*[*ṁ*]*gila-kuchimhā V*[*a*]*su*[*gu*]*t*[*o*] *m*[*o*]*cito Mahādev*[*e*]*naṁ*. I thank Gregory Schopen for his help in rereading the inscription from rubbings and photographs; for the photographs, I thank Sonya Quintanilla for her generosity. For the most part I follow the reading and understanding of Sircar (1961: 207), taken into account in Lüders (1963: viiic and 155–158 [B 62]), which see for other references. Earlier readings and sometimes very different interpretations of the inscription are to be found in Cunningham (1879: 142 [#66]), Hultzsch (1886: 76 [#156]), Barua and Sinha (1926: 61–62); see also Barua (1934: 78–81). The translation is that of Lüders (1963: 156).

28. I frame the expression thus since there are considerable paleographical and other issues here as well.

29. See Lüders (1941: 73–79≈1963: 156–158).

30. Lüders (1963: 158) says Mahādeva "is clearly the same person, who in a different inscription . . . receives the attribute '*bhagavat*.' Thus it must be the name of the Buddha." The inscription to which Lüders refers is his B 81 (p. 180), which reads: *(ba)huhathika āsana (bhaga)vato mahādevasa* (The seat Bahuhathika of the Blessed One Mahādeva). Concerning this, Lüders says "Bhagavat Mahādeva to whom the stone seat is here ascribed can scarcely be someone else than the historical Buddha. . . ." Hultzsch (1886: 76, n. 2) was apparently the first to suggest that Mahādeva refers to the Buddha (or as he says, Mahāsatta or Bodhisatta), referring to this inscription.

31. Lüders 1963: 158. The Chinese *dàshén* is given as equivalent to *mahādeva* in *Mahāvyutpatti* §3582, although this is a quite late Chinese equivalent. A much earlier example of the use of *dàshén* to refer to the Buddha is found in the *Xuanyan ji*, an entirely Chinese work of the literatus Liu Yiching (403–444), author of the famous *Shishuo xinyu* ("A New Account of Tales of the World," in Richard Mather's translation). The passage is quoted in the *Bianzheng lun* of Falin (T. 2110 [LII] 540b3), translated by Gjertson (1981: 297), and slightly differently in (1989: 21). Since this is by no means even a reflex of any Indian text, I leave it out of consideration here. It may be that there are one or two such usages in texts that may rightly be considered translations of Indic originals, but if so, they are rarities.

32. T. 207 (IV) (30) 529a18–b8, a fifth-century Chinese translation. The text was translated by Chavannes (1910–1911: ii.51–52 [#186]).

33. John Strong (private communication) makes the intriguing suggestion that *mahādeva* here is to be understood in a comparative sense: everyone else appeals to his respective god, *deva*, but the Buddhist trumps them all by claiming access to a "great god," *mahādeva*, the Buddha.

34. The issue of the gap between the visual evidence on the Bhārhut stūpa and extant Buddhist literature requires a brief comment. There are many examples at Bhārhut of narratives for which we have, at best, only very uncertain textual evidence. Such narrative illustrations are often claimed to represent "local" traditions, as if there were some fundamental typological difference between stories that have managed to circulate widely or have been recorded in some surviving textual source and those that have not. I find this putative distinction problematic. To mention only one objection, it is well known that the record we have of the Indian Buddhist textual tradition (treating this complex as a unity for the moment) is drastically partial—in fact, it is so incomplete that we can hardly even sense how fragmentary it truly is. From this perspective, to state that some narrative illustration at Bhārhut appears to depict a story unknown elsewhere is to state no more than that our extant written textual record does not duplicate the "textual record" we find recorded on the stones of the stūpa in visual form. When, as in the present case, an illustration is accompanied by an inscription that labels its contents, this may be able to confirm a suggested identification with a written tradition, point us toward some written narrative, or, as here, suggest that we should hesitate to identify the depicted scene precisely with any known story. How we treat this evidence in concert with our written literary sources will depend on what sorts of conclusions we hope to be able to draw, but just as surely as we cannot forge links where none exist, we likewise cannot dismiss evidence simply because its form is not written on palm leaf or paper. The crucial question in cases like the present one is whether the evidence we have is evidence relevant to the problem with which we wish to associate it, or whether, more cautiously, we must content ourselves with an indication of superficial points of similarity and stop there. The present example most probably belongs in the latter category.

Chapter 13: Incest in Indian Buddhist Culture

1. Mair (1986: 19) states that "students of folklore have correctly pointed out striking similarities between this story [of Mahādeva from the *Vibhāṣā* and its dependent accounts] and the Oedipus myth," but I regret that I am not aware of any such published remarks.

2. To be sure, such things are not found only in Buddhist literature. For instance, in one Jaina text we find an interesting, although obscure, reference to father-daughter incest. Alsdorf (1965: 24; and 1980: 21) refers to a story from the *Uttarajjhayaṇa-Nijjutti* 137, 138 (not available to me), in which the following verse is found: "*nava māsa ku(c)hīe dhāliyā pāsavaṇe pulise ya maddie* | *dhūyāē gehiē haḍē salaṇaē asalaṇaē ya jāyae* ||." On the basis of Alsdorf's French and German renderings, I understand: "For nine months I

carried her in my breast, / I wiped up her urine and excrement / my daughter has stolen my husband / what should have been my refuge has become my non-refuge." No doubt there are many stories in Jaina literature that would draw our attention in this regard; see Granoff (1994) and the remarks below on the story of Utpalavarṇā.

Notice that the stories in Bhayani (1994) seem to be only marginally Oedipal or Oedipal in another sense: a son kills his father, but not in order to possess his mother. Other Indian materials are discussed by Goldman (1978), to whose work I will return below. See also the materials collected by Doniger (1975: 25–26; 29–31; 33–35), although at least the passage in *Bṛhadāraṇyaka Upaniṣad* 1.4.3–4 is Oedipal only in a rather abstract way. For Prajāpati's incest with his daughter Uṣas, see Jamison (1991: 289–303).

I owe to Ms. Lilian Handlin a reference to two Pāli Jātakas that contain the only South Asian Buddhist literary references to father-daughter incest that I know, although here the father only pretends to importune his daughter in order to satisfy himself as to her chastity. The two stories, the *Paṇṇika-Jātaka* (§102) and the *Seggu-Jātaka* (§217), are almost identical in the relevant particulars, see Fausbøll (1877–1896: i.411–412, ii.179–180), translated in Cowell et al. (1895–1907: i.244–245, ii.126). A lay devotee greengrocer has a lovely and virtuous daughter, but she was given to laughing or smiling such that he wonders about her virginity. In order to test her, he takes her to a forest and "as if bent on lust, speaking secret words to her took her hand," according to one version (Fausbøll 1877–1896: i.411.17–18: *kilesanissito viya hutvā rahassakathaṁ kathetvā taṁ hatthe gaṇhi*), while in the other "he took her hand as if he lustfully desired her" (ibid.: ii.179.27–180.10: *kilesavasena icchanto viya hatthe gaṇhi*). In both cases the girl wails and protests, at which point her father confesses his desire to certify her virginity (*komārika, kumārikādhamma*—on the latter word, see Cone 2001: 712, s.v. kumārika and kumārikādhamma). In one she answers, "I am, father, [a virgin]; I have looked upon no man with lust" (Fausbøll 1877–1896: i.411.22–23: *āma tāta atthi mayā hi lobhavasena na koci puriso olokitapubbo*), while in the other she says, "I am indeed a virgin, father, and I know nothing of the ways of sexual love" (ibid.: ii.180.15–16: *āma tāta kumārikā yevāhaṁ nāhaṁ methunadhammaṁ nāma jānāmi*). For a discussion of the correct reading a few lines before, see Cone (2001: 712a, s.v. kumārika). Her father is satisfied and consents to give her in marriage without fear that any ill repute will come to his family from the match.

3. Filliozat (1971) refers to *Caṇḍamahāroṣaṇatantra*, IV.18–19; see George (1974: 23–24; 59). La Vallée Poussin apparently referred to this or something like it when, in his discussion of "Tantrism" in the *Encyclopedia of Religion and Ethics*, he wrote (quoted by George [1974: 3]): "The most conspicuous topic of this literature is what is called the *strīpūjā*, worship of women: disgusting practices both obscene and criminal, including incest, are part of this *pūjā*, which is looked upon as the true 'heroic behavior' (*duḥkharacharya*) of a *bodhisattva*, and the fulfillment of the perfect virtues." Compare also the passage from the Tibetan Rdzogs chen text *Sangs rgyas rdo rje sems dpa'i dgos pa Kun grol yangs pa'i rgyud*, "discovered" by Rig 'dzin Rgod kyi ldem phru can (1337–1408) and translated by Kapstein (1992: 244; text in n. 17 on p. 266): "The wide-open universal ground is dharmakāya-as-mother, and uncontrived awareness is dharmakāya-as-son. If

the son's mnemic engagement is not lost, then, meeting with the mother, bliss is won," *kun gzhi yangs pa chos sku'i ma* || *bcos med rig pa cho sku'i bu* || *bu yi dran pa ma shor na* || *ma dang 'phrad nas bde ba thob* ||. The key expression is *ma dang 'phrad nas*; Jäschke (1881: 359a, s.v. 'phrad pa) translates the expression *sngar nga dang phrad pa'i 'og tu* as "not until they have met me (sensu obscoeno)."

4. I refer to chapter 5 of the *Guhyasamājatantra*, verses 5–6, in Matsunaga (1978: 15); and see a translation in Snellgrove (1987: 171):

mātṛbhaginīputrīś ca kāmayed yas tu sādhakaḥ |
*sa siddhiṁ vipulāṁ gacchen mahāyānāgradharmeṣu** ||
mātaraṁ buddhasya vibhoḥ kāmayan na ca lipyate |
sidhyate tasya buddhatvaṁ nirvikalpasya dhīmataḥ ||

* I follow Matsunaga (2000: 26, n. 4, and the readings in 1978: 15, n. 27), in preference to the edition's °*dharmatām*.

5. For other reasons I leave entirely out of consideration such passages as the often-cited *Abhidharmakośabhāṣya ad Abhidharmakośa* III.15 (and see *Yogācārabhūmi*, Bhattacharya [1957: 23.3ff.]), in which reference is made to the fetus's Oedipal hatred of the parent of the opposite sex. This surely requires separate treatment, but of a rather more informed sort than that in Obeyesekere (1990: 163–167).

My suggestion of a separate treatment appropriate to Tantric materials is unrelated to chronology. I in no way assume such Tantric texts to be later than those non-Tantric materials with which we are concerned. Incidentally, although the *Jifayue sheku tuoluoni jing* contains a "magic spell," there is nothing Tantric about it—it belongs to an entirely conventional Mahāyāna scriptural genre.

6. *Aṅguttara-Nikāya*, V (Pañcaka-Nipāta), 6 (Nīvaraṇa-Vagga), 55 (Mātāputtā). Morris and Hardy (1885–1900: iii.67,17–68,8) = DPG 37: 62–63. The translation is a modified version of Hare (1934: 55). The commentary *Manorathapūraṇī* mentions nothing about this story. Although they do not mention this passage, Fišer (1993); Sugimoto (1993); and Fukunaga (1990: 299–320) contain some of the few serious considerations of sexual discussions in Pāli literature. See also the detailed but rather humorless discussion of the first *pārājika* in Hirakawa (1993: 139–207).

7. I translate with "opportunity for corruption" the word Hare renders "amorousness." *A Critical Pāli Dictionary* s.v. otāra (Trenckner et al. 1924–: 716) has under meanings 3 b and c the definitions "opportunity, chance (for attack), a weak spot, moral weakness," and the like. However, for definition 4, under which the present passage is classified, the editors suggest: "fixing upon (in a psychological sense), hence: affection, infatuation (rare)." They also note that exactly the same stock phrase is found in the Vinaya (Oldenberg 1897–1883: v.132,24–26), where Horner (1938–1966: vi.212) has rendered simply "desire." I am not convinced, however, that the meanings suggested under definition 4 are any more defensible than those under 3 b and c. That is, the logic that companionship and intimacy lead to opportunities for moral lassitude is quite as easy (if not easier) to understand (for me, anyway) as the idea that they lead to infatuation. Note that the only

other passage cited by the *Critical Pāli Dictionary* in this context is Buddhaghosa's interpretation of *Mahāparinibbāna-sutta* 5.9 (*Dīgha-Nikāya* ii.141.15, commentary in *Sumaṅgalavilāsinī*, Rhys Davids, Carpenter, and Stede 1886–1932: ii.583.3–5=DPG 5: 156.10–12), which has almost precisely the same sequence, as follows: *mātugāmena pana ālāpasallāpe* sati vissāso hoti, vissāse sati otāro hoti, otiṇṇacitto sīlavyasanaṁ patvā apāyapūrako hoti* (*the PTS text has *ālāpe* for *ālāpasallāpe*). The point seems to be that conversation with women leads to intimacy, and that such intimacy in turn leads to opportunities for sexual liaison, that is, to violate the disciplinary rule. In the examples cited by the *Critical Pāli Dictionary* under definition 2 b for the past participle *otiṇṇa*, at least that from Vin. iii.120,33, seems, once again, to possibly support this interpretation.

8. In light of note 7, it may be better to translate *otiṇṇacitto* significantly more strongly here as "with minds opened to corruption," rather than simply following the interpretation of the *Critical Pāli Dictionary* (Trenckner et al. 1924–) s.v. otiṇṇa.

9. Here is repeated the above description verbatim.

10. *Paramatthajotikā* II, *ad Sutta-Nipāta* 207 (*Munisutta*). Smith (1916–1918: i.254,11–255,7); DPG 54: 214,3–18. On the authorship of this commentary, see von Hinüber (1996: 129–130, §255–259). This passage is mentioned briefly by Oikawa (2002: 70–71).

11. Oikawa (2002: 71) writes, "They built a bad reputation and returned to a secular life." The key expression here is *agāramajjhe vasiṁsu*; I follow the definition in the *Critical Pāli Dictionary* (Trenckner et al. 1924–) I.16a.

12. The verse is found also in the Pāli *Jātaka* (Fausbøll 1877–1896: iv.118,22–23) in a variant form:

> *visaṁ yathā halāhalaṃ telaṁ ukkaṭṭhitaṁ* yathā* |
> *tambalohavilīnaṁ va kāmā dukkhatarā tato* ||

*The spelling of this word fluctuates; forms include *pakkutthita*, *ukkathita*, *ukkatthita*, *ukkuttika*, *pakkudhita*, and perhaps others.

13. *Aṅguttara-Nikāya* V.6.55 (Morris and Hardy 1885–1900: iii.68.28–30): *mātugāmaṁ yeva sammā vadamāno vadeyya samantapāso mārassā ti.*

14. One may, for convenience, consult Wilson (1996) and Sponberg (1992), although both require considerable reevaluation.

15. This may be something of what was intended in the brief comment of Liz Wilson (1996: 202, n. 37), who in her study of "horrific figurations of the feminine" remarked on this passage: "As a biological instinct, sexual desire can lead to such antisocial behavior as incest."

16. I. B. Horner (1930: 276–277), in reference to this *sutta*, said the following: "A record of the incestuous behavior of an almswoman and an almsman, mother and son, who had both been keeping Vassa at Sāvatthi, appears in the Anguttara; it is the occasion of a long discourse by Gotama on the fascinating chains held by women to bind men. Had the incident been set down in the Vinaya, a rule prohibiting the immediately preceding circumstances would have been made but not one forbidding the thing itself." When Sponberg (1992: 20) cites the text, he entirely ignores the prior section that refers to the incest.

17. We should recall here what has been called the "quicksand" analogy. Frequent mention of quicksand and its dangers in literature of the American West does not translate into a corresponding frequency of genuine encounters in the real American West. The hold that certain topics have on the imagination determines the frequency of their appearance, and thus the frequency with which mother-son incest actually occurs need bear no necessary relation to the frequency with which it is depicted—although the *imagining* of the act itself and the frequency with which *this* takes place *is* significant. The corollary is true as well: a paucity of references does not prove the rarity of a phenomenon, but only a lack of interest or awareness, a fact to which modern feminist and subaltern studies have in some respects sensitized us.

18. Nevertheless, we may note that this commentary does provide a rationale for the initial ordination of the pair, which seems to have nothing to do with religious intention and everything to do with the fact that the family was deprived of its breadwinner. It also paints a believable picture of their daily contact, their sharing the alms they receive, and, essentially, gossiping, but it goes no further than does the *Aṅguttara* toward explaining how mother and son might actually fall into a sexual relationship.

19. The absence of a Chinese translation is not significant; large portions of the *Aṅguttara-Nikāya* in particular have no parallels in Chinese.

20. Obeyesekere 1990: 162. Notice in this regard also the tale in Parker 1914: 193–199, "The Wax Horse."

21. Twitchell 1987: xiii.

22. Leavitt 1990: 984, n. 1.

23. The general cultural background justifying this is found not only in Brahmanical literature, but in Buddhist as well. Thus, for instance, while we read in the *Mahāvastu* (Senart 1882–1897: III.265,17–18, translated in Jones 1949–1956: 3.254): "Women will come, my son, who are venerable, gracious and beautiful, to make obeisance to the Exalted One, and these, my son, you must regard as you would your mother," in the *Saṃyutta-Nikāya* (iv.110–111 = 35.127[4], Bhāradvāja) we find the Buddha saying (Bodhi 2000: 1197): "Come, bhikkhus, toward women old enough to be your mother set up the idea that they are your mother; toward those of an age to be your sisters set up the idea that they are your sisters; towards those young enough to be your daughters set up the idea that they are your daughters." The commentary *Sāratthappakāsinī* in DPG 31: 39.20–21 specifies that it is not permissible to have thoughts of attraction to any of these three worthies. Precisely the same statement as that in the *Saṃyutta-Nikāya* is also found in the Chinese *Sūtra in 42 Sections*; see Sharf (1996: 368, §27).

24. For details on this story and a cross-cultural comparison with the biblical story of Abraham and Sarah and its Jewish exegesis, see Silk (2008d).

25. We may note also the rather odd story of the origin of the influential Licchavi clan, namely, that its founders are brother and sister, married to each other. However, these twins are born as a single lump of meat, which subsequently divides itself. After abandonment by the queen of Benares, this lump is found by an ascetic, who cares for the twins, before passing them on to some cowherds. When entrusting them, he stipulates that they are to be married to each other, and this is indeed what transpires. For a

translation of the story from the *Papañcasūdanī*, commentary to the *Majjhima-Nikāya*, see Deeg (2004: 128–131).

26. Rhys Davids and Carpenter 1890–1911: i.92,21–22 (III.1.16): *te jātisambheda-bhayā sakāhi bhaginīhi saddhiṁ saṁvāsaṁ kappesuṁ*, [27–29:] . . . *kappenti.*

27. The expression *sadṛśāt kulāt kalatram ānītam* is common in the *Divyāvadāna* and elsewhere; see Hiraoka (2002: 157). For the Pāli *Jātaka*, see Fick (1920: 52).

28. Rhys Davids and Carpenter 1886: i.260.15–19=DPG 4: 210.14–17. Cf. the translation in Thomas (1949: 8), with which I disagree on several points. Note, however, his remarks on the parallels with the *Rāmāyaṇa* on pp. 10–12.

29. T. 1 (20) (I) 82c22–83a4 (*juan* 13), translated by Sueki Fumihiko in Okayama et al. (2001: 157–158). Cf. T. 20 (I) 260a25ff. This belongs to the Dharmaguptaka sect.

30. T. 1 (20) (I) 83a1–2 (*juan* 13).

31. For details on this reading, see Silk 2008d.

32. Sanskrit in Gnoli (1977: 29.19–31.1), the corresponding Tibetan in Derge Kanjur 1, *'dul ba, ga* 271a–272a7; sTog Kanjur 1, *'dul ba, ga* 372b3–373a3. In Chinese the same is found in T. 1450 (XXIV) 104b18–c16 (*juan* 2) and T. 191 (III) 937a22–b10 (*juan* 2), both renderings of the *Saṁghabhedavastu*. This story is repeated in the Tibetan *Abhiniṣkramaṇa-sūtra*, a sūtra entirely distinct from the scripture of the same name preserved in Chinese; the wording is identical with that in the corresponding portion of the Tibetan translation of the *Saṁghabhedavastu* (Derge 301, *mdo sde, sa*, 121a3–122a1; where I have omitted a few lines from the *Saṁghabhedavastu* text=Gnoli [30.3–16], the text in the corresponding *Abhiniṣkramaṇa-sūtra* is continuous; that is, it omits precisely the material I have skipped). For an outline of the Tibetan *Abhiniṣkramaṇa-sūtra*, and a few remarks on its relation to the *Saṁghabhedavastu*, see Matsuda (1990). Csoma (1833) is based on this sūtra, and his paraphrase of the present episode is found on p. 33.

33. T. 1450 (XXIV) 104b24–25 (*juan* 2): "We are young yet have no wives; day and night we suffer—how could we not be gaunt?" It is interesting to compare here a few lines from the Latin poet Catullus. He writes in 88.1–2 (I cite the translation of Ulysses K. Vestal, published by the Theatrum Pompei Project, http://www.theaterofpompey.com): "What does the man do, Gellius, who with his mother and sister is sexually aroused, and after his tunics have been cast aside stays awake at night?" The next verse continues:

> Gellius is thin: why not? For whom there's so good a mother
> and so vivacious and so vibrant a sister
> and so good an uncle and [a world] so entirely full of girls
> of his own kin, for what reason should he cease being scrawny?
> Although he touches nothing, unless to touch what it is not allowed,
> as much as you like for what reason he should be thin you will find.

34. *vaimātṛkābhir bhaginībhiḥ*, as opposed to *svakasvakā bhaginīḥ*. The relevant Tibetan translations likewise distinguish *rang rang gi sring mo* from *mas dben gyi sring mo*, respectively. T. 1450 (XXIV) 104b25–27 (*juan* 2): "Then the sage told them: 'Marriage

together with your younger sisters is acceptable.' The princes replied: 'We didn't know whether we should accept them or not.' The sage said: 'As long as you do not share a mother, it is generally permitted.'" T. 191 (III) 937a29–b1 (*juan* 2) is a bit less clear, specifying only the prohibition: "The sage said: 'You must not have sexual relations with your own elder sister(s); as for others, you may do as you please.'"

35. I interpret the relation in this direction since we know from the existence of parallels that the basic story was well-established mythology. Were this not so, we might naturally wish to hypothesize that concerns over marriage regulations were paramount, and a somewhat radical and over-the-top story of incest was (merely) borrowed to emphasize and legitimize the case. Still, there may be more to be said on this question.

36. Senart 1882–1897: i.351.2–4, reprised on 8–9. For my reading of the passage, see Silk 2007a.

37. This Chinese scripture collects materials from multiple sources, for which it often offers sectarian attributions, but not in the present case. T. 190 (III) 675c10–13 (*juan* 5). Compare the translation in Beal (1875: 22), who I believe has misunderstood the last clause: "and so at first they desired to do, but on second thoughts they feared to pollute their race by such intermarriages." This appears to be the opposite of the true meaning. Note, once again, that this text is entirely distinct from the *Abhiniṣkramaṇa-sūtra* preserved in Tibetan and cited above.

38. *Dhammapada* commentary XV.1 (H. C. Norman 1906–1914: iii.255,7–8); and *Jātaka* §536 (Kuṇāla); Fausbøll (1877–1896: v.413,1) = Bollée (1970: 1.22–2.1*e*): *ye soṇasigālādayo viya attano bhaginīhi saddhiṁ vasiṁsu.* The passage is translated in Burlingame (1921: iii.70–71) and Cowell et al. (1895–1907: v.219), and see the note in Bollée (1970: 80).

39. Many years ago, when I mentioned in casual conversation what I thought was the generally agreed idea that the patterns of cross-cousin marriage found in some Indian life stories of the Buddha owe their origins to Dravidian influences (see Emeneau 1939, Trautmann 1973), the Pāli specialist Sakamoto-Gotō Junko strongly disagreed, suggesting, as I understood her then, that the source of such ideas was rather Iran. I do not know if she had in mind the legend mentioned here (concerning which, at that time, I myself was completely ignorant), and as far as I know she has never presented her idea formally. It would certainly be worth pursuing.

40. It is true that in South India uncle-niece marriage is practiced. As far as I know, however, aunt-nephew unions are viewed differently, as we might expect in a patriarchal society.

41. Fausbøll 1877–1896: iv.105,1–16, §458 (Udaya-Jātaka); and see the translation in Cowell et al. (1895–1907: iv.67).

42. Fausbøll (1877–1896: iv.105,1–2): *jātibrahmacārī pana ahosi supinantena pi methunadhammaṁ na jānāti.*

43. *Jātaka* §458 (Udaya). Fausbøll (1877–1896: iv.105,9–16) = DPG 73: 94.9–140).

44. See Silk (2003a) for some remarks on Mahā-Kāśyapa (the Sanskrit form of Pāli Mahā-Kassapa).

45. See the Mūlasarvāstivāda Vinaya's *Bhikṣuṇīvinayavibhaṅga*, Derge Kanjur 5, *'dul ba, ta*, 31a6–37b1 (the end point here somewhat arbitrarily picked, as the story continues), equivalent to Chinese T. 1443 (XXIII) 909b1–910b22 (*juan* 1), the Tibetan translated in Ralston (1882: 190–199); and see Sylvain Lévi's summary from Chinese in Chavannes (1910–1912, 1934: iv.151), this representing a quite elaborated version. Also found in the *Abhiniṣkramaṇa-sūtra* T. 190 (III) 862a29–866a15 (*juan* 45–46), of which Beal (1875: 316–318) is an extremely condensed paraphrase; the *Zachouyu jing* (T. 207 [IV] 524b20–c28), translated in Chavannes (1910–1912: ii.16–19); and the *Bodhisattvāvadānakalpalatā*, summarized in Black (1997: 295–297), and probably elsewhere too.

In light of our various investigations, it is quite interesting (although it would be too much to say ironic) to notice that the *Bhikṣuṇīvinayavibhaṅga* (Derge Kanjur 5, *'dul ba, ta*,136a6; Chinese lacks any equivalent in 910a–b) emphasizes the platonic nature of the relationship between Nyagrodhaja (Kāśyapa) and his wife Bhadrā by saying that they live together as mother and son, *ma dang bu gnyis ji lta ba bzhin du 'khod do* (see Ralston 1882: 197–198).

46. The story in Pāli appears almost identically in the commentaries to the *Aṅguttara-Nikāya, Manorathapūraṇī* in DPG 41: 139–140; Walleser and Kopp (1924–1957: i.175.5–178.7), the *Saṁyutta-Nikāya, Sāratthappakāsinī* in DPG 30: 168–169; Woodward (1929–1937: ii.191.13–194.1), this summarized by Hecker in Nyanaponika and Hecker (1997: 109–111), the *Theragāthā, Paramatthadīpanī* V in DPG 62: 362–363; Woodward (1940–1959: 3.130); paraphrased in Rhys Davids (1913: 359–360), and the *Apadāna, Visuddhajanavilāsinī* in Burmese DPG 64: 267–269; Godakumbura (1954: 260). The translation of Oikawa (1987: 14–16) refers to the first three of these sources.

47. Jātakas §328 (Ananusociya); Fausbøll (1877–1896: iii.93,13–94,20); translated in Cowell et al. (1895–1907: iii.62–63) and §531 (Kusa); Fausbøll (1877–1896: v.282,16–283,28), with the tale then continuing in a quite different direction, translated in Cowell et al. (1895–1907: v.144–145); see also Chopra (1966: 162). An attempt to plot the textual evolution of the Kusa story is found in Itō (1996: 133). *Dhammapada-aṭṭhakathā* XVI.5, *Anitthigandhakumāra-vatthu* (H. C. Norman 1906–1914: iii.281–282; translated in Burlingame 1921: iii.86–87).

Chapter 14: The Story of Utpalavarṇā

1. Burlingame's remark (1921: 2.127, n. 1), as the opinion of one well versed in Buddhist narrative, is worth noticing: "[The] story of Uppalavaṇṇā's career before her adoption of the religious life [is] one of the most extraordinary stories in Buddhist literature." Another entirely different although equally remarkable story of the life of Utpalavarṇā is found in the so-called *Sūtra of the Wise and the Foolish*, for which see conveniently—although at some remove from the Chinese original—Frye (1985: 128–132). For comparative notes, see Penzer (1924–1928: II.120–124), although he dismisses our story as uncharacteristic, the sexual advances of the woman not being rejected as they generally are in the materials he cites.

2. In such a future study, close attention should be paid to the Jaina story of Kuberadatta and Kuberadattā, found in the *Vasudevahiṇḍī*, edited in Caturvijay and Punyavijay

(1930–1931: 10.27–12.12), and translated in Jain (1977: 564–566), Hemacandra's *Pariśiṣṭaparvan* (2.224–314, edited in Jacobi [1932: 65–73, summarized on pp. xxviii–xxxix], and translated in Hertel [1908: 68–78]), and Udayaprabha Sūri's *Dharmābhyudaya-mahākāvya*, translated in Granoff (1994: 24–26), as well no doubt as in other texts too. According to Granoff, stories of incest and other intentionally shocking themes are quite common in Jaina narrative literature. Note that long ago Winternitz in his *History of Indian Literature* (1927: 508—and likely in the 1920 German original as well) mentioned that "the story of the twins Kuberadatta and Kuberadattā, the children of the courtesan Kuberasenā, is a kind of Oedipal tragedy." Also note the possible connection, at least conceptual if not historical, with the tale, recorded twice with slight variations in Crooke and Chaube (2002: 242–243, §204 and 388–389, §105), in which a woman ends up sleeping with her son. For Utpalavarṇā in a Chinese Dunhuang manuscript, see Chen (1974: 719–724, "Lianhuaseni chujia yinyuan ba").

3. Pruitt (1998b: 189.6–32; old page numbers 195–196). The translation is basically that of Pruitt (1998a: 247–248), but I have made a number of changes, both stylistic and substantive. The footnotes to the translation are mine.

4. See Silk 2008b.

5. Evidently by a slip, Pruitt omitted a translation of the words *taṁ dhātiyā hatthe adāsi*.

6. Derge Kanjur 3, *'dul ba, nya* 216a3–226a3; sTog Kanjur 3, *'dul ba, ja* 475a2–489a6. Its Chinese equivalent is found in T. 1442 (XXIII) 897a23–899a17 (*juan* 49), which is considerably abbreviated in comparison with the Tibetan version. Although this in itself cannot be taken as evidence that it is the translation that abridged the text, examples elsewhere suggest that this was probably the case and that the Tibetan version represents more closely some version in circulation in India. The Tibetan version was translated, indirectly from von Schiefner's German (which I have not been able to consult), in Ralston (1882: 206–215).

7. The crucial point here is that, lacking a son, Utpalavarṇā's father will have no one to offer him the *piṇḍas*, the post-mortem offerings, and thus he must both acquire a son for his own future weal and a husband for his daughter. The text specifies that the boy fills this role with the technical term *(d)mag pa* (Derge 216b1; sTog 475b2), something like "uxorilocal bridegroom." The young man is stated to be an orphan, but the possible legal significance of this is not clear to me. It does not appear that he is being adopted, although a boy without parents, either an orphan or one abandoned, may give himself for adoption (called *svayaṁdatta*). The restrictions on marriage of adopted sons would, however, rule out any subsequent union with the woman who would become a sister. Therefore, I believe that the young man here is not being adopted, but simply accepted as son-in-law. See Sarkar (1891: 387–388); the detailed studies of Kane (1968–1977: III.662–699); and Silk (2008b).

Notice further the likelihood that, since the daughter apparently has no brother, she will become the *putrikā*, "appointed daughter," whose firstborn son would become heir to her sonless father, rather than succeed to his own father's line as is usual. It may be that since the prospective husband here is an orphan, this would make little difference to him or even be a preferred situation; see here Jamison (1996: 302, n. 62) and the lengthy discussion in Schmidt (1987: 30–75), which incidentally also touches on Iranian customs, including close-kin marriage.

8. I believe the verb *nongs*, which I have tentatively translated in the negative as "without objection," is being used idiomatically here, but I am ignorant of its exact meaning.

9. The Chinese translation, being quite a bit shorter than the version preserved in Tibetan, contains little of the detail found in the latter. Here, for instance, Chinese has only the following: "Not long after that time, Utpalavarṇā's father sickened and died. Sometime after that, her mother could not maintain her determination, and by and by she engaged in private and secret sexual intercourse with her son-in-law."

Although on the whole excellent, Ralston's translation from Tibetan quite often paraphrases the text, as it does here. For the most part this process appears intended more to avoid prolixity than simply to bowdlerize, although salacious passages are consistently omitted.

10. Evidently the servant girl, but the text is not entirely clear here.

11. Although the pronouns are perhaps a little confusing in English, of course she refers to her husband having sex with her mother, her husband's mother-in-law, not with their infant daughter.

12. In the region Mathurā, and presumably in Gandhāra as well, it was traditional for both Indian and Scythian men to cover the head with a turban or cap, respectively, but it does not appear that women always did so; see Salomon (1989: 40).

13. The term I translate "courtesan" here and below is *'jud mthun ma*, which I believe to represent Sanskrit *gaṇikā*, so attested in the dictionary of Tshe ring dbang rgyal, Bacot (1930: 55a3). It may simply mean "prostitute," but I believe that the reference is rather to women who are organized into a higher-status group than what we might understand as independent prostitutes (*rūpājīvā*, for instance), although quite clearly the distinctions in nuance among the many synonyms—according to Sternbach (1965: 199, n. 2) 330 synonyms have been identified—can hardly have been consistently applied. Even were our text available in Sanskrit, it is not certain we would have much to say about the exact nuance of the word. As an example of such difficulties, notice that in the *Milindapañha* episode referred to below, the prostitute Bindumatī refers to herself as *ahaṁ . . . gaṇikā rūpūpajīvinī antimajīvikā*, all in apposition (Trenckner 1880: 122.2–3).

14. It appears, then, that Utpalavarṇā has accepted a promotion from an ordinary prostitute into the high-class category of courtesan. We should note that, at least according to the scheme set forth in the commentary to the *Kāmasūtra* (VI.6.50; Sharma [1997: 1118]; cf. Daniélou [1994: 482]), within the category of prostitute (*veśyā*), further specified by the commentator as *rūpājīvā* (literally, a woman who makes her living from her looks), is included an unchaste woman (*kulaṭā*) and an independent woman (*svairiṇī*). The first is defined as a woman who leaves her home out of fear of her husband and secretly has sex with another, the second as one who despises (or simply rejects?) her husband and has sex with another in her own home or in that of another—*kulatā yā*

patibhayād gṛhāntaraṁ gatvā pracchannam anyena saṁprayujyate | *svairiṇī yā patiṁ tiraskṛtya svagṛhe 'nyagṛhe vā saṁprayujyate.* If our Buddhist authors also understood the classification of prostitute as including what we might see as adulterous women (since there is no implication of monetary recompense for sex here), Utpalavarṇā should already be classified as a prostitute, that is as a *veśyā*, although she has not yet been paid for sex as such. Note also the distinction made in verse 27 of the *Rasaratnahāra* of Śivarāma Tripāṭhin, quoted in Sternbach (1953: 20, §54), an eighteenth-century text that contrasts the promiscuity of the *kulaṭā*, who has sex with many men, with the greed of the *sāmānyā*, who will have sex with anyone for money: *kulaṭā bahupuṁrāgā veśyādeśyā prakāśataḥ* | *lobhena sarvapuṁrāgā sāmānyā kathitā budhaiḥ* ||.

15. The text has *chang gral du tshogs shing*, which may mean little more than "gathered around the bar."

16. Ralston takes *mi sdug pa thob pa* as a proper name, for which he suggests the reconstruction Aniṣṭaprāpta. The Chinese translation, however, takes the form as descriptive (897c12) *zuò bùjìngguān chéng*. In addition, the Tibetan text itself just a bit below has the expression *spos 'tshong gi khye'u che ge mo zhig* (the perfumer's son so-and-so), confirming that *mi sdug pa thob pa* is a description rather than a name.

17. This list contains as its last item a very troublesome term, in Tibetan *rma 'byed pa*, which perhaps corresponds to Sanskrit *vraṇabhaṅga*, a term that in its turn appears to parallel Pāli *vanabhaṅga*. Close to the same overall expression appears in the *Samāhitā Bhūmi* of the *Yogācārabhūmi*, as edited by Delhey (2002, §2.2.2.1.1): *yā strīsahagatā śubhatāṣṭasthānasaṁgṛhītā yair aṣṭābhiḥ sthānaiḥ strī puruṣaṁ badhnāti tadyathā nṛttena gītena hasitena prekṣitena varṇena sparśena ākalpena vraṇabhaṅgena ca.* My query about this word generated a series of discussions in March 2004 both privately and on the Indology list (for the archive, see http://www.ucl.ac.uk/~ucgadkw/indology.html, under the title "stock phrase about women?"). Since Martin Delhey has already attempted to solve the problem (2002: 380, n. 137), I refrain from repeating here what he has already said, and the new issues he will surely address when he revises his thesis for publication. In any event, my translation of *rma 'byed pa* / **vraṇabhaṅga* here remains no more than a wild guess.

18. Probably this indicates her possession of the perfumer's son; perhaps she is mockingly suggesting that she proposed marriage to him. See Silk 2007c.

19. The text is not entirely clear here, using only a pronoun that seems to suggest that the perfumer's son is still the subject of the discussion. The concern expressed immediately below, however, that the presence of a young child makes a woman less attractive to men, seems rather to suggest that Utpalavarṇā resumed (or continued) the life of a prostitute. While these two interpretations are not necessarily mutually incompatible, I may have misunderstood the text here.

20. In the expression *bdag cag gnyis kyi bu mo phan tshun sha glag bya ste*, I take the term spelled in the Derge edition *sha glag* and in sTog *sha klag* as *sha lag*, meaning an agreement to marry, or matchmaking. The Chinese appears to paraphrase the whole discussion, saying (897c25): "If we have a boy and girl, they must certainly marry."

21. See Silk 2008b.

22. A stock expression *mitrāmitramadhyamā lokāḥ* is found, for instance, in the *Cīvaravastu* of the Mūlasarvāstivāda Vinaya; see Dutt (1939–1959: III.2.5.4).

23. The last clause, *sems can dmyal ba la gzhol bar 'gyur bar ma byed cig*, is not clear to me. Perhaps it means: "Don't let this cause you to go to hell."

24. I do not understand the precise meaning of the expression *rgyal ba'i skyob pa'i nyan thos ma.*

25. I do not understand this line well: *ming por gyur nas da ltar khyo 'di yin.*

26. Parallel versions of the same story also contain equivalents to this verse, for instance in the *Vasudevahiṇḍī* in Prākrit, apparently in prose in Caturvijay and Punyavijay (1930–1931: 12.1–3), and translated in Jain (1977: 566), and in the *Pariśiṣṭaparvan* of Hemacandra in Sanskrit, where it is spoken by Kuberadattā, sister and wife of Kuberadatta, to the son of the Kuberadatta by their mother Kuberasenā. This second version, in Jacobi (1932, verses 294–296), reads:

> You are my brother, my son, my husband's younger brother,
> My nephew, my uncle, my grandson, young child.
> And your father, my lad, is my uterine brother,
> My father, grandfather, husband, son, and father-in-law.
> And your mother, my lad, is my mother, grandmother,
> My brother's wife, daughter-in-law, mother-in-law, and co-wife—alas!

The identifications are justified in the verses that follow: he is her son, for instance, since he is the son of her husband (although biologically, of course, she is not his mother, and thus he is not her biological son).

Such verses are found widely in European literature as well, as in the following medieval French example of a tomb inscription. I cite from Archibald (2001: 123), but see also Rank (1992: 296–297); Taylor (1938: 25–26); and Baum (1916: 605–607, n. 70).

> *Cy-gist la fille, cy-gist le père,*
> *Cy-gist la sœur, cy-gist le frère,*
> *Cy-gist la femme et le mary,*
> *Et si n'y a que deux corps ici.*

> Here lies the daughter, here lies the father,
> Here lies the sister, here lies the brother,
> Here lies the wife and the husband,
> And there are only two bodies here.

It has been suggested by those who have studied European examples of such verses, and similar "riddles" in verse or not, that some of them at least reflect actual family arrangements.

27. A set of verses almost precisely parallel to these is found in Pāli in the *Theragāthā*; see verses 1150–1154 in Oldenberg and Pischel (1883: 104, with corrections to verse 1152 on pp. 231 and 237), with translations in Rhys Davids (1913: 383–384) and

K. R. Norman (1969: 106). These verses are attributed to Mahā-Moggallāna, our very same Mahā-Maudgalyāyana, and said by the commentary to have been spoken in response to a prostitute who sought to lure him. I do not know of the verses appearing elsewhere; there are no parallels listed in Mizuno (1993: 34), but he misses the present occurrence as well, although his generally exhaustive listings do claim to take into account T. 1442, as noted on his p. 4—a rare oversight in the work of this careful and exacting scholar.

28. The line is difficult to understand; see K. R. Norman (1969: 282 on 1150). It appears to me that the Pāli commentator also did not understand the line.

29. In the verse line *rgyun lam dgu nas rtag tu ni*, I have not been able to identity the compound *rgyun lam*. Note that the Pāli parallel has *nava sotāni*, and *rgyun* by itself can translate Sanskrit *srotas*. Moreover, in light of the parallel, contextually, and in view of the Chinese translation (898b24: *jiǔkǒng*), the meaning is plain enough. My friend Harunaga Isaacson has brought to my attention the occurrence in *Aṣṭāṅgahṛdaya* cikitsāsthāna 15.1 of the word *srotamārga*, which would correspond, element by element, to *rgyun lam*, but whether this has the significance we seek here and whether this word might stand behind our Tibetan translation remain unclear.

30. The Tibetan text's *dbyar du* might be understood to refer to summer, and the image of a cesspool stinking on a hot summer's day certainly creates a strong impression. But the sense seems rather more likely to be as I have translated it, with the picture of the cesspool overflowing thanks to excessive rainfall, with its contents sloshing about everywhere.

31. The image of an elephant in the mud as a metaphor for humans mired in transmigration is found elsewhere, for example in the *Divyāvadāna*; see Cowell and Neil (1886: 181.4): *kāruṇyād uddhṛto duḥkhāj jīrṇaḥ paṅkād iva dvipaḥ* (out of compassion he lifted me out of suffering, like an old elephant out of the mud). In the Pāli parallel, this verse differs and in fact constitutes the beginning of the woman's response. While slightly different, lines cd read *ettha ceke visīdanti paṅkamhi va jaraggavo* (and some here sink down like an old bull in mud). In the context of the structure of the Pāli poem, it is hard to make sense of this line, although in isolation its syntax is clear enough.

32. This, after her conversion, is the first time the text refers to Utpalavarṇā with the respectful term **kuladuhitṛ*.

33. In this context *khyim thab*, probably **pati*, might better be translated "master."

34. The Buddha's foster mother; she is the head of the order of nuns. Notice the implication here that written letters were used rather ordinarily, something we saw implied in the story of Dharmaruci and elsewhere, and also that Mahāprajāpatī, a woman, was probably imagined as literate.

35. In this context *'jud mthun ma*, although it usually renders the rather high-class term *gaṇikā*, may nevertheless be better translated "whore."

36. On this set of examples, see Bloomfield 1920: 339–343.

37. This is a very common verse, standard in such contexts, and indeed, the broader context itself is constructed here from a series of clichés that are regularly used to narrate such stories and to characterize those of high spiritual attainments.

38. So I understand *gcer bu pa'i nyan thos ma*.

39. Perhaps *pravrājaka, vratin, mahātman*?

40. A considerably different story of the background life of Uppalavaṇṇā, but with some common elements, may be found in the commentary to the *Aṅguttara-Nikāya*, conveniently translated in Bode (1893: 540–552).

41. Something of the syntax of the last sentence escapes me, namely, the role of *rang sangs rgyas bye ba phrag 'bum bas* (thanks to the hundreds of thousands of lone buddhas?); I omit it from the translation.

42. The references to the caravan journey between Gandhāra and Mathurā, for instance, may give the impression that we are talking here of a few days travel. In fact, the two places are rather distant (see Bajpai 1989), and the relevant time frame thus collapsed here. The distance from Taxila to Mathurā is something less than 600 miles, and while I do not know exactly how quickly a caravan would have been expected to travel, at an absolute minimum the journey would have taken a month, and more probably several. In addition to this time compression, the absence of any reference to events other than those of the primary story line gives a rather one-dimensional feel to the narrative.

43. Pruitt (1998b: 75, translated in 1998a: 100–102); and see Rhys Davids (1909: 52).

44. And indeed that the Mūlasarvāstivāda version is an elaboration rather than the Theravāda version an abbreviation seems much more likely.

45. Ralston (1882: liv). For the *Gesta Romanorum* referred to by Ralston, see Swan (1876). He may have had in mind here a tale such as the thirteenth in the collection, a story of mother-son incest, out of which a daughter is born, whom the mother immediately murders.

46. The proverbial equality with which courtesans treat their customers is illustrated, for example, in the verses cited by Sternbach (1953: 71–72, §§351–358, as well as 123, §626).

47. See Trenckner (1880: 121–122), translated in Horner (1963–1964: I.170–171). Burlingame (1917) is a study of the Act of Truth in general and, inter alia, a study and translation of the series in the *Milindapañha* in which this episode appears, a set of passages which he refers to (p. 437) as the "*locus classicus* of the Act of Truth." It is very interesting to note the observation of Brown (1968: 172): "Women, as far as I have observed, have to base an Act of Truth on the perfection of their sex life."

48. On child abandonment, see Silk 2008b.

49. Like all such texts, the *Mārkaṇḍeya Purāṇa* is hardly datable, but as it is perhaps one of the older Purāṇas, it may belong to the third quarter of the first millennium C.E.

50. *Mārkaṇḍeya Purāṇa* I.40: *tapasyaṁtaṁ nagendrasthaṁ yā vaḥ kṣobhayate balāt* | *durvāsasaṁ muniśreṣṭhaṁ tāṁ vo manye guṇādhikām* ||. My translation is indebted to that of Pargiter (1913: 4–5).

51. See *Mārkaṇḍeya Purāṇa* I.41–53 in *Śrīmārkaṇḍeyamahāpurāṇam / The Mārkaṇḍeyamahāpurāṇam* (Delhi: Nag Publishers, 1983?), a reprint of that published in Bombay by Veṅkaṭeśvara Press, 1910. My translation owes a great deal to that of Pargiter (1913: 5), as well as to the kind corrections of Harunaga Isaacson.

52. I do not intend to allude here to the profound dispute as to whether Buddhist practice leads one to approach liberation gradually or suddenly. The point is rather that the conversion experience itself, the moment when one realizes the truth of the Buddhist message, must be instantaneous, a viewpoint that I suggest the structure of the story here supports.

53. It is worth considering how an audience familiar with Indian rhetoric would have seen the dynamics in this story. For instance, when Utpalavarṇā begins her process of seducing the perfumer's son, one key feature of her temptation is to lead him to believe that she herself is paying for the medicines for her ailing lover. Her position as an available woman is made clear: she is unmarried and has a young lover. But one of the well-known tricks of the courtesan, according to Indian erotic literature, is her capacity to seduce and then bleed dry her lovers, keeping them only so long as they have money. By having her servant girl tell the perfumer's son that Utpalavarṇā herself is paying for the ill man's medication, the authors move beyond the genre's conventional pattern of deceit. The perfumer's son is deceived, but the motivation for the deception is not quite what it would usually be. The reader, moreover, knows what the perfumer's son does not, namely, that the scam is a rather sophisticated sort of double cross: Utpalavarṇā pretends not to be interested in money because she is interested in very much more than the limited amount she would be able to extract from one lover (who, we recall, does not actually even exist). It is hard to say whether this move was intended to persuade an audience that since such a clever, shrewd woman as Utpalavarṇā ultimately saw the light of the Buddhist truth, becoming as the sequel explains a prominent Buddhist nun, then those in the audience should likewise pledge their allegiance to the Buddhist way. It may rather be that some elements of the narrative should simply be read as entertainment, rather than as contributing directly to the final theological message.

Chapter 15: The "Indian Oedipus"

1. A general bibliography would be difficult to compile and not very useful unless completely annotated. For some focused essays, see the collection in Edmunds and Dundes (1984); for South Asian materials, extensive discussion from the point of view of psychoanalytical anthropology has been given by Obeyesekere (1990: 71–214; and see slightly earlier 1989). Freud's own basic statement is to be found in (1953: 260–266; and reprinted in this or other translations in numerous places). An influential early study was Rank (1992; originally published in German in 1912). As one example of reflections on the problem, see the essays collected in Pollock and Ross (1988). Although the idea of gathering folkloric evidence is a good one, the utility of Johnson and Price-Williams (1996) is doubtful, at least to judge by the accuracy with which the Asian materials known to me are reported; the Mahādeva story in the *Konjaku monogatari*, which is, as we know, a literary recasting of an Indian story, and the story of Ajātaśatru, found in a Chinese scripture of mixed Central Asian-Chinese origins (see Silk 1997), are both cited as Japanese evidence, for instance.

2. Ramanujan (1984, a revision of 1972). In addition to the studies cited below, some authors make frequent mention of Devereux (1951). However, his article is devoted entirely to speculations about two stories from the *Mahābhārata* as retold in Meyer (1930); whatever the merits of Devereux's article at the time of its publication, it has been superseded by later studies, most significantly those of Ramanujan (1972, 1984) and Goldman (1978, 1982, 1993).

3. Ramanujan (1972: 132 = 1984: 237). This is very similar in most of its main features to a story collected by Karve (1950) in Maharashtra, both stories clearly belonging to the same tradition. Karve is not clear about just where she collected her story, saying only that she heard it from a woman of the Maratha Hindu butcher caste. The geographic proximity of North Karnataka and Maharashtra makes one strongly suspect contact between the two tale traditions. Another story is found in D'Penha (1892). From Salsette (a region north of Bombay—though no information is given about the collection of the story, its original language, and so on), it is notable for the mother-son incest theme, predicted to the protagonist by a fortune-teller (her own mother!), and the eventual revelation of all through the swaddling sari. (In this story the woman ultimately decides to maintain the relationship!) Ramanujan (1984: 238) also refers to several other folklore collections in Kannada, to which I do not have access. It is striking that, in precisely the regions in which these stories were collected, several forms of close-kin marriage are traditionally practiced, predominantly uncle-niece and cross-cousin matches. The possible connection between this sociological fact and the imaginative world of the tales deserves to be explored.

4. Ramanujan 1984: 253. For Ramanujan (1984: 252), Indian tales differ from the Greek in that "[i]nstead of sons desiring mothers and overcoming fathers (e.g., Oedipus) and daughters loving fathers and hating mothers (e.g., Electra), most often we have fathers (or father-figures) suppressing sons and desiring daughters, and mothers desiring sons and ill-treating or exiling daughters or daughter-figures." Karve's tale, however, does not present the story this way, the whole encounter being fated; the marriage between mother and son is motivated by neither one of them but by the son's adoptive parents.

5. Ramanujan 1972: 132 = 1984: 238. We must not overlook the importance, pointed out by Ramanujan (1984: 241), of the vector through which the stories are told. The folktales he and others have noted are told by women to girls. Unfortunately, when dealing with materials for which we have only literary sources, such potentially important contextualizing information is forever beyond our grasp. It is another, equally interesting, question just what happens when a tale moves from the oral to the written (although there is certainly no guarantee that this is what happened in our case here).

6. Other attempts to adjust Ramanujan's visual models to different situations include those in Johnson and Price-Williams (1996).

7. The *Sangoku denki* account seems in many ways to resemble the *Konjaku* version, although the facts are not as explicitly stated.

8. Archibald (2001: 102) writes: "In classical stories mother-son incest seems to be fairly rare, and is always presented as the most shocking relationship, but when it is delib-

erate on the part of the mother it is regarded as particularly monstrous; it never seems to be initiated knowingly by the son. . . .”

Chapter 16: Joseph and the Wife of Potiphar

1. For a most interesting study of rabbinic interpretations of the story of Joseph and Potiphar, see Kugel (1990).

2. Genesis 39:4–6.

3. Bloomfield 1923. See also Penzer (1924–1928: II.120–124), who at the time of writing had not yet seen Bloomfield's article.

4. As an example of this type, see *Pārśavanāthacarita* (Harigovinddas and Bechardas 1912: 185) III.402c, and Bloomfield (1923: 152; 1919: 85).

5. Bloomfield (1923: 144) noting and translating the epigram edited by Böhtlingk in his *Indische Sprüche* (1870–1873: iii.222, §5743): *rājapatnī guroḥ patnī mitrapatnī tathaiva ca | patnīmātā svamātā ca pañcaitā mātaraḥ smṛtāḥ* ||.

6. *Jātaka* §472, in Fausbøll (1877–1896: iv.190.3–10) = DPG 73: 169.3–8. The full passage is Fausbøll (1877–1896: iv.189.15–190.19); translated also in Cowell et al. (1895–1907: iv.118); in Bloomfield (1923: 146); and by Yukihiro and Mamiko Okada in Nakamura (1982–1988: 6.186–187).

7. Although I may be over-reading here, I think the text is offering two reasons for the impossibility of the affair: (1) she is his mother; (2) she's married, and so off limits in any case.

8. In the commentary to the *Dhammapada* (H. C. Norman 1906–1914: iii.181.19–182.1), this is all reduced to just a few words. The chief consort is stated to be a co-wife with Mahāpaduma's mother (*mahāpadumakumārassa bodhisattassa mātu sapattī rañño aggamahesī*) and to have importuned him to immorality (*asaddhammena nimantetvā*), a suggestion that he refuses. See the translation in Burlingame (1921: iii.22).

9. He uses two words which I have clumsily distinguished in translation, *ammā* (“mom”) and *mātā* (“mother”). Although certainly it is true that *ammā* is commonly used in addressing any woman, I think the context makes clear that it is used here to show relationship. An unintended artifact of my English may be the implication that there is a difference in levels of formality between the two words. There appears to be no such distinction in Pāli. Rather, *ammā* is frequently used in the vocative, while *mātā* seems not to be used in that case at all.

10. It may be of interest in this context to note an idea detected among the Nuer by E. E. Evans-Pritchard, although certainly without any suggestion that the same dynamic is necessarily at work in India. As Héritier (1982: 155) puts it: “[A]dultery with a wife of one's father other than one's mother is particularly shocking insofar as the father has sexual relations with both of his wives, and so transmits to the mother something of the son's sexual contact with the co-wife.”

11. Cowell and Neil 1886: 407.5–24 = Mukhopadhyaya 1963: 107.6–108.6. The passage is translated in Strong (1983: 270–271); Mukhopadhyaya (1963: xli–xlii); as well as by other scholars, perhaps first by Burnouf (1844: 405), which appears in English in

Stephens (1911: 82). For a bibliography, see Hiraoka (2002: 63–64), to whose list of translations add that in Hertel (1908: 252–253); a recent version by Sadakata (2000: 31); and now Hiraoka 2007: II.407. The passage is treated by Bloomfield (1923: 147–148).

A translation of the Tibetan version of the story, *Ku ṇā la'i rtogs pa brjod pa* (Tōh. 4145, Otani 5646), is found in Okamoto (1999), with the portion parallel to the passage translated here on pp. 87–88.

12. This verse is uncharacteristically poetic for this literature, the style of Kuṇāla's response being more typical. In the first two *pada*s in particular, the poet plays with the sense of eyes and vision in almost every other word, while in the second two *pada*s an intense sense of burning heat is conveyed. Okamoto Kensuke (2006) has recently discovered three verses in the *Kuṇālāvadāna* precisely parallel to verses in the latter portion of Aśvaghoṣa's *kāvya*, the *Buddhacarita*, heretofore lost in Sanskrit. Since the *Buddhacarita* is one of the masterworks of Indian *kāvya*, and the *Divyāvadāna* generally considered a rather prosaic work from a literary point of view, Okamoto's discovery and examples such as this verse raise some interesting questions about the literary qualities and status of the *Divyāvadāna*.

13. The identical verse is found in the *Aśokāvadānamālā* (Bongard-Levin and Volkova 1965:14, verse 26), where *pada* d reads *dāvāgninā prajvalate va vṛkṣaṁ*, in which *vṛkṣaṁ* should probably be considered a *lectio facilior* for the *Divyāvadāna*'s *kakṣam*.

14. I have taken a slight license with the last term; *apāya*, strictly speaking, refers to any of the unfavorable rebirths, including not only hell but the animal and hungry ghost realms as well, and in some lists demons too. Note that Kuṇāla's reference to Tiṣyarakṣitā as his mother in this passage is, if anything, even clearer in the Chinese translations: T. 2043 (L) 144b27 (*juan* 4), trans. Li 1993: 65: "You are a mother to me, and I am a son to you," and T. 2042 (L) 108b8 (*juan* 3), translated by Pryzluski (1923: 283): "Vous qui devez être [pour moi] une mère, comment pouvez-vous ressentir à l'égard de votre fils un sentiment passionné?" Kuṇāla in his verse uses the word *jananī* to refer to Tiṣyarakṣitā as his mother. Kuṇāla's birth mother is Padmāvatī, and thus Tiṣyarakṣitā as a co-wife of Aśoka is superior to Kuṇāla's mother and at the same time something like a stepmother to Kuṇāla himself. While we might expect at least on the basis of its etymology that *jananī* should mean birth mother (genetrix), which could not be applied to Tiṣyarakṣitā, there is ample evidence that the word is actually used in a looser sense. See, for instance, *Samarādityasaṁkṣepa* (Jacobi 1906: 167) 5.108d, where it is also used by a stepson to a stepmother (Bloomfield 1923: 152). Note that Karve (1943–1944: 71) has remarked on the uses of *mātṛ* and *ambā* for both natural mother and stepmother in the *Mahābhārata*. Hertel (1908: 252, n. 2) clearly stated: "Die Gemahlinnen eines Mannes werden alle als Mütter auch der Söhne ihrer Nebenfrauen betrachtet." In Kuṇāla's reply verse to the following verse of Tiṣyarakṣitā, the printed text of Cowell and Neil appears to have him once again use the vocative "mother" to Tiṣyarakṣitā, but the text must be corrected to read *āśu* for *māta*, a suggestion I owe to Michael Hahn.

15. Cowell and Neil print *tatas tiṣyarakṣitā tatkālam alabhamānā kruddhā kathayati.* I accept the suggested emendation of de Jong (1987: 112) of *tatkālam* to *tatkāmam*, in accord with the Chinese reading (T. 2043 [L] 144c1 [*juan* 4]) *bùsuìyì*. Note also, however, Hertel (1908: 252, with n. 3), who reads *tatkāyam* and translates: "Darauf sagte Tiṣyarakṣitā, wütend darüber, dass sie seinen Leib nicht erlangt hatte." This, while it seems to me less likely, is not impossible.

16. T. 2300 (LXX) 455b21–22 (*juan* 5), translated in Demiéville 1932: 34.

17. Bloomfield 1923: 152, with the text in Hertel 1917: 25, verses 175–176, with translation p. 480.

18. Bloomfield 1923: 165, with the text in Hertel 1917: 10–11, verses 25–32, with translation p. 33–34.

19. Hertel 1917: 11, verse 27: *deva tvajjananī daṣṭā mahālakṣmīr mahāhinā.*

20. Ibid.: verses 30–31: *kāmasarpeṇa daṣṭāhaṁ naṣṭā tan mama cetanā* || *tato nijāṅgasaṁśleṣapīyūṣais tvaṁ niṣiñca mām* | *yena śīghram avāpnomi jīvitaṁ jīviteśvara* ||.

21. Ibid.: verse 32: *śrutveti vacanaṁ tasyāḥ karṇayor vajrasaṁnibham* | *jhampāṁ dattvā gavākṣeṇa pālaḥ svāvāsam āyayau* ||.

22. Durgaprasād 1903: 21 (7.57–59), translated Penzer 1924–1928: I.79.

23. Durgaprasād 1903: 146 (33.40), translated Penzer 1924–1928: III.109–110. The reference in Bloomfield (1923: 161 to 30.40) is a misprint.

24. Durgaprasād 1903: 76–77 (20.118–123), translated Penzer 1924–1928: II.105.

25. Her words are quite direct; see Durgaprasād (1903: 77 [20.151]): *bhaja sundarakādyāpi māṁ tvadāyattajīvitām*, translated in Penzer (1924–1928: II.109): "Sundaraka, enjoy me even now, for my life depends on you." Perhaps a more colloquial translation, or at least one into a more modern idiom, might run: "Sundaraka, quick, take me right now or I'll die!" The imperative *bhaja*, while not as vulgar as some expressions, is forceful.

26. Durgaprasād 1903: 77 (20.152): *maivaṁ vādīr na dharmo 'yaṁ mātā me gurupatny asi.* Note here again the implied equivalence of guru and father.

27. Ibid. (20.154): *mātar maivaṁ kṛthā hṛdi tat* | *gurutalpābhigamanaṁ kutra dharmo bhaviṣyati* ||.

28. This is one of a number of closely related forms including *gurvaṅganāgama*, *gurutalpaga*, *gurutalpa*, *gurutalpagamana*—see Kane (1968–1977: IV.23–25), where he outlines the discussions of this sin in the legal (dharma) literature.

29. Jātaka 431: Fausbøll (1877–1896: iii.496–501), translated in Cowell et al. (1895–1907: iii.295–297).

30. Jātaka 431 (Hārita). Fausbøll (1877–1896: iii.498,1–16) = DPG 72: 440.6–16.

31. The expression indicates that the ascetic can provide merit for those who are generous to him. He is like a field, and those who plant in that field will reap its fruits of merit, useful, for instance, to better one's future rebirth.

32. This must be the sense of *muṭṭhi-mañcaka*, but I do not know that the compound is found elsewhere. Fausbøll prints the variant *khuddaka-mañjuka*, which while

obviously corrupt (DPG has *khuddaka-mañcaka*) suggests an understanding of the first member of the compound (literally, "fist" or "small amount, i.e., fist-full"). Parallels suggest the same: *Jātaka* i.304,16: *cullasayana*; ii.274,12: *nīcamañcaka.*

33. The word *visabhāgārammaṇa* is defined by the *Pali-English Dictionary* (Rhys Davids and Stede 1921–1925: 639b) as "pudendum muliebre," which appears to be correct. See the passage at *Papañcasūdanī* I.66,19 (*athassa gāme piṇḍāya carato visabhāgārammaṇe kileso uppajji so taṁ vipassanāya vikkhambhetvā vihāraṁ agamāsi*), as well as a number of cases in the *Jātaka* itself (i. 303,16, 19; 304,27, and see line 21: *visabhāgarūpārammaṇa*). This appears also to be what is intended by Matsumoto Shōkei in Nakamura (1982–1988: 5.212): "isei no shintai ni yotte (idai na hito) no me ga kuranda."

34. The text is very clear; although he took her hand, they drew the screen together—the verb is plural: *tāvad eva sāṇiṁ parikkhimpiṁsu.*

35. The text seems to be euphemistic here: *lokadhammaṁ sevitvā.*

36. Fausbøll (1877–1896: iii.499,5–8)=DPG 72: 441.3–5: *bodhisatto hi ekaccesu ṭhānesu pāṇātipāto pi adinnādānam pi kāmesu*[1] *micchācāro pi surāmerayamajjapānam*[2] *pi hoti yeva atthabhañjakavisaṁvādam*[3] *pana*[4] *purakkhatvā musāvādo nāma na hoti.*[5] (1) PTS *omits kāmesu*, (2) PTS *surāpānam*, (3) DPG *°bheda° for °bhañja°*, (4) DPG *omits*, (5) PTS *hosi.*

37. Unlike Sanskrit, Pāli has no dual verb forms.

38. The parallels are found in Jātaka 66 (Mudulakkhaṇa) Fausbøll (1877–1896: i.304,17–29); translated by Cowell et al. (1895–1907: i.163); and Jātaka 251 (Saṁkappa) Fausbøll (1877–1896: ii.274,10–275,9); translated by Cowell et al. (1895–1907: ii.191–192). Another story that should be taken into account in any future comparative investigation of these tales is number fifty-two in the *Sheng jing* (T. 154 [III] 105b [*juan* 5]), the story of the ascetic Bojie (Pulleyblank 1991 pa^{h}-kɨap), *Foshuo xianren bojie jing.*

39. T. 203 (IV) 492b29–c16 (*juan* 9), §109. My translation owes much to Chavannes (1910–1911: iii.419–420). Cf. also Willemen (1994: 223–224). I owe my knowledge of this story, which I had initially overlooked, to the kindness of Prof. Ishii Kōsei of Komazawa Junior College, who has also referred to the story in Ishii (1996). He relates this story to another in the *Nihon Ryōiki* (II.3), for which see the translation in Nakamura (1973: 161–163); and earlier, in German, in Bohner (1934: 109–110).

40. The story is translated in Tawney (1895: 49–53), with a Sanskrit edition and German translation in Hoffmann (1974: 127–136). The same basic tale appears repeated in folklore collections as well; for a Ceylonese example, see Parker (1914: 193–199), "The Wax Horse"; this contains notes of other parallels, including one from Kashmir, attesting to the very wide geographic range of the story. Compare also a North-Central story, "The Discarded Princess," told by a brahmin of Aksauli, Mirzapur, a region south of Benares, in Crooke and Charbe (2002: 203–204; originally published in *North Indian Notes & Queries* in 1895).

41. If, as the psychoanalytical theory appears to demand, both the vectors of desire and of aggression combine to compose the complex, we are not comparing apples and oranges when we discuss stories of intergenerational sexual relations together with those of intergenerational aggression or even violence.

Chapter 17: Further Dimensions of the Oedipal in India

1. Dutt 1939–1959: iii.2.8,8–10; Raghu Vira and Lokesh Chandra 1974a: folio 794=241a2–3: *sā naimittikena dṛṣṭvā vyākṛtā putraṁ janayiṣyati sa pitaraṁ jīvitād vyaparopya svayam eva paṭṭaṁ baddhvā rājyaṁ kārayiṣyatīti*; and see Ralston (1882: 78). References to this prophecy appear several more times in the same story: 11.5–6 (Ralston 81), 15.12–13 (Ralston 84–85).

2. Dutt 1939–1959: iii.2.13,14–16; Raghu Vira and Lokesh Chandra 1974a: folio 796=242a10: *bhavantaḥ yo hi putraḥ pitaraṁ ghātayati sa rājyahetoḥ yadi me putro bhaviṣyati tasyā jātasyaivāhaṁ paṭṭabandhaṁ kariṣyāmīti*; and see Ralston (1882: 83).

3. The dating of Purāṇas is a nightmarishly complex business; see Rocher (1986: 100–103).

4. *Brahma-Purāṇa*, Adhyāya 92. Schreiner and Söhnen (1987: 317–319). In making my translation, I have been much assisted by the summary in Söhnen and Schreiner (1989: 157). The same authors comment on the general characteristics of the *Gautamī-māhātmya* in their introduction, pp. xxxi–xxxii. Subsequently, I was able to compare my translation with that in Board of Scholars (1986: 840–844), a complete translation of the *Gautamī-māhātmya*, thanks to which I was able to correct a number of oversights. Finally, I am grateful for the careful comments of Harunaga Isaacson. For purposes of flow, I have treated the text's "Brahmā said" simply as the narrative voice and not translated it.

5. To this we may compare *Manu* XI.48, which says (Bühler [1886: 439–440]): "Some wicked men suffer a change of their (natural) appearance in consequence of crimes committed in this life, and some in consequence of those committed in a former (existence)" (*iha duścaritaiḥ kecit kecit pūrvakṛtais tathā* | *prāpnuvanti durātmāno narā rūpaviparyayam* ||). I do not believe, however, that Manu imagines that the karmic recompense for evil actions will appear, disappear, and reappear continually within one and the same lifetime, not to mention on a daily basis, as our text depicts happening. Nevertheless, the general notion is the same, of the visible physical manifestation of inner evil.

6. As Söhnen and Schreiner (1989: 157, n. 1) suggest, we may have to do with a "reverse Sanskritization" here. The name Sanājjāta (which itself is probably to be understood as a Sanskrit formation) appears to be taken here as if it were Middle Indic and -jj- Sanskritized into -dy-. That the penultimate vowel length is different appears to have been a matter of little import.

7. This is not to say that Buddhist cultures entirely lack similarly salvific pilgrimage locations. For a very interesting case of pilgrimage to an icy Tibetan mountain lake, immersion in which is said specifically to erase the sin of incest, see the fine paper by Buffetrille (1998); now in English (2004).

8. In the *Brahma-Purāṇa*, Adhyāya 81, Schreiner and Söhnen 1987: 296–297; and summarized in Söhnen and Schreiner 1989: 146.

9. In this context, we may compare the verse in Böhtlingk (1870–1873, § 4805): *mātṛvat paradārāṁś ca paradravyāṇi loṣṭavat* | *ātmavat sarvabhūtāni yaḥ paśyati sa paśyati* ||, (Who sees other women as his mother, the wealth of others as a lump of dirt, all beings as himself, he [truly] sees). The *Mahābhārata* has (13.132.11): "Those men who always

relate to the wives of others as to their [own] mother, sister and daughter go to heaven" (*mātṛvat svasṛvac caiva nityam duhitṛvac ca ye* | *paradāreṣu vartante te narāḥ svargagāminaḥ* ||). Examples such as these, which refer in the first place to ordinary displays of respect, only reinforce the obvious conclusion that sexual relations with a mother, sister, or daughter is almost unthinkable.

10. I thus think the expression in Söhnen and Schreiner (1989: 146), that he "resorted to dispassionate indifference," is, in this context, a bit weak.

11. *Brahma-Purāṇa*, Adhyāya 81, verse 15cd: *itaḥ strīnāmadheyaṁ yan mama mātṛsamaṁ matam.*

12. Ibid., verse 20: *mahāpātakinaḥ kecid gurudārābhigāminaḥ* | *atrāplavanamātreṇa dhautapāpā bhavantu te* ||.

13. I am grateful to Karen Muldoon-Hules for this insight.

14. Brāhma-khaṇḍa, *Setumāhātmya*, Adhyāya 35, vv. 3–24. I have used a text input by Harunaga Isaacson. For a printed edition, see *Śrīskandhamahāpurāṇam / The Skandhamahāpurāṇam* (Delhi: Nag Publishers, 1986–1987), a reprint of that published in Bombay by Veṅkaṭeśvara Press, 1908–1910. A short summary of the episode is given in Italian in Vallauri (1938: 368). I am most grateful to Harunaga Isaacson for his suggestions on my translation.

15. The five are killing a brahmin, drinking intoxicants, theft, incest, and associating with one who does such things.

16. The verse, cited by Böhtlingk (1870–1873, § 4809), occurs frequently, for example in Manu 2.215: *mātrā svasrā duhitrā vā na viviktāsano bhavet* | *bālavān indriyagrāmo vidvāṁsam api karṣati* ||.

17. Naturally, this need not prevent our simultaneous appreciation of a story as also transcending its context, as being both a product and representative of a specific time and place and a universal artifact that embodies and exhibits common human insights.

Chapter 18: The Medieval European Oedipal Judas

1. If Taylor (1938: 25) is right that the riddle in a tenth-century manuscript refers to Judas and Cyborea, the date of the story could be pushed back further still—but this identification is far from certain. The riddle reads:

> *Porto filium filii mei / mariti mei fratrem, / alterum unicum filium meum.*
> I carry the son of my son,
> [This son who is] My husband's brother [that is, my son is my husband, so my second child is the son of my son],
> My one and only other son [since I have two sons, but they in fact are brothers, as well as father and son].

I do not completely understand this verse, despite the good advice of a number of colleagues, and offer the translation with hesitation.

2. Baum 1916: 482–483. For a translation of the *Golden Legend* version, see Voragine (1941: 172–174, February 24; the work is arranged according to saints' days). For translations of individual stories of this type, see Edmunds (1985: 61–67, 89–93, 138–141, 144–148, 155–160, 197). See also the early study of Rand (1913). For English versions (although examples were of course also studied by Baum), see, among others, Axton (1990). Note that the Latin *Legenda aurea* is also known under its French title, *Légende dorée*, and its author as Jacques de Voragine. An English version was published by William Caxton in 1483 under the title *The Golden Legend or Lives of the Saints.* Many have noticed and studied the story, including the psychoanalyst Rank (1992: 277–282); he interprets numerous details in a correspondingly psychoanalytical manner, as he does the mass of materials he examined in his remarkable book.

3. Edmunds 1976: 149.

4. In the following, as I hope everywhere, I have tried to remain particularly conscious of the warning voiced by my teacher, Luis Gómez (1985), that comparisons, to be meaningful, must be systemic and not isolated. One must see phenomena as parts of a whole, not as individual objects to be compared to one another willy-nilly. Nevertheless, since, in the present case in any event, the goal is less to compare than to explore different ways of appreciating one set of materials, I feel secure in this approach, while remaining aware that I have not fully appreciated the role and function of the Judas story in the medieval Christian world.

5. Another factor to keep in mind: in the period of concern to us in ancient India, Sanskrit was already a learned language, not a mother tongue. Thus, the only people who were able to read Sanskrit, the language in which literature like the *Vibhāṣā* was written, or to understand it if it were read or recited to them, were much more specifically educated than most literate individuals of our own time, for whom reading is an ordinary and common skill.

6. Hahn 1980: 227.

7. For a general overview of the legal situation, see the first chapter of Archibald (2001: 9–52), as well as the excellent de Jong (1989); and Boureau (1986: 35–36). For a broader discussion of the many sides of the issue, see Archibald (2001 passim). One might see also Méla (1992), who sets the Judas-Oedipus story in a context of twelfth- and thirteenth-century literature, which he sees as pervasively Oedipal.

8. Baum 1916: 604–606.

9. Ibid.: 607.

10. For a brief introduction to relatively recent scholarship on antisemitism during this period, see Berger (1997); and for an accessible, though dated, survey see Trachtenberg (1943). I have seen this connection discussed in the literature only by Boureau (1986: 33, and passim). For a general consideration of Judas and antisemitism, see Maccoby (1992, especially chapter 7, "Judas and the Growth of Antisemitism").

11. Baum 1916: 481, 526. While many of these versions may ultimately depend on the *Legenda aurea*, some do not.

12. Boureau 1986: 25–26.

13. Edmunds 1976: 154; and see Edmunds 1985 for translations of these modern tellings. Note also that the mid-twelfth century marked the beginning of the blood libel,

in which Jews were accused of using the blood of Christian children to make matzo, an accusation that refers directly to the belief that Jews murdered Jesus. (There is a case in England in 1144, in Würzburg in 1147.) Since Judas is the archetypal Jew responsible for that murder, it is again hard to imagine that there should be no connection whatsoever between the sudden popularity of the Oedipal Judas legend and the blood libel in the eleventh and twelfth centuries.

14. Reider 1960: 521–522.

15. Baum 1916: 571. His only sympathetic remark comes at the end of his essay, when he comments about the possibility that the legend was still in his day circulating orally in Europe (which we now know it was) as follows (631–632): "But as civilization advances such legends tend to die out; as what we call the 'modern interpretation of the Bible' gains more adherents, the somewhat bigoted and entirely unchristian hatred of Judas which this legend represents must decline." The hatred of Judas may indeed have declined, if only as a function of a general decline in the type of education that would familiarize people with the legend.

16. See, for instance, Glassman (1975) on England. The phenomenon is also well known in Japan, where Jews have never lived in significant numbers, making antisemitism there all the more an example of mindless hatred of the unknown Other. On Japan, see Goodman and Miyazawa (1995).

Baum's England is also an England in which (it is true, in a time after Baum wrote) prominent members of the royal family were active sympathizers of Hitler and the Nazi regime. Naturally, it is not my intention to tar the English nation as a whole with the brush of accusations of antisemitism; I owe my very existence to the generosity of wartime Britain, which saved my German Jewish refugee mother from the genocidal onslaught of Hitler's SS. This is a debt that can never be repaid, and it is the farthest thing from my mind to imply by my observations about Baum's pride in the English preservation of the Judas story any corresponding lack of appreciation for the generosity—spiritual as well as material—of the English as a nation.

17. It is worth noticing a remarkable observation regarding a scholar whose work I will discuss in a moment. In his "Foreword" to Ohly's study of guilt, *The Damned and the Elect*, a work which focuses primarily on Judas, George Steiner wrote (1992: xiii–xiv):

> It is ironic that Dr Friedrich Ohly's work itself lies under a certain shadow. Nowhere does he bring himself to touch on the obvious central crux that, of the disciples, only Judas is, by his very name, defined as a Jew. It is in the name of Judas' alleged betrayal and of the deicide which it provokes, that Jews were hounded to pitiless death from those very times onward in which Judas looms in Christian literature and iconography. It is countless Jewish men, women and children who suffered ostracism and martyrdom in the black light of Judas' fate as it has been proclaimed and imaged by Christianity. Half a century after Auschwitz, it seems as if German scholarship is still lamed when it draws near the

> unspeakable; a condition which gives to this essay on "life and guilt" a constraining pathos.

Steiner's observations obviously intend to refer to multiple aspects of the Judas legend, not only those traditions that give to his life an incestuous patricidal past.

Baum noted (1916: 481, n. 1) that medieval art does not depict the Oedipal Judas, although ample attention is given in particular to depictions of the death of Judas, concerning which the Gospels themselves convey conflicting accounts. Note, however, that at least one Middle High German *Life of Judas*, dated to 1330, contains marginal illustrations—plates 1–4 in Ohly (1992: 18–21, with text and translation on pp. 143–149). Boureau (1986: 34) is more precise, saying that there is no public iconographic depiction, in windows, frescos, or paintings. Concerning the iconography of Judas, see, for instance, Sullivan (1998); and the interesting Mellinkoff (1982).

18. Rand (1913: 312); and followed by others, such as Baum (1916: 628); and Reider (1960: 518).

19. Baum 1916: 629. For a survey of the idea of Antichrist in the medieval period, see McGinn (1994: 114–199); and in much greater detail, Emmerson (1981). The idea that the Antichrist will belong to the tribe of Dan is detailed in Bousset (1896: 171–174) and noted repeatedly from medieval sources by Emmerson. I do not ignore here the idea that, for instance, in the period after the Reformation, some Protestants saw the Catholic pope as the Antichrist. Nor do I suggest that the Antichrist was always identified as a Jew, just that this was also a possible association.

20. I quote Archibald 2001: 111–113. The version in the *Legenda aurea*, though a bit later, is very similar; see Voragaine (1941: 177–190, March 12). See also Baum (1916: 595–597). There is a quite substantial scholarly literature on Hartmann and the *Gregorius.*

21. Ohly 1992: 4–5, and for the general theme, passim.

22. Ibid.: 9.

23. Ibid.: 29.

24. Ibid.: 31. This is clearly the view of Saint Augustine, who says in the *City of God* (*De civitate Dei* I.17, quoted by Ohly 1992: 35), with reference to Judas' suicide, "For by despairing of God's mercy he repented to his own destruction and left himself no room for saving penitence." As Ohly comments, "the worst sin of all is to withdraw from grace."

25. I do not mean to say there is only one way: certainly one could understand these stories as, among other things, also urging Christians toward a deeper, more sincere, and more devoted faith, which may be the point about Peter mentioned below. This would not contradict the other, antisemitic or at least anti-Jewish message I have been emphasizing. There are also those who argue that it is even possible to see parallels between the way Judas is portrayed and the portrayal of Jesus himself, for instance Reider (1960: 522ff.), referring to the work of Theodor Reik, *Der eigene und der fremde Gott* (1923).

26. Boureau 1986: 33.

27. Ohly 1992: 40.

28. Archibald 2001: 119–120. This is based on a seventeenth-century Old Russian version. Another version is translated in Edmunds (1985: 188–192). See also Baum (1916: 597–598); and Rank (1992: 279–281), for whom, for instance, the murder of the priests represents patricide.

29. Another remarkable element of the Andreas story, while certainly only by chance, parallels the Dharmaruci story as well. One version of the legend contains the following full text, found in Edmunds (1985: 190–191):

> His mother sent him to the city of Crete to look for his spiritual father to confess to him all his sins. But the priest did not forgive him his many sins. And he, Andrej, beat this spiritual father of his to death with the church lectern and secretly left the church alone. He went to another spiritual father, confessed to him also all the sins he had committed from his childhood to the present day, including fornication and incest. The priest did not forgive him, but said to Andrej: "It is not fitting for us to take such sins on our soul." And Andrej spoke, saying: "Christ came into the world to call sinners to repentance, while you, priest, do not want to forgive me my sins." It is said in the Gospel: "What you condemn on earth shall be condemned in heaven; what you forgive on earth, shall be forgiven in heaven." But the priest said: "I do not want to carry such a sin on myself, for a person who committed the sin will not get forgiveness." And Andrej killed this priest also and dragged him out of the church with his belt. Similarly, he went to a third priest and confessed all his sins to him. He too did not forgive him his many sins. Andrej beat the third priest to death as well with the church lock. And Andrej said to himself: "I will go to the city of Crete; there is a bishop there. He will accept me for repentance for he is sagacious and God-fearing and will forgive me. If he does not forgive me, I will go to a distant land to the tsar's camp and raise a great army and burn the city of Crete and take the people into slavery and kill the bishop." God is good and a lover of man, not wanting death for sinners and expecting their repentance. And Andrej came to the city of Crete and went to the bishop. The bishop received him and ordered that Andrej's mother be found. The bishop, seeing Andrej with strengthened courage, that he wanted to be chosen a vessel of God, began to question him in private. Andrej confessed his sins to the bishop in order, committed from his youth to his old age. And the bishop feared the judgement of God and death and sent him for his mother. And Andrej came with his mother to the bishop. The bishop, instructing them spiritually and at length, released them.

We cannot help but be immediately reminded here of the serial arson of Dharmaruci who, after his requests for ordination have been denied, finds eventual acceptance when the future Buddha himself offers him a sort of status, although as I have suggested, not genuine monastic ordination. The parallel is far from perfect, but the resonance is remarkable nonetheless, serving as it does in both contexts to emphasize the transformative power of true repentance.

30. Goldman 1978: 364.

31. Baum 1916: 608; see also 586–603.

32. Ibid.: 615. See further pp. 617–621, at the end of which Baum is entirely agnostic as to which theory—popular or learned origin—he favors.

33. Ibid.: 609 says, "No reputable church writer, except Jacopo [da Voragine, author of the *Legenda aurea*], gives it his sanction by repeating it or alluding to it." See also Boureau (1986: 34).

34. The *Kathāsāritsāgara* itself, of course, collects and compiles previously composed narratives, in which sense it might be problematic to term the text "creative." Rather, the point I wish to make is that much of the material collected in this massive text has as its sole or main goal entertainment; it is fiction for fiction's sake, pleasure reading (even if it claims, explicitly or implicitly, a didactic value, as is the case for instance with the *Hitopadeśa*).

Chapter 19: Why Incest Taboos?

1. See, as just a few examples among the many, Rank (1992), Archibald (2001), and more generally Twitchell (1987). For a series of essays on various literary examples from medieval to contemporary, see Barnes (2002). Considerably less "elevated" in tone is Miles (1973), which seems, in fact, little more than an excuse to quote lengthy passages of Victorian incest-themed pornography. For this and broader themes of "sexual perversion" in medieval literature, see the essays in Buschinger and Spiewok (1994). In addition, a number of more focused studies on eighteenth- and nineteenth-century literature deal with the incest theme in particular.

2. See the excellent study of Archibald 2001.

3. The quotations are from Thorslev 1965: 42–44.

4. Richardson 1985: 744.

5. See Thornhill (1991: 247). Héritier (1994) appears to be correct, however, that very little attention has been given to issues of homosexual incest, a gap her study attempts to fill. I do not know if the decade since the publication of her book has seen further work on this subject.

6. Miller 1997: 15.

7. Some prohibitions are so detailed, such as those expounded by the medieval Church (see de Jong [1989]), that even those within the group they claim to model sometimes need to study them. They were, moreover, frequently broken, often through ignorance. Such prohibitions clearly are not maintained by disgust. But perhaps here Miller intends only the basic incest taboos, for example, those concerning the nuclear family?

8. On the notion of attraction to the disgusting, see Miller (1997: 22, 111).

9. The fascination with incest does not, of course, necessarily reflect any actual rate of its occurrence. (One may get some sense of present-day fascinations with incest, in a most vivid manner, if one makes the mistake of doing a web search for "brother-sister incest.")

10. Miller 1997: 2.

11. Rozin, Haidt, and McCauley 2000: 642; see also Haidt et al. 1997. Note that Miller (1997: 48–49) does not entirely agree with this view. For further studies, see also Haidt and Hersh (2001), and of course the bibliographies to all these works.

12. See Plato's *Republic* IX.571; Ovid's *Metamorphoses* (VII.386–387; translated by Mandelbaum 1993: 225): "where fate would have depraved Menephron mate with his own mother—the incestuous way of wild beasts," and even more clearly X.324–329 (Mandelbaum, p. 339): "the other animals pursue delight and mate without such niceties. There's nothing execrable when a heifer is mounted by her father; stallions, too, mate with their daughters; and a goat can choose to couple with his child; the female bird conceives from that same seed which fathered her. Blessed are those who have that privilege"; and Chaucer's "The Parson's Tale" (Sequitur de Luxuria §77): "the coming together of those that are akin, or of those that are related by marriage, or else of those whose fathers or other kindred have had intercourse in the sin of lechery; this sin makes them like dogs that pay no heed to relationship."

13. Sometimes these ideas appear in very interesting ways. Tambiah (1969: 428) reports on a northeastern Thai village in which couples guilty of incest (here second cousins) may expiate their offense by eating like dogs, thus misleading the "punishing moral agents into thinking that they are not humans but animals," and therefore not to be punished for behaving in a fashion that is natural to dogs. As Tambiah reports (p. 435): "The dog is regarded as the incestuous animal *par excellence*; canine parents and children copulate."

14. See Shepher 1983: 104–107. For a look at some of the complications with zoo populations, see Lacy et al. (1993).

15. See Pusey and Wolf (1996), and for the point about genetic matching p. 202, referring to the case of the splendid fairy wren, in which 25 percent of breeding pairs are close relatives (compared to the 5 percent normal for other birds), suggesting close inbreeding. However, 60 percent of progeny in nests were sired by nonresident males, bringing the actual level of inbreeding to the common 5 percent, something that could never be known even through close observation, but only through molecular techniques. For further details (and, of course, further complications), see Rowley et al. (1993). More generally one may see many of the essays collected in Thornhill (1993).

16. Miller 1997: 8.

17. See Hejmadi et al. (2000), dealing specifically with a comparison of American and Indian reactions to certain facial expressions, including that indicative of disgust.

18. See, as one example of the difficulties in making such a claim, Thornhill (1991), and particularly the discussions added to her main paper. Regarding the question of whether we should avoid the singular formulation "the incest taboo," while it is true that there is a variety of configurations, perhaps as many as there are cultures or subcultures, there does seem to be one overarching and unifying concept behind such variant articulations, which might well justify speaking of "the" taboo in the singular. For a discussion, see Wolf (1995: 499–501).

19. Regarding hard evidence for genetic damage brought about by close-kin inbreeding, it is interesting to note that there is considerable research on this topic in the Indian context, thanks to the patterns of consanguineous marriage typical in some areas

of South India. See the bibliography available for download at http://www.consang.net/bibliographies/demography/Demography%20Asia%20South%20India%20South.pdf. As examples, see Bittles et al. (1987) and Bittles (2002). The data, interestingly enough, are ambiguous concerning the actual occurrence of cumulative genetic damage through inbreeding, the picture being complicated by numerous other factors.

20. Of course, the confusion is not pervasive. Willner (1983: 136), for instance, wrote very clearly: "Both Western legal and traditional anthropological definitions of incest represent it as the intersection of three sets: a set of sexual behaviors, a set of kinship categories and a set of prohibitions."

21. One may compare the distinction offered by Leavitt (1990: 984, n. 1):

> The term "incest taboo" (cultural rules prohibiting sexual relations between relatives) is not the same as "incest avoidance" (the circumvention, through various unconscious processes, of sexual relations among relatives). Nor does "incest taboo" or "incest avoidance" have the same meaning as "inbreeding avoidance" (the circumvention of procreation with partners who are homozygotic; mates who have identical rather than different alleles at one or more loci in homologous chromosome segments).

22. See Silk 2008a.

23. Fox 1980: 2.

24. Women may, in some contexts, seek economic or social benefits from marriages, but genetic benefits from breeding. This may lead them to choose marriage partners and sexual mates differently. Males may, naturally, have complementary variant concerns relevant to their choice of wife and mating partner(s). Tensions motivate men and women variably in this regard, such as the fact that men may, with little investment, father many children, while an individual woman can create and nurture comparatively few.

25. In the context of Indian technical literature, the distinction is in fact made explicit, with discussions of permissible marriages separate from definitions of women with whom sexual relations are forbidden (the latter termed *agamyā*). See Silk 2008a.

26. Arens 1985: 28.

27. It is possible that it is a failure to appreciate this point that leads Haig (1999) to make some odd suggestions. Although he begins his paper cautiously, saying (84) "My principal aim is to be clear about what the underlying theory would predict if sexual aversions and desires were determined by the costs of inbreeding rather than to make a judgment on the larger question whether evolved aversions actually exist," in the end (97) he appears to want to explain "the reason why sexual aggression by sons toward mothers is so rare" at least partly on the basis of a struggle for dominance between alleles inherited from mother and father: "A son's paternal alleles are equally likely to be present in his own gametes and his genetic father's gametes. When there is a high probability that a mother's future offspring will have the same father as the son, the son's paternal alleles gain more from the father conceiving a child because this avoids the costs of inbreeding." Such an approach seems to me untenable, assuming as it does a nearly totally mechanistic decision-making

process on the cellular level. (I am, however, unable to judge the utility of Haig's proposed mathematical models, which I take to be the main contribution of the study.)

28. Thornhill 1991: 248.

29. As an example, we may cite Durham's view (1991: 316) that there are only five possibly viable arguments explanatory of incest taboos:

> (1) Family harmony or disruption theory—the idea that incest taboos prevent competition within families, upon which stable social orders are built.
>
> (2) Group alliance or cooperation theory—incest taboos promote beneficial cooperation between families.
>
> (3) Psychoanalytic theory (Freud)—incest taboos protect against universal incestuous wishes, which would otherwise challenge the social order.
>
> (4) Aversion theory (Westermarck)—aversion develops from an early age, expressed as moral disgust.
>
> (5) Inbreeding theory—incest taboos limit inbreeding and therefore limit its possible genetic damage.

30. Westermarck 1921: ii.192–193.

31. These are the most frequently cited cases, studied originally by Joseph Shepher (1983); Arthur P. Wolf (1995); and Justine McCabe (1983). Wolf's 1995 volume, a summation of his many previous works as well as the work of others, contains the most detailed and closely argued assessment yet of all known evidence. The results of these scholars are invoked (not always in directions favored by their authors) time and again by others, among whom see as examples Spain (1987); and Leavitt (1990). Any future approach to this topic will have to start now with Wolf's monumental work.

32. For Bevc and Silverman (2000: 159), for instance: "Early sustained cohabitation between siblings operates as a barrier specific to potentially reproductive acts rather than as a general suppressor of sexual interest."

33. Shields 1993: 146.

34. As van den Berghe (1983: 92) notes, "It is clear that panmixia [random mating] seldom if ever exists in nature. A variety of barriers set limits on both outbreeding (at the limit, barriers against interspecific mating, but also spatial barriers to mating between populations of the same species) and inbreeding (between close relatives)." This is to say, demography and dispersal—environmental factors—determine which potential mates are available, but choice beyond that, i.e., nonrandom mating, must be (Shields 1993: 163) "caused, at least in part, by increased reproductive success associated with the observed choices."

35. Shields 1993: 147, quoting Ralls et al. 1986: 51.

36. This *r* is related to, but different from, the coefficient used to numerically calculate inbreeding, the symbol for which is *f* or *F*, the so-called inbreeding coefficient developed in the 1920s by Sewall Wright; see Durham (1991: 300–301 et seq.). The *r* and *F* values are usually not the same because Wright took into account nonrandom factors including general populational inbreeding; in other words, *F* does not necessarily assume that any initial breeding pair is entirely unrelated. For a corrected formula, see Bittles (2002: 94).

37. Some of the complexity here may be appreciated by noting the observation of Richard Dawkins (in van den Berghe 1983: 106):

> Paradoxically, the risk from highly lethal recessive genes is less than that from genes whose clinical effect is slight. Highly lethal genes kill fetuses before they have time to impose rearing costs on their parents (and before they are big enough to be recorded in the clinical statistics, which may be partly why the observed incidence of inbreeding depression is somewhat lower than the naive theoretical expectation). Worst of all are weakly deleterious genes that kill or sterilize young adults after the end of the costly rearing period (remember that "costs" to parents are "opportunity costs," measured in lost future opportunities to rear other, healthier children).

38. Lacy et al. 1993: 354. There remains the question of just what inbreeding means, and the extent to which communities in the distant past would have been outbred in any biologically and genetically meaningful sense. If we assume relatively small and isolated populations in some distant point in the prehistoric past, then the breeding populations over time would have quickly become highly inbred from an absolute perspective. (We may disregard the effects of genetic drift, through which even those who share common ancestors do to some extent genetically drift apart over time.) This would be an inevitable result of the limited gene pool. Some scholars have suggested that for such populations, significant dangers could accrue of precisely the opposite sort, namely, outbreeding depression. We must likewise consider that only gross genetic defects would or could have been noticeable and in any way connected with their ultimate cause. A general decrease in fitness defined as lower overall viability in the long run could hardly be noticeable, or if noticed, causally identified. What would be noticed is stillbirths and visible physical abnormalities. (One should remember, however, that in primitive circumstances, ill health from all causes would occur at a rather high rate, and the specific etiology in any particular case or class of cases might never be identified.) Such defects can result from the expression of recessive alleles, but there are many other types of genetic expression which can arise from the same mating patterns that are not visible, or not quickly so. This suggests that any putative recognition of a simple connection between certain procreative configurations and what we would call inbreeding depression could be hard to maintain.

39. On this, see Olivelle (2002, especially 31–36, and with reference to Tambiah [1969]). Olivelle sees a parallel between permissible marriages and permitted foods. Of course, even the types of distant matches disfavored by the Brahmanical law books would not give rise to genetic abnormalities; we are speaking rather of matings across species boundaries, for instance (although this in its turn is complicated by the reciprocal definition of species as that grouping within which interbreeding is possible).

40. Thornhill 1990: 155.

41. For reasons I do not understand, Wolf (1995: 504, 508) seems to flatly contradict himself on this matter. He first says, "I doubt very much the claim that primitive hunters and gatherers recognized the dangers of inbreeding . . . ," but only a few pages later: "My guess is that the inbreeding hypothesis"—concerning which he said a few lines above

"our tendency to avoid childhood associates is explained by the dangers of inbreeding"—"will prove correct. . . ."

42. We need hardly be ashamed of our inability to provide an answer to this question. Arthur Wolf wrote (1995: 2): "I do not after 25 years of thinking about the problem know why it is that intimate childhood association inhibits sexual attraction, but I do claim to have the evidence necessary to show that it does."

One of the key problems facing the Westermarck theory in almost any form is not that of verifying its explanatory coherence empirically, but rather of identifying a mechanism through which the posited aversion would function. If children and the adults who raised them, or children reared together, avoid sexual contact later in life, how does this come about? One postulate focuses on olfactory detection of the major histocompatability complex (MHC) phenotype; see Hendrix and Schneider (1999). For studies relevant to the MHC hypothesis, see, in addition to those cited below, Schneider and Hendrix (2000); Weisfeld et al. (2003); Penn and Potts (1998, 1999); Yamazaki et al. (1988). According to this hypothesis, relatives may recognize each other, and avoid sexual contact because of an evolutionarily conditioned aversion to the possibility of motivating genetic defects, with smell carried by the familially conditioned MHC phenotype as the medium of such recognition. But this is only half the answer. It may be that a child's aversion to sexual relations with a parent (or sibling) is conditioned in the formative years, perhaps through an olfactory signal, but this does not explain the corresponding parental aversion to sex with a child. The parent cannot be conditioned in the way the basic Westermarck theory predicts children are conditioned. However, for Hendrix and Schneider (1999: 205–206), "Because children receive half of their MHC genes from each parent . . . their scents are likely to be somewhat similar to those of . . . parents and siblings." That is, parents may recognize those children with whom they are forbidden to have sexual relations on the basis of shared genotypes. While this appears to solve one problem, it creates another. For if this hypothesis were correct, Westermarck would be wrong, since what he has predicted is not that related individuals, those who share genetic material, will avoid sexual relations, but that those raised together in close proximity will do so. The problem of parental aversion to sexual contact with children is a difficult one, but at least with regard to siblings the case seems watertight (Bevc and Silverman 2000: 152).

While the mechanism of recognition though the MHC appears to have been correctly identified, the key factor is early childhood propinquity. According to Lieberman et al. (2003: 820), while smells work as signals telling us with whom we can and cannot have sexual relations, they do not do so based on common genetic inheritance, but rather on familiarization patterns caused by early propinquity, the study concluding that the longer the period of co-residence, the stronger the effect. With their focus on perceptions of moral wrongness in others, Lieberman et al. (2003: 823) suggest that the degree of relatedness is not significant, and only length of co-residence is a statistically significant predictor of moral wrongness associated with third-party sibling incestuous behaviors. They subsequently (2003: 835) conclude that Westermarck was right after all; because the effect holds whether coresiding individuals are genetically related or not, these results undermine the hypothesis that human kin recognition—for siblings at least—involves using the MHC or phenotypic markers in oneself as a template for kin recognition.

43. This is precisely the suggestion of Westermarck himself (1921: ii.193); see also Wolf (1995: 509, 513).

44. I say "extending" since, as I have suggested above, there seems to be no doubt that human strategies of inbreeding avoidance predate any incest taboos, if only because nonhuman animals have been shown likewise to engage in inbreeding avoidance strategies (in parallel with schemes to avoid excessive outbreeding). Scholars who study the genetic effects of consanguineous mating generally consider unions of $F \geq 0.0156$, namely, those between second cousins or closer, to be in the class of those prone to produce genetic abnormalities. Beyond this degree of affinity, the genetic influence of such unions would differ only slightly from that of the general population.

45. Nancy Thornhill (1991: 261, n. 4) has "proposed that societal rules regulating mating and marriage between relatives (affinal and genetic) are evolutionarily different from the avoidance of mating between close kin, and that rule makers must rely on measures other than natural avoidance for enforcement." With this I can certainly agree. However, she goes on to argue that the real basis of incest avoidance rules in societies is to keep women sexually isolated and avoid concentrations of wealth other than those of the rulers (1990: 155). See also Walter (2000: 485), for whom things like incest taboos "are not instituted for the purpose of preventing inbreeding[;] they are instituted for the purpose of establishing and maintaining valued and necessary political alliances."

46. This despite the efforts of those such as Spain (1987, 1988) to defend a (neo-)Freudian position as in harmony with at least some of the ideas of Westermarck.

47. Freud in *A General Introduction to Psychoanalysis*, as cited by Wolf 1995: 1.

48. *Totem and Taboo*, as cited in Wolf 1995: 11.

49. Westermarck 1921: 2.203; and cited by Wolf 1995: 12; he goes on to ask whether "the exceptional severity with which parricide is treated by many law books proves that a large number of men have a natural propensity to kill their parents." This, of course, is precisely what Freud *would* maintain.

50. As Wolf (1995: 490) points out, Freud himself, in his "Three Essays on Sexuality," very clearly stated that acceptance of the importance of the Oedipus complex "has become the shibboleth that distinguishes the adherents of psychoanalysis from its opponents."

51. Richardson 2000: 570.

52. Archibald 2001: 231.

Chapter 20: Forging Mahādeva

1. Ramanujan 1984: 244, 253.

2. Goldman 1978: 327. For further of Goldman's investigations, see his 1982 and 1993 studies.

3. Ibid.: 337. See also the detailed reflections of Obeyesekere (1990: 71ff.).

4. Goldman 1978: 329.

5. Ibid.: 369, n. 24.

6. For greater detail on the story, see Hart (1980: 123–125).

7. Goldman 1978: 370.

8. Ibid.: 364.

9. See Patañjali's *Mahābhāṣya* (Kielhorn 1965: 112) *ad Aṣṭādhyāyī* III.2.88 (where we find *mātṛhan, pitṛhan, bhrātṛhan*), and for the *Atharva Veda*, see the Paippalāda recension IX.22.7 and XIX.46.14. I thank my colleague Stephanie Jamison for helping me locate the *Atharva* references.

10. *Kauṣītaki Upaniṣad* III.1 (Olivelle 1998: 346): *sa yo māṁ veda na ha vai tasya kena cana karmaṇā lomo mīyate . . . na mātṛvadhena na pitṛvadhena.*

11. Obeyesekere 1990: 105.

12. Obviously a very clear example of this concerns the caste system. I plan to offer some observations on the rather wide range of Indian Buddhist attitudes to outcastes in the not-too-distant future.

13. There are, of course, other possible dimensions to the "Indianness" of the Dharmaruci story. One approach to this issue is to begin with a catalogue of the chief story motifs identifiable in the *Divyāvadāna* story of Dharmaruci, as classified according to standard categories employed by folklore scholars; see Thompson (1956–1958); and Thompson and Balys (1958): T 452: Professional go-between; T 452.1: Mother acts as procuress of bedmate for her son; T 412: Mother-son incest; N 365.1: Boy unwittingly commits incest with his mother; H 110: Identification by cloth or clothing (it is not clear whether we should class this as H 112 or H 119); S 22: Patricide; T 92.9.1: Patricide because of father-son rivalry for girl's love; S 111.1: Murder with poisoned bread; K 1510.1: Adulteress kills home-coming husband; S 115: Murder by stabbing; (? Murder to prevent detection of previous crime); S 22 B (New?): Matricide; R 325.3: Saint offers murderer refuge.

When we compare this listing with elements of Ramanujan's Indian Oedipal tales, we notice first and foremost that the latter do not involve any murder (although they do include a suicide), so many of these motifs are not present at all, despite the broad overall similarities between the stories. Ramanujan's list of the chief motifs in his tales is as follows (1984: 242): A 463.1 (The Fates); M 301 (The prophets [astrologers]); M 344 (Mother-son incest prophecy); M 370 (Vain attempts to escape fulfillment of prophecy); M 371 (Exposure of child to avoid fulfillment of prophecy); S 331 (Exposure of child in boat [floating chest]); R 131.3.1 (Shepherd rescues abandoned child); T 412 (Mother-son incest); N 101 (Inexorable fate); H 51 (Recognition by scar).

Although not noted in this list, one possibly characteristically Indian feature of such stories is the identification by cloth. Both in Ramanujan's tale (and Karve's almost identical version) and in the most detailed of ours, that of the *Divyāvadāna*, the fact that incest has taken place is revealed through a piece of cloth, in both cases actually an article of clothing. In Ramanujan's and Karve's folktales it is a sari used as a swaddling cloth, and the revelation is inadvertent; in the Dharmaruci story the mother exchanges clothing with her son, with the full and conscious intention of alerting him to the truth of their relationship.

There are several instances of a similar conceit in Indian poetic literature. A verse quoted in the twelfth-century anthology *Subhāṣitaratnakoṣa* (Jeweled Treasury of Fine Words) begins (verse 847ab, trans. Ingalls [1965: 260], text Kosambi and Gokhale [1957: 155]): "The other night from our exchange of love / my friend departed wearing by mistake my robe." The translator, Daniel Ingalls, comments (1965: 527): "Garments were exchanged for sentimental reasons and also simply by mistake." Another example is found in the *Gītagovinda* (Love Song of the Dark Lord) of Jayadeva, which contains the following verse (Miller [1977: 199]; but cf. Siegel [1978: 270, 302]. Found only in the longer recension as 7.41/42, edited in Quellet [1978: 94–95]): "In the morning, seeing her dark scarf on himself, / His yellow cloth on her quivering chest, and Rādhā's alarm, / He laughs freely within the circle of friends; / As he pulls from her eyes the cloth quivering with shame / On Rādhā's face, his mouth sweetly smiles. / Let Nanda's son be bliss for the world!" Siegel comments (1978: 270, n. 156): "Rādhā is wearing Kṛṣṇa's yellow garment and he is wearing her blue garment. The implication is that, dressing together in the dark after lovemaking, they mistakenly put on each other's clothes. The friends laugh at dawn when they discover the mistake, when they see this evidence of the lovemaking. In later poetry about the love-play of Rādhā and Kṛṣṇa the exchange of clothes became a conventional theme and the lovers do so consciously." Taken together with the episode in the story of Dharmaruci and in Ramanujan's folktale, it is possible that there may be some further and more significant connection between exchange of cloth or clothing and sexual relations.

As has been demonstrated by John Boswell, in Europe it was a common literary trope, and very likely a common practice, to place with an abandoned baby some token which would facilitate future identification. The types of tokens that were left with abandoned infants included swaddling clothes; see Boswell (1988: 126). In the twelfth-century *lai* by Marie de France titled *Fresne*, the main character Fresne offers her birth-token cloth as a bed covering for the bridal couple on the wedding night, which allows the in-time discovery of a potentially incestuous situation (ibid.: 368–370).

14. See Silk forthcoming b.

15. Mair 1986: 19–20.

16. Cf. Bareau (1957: 242), who says of the *Vibhāṣā* story: "Although we cannot place much faith in this account, it nevertheless seems that the controversy in question had its origins in certain facts judged scandalous by a group of monks." The key question is who judged what to be scandalous, and when. Is the problematic our texts describe to be properly attributed, as they do, to some time in their distant past, or rather to a time contemporaneous with the composition of the texts themselves?

17. I would only quibble that it is not quite correct to refer to a story for which we have purely literary evidence as, technically, a "folktale." It would be safer to refer to it as simply a "tale" or "story."

18. Doniger 1996: 212; and 1994. Doniger is concerned for the most part with Purāṇic mythologies. These are mythologies in which, for instance, the female Chāyā (Shadow) deceives Vivasvant (Sun) into believing she is his wife Saṁjñā, for as Saṁjñā's "shadow" she resembles her, but she also discusses a story in which a god seduces a mortal woman by masquerading as her husband. See Goldman (1978: 360): "Undoubtedly

the least disguised myth of oedipal incest and its punishment in the Sanskrit epics is the well known and often repeated story of the god Indra, the great sage Gautama, and the latter's wife Ahalyā." Goldman goes on to discuss the story.

19. For what it is worth, such a reading appears to conform to the expectations of at least one contemporary scholar. Lily de Silva (2001: 13), albeit in a rather different context, felt that "incest is a far more heinous crime than even matricide and patricide."

20. Faure 1998: 281.

21. See Silk 2008a.

22. *Abhidharmakośa* and *bhāṣya* IV.74ab (Pradhan 1975: 244.13–18); and see Yaśomitra's commentary in Wogihara (1936: 406.10–12). The passage is translated in La Vallée Poussin (1923–1931: iv.157), with valuable notes, including reference to parallels.

Glossary

Apidamo dapiposha lun 阿毘達磨大毘婆沙論
Apidamozang xianzong lun 阿毘達磨藏顯宗論
āyìduō 阿逸多
Bianzheng lun 辯正論
Bojie 撥劫
bùsuìyì 不遂意
Buzhiyi lun 部執異論
Buzhiyilun shu 部執異論疏
chānghuì 倡穢
chitsu 帙
Chōzen 澄禪
Chūkan 中觀
Chuyao jing 出曜經
Cien 慈恩
Da Zhidu lun 大智度論
daiippen 第一編
Dainihon Bukkyō Zensho 大日本佛教全書
Dainihon Zokuzōkyō 大日本續藏經
Dajue 大覺
dàshén 大神
Datang Xiyuji 大唐西域記
Datian 大天
dùchūjiā 度出家
Falin 法琳
Fenbie gongde lun 分別功德論
Foshuo xianren bojie jing 佛説仙人撥劫經
genbun 原文
gèng hào tārén 更好他人
Gentō 玄棟
Guan Xukongzang pusa jing 觀虛空藏菩薩經
Hōbutsushū 寶物集
Ji 基
jiā 家
jiāotōng 交通
Jiatouluo 加偸邏
Jifayue sheku tuoluoni jing 集法悦捨苦陀羅尼經
Jinglü yixing 經律異相
jiǔkǒng 九孔
Jizang 吉藏
Kaiyuan shijiao lu 開元釋教録
kan 函
Konjaku monogatarishū 今昔物語集
Kuiji 窺基
kyō 経
kyūsatsu 九冊
Lianhuaseni chujia yinyuan ba 蓮花色尼出家因縁跋
Liu Yiching 劉義慶
Makadaiba akugyōji 摩訶提婆惡行事
Minobusan 身延山
Mohetipo 摩訶提婆
mójié(dà)yú 摩竭(大)魚
mǔ 母
Mulian 目連
nāmó fó 南無佛
nanakan 七卷
Nihon Ryōiki 日本靈異記
Pishe 毘闍
Piyueluo 毘悦羅
qí zǐ zhǎngdà rǎnhuì yú mǔ 其子長大, 染穢於母
rǎnhuì 染穢
ron 論
Sangoku denki 三國傳記
Sanlun xuanyi 三論玄義
Sanron gengi kennyūshū 三論玄義檢幽集

satsu 冊
setsuwa bungaku 説話文学
Sheng jing 生經
Shibabu lun 十八部論
Shishuo xinyu 世説新語
Sifenlü xingshichao pi 四分律行事鈔批
sītōng 私通
suì 歳
Taira Yasuyori 平康頼
Tenjiku no Daiten no koto 天竺ノ大天ノ語
tō 套
Tsuini shukke wo motomu sō soku yurusu 遂ニ出家ヲ求ム僧即免ス
wàidào 外道
Xuanyan ji 宣驗記
Yibu zonglun lun 異部宗輪論
Yibuzonglunlun shuji 異部宗輪論述記
yú 於
Yuqieshidilun lüezuan 瑜伽師地論略纂
Zabaozang jing 雜寶藏經
Zachouyu jing 雜譬喩經
zàng 藏
Zapiyu jing 雜譬喩經
zenchishiki 善知識
Zhetatuo 遮他陀
zuò bùjìngguān chéng 作不淨觀成

Works Cited

Akanuma Chizen 赤沼智善. 1931. *Indo bukkyō koyū meishi jiten* 印度佛教固有名詞辭典. Reprint: Kyoto: Hōzōkan 法蔵館, 1967.

Allchin, Raymond, Bridget Allchin, Neil Kreitman, and Elizabeth Errington, eds. 1997. *Gandharan Art in Context: East-West Exchanges at the Crossroads of Asia*. Cambridge: The Ancient India and Iran Trust.

Alsdorf, Ludwig. 1965. *Les Études Jaina: État présent et taches futures*. Paris: Collège de France.

———. 1980. "Ardha-Māgadhī." In *Die Sprache der ältesten buddhistischen Überlieferung / The Language of the Earliest Buddhist Tradition*, ed. Heinz Bechert, 17–23. Symposien zur Buddhismusforschung II. Abhandlungen der Akademie der Wissenschaften in Göttingen, Philologish-historische Klasse, Dritte Folge 117. Göttingen: Vandenhoeck & Ruprecht.

Anonymous. 1984. *Inauguration du buste de Constantin Regamey*. 19 mai 1983. Publications de l'Université de Lausanne 58. Lausanne: Librairie Payot, Librairie de l'Université.

Archibald, Elizabeth. 2001. *Incest and the Medieval Imagination*. Oxford: Clarendon Press.

Arens, W. 1985. *The Original Sin: Incest and Its Meaning*. New York: Oxford University Press.

Axton, Richard. 1990. "Interpretations of Judas in Middle English Literature." In *Religion in the Poetry and Drama of the Late Middle Ages in England*, eds. Piero Boitani and Anna Torti, 179–197. Cambridge: D. S. Brewer.

Bacot, J[acques]. 1930. *Dictionnaire Tibétain-Sanskrit par Tse-ring-ouang-gyal (Che riṅ dbaṅ rgyal)*. Buddhica, Deuxième série, Documents, Tome 2. Paris: Librarie Orientaliste Paul Geuthner.

Bajpai, Shiva G. 1989. "Mathurā: Trade Routes, Commerce, and Communication Patterns, from the Post-Mauryan Period to the End of the Kuṣāṇa Period." In *Mathurā: The Cultural Heritage*, ed. Doris Meth Srinivasan, 46–58. New Delhi: American Institute of Indian Studies.

Balk, Michael. 1984. *Prajñāvarman's Udānavargavivaraṇa*. Bonn: Indica et Tibetica Verlag.

Banerjee, Anukul Chandra. 1977. *Two Buddhist Vinaya Texts in Sanskrit*. Calcutta: The World Press Private Limited.

Banning, Anne. 1989. "Mother-Son Incest: Confronting a Prejudice." *Child Abuse & Neglect* 13, no. 4: 563–570.

Bapat, P[urośottam] V[iśvanath], and A[kira] Hirakawa. 1970. *Shan-Chien-P'i-P'o-Sha: A Chinese Version by Saṅghabhadra of Samantapāsādikā*. Bhandarkar Oriental Series 10. Poona: Bhandarkar Oriental Research Institute.

———, and V[asudev] V[ishvanath] Gokhale. 1982. *Vinaya-sūtra*. Tibetan Sanskrit Works Series 22. Patna: Kashi Prasad Jayaswal Research Institute.

Bareau, André. 1954–1956. "Trois Traités sur les Sectes Bouddhiques attribués à Vasumitra, Bhavya et Vinītadeva." *Journal Asiatique* 242, no. 2: 229–266; 244, no. 2: 167–200.

———. 1955a. *Les Premiers Conciles Bouddhiques*. Annales du Musée Guimet, Bibliothèque d'Études 60. Paris: Presses Universitaires de France.

———. 1955b. *Les Sectes Bouddhiques du Petit Véhicule*. Publications de l'École française d'Extrême-Orient 38. Paris: École française d'Extrême-Orient.

———. 1957. "Les controverses relatives à la nature de l'Arhant dans le Bouddhisme ancien." *Indo-Iranian Journal* 1, no. 3: 241–250.

———. 1971. *Recherches sur la Biographie du Buddha dans les Sūtrapiṭaka et les Vinayapiṭaka Anciens:* II. *Les derniers mois, le Parinirvāṇa et les Funérailles*. Vol. 2. Publications de l'École française d'Extrême-Orient 77. Paris: École française d'Extrême-Orient.

Barnes, Elizabeth. 2002. *Incest and the Literary Imagination*. Gainesville: University of Florida Press.

Barth, Auguste. 1899. Review of Senart 1882–1897. *Journal des Savants* (August, September, October 1899): 453–469, 516–531, 622–631. Reprinted in *Quarante Ans d'Indianisme: Oeuvres de Auguste Barth*, Tome V, 1–43. Paris: Libraire Ernest Leroux, 1927.

Barua, Benimadhab. 1934. *Barhut*. Vol. 2. Indian Research Institute Publications, Fine Arts Series 1 Calcutta: Satis Chandra Seal/Indian Research Institute. London, A. Probsthain.

———, and Kumar Gangananda Sinha. 1926. *Barhut Inscriptions*. Calcutta: University of Calcutta.

Baum, Paull Franklin. 1916. "The Mediaeval Legend of Judas Iscariot." *Publications of the Modern Language Association of America* 31, no. 3 (New Series 24, no. 3): 481–632.

Beal, Samuel. 1875. *The Romantic Legend of Śākya Buddha*. London. Reprint: Delhi: Motilal Banarsidass, 1985.

Bechert, Heinz. 1958. "Über das Apadānabuch." *Wiener Zeitschrift für die Kunde Süd- und Ostasiens* 2: 1–21.

Bell, Vikki. 1993. *Interrogating Incest: Feminism, Foucault and the Law*. London: Routledge.

Berger, David. 1997. *From Crusades to Blood Libels to Expulsions: Some New Approaches to Medieval Antisemitism*. New York: Touro College Graduate School of Jewish Studies.

Bernhard, Franz. 1967. "Zur Textgeschichte und Interpretation der Strophen: Dhammapada 294, 295." *Festschrift für Wilhelm Eilers*, 511–526. Wiesbaden: Otto Harrassowitz.

Bevc, Irene, and Irwin Silverman. 2000. "Early Separation and Sibling Incest: A Test of the Revised Westermarck Theory." *Evolution and Human Behavior* 21: 151–161.

Bhattacharya, Vidhushekhara. 1957. *The Yogācārabhūmi of Ācārya Asaṅga: The Sanksrit Text Compared with the Tibetan Version*. Calcutta: The University of Calcutta.

Bhayani, H. C. 1994. "Some Ancient Indian Versions of Oedipus." In *Jainism and Prakrit in Ancient and Medieval India: Essays for Prof. Jagdish Chandra Jain*, ed. N. N. Bhattacharyya, 151–161. Delhi: Manohar.

Bittles, A[lan] H[olland]. 2002. "Endogamy, Consanguinity and Community Genetics." *Journal of Genetics* 81, no. 3: 91–98.

———, A. Radha Rama Devi, H. S. Savithri, Rajeswari Sridhar, and N. Appaji Rao. 1987. "Consanguineous Marriage and Postnatal Mortality in Karnataka, South India." *Man* 22, no. 4: 736–745.

Black, Deborah. 1997. *Leaves of the Heaven Tree: The Great Compassion of the Buddha.* Berkeley: Dharma Publishing.

Bloomfield, Maurice. 1920. "Notes on the Divyāvadāna." *Journal of the American Oriental Society* 40: 336–352.

———. 1923. "Joseph and Potiphar in Hindu Fiction." *Transactions and Proceedings of the American Philological Association* 54: 141–167.

———. 1926. "Organized Brigandage in Hindu Fiction." *The American Journal of Philology* 47, no. 3: 205–233.

Board of Scholars. 1986. *Brahma Purāṇa*. Part IV. *Gautamī-māhātmya*. Ancient Indian Tradition and Mythology 36. Delhi: Motilal Banrsidass.

Bode, Mabel. 1893. "Women Leaders of the Buddhist Reformation." *Journal of the Royal Asiatic Society of Great Britain and Ireland* (July 1893): 517–566; (October 1893): 763–798.

Bodhi, Bhikkhu. 2000. *The Connected Discourses of the Buddha: A New Translation of the Saṁyutta Nikāya*. Boston: Wisdom Publications.

Bohner, Hermann. 1934. *Legenden aus der Frühzeit des Japanischen Buddhismus: Nippon-koku-gembō-zenaku-ryō-i-ki*. Textband. Mitteilungen der Deutschen Gesellschaft für Natur- und Völkerkunde Ostasiens 27. Tokyo: Deutsche Gesellschaft für Natur- und Völkerkunde Ostasiens.

Böhtlingk, Otto. 1870–1873. *Indische Sprüche*. St. Petersburg. Reprint: Wiesbaden: Antiquariat Otto Harrassowitz, 1966.

———, and Rudolph Roth. 1855–1875. *Sanskrit-Wörterbuch*. 7 vols. St. Petersburg: Kaiserlichen Akademie der Wissenschaften.

Bollée, W[illem] B. 1970. *Kuṇālajātaka: Being an Edition and Translation*. London: Luzac & Company.

Bongard-Levin, Gregory M., and O. F. Volkova. 1965. *The Kunala Legend and an Unpublished Asokavadanamala Manuscript*. Calcutta: Indian Studies Past and Present.

Bosson, James E. 1969. *A Treasury of Aphoristic Jewels: The Subhāṣitaratnanidhi of Sa Skya Paṇḍita in Tibetan and Mongolian*. Indiana University Publications, Uralic and Altaic Series 92. Bloomington: Indiana University.

Boswell, John. 1988. *The Kindness of Strangers: The Abandonment of Children in Western Europe from Late Antiquity to the Renaissance*. New York: Pantheon Books.

Boublil, M. 2002. "L'absence de Thésée ou le couple monoparental mère-fils à l'épreuve du temps." *Neuropsychiatrie de l'Enfance et de l'Adolescence* 50: 58–61.

Boureau, Alain. 1986. "L'incest de Judas: Essai sur la genèse de la haine antisémite au xiie siècle." *L'amour de la haine = Nouvelle Revue de Psychanalyse* 33: 25–41.

Bousset, W[ilhelm]. 1896. *The Antichrist Legend: A Chapter in Christian and Jewish Folklore.* Trans. A. H. Keane. London. Reprint: New York: AMS Press, 1985.

Brough, John. 1957. "Some Notes on Maitrakanyaka: Divyāvadāna XXXVIII." *Bulletin of the School of Oriental and African Studies* 20: 111–132. Reprinted in *John Brough: Collected Papers,* eds. Minoru Hara and J. C. Wright, 159–180. London: School of Oriental and African Studies, University of London, 1996.

Brown, W. Norman. 1968. "The Metaphysics of the Truth Act *(*Satyakriyā).*" In *Mélanges d'Indianisme, a la mémoire de Louis Renou,* 171–177. Publications de l'Institut de Civilisation Indienne, série in-8°, fasc. 28. Paris: Éditions E. de Boccard.

Buffetrille, Katia. 1998. "Pèlerinage et inceste: Le cas de Mchod rten nyi na." In *Tibetan Mountain Deities, Their Cults and Representations,* ed. Anne-Marie Blondeau, *19–42.* Papers Presented at a Panel of the 7th Seminar of the International Association for Tibetan Studies, Graz 1995. Proceedings of the 7th Seminar of the International Association for Tibetan Studies, Graz 1995, vol 6. Österreichische Akademie der Wissenschaften, Philosophisch-historische Klasse, Denkschriften 266. Veröffentlichungen zur Sozialanthropologie 3. Vienna: Verlag der Österreichischen Akademie der Wissenschaften.

———. 2004. "Pilgrimage and Incest: The Case of Chorten Nyima (mchod rten nyi ma) on the Tibeto-Sikkimese Border." *Bulletin of Tibetology* 40, no. 1: 5–38.

Bühler, Georg. 1886. *The Laws of Manu.* The Sacred Books of the East 25. Oxford. Reprint: Delhi: Motilal Banarsidass, 1970.

Burlingame, Eugene Watson. 1917. "The Act of Truth (saccakiriya): A Hindu Spell and Its Employment as a Psychic Motif in Hindu Fiction." *Journal of the Royal Asiatic Society of Great Britain and Ireland* (July 1917): 429–467.

———. 1921. *Buddhist Legends.* Harvard Oriental Series 28, 29, 30. Cambridge, MA. Reprint: London: The Pali Text Society, 1979.

Burnouf, Eugēne. 1844. *Introduction à l'Histoire du Buddhisme Indien.* Paris: Imprimerie Royal.

Buschinger, Danielle, and Wolfgang Spiewok, eds. 1994. *Sexuelle Perversionen im Mittelalter / Les Perversions sexuelles au Moyen Age.* XXIX. Jahrestagung des Arbeitskreises "Deutsche Literatur des Mittelalters," / 29ème Congrès du Cercle de travail de la littérature allemande au Moyen Age (Greifswald/Deutschland-Allemagne) (Brugge/Belgien-Belgique, 22–25 September 1994). WODAN, Greifswalder Beiträge zum Mittelalter / Etudies médiévales de Greifswald 46. Serie 3, Tagunsbände und Sammelschriften / Serie 3, Actes de colloques et ouvrages collectifs 26. Greifswald, Germany: Reineke-Verlag.

Caturvijay Muni, and Punyavijay Muni. 1930–1931. *Vasudevahiṇḍiprathamakhaṇḍam.* Bhavnagar. Reprint: Gandhinagar: Gujarat Sahitya Akadami, 1989.

Chab spel tshe brtan phun tshogs. 1987. *Mkhas pa lde'us mdzad pa'i Rgya bod kyi chos 'byung rgyas pa.* Lhasa: Bod ljong mi dmangs dpe skrun khang.

Chavannes, Emmanuel Édouard. 1910–1911, 1934. *Cinq Cents Contes et Apologues extraits du Tripiṭaka chinois et traduits en Français.* Paris: Ernest Leroux.

Chen Yinke 陳寅恪. *1974. Chen Yinke xiansheng lunwenji* (xia) 陳寅恪先生論文集 (下). Taibei: Sanrenxiang chubanshe 三人行出版社.

Chimpa, Lama, and Alaka Chattopadhyaya. 1980. *Tāranātha's History of Buddhism in India.* Calcutta: K. P. Bagchi & Company.

Chopra, Tilak Raj. 1966. *The Kuśa-Jātaka: A Critical and Comparative Study.* Alt- und Neu-Indische Studien 13. Hamburg: Cram, De Gruyter & Co.

Clarke, Shayne Neil. 1999. "Pārājika: The Myth of Permanent and Irrevocable Expulsion from the Buddhist Monastic Order: A Survey of the Śikṣādattaka in Early Monastic Buddhism." Master's Thesis, University of Canterbury.

———. 2000. "The Existence of the Supposedly Non-existent *Śikṣādattā-śrāmaṇerī:* A New Perspective on *Pārājika* Penance." *Bukkyō Kenkyū* 佛教研究 29: 149–176.

Cole, Alan. 1998. *Mothers and Sons in Chinese Buddhism.* Stanford: Stanford University Press.

Cone, Margaret. 2001. *A Dictionary of Pāli.* Part I: a–kh. Oxford: The Pali Text Society.

Cousins, Lance S. 1991. "The 'Five Points' and the Origins of the Buddhist Schools." In *The Buddhist Forum.* Vol. II: *Seminar Papers 1988–1990,* ed. Tadeusz Skorupski, 27–60. London: School of Oriental and African Studies, University of London.

Cowell, Edward Byles, et al. 1895–1907. *The Jātaka, or Stories of the Buddha's Former Births.* Cambridge. Reprint London: The Pali Text Society, 1981.

———, and Robert Alexander Neil. 1886. *The Divyāvadāna: A Collection of Early Buddhist Legends.* Cambridge. Reprint: Amsterdam: Oriental Press / Philo Press, 1970.

Crooke, William, and Pandit Ram Gharib Chaube. 2002. *Folktales from Northern India.* Ed. Sadhana Naithani. Santa Barbara: ABC-Clio. Reprints materials from *North Indian Notes & Queries* 1892–1896 and *Indian Antiquary* 1924–1926.

Cross, F. L., and Elizabeth A. Livingstone, eds. 1997. *The Oxford Dictionary of the Christian Church.* 3rd ed. Oxford: Oxford University Press.

Csoma de Kőrös, Alexander. 1833. "Origin of the Shakya race translated from the ལ (La), or 26th volume of the mDo class in the Ká-gyur, commencing on the 161st leaf." *Journal of the Asiatic Society of Bengal* 2: 385–392. Reprinted in *Tibetan Studies,* Collected Works of Alexander Csoma de Kőrös, 27–34. Budapest: Akadémiai Kiadó, 1984.

Cunningham, Alexander. 1879. *The Stûpa of Bharhut: A Buddhist Monument ornamented with numerous sculptures illustrative of Buddhist Legend and History in the third century B.C.* London. Reprint: Varanasi: Indological Book House, 1962.

Daniélou, Alain. 1994. *The Complete Kāma Sūtra.* Rochester, VT: Park Street Press.

Das, Sarat Chandra, and Hari Mohan Vidyābhūṣaṇa (and Satis Chandra Vidyābhūṣaṇa). 1888–1918. *Bodhisattvāvadānakalpalatā.* Bibliotheca Indica 124. Calcutta: Baptist Mission Press.

Davenport, John T., with Sallie D. Davenport and Losang Thoden. 2000. *Ordinary Wisdom: Sakya Pandita's Treasury of Good Advice.* Boston: Wisdom Publications.

Deeg, Max. 2004. "Legend and Cult—Contributions to the History of Indian Buddhist Stūpas. Part Two: The 'Stūpa of Laying Down the Bows.'" *Buddhist Studies Review* 21, no. 2: 119–149.

Delhey, Martin. 2002. "*Samāhitā Bhūmiḥ*: Das Kapitel über die meditative Versenkung im Grundteil der Yogācārabhūmi." Ph.D. diss., University of Hamburg.

Demiéville, Paul. 1932. "L'origins des sectes bouddhiques d'après Paramārtha." *Mélanges chinois et bouddhiques* 1: 15–64.

———. 1951. "A Propos du Concile de Vaiśālī." *T'oung Pao* 40, nos. 4–5: 239–296.

Desens, Marliss C. 1994. *The Bed-Trick in English Renaissance Drama: Explorations in Gender, Sexuality, and Power.* Newark, NJ: University of Delaware Press.

Devereux, George. 1951. "The Oedipal Situation and Its Consequences in the Epics of Ancient India." *Samīkṣā: Journal of the Indian Psychoanalytic Society* 5, no. 1: 5–13.

Doniger (O'Flaherty), Wendy. 1975. *Hindu Myths: A Sourcebook Translated from the Sanskrit.* Harmondsworth, Middlesex: Penguin Books.

———. 1993. "When a Lingam Is Just a Good Cigar: Psychoanalysis and Hindu Sexual Fantasies." In *The Psychoanalytic Study of Society* 18, eds. L. Bryce Boyer, Ruth M. Boyer, and Stephen M. Sonnenberg, 81–103. Hillsdale, NJ: The Analytic Press.

———. 1994. "Speaking in Tongues: Deceptive Stories about Sexual Deception." *Journal of Religion* 74, no. 3: 320–337.

———. 1996. "Enigmas of Sexual Masquerade in Hindu Myths and Tales." In *Untying the Knot: On Riddles and Other Enigmatic Modes*, eds. Galit Hasan-Rokem and David Shulman, 208–223. New York: Oxford University Press.

———. 2000. *The Bedtrick: Tales of Sex and Masquerade.* Chicago: The University of Chicago Press.

———, and Sudhir Kakar. 2002. *Kamasutra.* Oxford: Oxford University Press.

Dorji, Tseten. 1974. F*ive Historical Works of Tāranātha (Rgya gar chos 'byuṅ, Kahna pa'i rnam thar, Bka' babs bdun gyi rnam thar, O rgyan rnam thar Rgya gar ma, and Sgrol ma'i rnam thar).* Reproduced from impressions of nineteenth-century Sde-dge blocks from the library of Ri-bo-che Rje-druṅ of Padma-bkod. Lohit, Arunachal Pradesh: Tibetan Nyingmapa Monastery.

D'Penha, Geo. Fr. 1892. "Folklore in Salsette: No. 12: The Fortune-teller's Daughter." *The Indian Antiquary* (Feb. 1892): 45–47.

Draper, Patricia, and Henry Harpending. 1982. "Father Absence and Reproductive Strategy: An Evolutionary Perspective." *Journal of Anthropological Research* 38, no. 3: 255–273.

Durgaprasād (and Kāshināth Pāṇḍurang Parab). 1903. *Kathāsaritsāgara.* 2nd ed. Bombay. Reprint: Delhi: Motilal Banarsidass, no date.

Durham, William H. 1991. *Coevolution: Genes, Culture, and Human Diversity.* Stanford: Stanford University Press.

Durt, Hubert Luc Ghislain. 1980. "Mahalla/Mahallaka et la Crise de la Communauté après le Parinirvāṇa du Buddha." In *Indianisme et Bouddhisme: Mélanges offerts à Mgr Étienne Lamotte*, 79–99. Publications de l'Institut Orientaliste de Louvain 23. Louvain: Université Catholique de Louvain, Institut Orientaliste.

Dutt, Nalinaksha. 1939–1959. *Gilgit Manuscripts.* 4 vols. in 9 parts. Srinagar and Calcutta: J. C. Sarkhel at the Calcutta Oriental Press.

Dutton, Donald G., and Stephen D. Hart. 1992. "Evidence for Long-term, Specific Effects of Childhood Abuse and Neglect on Criminal Behavior in Men." *International Journal of Offender Therapy and Comparative Criminology* 36, no. 2: 129–137.

Edgerton, Franklin. 1953. *Buddhist Hybrid Sanskrit Grammar and Dictionary.* 2 vols. New Haven: Yale University Press.

Edmunds, Lowell. 1976. "Oedipus in the Middle Ages." *Antike und Abendland* 22, no. 2: 140–155.

———. 1985. *Oedipus: The Ancient Legend and Its Later Analogues.* Baltimore: The Johns Hopkins University Press.

———, and Alan Dundes, eds. 1984. *Oedipus: A Folklore Casebook.* New York: Garland Publishing.

Eggeling, Julius. 1882–1900. *The Śatapatha-Brâhmaṇa, according to the text of the Mâdhyandina school.* The Sacred Books of the East 12, 26, 41, 43, 44. Oxford: Clarendon Press.

Eimer, Helmut. 1983. *Rab Tu 'Byuṅ Ba'i Gzi.* 2 vols. Asiatische Forschungen 82 Wiesbaden: Otto Harrassowitz.

Emeneau, M[urray] B. 1939. "Was There Cross-cousin Marriage among the Śākyas?" *Journal of the American Oriental Society* 59: 220–226.

Emmerson, Richard Kenneth. 1981. *Antichrist in the Middle Ages: A Study of Medieval Apocalypticism, Art, and Literature.* Seattle: University of Washington Press.

Ėndon, D[andaryn]. 1989. *Skazochnye Syuzhety v Pamyatnikakh Tibetskoĭ i Mongol'skoĭ Literatur.* Moskow: Nauka.

Enomoto Fumio 榎本文雄. 1993. "*Basharon* no bonbun shahon danpen" 『婆沙論』の梵文写本断片 [A manuscript fragment of the *Vibhāṣā* in Sanskrit]. *Indogaku Bukkyōgaku Kenkyū* 印度学仏教学研究 42, no. 1: 495–490 (sic).

———. 1996. "A Sanskrit Fragment from the Vibhāṣā Discovered in Eastern Turkestan." *Sanskrit-Texte aus dem buddhistischen Kanon: Neuentdeckungen und Neueditionen* III, 133–143. Sanskrit-Wörterbuch der buddhistischen Texte aus den Turfan-Funden Beiheft 6. Göttingen: Vandenhoeck & Ruprecht.

Faure, Bernard. 1998. *The Red Thread: Buddhist Approaches to Sexuality.* Princeton: Princeton University Press.

Fausbøll, Michel Viggo. 1877–1896. *The Jātaka, Together with Its Commentary.* London: Trübner & Co.

Feer, Henri Léon. 1878. "Études boudhiques. Maitrakanyaka-Mittavindaka, la piété filiale." *Journal Asiatique* 7th ser., no. 11: 360–443.

———. 1883. *Fragments Extraits du Kandjour.* Annales du Musée Guimet 5. Paris: Ernest Leroux.

Fick, Richard. 1920. *The Social Organisation of North-East India in Buddha's Time.* Trans. Shishirkumar Maitra. Calcutta. Reprint: Delhi: Indological Book House, 1972.

Filliozat, Jean. 1971. "Le Complexe d'Oedipe dans un Tantra Bouddhique." In *Études Tibétaines dédiées à la mémoire de Marcelle Lalou,* 142–148. Paris: Librarie d'Amerique et d'Orient Adrien Maisonneuve. In English: "The Oedipus Complex in a Buddhist Tantra." *Religion, Philosophy, Yoga: A Selection of Articles by Jean Filliozat*, 429–438. Trans. Maurice Shukla. Delhi: Motilal Banarsidass, 1991.

Finkelhor, D. 1979. *Sexually Victimized Children*. New York: The Free Press.

Fišer, Ivo. 1993. "Pāli *vinaya* and Sanskrit *kāma-śāstra*." *Studies on Buddhism in Honour of A. K. Warder*, 57–65. South Asian Studies Papers 5. Toronto: University of Toronto, Centre for South Asian Studies.

Fox, Robin. 1980. *The Red Lamp of Incest*. New York: E. P. Dutton.

Frances, Vera, and Allen Frances. 1976. "The Incest Taboo and Family Structure." *Family Process* 15, no. 2: 235–244.

Frauwallner, Erich. 1952. "Die buddhistischen Konzile." *Zeitschrift der Deutschen Morgenländischen Gesellschaft* 102, no. 2: 240–261.

Freud, Sigmund. 1953. *The Interpretation of Dreams*. The Standard Edition of the Complete Psychological Works of Sigmund Freud IV. London: The Hogarth Press. A translation of *Die Traumdeutung*. Leipzig/Vienna: Franz Deuticke, 1900.

Frye, Richard N. 1985. "Zoroastrian Incest." In *Orientalia Iosephi Tucci Memoriae Dicata*, eds. G. Gnoli and L. Lanciotti, 445–455. Serie Orientale Roma 56/1. Rome: Istituto Italiano per il Medio ed Estremo Oriente.

Fukunaga Katsumi 福永勝美. 1990. *Bukkyō igaku jiten* 仏教医学事典. Tokyo: Yūzankaku Shuppan 雄山閣出版.

George, Christopher S. 1974. *The Caṇḍamahāroṣaṇa Tantra: Chapters I–VIII: A Critical Edition and English Translation*. American Oriental Series 56. New Haven: American Oriental Society.

Ghosh, Arabinda. 1978. *Remains of the Bharhut Stūpa in the Indian Museum*. I. M. Monograph 9. Calcutta: Indian Museum.

Gjertson, Donald E. 1981. "The Early Chinese Buddhist Miracle Tale: A Preliminary Survey." *Journal of the American Oriental Society* 101, no. 3: 287–301.

———. 1989. *Miraculous Retribution: A Study and Translation of T'ang Lin's* Ming-pao chi. Berkeley: Centers for South and Southeast Asia Studies, University of California at Berkeley.

Glassman, Bernard. 1975. *Anti-Semitic Stereotypes without Jews: Images of the Jews in England 1290–1700*. Detroit: Wayne State University Press.

Gnoli, Raniero. 1977. *The Gilgit Manuscript of the Sanghabhedavastu: Being the 17th and Last Section of the Vinaya of the Mūlasarvāstivādin*. Serie Orientale Roma 49/1. Rome: Istituto Italiano per il Medio ed Estremo Oriente.

Godakumbura, C[harles] E[dmund]. 1954. *Visuddhajanavilāninī, Apadāna Commentary*. London: The Pali Text Society.

Goldman, Robert P. 1978. "Fathers, Sons and Gurus: Oedipal Conflict in the Sanskrit Epics." *Journal of Indian Philosophy* 6, no. 4: 325–392.

———. 1982. "Matricide, Renunciation, and Compensation in the Legends of Two Warrior-Heroes of the Sanskrit Epics." *Indologica Taurinensia* 10: 117–131.

———. 1993. "Transsexualism, Gender, and Anxiety in Traditional India." *Journal of the American Oriental Society* 113, no. 3: 374–401.

Gómez, Luis O[scar]. 1985. "Contributions to the Methodological Clarification of Interfaith Dialogue among Christians and Buddhists." In *The Cross and the Lotus: Christianity and Buddhism in Dialogue*, ed. G[ary] W. Houston, 127–208. Delhi: Motilal Banarsidass.

———. 1996. *Land of Bliss: The Paradise of the Buddha of Measureless Light. Sanskrit and Chinese Versions of the Sukhāvatīvyūha*. Honolulu: University of Hawai'i Press.

Gonda, Jan. 1977. *Medieval Religious Literature in Sanskrit*. A History of Indian Literature II.1. Wiesbaden: Otto Harrassowitz.

Goodman, David G., and Masanori Miyazawa. 1995. *Jews in the Japanese Mind: The History and Uses of a Cultural Stereotype*. New York: Free Press.

Granoff, Phyllis. 1994. "Life as Ritual Process: Remembrance of Past Births in Jain Religious Narratives." In *Other Selves: Autobiography & Biography in Cross-Cultural Perspective*, eds. Phyllis Granoff and Koichi Shinohara, 16–34. Oakville, Ontario: Mosaic Press.

Hahn, Thomas. 1980. "The Medieval Oedipus." *Comparative Literature* 32, no. 3: 225–237.

Haidt, Jonathan, and Matthew A. Hersh. 2001. "Sexual Morality: The Cultures and Emotions of Conservatives and Liberals." *Journal of Applied Social Psychology* 31, no. 1: 191–221.

———, Paul Rozin, Clark McCauley, and Sumio Imada. 1997. "Body, Psyche, and Culture: The Relationship between Disgust and Morality." *Psychology and Developing Societies* 9, no. 1: 107–131.

Haig, David. 1999. "Asymmetric Relations: Internal Conflicts and the Horror of Incest." *Evolution and Human Behavior* 20: 83–98.

Hara Minoru 原実. 2002. "Kodai Indo no joseikan (1)" 古代インドの女性観 (1) [Women in ancient India 1]. *Journal of the International College for Advanced Buddhist Studies/Kokusai Bukkyō Daigakuin Daigaku Kenkyū Kiyō* 国際仏教大学院大学研究紀要 5: 1–40 (230–191).

———. 2003. "Kodai Indo no joseikan (2)" 古代インドの女性観 (2) [Women in ancient India 2]. *Journal of the International College for Advanced Buddhist Studies/Kokusai Bukkyō Daigakuin Daigaku Kenkyū Kiyō* 国際仏教大学院大学研究紀要 6: 1–42 (232–191).

Hare, Edward M[iles]. 1934. *The Book of the Gradual Sayings* III. Reprint. London: The Pali Text Society, 1973.

Harigovinddas, Shravak Pandit, and Shravak Pandit Benchardas. 1912. *The Parshavath Charitra of Shree Bhava Deva Suri*. Yashovijaya Jaina Granthamala 32. Benares: Harishchand Bhurabhai.

Hart, George L., III. 1980. "The Theory of Reincarnation among the Tamils." In *Karma and Rebirth in Classical Indian Traditions*, ed. Wendy Doniger O'Flaherty, 116–133. Berkeley: University of California Press.

Hejmadi, Ahalya, Richard J. Davidson, and Paul Rozin. 2000. "Exploring Hindu Indian Emotion Expressions: Evidence for Accurate Recognition by Americans and Indians." *Psychological Science* 11, no. 3: 183–187.

Hendrix, Lewellyn, and Mark A. Schneider. 1999. "Assumptions on Sex and Society in the Biosocial Theory of Incest." *Cross-Cultural Research* 33, no. 2: 193–218.

Héritier, Françoise. 1982. "The Symbolics of Incest and Its Prohibition." Trans. John Leavitt. In *Between Belief and Transgression: Structuralist Essays in Religion, History, and Myth*, eds. Michel Izard and Pierre Smith, 152–179. Chicago: University of Chicago Press.

———. 1994. *Les Deux Sœurs et Leur Mère: Anthropologie de l'Inceste*. Paris: Éditions Odile Jacob.

Hertel, Johannes. 1908. *Ausgewählte Erzählungen aus Hēmacandras Pariśiṣṭaparvan*. Bibliothek morgenländischer Erzähler 1. Leipzig: Wilhelm Heims.

———. 1917. *Jinakīrti's "Geschichte von Pāla und Gopāla."* Berichte über die Verhandlungen der Königlich Sächsischen Gesellschaft der Wissenschaften zu Leipzig, Philologish-historische Klasse 69/4. Leipzig: B. G. Teubner.

Hetherton, Jacquie. 1999. "The Idealization of Women: Its Role in the Minimization of Child Sexual Abuse by Females." *Child Abuse and Neglect* 23, no. 2: 161–174.

Hinüber, Oskar von. 1996. *A Handbook of Pāli Literature*. Berlin. Reprint: New Delhi: Munshiram Manoharlal, 1997.

Hirakawa Akira 平川彰. 1993. *Nihyaku gojikkai no kenkyū* 二百五十戒の研究 I. Hirakawa Akira Chosakushū 平川彰著作集 14. Tokyo: Shunjūsha 春秋社.

——— 平川彰 et al. 1973. *Index to the Abhidharmakośabhāṣya (P. Pradhan Edition)*. Part One: *Sanskrit-Tibetan-Chinese*. Tokyo: Daizo Shuppan.

Hiraoka Satoshi 平岡聡. 2000. "Butten ni tokareru 'boshi sōkan' setsuwa: Indo genten to sono Chūgoku-Nihonteki hen'yō" 仏典に説かれる「母子相姦」説話: インド原典とその中国・日本的変容 [Buddhist stories of mother-son incest]. *Kyōto Bunkyō Daigaku Ningengaku Kenkyūjo: Ningengaku Kenkyū* 京都文教大学人間学研究所人間学研究 1: 23–36.

———. 2002. *Setsuwa no kōkogaku: Indo bukkyō setsuwa ni himerareta shisō* 説話の考古学: インド仏教説話に秘められた思想. Tokyo: Daizō shuppan 大蔵出版.

———. 2007. *Budda ga nazo toku sanze no monogatari:* Diviya Avadāna *zenyaku* ブッダが謎解く三世の物語 『ディヴィヤ・アヴァダーナ』全訳. 2 vols. Tokyo: Daizō shuppan 大蔵出版.

Hoffmann, Ingeborg. 1974. "Der Kathākośa: Text und Übersetzung mit bibliographischen Anmerkungen." Ph.D. diss., Department of Philosophy, Ludwig-Maximillians University, Munich.

Hora, Sunder Lal. 1955. "Fish in the Jātaka Sculptures." *Journal of the Asiatic Society, Letters* 21, no. 1: 1–13.

———, and S. K. Saraswati. 1955. "Fish in the Jātaka Tales." *Journal of the Asiatic Society, Letters* 21, no. 1: 15–30.

Horner, Isaline Blew. 1930. *Women under Primitive Buddhism: Laywomen and Almswomen* New York: Routledge.

———. 1938–1966. *The Book of the Discipline (Vinaya Piṭaka)*. London: The Pali Text Society.

———. 1963, 1964. *Milinda's Questions*. Sacred Books of the Buddhists 22, 23. Reprint: Oxford: The Pali Text Society, 1990.

Hultzsch, Eugen. 1886. "Ueber eine Sammlung indischer Handschriften und Inschriften." *Zeitschrift der Deutschen Morgenländischen Gesellschaft* 40: 1–80.

Ikegami Junichi 池上洵一. 1976. *Sangoku denki* (jō) 三国伝記 (上). Chūsei no bungaku 中世の文学1/6. Tokyo: Miyai shoten 三弥井書店.

Ingalls, Daniel H[enry] H[olmes]. 1965. *An Anthology of Sanskrit Court Poetry: Vidyākara's "Subhāṣitaratnakoṣa."* Harvard Oriental Series 44. Cambridge, MA: Harvard University Press.

Ishihama Yumiko, and Yoichi Fukuda. 1989 *A New Critical Edition of the* Mahāvyutpatti. Studia Tibetica 16. Materials for Tibetan-Mongolian Dictionaries 1 (Tokyo: Toyo Bunko).

Ishii Kōsei 石井公成. 1996. "Ihatsu o ireta hako: *Nihon Ryōiki* chū-kan san-en no saikentō" 遺髪を入れた筥『日本霊異記』中巻三縁の再検討 [A basket filled with hair of the deceased: A reexamination of *Nihon Ryōiki* 2.3]. *Komazawa Tanki Daigaku Bukkyō Ronshū* 駒澤短期大學佛教論集 2: 63–76.

Itō Chikako 伊藤千賀子. 1996. "Kuśa Jātaka (Shūtaishi honjō) ni tsuite" クシャ・ジャータカ (醜太子本生) について [On the Kusa-Jātaka (The Ugly Prince)]. *Indogaku Bukkyōgaku Kenkyū* 印度学仏教学研究 44, no. 2: 130–133 (851–848).

Iwamoto Yutaka 岩本裕. 1968. *Mokuren densetsu to urabon* 目連傳說と盂蘭盆. Bukkyō Setsuwa Kenkyū 佛教説話研究. Vol. 3. Kyoto: Hōzōkan 法藏館.

———. 1978. *Kaitei zōho bukkyō setsuwa kenkyū josetsu* 改訂増補仏教説話研究序説. Bukkyō Setsuwa Kenkyū 佛教説話研究, Vol. 1. Tokyo: Kaimei shoin 開明書院.

Jacobi, Hermann [Georg]. 1906. *Samaraditya Samkshepa*. Ahmedabad: Saraswati Printing Press.

———. 1932. *Sthavirāvalīcarita or Pariśiṣṭaparvan: Being an Appendix of the Triṣaṣṭiśalākāpuruṣacarita by Hemacandra*. 2nd ed. Bibliotheca India 96. Calcutta: Asiatic Society of Bengal.

Jain, Jagdishchandra. 1977. *The Vasudevahiṇḍi: An Authentic Jain Version of the Bṛhatkathā*. L. D. Series 59. Ahmedabad: L. D. Institute of Indology.

Jamison, Stephanie W. 1991. *The Ravenous Hyenas and the Wounded Sun: Myth and Ritual in Ancient India*. Ithaca, NY: Cornell University Press.

———. 1996. *Sacrificed Wife Sacrificer's Wife: Women, Ritual, and Hospitality in Ancient India*. New York: Oxford University Press.

Jäschke, Heinrich August. 1881. *A Tibetan-English Dictionary*. London: Routledge & Kegan Paul.

Jinananda, B. 1961. *Upasampadājñaptiḥ*. Tibetan Sanskrit Works Series 6. Patna: Kashi Prasad Jayaswal Research Institute.

Johnson, Allen, and Douglass Price-Williams. 1996. *Oedipus Ubiquitous: The Family Complex in World Folk Literature*. Stanford: Stanford University Press.

Jones, J[ohn] J[ames]. 1949–1956. *The Mahāvastu*. Reprint: London: The Pali Text Society, 1973–1978.

Jong, Jan Willem de. 1987. "Notes on the Text of the Aśoka Legend." In *India and the Ancient World*, ed. Gilbert Pollet, 103–113. Orientalia Lovaniensia Analecta 25. Leuven: Department Oriëntalistiek.

———. 1997. *A Brief History of Buddhist Studies in Europe and America*. Tokyo: Kōsei Publishing Co..

Jong, Mayke de. 1989. "To the Limits of Kinship: Anti-incest Legislation in the Early Medieval West (500–900)." In *From Sappho to De Sade: Moments in the History of Sexuality*, ed. Jan Bremmer, 36–59. London: Routledge.

Kabata Ryōshun 賀幡亮俊. 1959. "Daiten no gojihihō ni tsuite: Shoki Indo Jōdo shisō to no kanren kara" 大天の五事非法について: 初期インド浄土思想との關連から. [The Five Theses of Mahādeva: Their connection with early Indian Pure Land thought]. *Indogaku Bukkyōgaku Kenkyū* 印度学仏教学研究 7, no. 2: 561–564 (166–169).

Kagawa Takao 香川孝雄. 1984. *Muryōjukyō no shohon taishō kenkyū* 無量寿経の諸本對照研究. Kyoto: Nagata Bunshōdō 永田文昌堂.

Kanakura Enshō 金倉圓照. 1962. *Indo chūsei seishi-shi* 印度中世精神史. Reprint: Tokyo: Iwanami Shoten 岩波書店, 1983.

Kane, P[andurang] V[aman]. 1968–1977. *History of Dharmaśāstra (Ancient and Medieval Religious and Civil Law in India)*. 2nd ed. 5 vols. Government Oriental Series B 6. Poona: Bhandarkar Oriental Research Institute.

Kapstein, Matthew. 1992. "The Amnesic Monarch and the Five Mnemic Men: 'Memory' in Great Perfection (Rzdogs-chen) Thought." In *In the Mirror of Memory: Reflection on Mindfulness and Remembrance in Indian and Tibetan Buddhism*, ed. Janet Gyatso, 239–269. Albany: State University of New York Press.

Karttunen, Klaus. 1997. *India and the Hellenistic World*. Studia Orientalia 83. Helsinki: Finnish Oriental Society.

Karve, Irawati. 1943–1944. "Kinship Terms and the Family Organization as Found in the Critical Edition of the Mahābhārata." *Bulletin of the Deccan College Research Institute* 5: 61–148.

———. 1950. "A Marathi Version of the Oedipus Story." *Man* 50, no. 99: 71–72.

Kashyap, Bhikkhu J. 1959. *Khuddakanikāya* VII: *The Apadāna* (II)*: Buddhavaṁsa-Caryāpiṭaka*. Nālandā Devanāgarī Pāli Series. Nalanda: Pali Publication Board.

Kasugai Shin'ya 春日井眞也. 1954. "*Gōsesetsuron* ni in'yō seraretaru Maga-Baramon ni tsuite" 業施設論に引用せられたるマガ婆羅門について [On the Maga-Brahman or *bram-ze-mchu-skyes* in the *Karmaprajñapti* or *Las gdags pa*]. *Indogaku Bukkyōgaku Kenkyū* 印度学仏教学研究 3, no. 1: 299–304.

———. 1960. "Ancient Iranian Religion as It Appears in Buddhist Texts: Its Polyandry and Religious Practices." In *Proceedings of the IXth International Congress for the History of Religions: Tokyo and Kyoto, 1958, August 27th – September 9th*, eds. Japanese Organizing Committee for the IX I.C.H.R., Science Council of Japan, International Association for the History of Religions, 112–115. Tokyo: Maruzen.

Katō Seishin 加藤精神. 1950. "Hakushuji Daiten no kenkyū" 舶主兒大天の研究 [A study of ship captain's son Mahādeva]. In *Ishii kyōju kanreki kinen bukkyō ronkō* 石井教授還曆起念　佛教論攷 (*Jōdogaku* 浄土學 22/23), 32–43. Tokyo: Taishō Daigaku Jōdogaku Kenkyūkai 大正大學淨土學研究會.

Kawasaki, Shinjo. 1975. "A Reference to Maga in the Tibetan Translation of the *Tarkajvālā.*" *Indogaku Bukkyōgaku Kenkyū* 印度学仏教学研究 23, no. 2: 1103–1097 (sic).

Kern, Hendrik [Johan Hendrik Caspar]. 1903. *Histoire de Bouddhisme dans l'Inde.* Trans. by Gédéon Huet. Annales du Musée Guimet, Bibliothēque d'Études 11, vol. 2. Paris: Ernest Leroux.

Kielhorn, Lorenz Franz. 1965. *The Vyākaraṇa-Mahābhāṣya of Patañjali. Adhāyas III, IV, and V.* Vol. 2. 3rd ed., rev. by Kashinath Vasudev Abhyankar. Poona: Bhandarkar Oriental Institute. First published in 1883.

Kirde, Signe. 2002. "Bibliographie zur Bodhisattvāvadānakalpalatā des Kṣemendra." In *Śikhisamuccayaḥ: Indian and Tibetan Studies,* eds. Dragomir Dimitrov, Ulrike Roesler, and Roland Steiner, 109–128. Wiener Studien zur Tibetologie und Buddhismuskunde 53. Vienna: Arbeitskreis für Tibetische und Buddhistische Studien Universität Wien.

Klaus, Konrad. 1983. *Das Maitrakanyakāvadāna (Divyāvadāna 38).* Indica et Tibetica 2. Bonn: Indica et Tibetica Verlag.

Koizumi Hiroshi 小泉弘. 1971. *Hōbutsushū: Chūsei koshahon sanshu* 宝物集〈中世古写本三種〉. Koten Bunko 古典文庫 283. Tokyo: Koten Bunko 古典文庫.

———, Yamada Shōzen 山田昭全, Kojima Takayuki 小島孝之, and Kinoshita Motoichi 木下資一. 1993. *Hōbutsushū, Kankyo no Tomo, Hirasan kojin reitaku* 宝物集· 閑居友· 比良山古人霊託. Shin Nihon Koten Bungaku Taikei 新日本古典文学大系 40. Tokyo: Iwanami shoten 岩波書店.

Kosambi, D[amodar] D[harmanand], and V[asudev] V[ishvanath] Gokhale. 1957. *The Subhāṣitaratnakoṣa, Compiled by Vidyākara.* Harvard Oriental Series 42. Cambridge, MA: Harvard University Press.

Koyama Ken'ei 小山憲榮. 1891. *Ibushūrinron jukki hotsujin* 異部宗輪論述記發軔. Kyoto: Bunseidō 文政堂.

Kroeber, A[lfred]. L. 1920. "Totem and Taboo: An Ethnologic Psychoanalysis." *American Anthropologist* 22, no. 1: 48–55.

———. 1939. "Totem and Taboo in Retrospect." *The American Journal of Sociology* 45, no. 3: 446–451.

Krug, Ronald S. 1989. "Adult Male Report of Childhood Sexual Abuse by Mothers: Case Descriptions, Motivations and Long-term Consequences." *Child Abuse & Neglect* 13, no. 1: 111–119.

Kugel, James L. 1990. *In Potiphar's House: The Interpretive Life of Biblical Texts.* New York: HarperSanFrancisco.

Kuijp, Leonard W[illem] J[ohannes] van der. 1996. "Tibetan Belles-Lettres: The Influence of Daṇḍin and Kṣemendra." In *Tibetan Literature: Studies in Genre,* eds. José Ignacio Cabezón and Roger R. Jackson, 393–410. Ithaca, NY: Snow Lion Publications.

Kuo, Li-ying. 1994. *Confession et contrition dans le bouddhisme chinois du Ve au Xe siēcle.* Publications de l'École française d'Extrême-Orient, Monographies 170. Paris: École française d'Extrême-Orient.

Lacy, Robert C., Ann Petric, and Mark Warneke. 1993. "Inbreeding and Outbreeding in Captive Populations of Wild Animal Species." In *The Natural History of Inbreeding and Outbreeding: Theoretical and Empirical Perspectives*, ed. Nancy Wilmsen Thornhill, 352–374. Chicago: The University of Chicago Press.

Lamotte, Étienne Paul Marie. 1944–1980. *Le Traité de la grande Vertu de Sagesse.* 5 vols. Publications de l'Institut Orientaliste de Louvain 25, 26, 2, 12, 24. Reprint: Louvain: Université de Louvain, 1970–1981.

———. 1947. "La Critique d'authenticité dans le Bouddhisme." In *India Antiqua*, 213–222. Leiden: E. J. Brill. English trans. Sara Boin-Webb, "The Assessment of Textual Authenticity in Buddhism." *Buddhist Studies Review* 1, no. 1 (1983–1984): 4–15.

———. 1956. "Buddhist Controversy over the Five Propositions." *Indian Historical Quarterly* 32, nos. 2–3: 148–162.

———. 1958. *Histoire du Bouddhisme Indien, des Origines à l'ére Śaka.* Bibliothēque du Muséon 43; Reprint Publications de l'Institut Orientaliste de Louvain 14. Louvain: Université de Louvain, Institut Orientaliste, 1976. English trans. Sara Webb-Boin. *History of Indian Buddhism: From the Origins to the Śaka Era.* Publications de l'Institut Orientaliste de Louvain 36. Louvain: Université Catholique de Louvain Institut Orientaliste, 1988. My references are to the French original.

Lariviere, Richard W. 1989. *The Nāradasmṛti.* 2 vols. University of Pennsylvania Studies on South Asia 4. Philadelphia: Department of South Asia Regional Studies, University of Pennsylvania.

Larson, Jane E. 1993. " 'Women Understand So Little, They Call My Good Nature "Deceit' ": A Feminist Rethinking of Seduction." *Columbia Law Review* 93: 374–472.

La Vallée Poussin, Louis de. 1909. "Councils and Synods (Buddhist)." In *Encyclopaedia of Religion and Ethics*, ed. James Hastings, vol. IV, 179–185. New York: Charles Scribner's Sons.

———. 1910. "The 'Five Points' of Mahādeva and the Kathāvatthu." *Journal of the Royal Asiatic Society* 1910: 413–423.

———. 1923–1931. *L'Abhidharmakośa de Vasubandhu.* Paris: Geuthner. Reprint: *Mélanges chinois et bouddhiques* 16. Brussels: Institut Belge des Hautes Études Chinoises, 1971.

———. 1929. "Notes Bouddhiques VII: Le Vinaya et la Pureté d'Intention," and "Note Additionnelle." *Académie Royale de Belgique: Bulletins de la Classe des Lettres et des Sciences Morales et Politiques*, 5e série, tome 15: 201–217; 233–234.

Lawson, Christine. 1993. "Mother-Son Sexual Abuse: Rare or Underreported? A Critique of the Research." *Child Abuse & Neglect* 17, no. 2: 261–269.

Leavitt, Gregory C. 1990. "Sociobiological Explanations of Incest Avoidance: A Critical Review of Evidential Claims." *American Anthropologist* 92, no. 4: 971–993.

Lee Ja-rang 李慈郎. 1998. "Konpon bunretsu no gen'in ni kansuru ichikōsatsu" 根本分裂の原因に関する一考察 [A reconsideration of the cause of the initial schism in Buddhist monasteries]. *Indo Tetsugaku Bukkyōgaku Kenkyū* インド哲学仏教学研究 5: 18–30.

———. 2000. "Daiten no 'goji' shuchō no haikei ni tsuite." 大天の「五事」主張の背景について [The background of Mahādeva's assertion of the five points.]. *Shūkyō Kenkyū* 宗教研究 324: 25–44.

———. 2001. "Shoki bukkyō kyōdan no kenkyū: Sanga no bunretsu to buha no seiritsu" 初期仏教教団の研究· サンガの分裂と部派の成立. Ph.D. diss., University of Tokyo.

Lee, Jong Cheol. 2001. *The Tibetan Text of the* Vyākhyāyukti *of Vasubandhu*. Bibliotheca Indologica et Buddhologica 8. Tokyo: The Sankibo Press.

Lévi, Sylvain. 1932. "Note sur des Manuscrits Sanscrits Provenant de Bamiyan (Afghanistan), et de Gilgit (Cachemire)." *Journal Asiatique* 220: 1–45.

Li, Rongxi. 1993. *The Biographical Scripture of King Aśoka*. BDK English Tripiṭaka 76–II. Berkeley, CA: Numata Center for Buddhist Translation and Research.

Lieberman, Debra, John Tooby, and Leda Cosmides. 2003. "Does Morality Have a Biological Basis? An Empirical Test of the Factors Governing Moral Sentiments Relating to Incest." *Proceedings of the Royal Society, London (Biological sciences)* 270: 819–826.

Lightfoot, J[ane]L[ucy]. 1999. *Parthenius of Nicaea: The Poetical Fragments and the Erōtika Pathēmata*. Oxford: Clarendon Press.

Lilley, Mary E. 1927. *Apadāna*. London: The Pali Text Society.

Lindtner, Christian. 1988. "Buddhist References to Old Iranian Religion." In *A Green Leaf: Papers in Honour of Professor Jes P. Asmussen*, 433–444. Acta Iranica 28. Deuxiēme Série: Hommages et Opera Minora XII. Leiden: E. J. Brill.

Lokesh Chandra. 1971. *The Collected Works of Bu-ston*, Part 24 (YA). Śata-Piṭaka 64. New Delhi: International Academy of Indian Culture.

Loutan-Charbon, Nicole. 1978. *Constantin Regamey, Compositeur*. Yverdon: Revue Musicale de Suisse Romande.

Lüders, Heinrich. 1941. *Bhārhut und die buddhistische Literatur*. Abhandlungen für die Kunde Morgenlandes 26–3. Leipzig. Reprint: Nendeln, Liechtenstein: Kraus Reprint, 1966.

———. 1963. *Bharhut Inscriptions*. Revised by E. Waldschmidt and M. A. Mehendale. Corpus Inscriptionum Indicarum 2.2. New Delhi: Archaeological Survey of India.

Maccomby, Hyam. 1992. *Judas Iscariot and the Myth of Jewish Evil*. London: Peter Halban.

Maeda Hisao 前田壽雄. 2003. "Hōnen ni okeru gyakubō no sukui" 法然における逆謗の救い [Salvation from the five grave offences and slandering the Dharma in Hōnen's thought]. *Indo Tetsugaku Bukkyōgaku* 印度哲学仏教学 18: 212–228.

Maeda Takashi 前田崇.1991. "Yugaron Bonbun Kenkyū: Ābhiprāyikārthagāthānirdeśa (Shakuishugi gata)" 瑜伽論梵文研究 Ābhiprāyikārthagāthānirdeśa (釈意趣義伽他). *Bunka* 文化 55, nos. 1–2: 62–92 (101–171).

Mair, Victor. 1986. "An Asian Story of the Oedipus Type." *Asian Folklore Studies* 45, no. 1: 19–32.

———. 1994. *The Columbia Anthology of Traditional Chinese Literature*. New York: Columbia University Press.

Malalasekera, George Peiris [Gunapala Piyasena]. 1938. *Dictionary of Pāli Proper Names*. London: The Pali Text Society.

Mandelbaum, Allen. 1993. *The Metamorphoses of Ovid*. New York: Harcourt Brace & Co.

Martin, Dan, with Yael Bentor. 1997. *Tibetan Histories: A Bibliography of Tibetan-Language Historical Works*. London: Serindia Publications.

Masson-Moussaieff, J[effrey]. 1971. "Obscenity in Sanskrit Literature: A Definition of the Term in the Ancient Indian Context." *Mahfil* 7, nos. 3–4: 197–207.

Masuda, Jiryo. 1925. "Origin and Doctrines of Early Indian Buddhist Schools: A Translation of the Hsüan-chwang Version of Vasumitra's Thesis." *Asia Major* 2: 1–78.

Matsuda Yūko 松田祐子. 1990 "Zōyaku Abhiniṣkramaṇa-sūtra kenkyū (jo)" 蔵訳 Abhiniṣkramaṇa-sūtra 研究（序）[A study of the Tibetan *Abhiniṣkramaṇa-sūtra*]. *Nihon Bukkyō Gakkai Nenpō* 日本仏教学会年報 55: 15–25.

Matsumoto Junko 松本純子. 2001. "*Karamaśataka* ni mieru hasō" *Karamaśataka* に見える破僧 [Saṅghabheda in the *Karmaśataka*]. *Indogaku Bukkyōgaku Kenkyū* 印度学仏教学研究 50, no. 1: 439–436 (90–93).

Matsunaga, Yukei 松長有慶. 1978. *The Guhyasamāja Tantra*. Tokyo: Toho Shuppan.

———. 2000. *Himitsu Jūe Tantora wayaku* 秘密集会タントラ和訳. Kyoto: Hōzōkan 法蔵館.

Matthews, Jane Kinder, Ruth Mathews, and Kathleen Speltz. 1991. "Female Sexual Offenders: A Typology." In *Family Sexual Abuse: Frontline Research and Evaluation*, ed. Michael Quinn Patton, 199–219. Newbury Park, CA: Sage Publications.

May, Jacques. 2001. "La carrière universitaire de Constantin Regamey." *Asiatische Studien/Études Asiatiques* 55, no. 2: 349–379.

McCabe, Justine. 1983. "FBD Marriage: Further Support for the Westermarck Hypothesis of the Incest Taboo?" *American Anthropologist* 85, no. 1: 50–69.

McGinn, Bernard. 1994. *Antichrist: Two Thousand Years of the Human Fascination with Evil*. New York: HarperSanFrancisco.

Mejor, Marek. 1992. *Kṣemendra's Bodhisattvāvadānakalpalatā: Studies and Materials*. Studia Philologica Buddhica, Monograph Series 8. Tokyo: The International Institute for Buddhist Studies.

Méla, Charles. 1992. "Oedipe, Judas, Osiris." In *L'imaginaire courtois et son double*, eds. Giovanna Angeli and Luciano Formisano, 17–38. Pubblicazioni dell'Università degli Studi di Salerno, sezione atti, Convegni, Miscellanee. Naples: Edizioni Scientifiche Italiane.

Mellinkoff, Ruth. 1982. "Judas' Red Hair and the Jews." *Journal of Jewish Art* 9: 31–46.

Meyer, Johann Jakob. 1930. *Sexual Life in Ancient India: A Study in the Comparative History of Indian Culture*. New York: E. P. Dutton & Co.

Miles, Henry. 1973. *Forbidden Fruit: A Study of the Incest Theme in Erotic Literature*. London: Luxor Press.

Miller, Barbara Stoler. 1977. *Love Song of the Dark Lord: Jayadeva's Gītagovinda*. New York: Columbia University Press.

Miller, William Ian. 1997. *The Anatomy of Disgust*. Cambridge, MA: Harvard University Press.

Mizuno Kōgen 水野弘元. 1967. "Bukkyō no bunpa to sono keitō" 仏教の分派とその系統 [Buddhist sects and their lineages]. In *Kōza Bukkyō III: Indo no Bukkyō* 講座仏教 III インドの仏教, 79–118. Tokyo: Daizō shuppan.

———. 1991. "*Pāri Hokkukyō*-ge no taiōhyō" 『パーリ法句経』偈の対応表 [A Comparative Study on the Pāli *Dhammapada*]. *Bukkyō Kenkyū* 佛教研究 20: 1–50.

———. 1993. "Chōrōge, Chōrōnige no taiōhyō" 長老偈, 長老尼偈の対応表 [A comparative study on the *Theragāthā* and the *Therīgāthā*]. *Bukkyō Kenkyū* 佛教研究 22: 3–83.

Morris, Richard, and Edmund Hardy. 1885–1900. *The Aṅguttara-Nikāya*. 2nd ed., revised by A. K. Warder. London: The Pali Text Society. Reprint: 1961.

Mukherjee, Diswadeb. 1966. *Die Überlieferung von Devadatta, dem Widersacher des Buddha, in den kanonischen Schriften*. Münchener Studien zur Sprachwissenschaft, Beiheft J. Munich: J. Kitzinger.

Mukhopadhyaya, Sujitkumar. 1963. *The Aśokāvadāna: Sanskrit Text Compared with Chinese Versions*. New Delhi: Sahitya Akademi.

Müller, Éduard. 1895. "Les Apadānas du Sud." *Actes du Diexième Congrès International des Orientalistes*, Session de Genève 1894, Part 2, 165–173. Leiden: E. J. Brill. Published under the name Éd. Müller-Hess.

———. 1896. "Die Legende von Dīpaṅkara und Sumedha." *Gurupūjākaumudī*, 54–58. Leipzig: Otto Harrassowitz.

Nakada Yorihide 仲田順英. 1995. "Ritsuzōchūni okeru Devadatta denshō ni tsuite: "Saṅghabhedavastu" o chūshin to shite" 律蔵中における Devadatta 伝承について："Saṅghabhedavastu" を中心として [Devadatta legends in the Vinaya texts]. *Taishō Daigaku Daigakuin Kenkyū Ronshū* 大正大学大学院研究論集 19: 312–291 (1–22).

Nakamura Hajime 中村元. 1982–1988. *Jātaka zenshū* ジャータカ全集. 10 vols. Tokyo: Shunjūsha 春秋社.

Nakamura, Kyoko Motomichi. 1973. *Miraculous Stories from the Japanese Buddhist Tradition: The* Nihon ryōiki *of the Monk Kyōkai*. Reprint: Richmond, England: Curzon Press, 1997.

Nanjio, Bunyiu. 1923. *The Laṅkāvatāra Sūtra*. Bibliotheca Otaniensis 1. Reprint: Kyoto: Otani University Press, 1956.

Näther, Volkbert. 1975. *Das Gilgit-Fragment Or. 11878A im Britischen Museum zu London*. Marburg: Erich Mauersberger.

———. 2003. "The Final Leaves of the Pravrajyāvastu Portion of the Vinayavastu Manuscript Found Near Gilgit: Part 2 Nāgakumārāvadāna." Ed. Volkbert Näther, rev. and trans. by Claus Vogel and Klaus Wille. In *Sanskrit-Texte aus dem buddhistischen Kanon: Neuentdeckungen und Neueditionen* IV, eds. Jin-il Chung, Claus Vogel, and Klaus Wille, 11–76. Sanskrit-Wörterbuch der buddhistischen Texte aus den Turfan-Funden Beiheft 9. Göttingen: Vandenhoeck & Ruprecht.

Nattier, Janice, and Charles S. Prebish. 1977. "Mahāsāṃghika Origins: The Beginnings of Buddhist Sectarianism." *History of Religions* 16, no. 3: 237–272.

Nishiwaki, Augustine Hiroshi. 1962. "The Dharma-Saṁgraha: A New Edition with Linguistic Commentary." Ph.D. diss., The Catholic University of America.

Nolot, Édith. 1991. *Règles de Discipline des Nonnes Bouddhistes*. Collège de France, Publications de l'Institut de Civilisation Indienne 60. Paris: Collège de France.

———. 1996. "Studies in Vinaya Technical Terms I–III." *Journal of the Pali Text Society* 22: 73–150.

———. 1999. "Studies in Vinaya Technical Terms IV–X." *Journal of the Pali Text Society* 25: 1–111.

Norman, H[arry] C[ampbell]. 1906–1914. *The Commentary on the Dhammapada*. Reprint: London: The Pali Text Society, 1970.

Norman, K[enneth] R[oy]. 1969. *The Elders' Verses I: Theragāthā*. London: The Pali Text Society. Reprint 1990.

———. 1992. *The Group of Discourses (Sutta-Nipāta)*. Volume II: *Revised Translation with Introduction and Notes*. Oxford: The Pali Text Society.

Nyanaponika Thera, and Hellmuth Hecker. 1997. *Great Disciples of the Buddha: Their Lives, Their Works, Their Legacy*. Boston: Wisdom Publications.

Obermiller, Eugene [Evgenni Eugen'evich]. 1931–1932. *History of Buddhism (Chos ḥbyung) by Bu-ston:* Part I: The Jewelry of Scripture. Part II: The History of Buddhism in India and Tibet. Materialien zur Kunde des Buddhismus 18, 19. Heidelberg. Reprint: Tokyo: Suzuki Research Foundation, 1964.

Obeyesekere, Gananath. 1989. "The Conscience of the Parricide: A Study in Buddhist History." *Man* 24, no. 2: 236–254.

———. 1990. *The Work of Culture: Symbolic Transformations in Psychoanalysis and Anthropology*. Chicago: The University of Chicago Press.

Ohly, Friedrich. 1992. *The Damned and the Elect: Guilt in Western Culture*. Trans. Linda Archibald. Cambridge: Cambridge University Press.

Oikawa Shinkai 及川真介. 1987. "Daikashō (Mahākassapa)" 大迦葉 (Mahākassapa). *Hokke Bunka Kenkyū* 法華文化研究 13: 1–24.

———. 2002. "Women and Men as Described in Pāli Commentaries." In *Buddhist and Indian Studies in Honour of Professor Sodō Mori*, 67–78. Hamamatsu: Kokusai Bukkyoto Kyokai.

Okamaoto Kensuke 岡本健資. 1999. "Kunāra ōji no monogatari: Ku-na-la'i rtogs pa brjod pa shiyaku (1)" クナーラ王子の物語—Ku-na-la'i rtogs pa brjod pa 試訳 (1) [A Japanese Translation of the Tibetan Text of *Kuṇālāvadāna* (1)]. *Indogaku Chibettogaku Kenkyū* インド学チベット学研究 4: 78–102.

———. 2006. "Three Parallel Verses in the *Buddhacarita* and the *Aśokāvadāna*." *Indogaku Bukkyōgaku Kenkyū* 印度学仏教学研究 54, no. 3: 1187–1191 (75–79).

Okayama Hajime 丘山新, Kamitsuka Yoshiko 神塚淑子, Karashima Seishi 辛嶋静志, Kanno Hiroshi 菅野博史, Sueki Fumihiko 末木文美士, Hikita Hiromichi 引田弘道, and Matsumura Takumi 松村巧. 2001. *Gendaigoyaku Agon kyōten: Jōagonkyō dai-yonkan* 現代語訳阿含経典 長阿含経 第 4 巻. Tokyo: Hirakawa shuppansha 平河出版.

Oldenberg, Hermann. 1879–1883. *The Vinaya Piṭakaṁ: One of the Principal Buddhist Holy Scriptures in the Pāli Language.* Reprint: London: The Pali Text Society, 1984.

———, and Richard Pischel. 1883. *The Thera- and Therī-gāthā: (Stanzas Ascribed to Elders of the Buddhist Order of Recluses).* Reprint: London: The Pali Text Society. 1990.

Olivelle, Patrick. 1998. *The Early Upaniṣads: Annotated Text and Translation.* New York: Oxford University Press.

———. 2002. *Food for Thought: Dietary Rules and Social Organization in Ancient India.* 2001 Gonda Lecture. Amsterdam: Royal Netherlands Academy of Arts and Sciences.

Pargiter, F[rederick] E[den]. 1913. *The Purāṇa Text of the Dynasties of the Kali Age.* London. Reprint: Varanasi: Chowkhamba Sanskrit Series Office, 1962. [Chowkhamba Sanskrit Series 19].

Parker, H[enry]. 1914. *Village Folk-tales of Ceylon.* Vol. 3. London: Luzac & Co.

Pāsādika, Bhikkhu. 1989. *Nāgārjuna's Sūtrasamuccaya: A Critical Edition of the Mdo kun las btus pa.* Fontes Tibetici Havnienses 2. Copenhagen: Akademisk Forlag.

Paul, Robert A. 1976. "Did the Primal Crime Take Place?" *Ethos* 4, no. 3: 311–352.

Penn, Dustin J., and Wayne K. Potts. 1998. "MHC-disassortative Mating Preferences Reversed by Cross-fostering." *Proceedings of the Royal Society, London (Biological Sciences)* 265: 1299–1306.

———. 1999. "The Evolution of Mating Preferences and Major Histocompatibility Complex Genes." *American Naturalist* 153, no. 2: 145–164.

Penzer, N[orman] M[osley]. 1924–1928. *The Ocean of Story being C. H. Tawney's Translation of Somadeva's Kathā Sarit Sāgara (or Ocean of Streams of Story).* London: Chas. J. Sawyer.

Pollock, George H., and John Munder Ross. 1988. *The Oedipus Papers.* Classics in Psychoanalysis, monograph 6. Madison, CT: International Universities Press.

Pradhan, Prahlad. 1975. *Abhidharmakośabhāṣyam of Vasubandhu.* Tibetan Sanskrit Works Series 8. Patna: K. P. Jayaswal Research Institute.

Prebish, Charles S. 1974. "A Review of Scholarship on the Buddhist Councils." *Journal of Asian Studies* 33, no. 2: 239–254.

Pruitt, William. 1998a. *The Commentary on the Verses of the Therīs (Therīgāthā-Aṭṭhakathā Paramatthadīpanī VI).* Oxford: The Pali Text Society.

———. 1998b. *Therīgāthā-aṭṭhakathā (Paramatthadīpanī VI) by Achariya Dhammapāla.* Oxford: The Pali Text Society.

Przyluski, Jean. 1923. *La Légende de l'Empereur Açoka.* Annales du Musée Guimet, Bibliothèque d'Études 31. Paris: Paul Geuthner.

Puiggali, Jacques. 1983. "La folie de Périandre, d'après Parthénios." *Fantasmes - Folie: Littérature, Médecine, Société* 5: 69–82.

Pulleyblank, Edwin G[eorge]. 1991. *Lexicon of Reconstructed Pronounciation in Early Middle Chinese, Late Middle Chinese, and Early Mandarin.* Vancouver: UBC Press.

Pusey, Anne, and Marisa Wolf. 1996. "Inbreeding Avoidance in Animals." *Trends in Ecology and Evolution* 11, no. 5: 201–206.

Quellet, Henri. 1978. *Le Gītagovinda de Jayadeva: Texte, Concordance et Index*. Hildesheim: Georg Olms Verlag.

Radermacher, L. 1942. "Eine Wandernde Novelle und Aristippos ΗΕΡΙ ΗΑΛΑΙΑΣ ΤΡΥΦΗΣ." *Rheinisches Museum für Philologie* 91, no. 2: 181–185.

Raghu Vira, and Lokesh Chandra. 1974a. *Gilgit Buddhist Manuscripts* (Facsimile Edition). Part 6. Śata-piṭaka Series, Indo-Asian Literatures 10 (6). New Delhi: International Academy of Indian Culture.

———. 1974b. *Gilgit Buddhist Manuscripts* (Facsimile Edition). Part 7. Śata-piṭaka Series, Indo-Asian Literatures 10 (7). New Delhi: International Academy of Indian Culture.

Raine, Adrian. 1993. *The Psychopathology of Crime: Criminal Behavior as a Clinical Disorder.* San Diego: Academic Press.

Ralls, K., P. H. Harvey, and A. M. Lyles. 1986. "Inbreeding in Natural Populations of Birds and Mammals." In *Conservation Biology: the Science of Scarcity and Diversity*, ed. M. E. Soulé, 35–56. Sunderland, MA: Sinauer Associates.

Ralston, W[illiam] R[alston] S[hedden]. 1882. *Tibetan Tales, Derived from Indian Sources. Translated from the Tibetan of the Kah-gyur by F. Anton von Schiefner, done into English from the German, with an Introduction.* London: Trübner & Co.

Ramanujan, A. K. 1972. "The Indian 'Oedipus.'" In *Indian Literature: Proceedings of a Seminar*, ed. Arabinda Poddar, 127–137. Simla: Indian Institute of Advanced Study.

———. 1984. "The Indian Oedipus." In *Oedipus: A Folklore Casebook*, eds. Lowell Edmunds and Alan Dundes, 234–261. New York: Garland Publishing.

Rand, Edward Kennard. 1913. "Mediæval Lives of Judas Iscariot." In *Anniversary Papers by Colleagues and Pupils of George Lyman Kittredge*, 305–316. Reprint: New York: Russell & Russell, 1917.

Rani, Sharada. 1977. *Buddhist Tales from Kashmir in Tibetan Woodcuts (Narthang Series of the Woodcuts of Kṣemendra's Avadana-Kalpalata)*. Śata-Piṭaka Series 232. Delhi: Jayyed Press; Published by Mrs. Sharada Rani.

Rank, Otto. 1992. *The Incest Theme in Literature and Legend: Fundamentals of a Psychology of Literary Creation.* Trans. Gregory C. Richter. Baltimore, MD: The Johns Hopkins University Press. [A translation of *Das Inzest-Motiv in Dichtung und Sage* (Leipzig/Vienna: Franz Deuticke, 1912).]

Régamey, Konstanty. 1938. *The Bhadramāyākāravyākaraṇa: Introduction, Tibetan Text, Translation and Notes.* The Warsaw Society of Sciences and Letters, Publications of the Oriental Commission Nr. 3. Warsaw: Nakładem Towarzystwa Naukowego Warswzawskiego Wydano z Zasiłku Funduszu Kultury J. Piłsudskiego.

Reider, Norman. 1960. "Medieval Œdipal Legends about Judas." *The Psychoanalytic Quarterly* 29, no. 4: 515–527.

Renou, Louis. 1975. *Grammaire Sanscrite.* 2nd corr. ed. Paris: Adrien Maisonneuve.

Rhoton, Jared Douglas. 2002. *A Clear Differentiation of the Three Codes: Essential Distinctions among the Individual Liberation, Great Vehicle, and Tantric Systems.* Albany: State University of New York Press.

Rhys Davids, [Caroline Augusta Foley]. 1909. *Psalms of the Early Buddhists.* Vol. I. *Psalms of the Sisters.* Reprint: London: The Pali Text Society, 1980.

———. 1913. *Psalms of the Early Buddhists.* Vol. II. *Psalms of the Bretheren.* Reprint: London: The Pali Text Society, 1980.

Rhys Davids, T[homas] W[illiam], and J[oseph] Estlin Carpenter. 1890–1911. *The Dīgha Nikāya.* Reprint: London: The Pali Text Society, 1975.

———, J[oseph] Estlin Carpenter, and William Stede. 1886, 1931, 1932. *The Sumaṅgala-Vilāsinī, Buddhaghosa's Commentary on the Dīgha Nikāya.* London: The Pali Text Society. Rhys Davids and Carpenter are responsible for vol. 1; Stede for vols. 2 and 3.

———, and William Stede. 1921–1925. *The Pali Text Society's Pali-English Dictionary.* Reprint: London: The Pali Text Society, 1979.

Richardson, Alan. 1985. "The Dangers of Sympathy: Sibling Incest in English Romantic Poetry." *Studies in English Literature, 1500–1900* 25, no. 4: 737–754.

———. 2000. "Rethinking Romantic Incest: Human Universals, Literary Representation, and the Biology of Mind." *New Literary History* 31, no. 3: 553–572.

Rocher, Ludo. 1986. *The Purāṇas.* A History of Indian Literature, vol. 2, fasc. 3.Wiesbaden: Otto Harrassowitz.

Rockhill, William Woodville. 1892. *Udānavarga: A Collection of Verses from the Buddhist Canon.* London: Kegan Paul, Trench, Trübner & Co.

———. 1907. *The Life of the Buddha and the Early History of His Order.* London: Kegan Paul, Trench Trübner & Co.

Roesler, Ulrike. 2002a. "The Great Indian Epics in the Version of Dmar ston Chos kyi rgyal po." In *Religion and Secular Culture in Tibet,* ed. Henk Blezer, with the assistance of Abel Zadoks, 431–450. Tibetan Studies II: Proceedings of the Ninth Seminar of the International Association for Tibetan Studies, Leiden 2000. Leiden: E. J. Brill.

———. 2002b. "Not a Mere Imitation: Indian Narratives in a Tibetan Context." In *Faces of Tibetan Religious Tradition and Contacts with Neighbouring Cultural Areas,* eds. Alfredo Cadonna and Ester Bianchi, 153–177. Florence: Leo S. Olschki.

Roth, Gustav. 1970. *Bhikṣuṇī-Vinaya: Manual of Discipline for Buddhist Nuns.* Tibetan Sanskrit Works Series 12. Patna: K. P. Jayaswal Research Institute.

Rowley, Ian, Eleanor Russell, and Michael Brooker. 1993. "Inbreeding in Birds." In *The Natural History of Inbreeding and Outbreeding: Theoretical and Empirical Perspectives,* ed. Nancy Wilmsen Thornhill, 304–328. Chicago: The University of Chicago Press.

Rozin, Paul, Jonathan Haidt, and Clark McCauley. 2000. "Disgust." In *Handbook of Emotions,* 2nd ed., eds. M. Lewis and J. M. Haviland-Jones, 637–653. New York: Guilford.

Ruegg, David Seyfort. 1990. "On the Authorship of Some Works Ascribed to Bhāvaviveka/Bhavya." In *Earliest Buddhism and Madhyamaka,* eds. David Seyfort Ruegg and Lambert Schmithausen. Panels of the VIIth World Sanskrit Conference: Kern Institute, Leiden: August 23–29, 1987. Vol. 2, 59–71. Leiden: E. J. Brill.

———. 1999. "Remarks on the Place of Narrative in the Buddhist Literatures of India and Tibet." In *India, Tibet, China: Genesis and Aspects of Traditional Narrative*, ed. Alfredo Cadonna, 193–227. Florence: Leo S. Olschki.

Sadakata Akira 定方晟. 2000. "Kunāra monogatari: Tekisuto to wayaku" クナーラ物語: テキストと和訳 [*Kuṇālāvadāna*: Text and Japanese translation]. *Tōkai Daigaku Kiyō (Bungakubu)* 東海大学紀要文学部 74: 11–43.

Saeki Kyokuga 佐伯旭雅. 1887. *Kandō Abidatsuma kusharon* 冠導阿毘達磨倶舎論. Photo reprint of woodblock edition. 3 vols. continuous pagination. Kyoto: Hōzōkan 法蔵館, 1978.

Saigusa Mitsuyoshi 三枝充悳. 1970. *Sanron gengi* 三論玄義. *Butten Kōza* 仏典講座 27. Tokyo: Daizō shuppan 大蔵出版.

Saitō Tatsuya 斉藤達也. 1998. "Gishin Nanbokuchō jidai no Ansokukoku to Ansokukei Bukkyōsō." 魏晋南北朝時代の安息国と安息系仏教僧 [The Country Anxi (安息) and the Buddhist Monks from It in the Wei-Jin Nanbeichao (魏晋南北朝) Periods]. *Journal of the International College for Advanced Buddhist Studies/Kokusai Bukkyō Daigakuin Daigaku Kenkyū Kiyō* 国際仏教大学院大学研究紀要 1: 117–141 (176–152).

Sakaki Ryōsaburō 榊亮三郎. 1916. *Mahāvyutpatti*. Kyoto: Kyōto Teikoku Daigaku Bunka Daigaku Sōsho 京都帝國大學文科大學叢書 3. Numerous reprints.

Salomon, Richard. 1989. "Daily Life in Ancient Mathurā." In *Mathurā: The Cultural Heritage*, ed. Doris Meth Srinivasan, 39–45. New Delhi: American Institute of Indian Studies.

———. 1999. *Ancient Buddhist Scrolls from Gandhāra: The British Library Kharoṣṭhī Fragments*. Seattle: University of Washington Press.

Sarkár, Golápchandra. 1891. *The Hindu Law of Adoption*. Tagore Law Lectures 1888. Calcutta: Thacker, Spink & Co.

Sasaki, Shizuka 佐々木閑. 1991. "Ritsuzō ni arawareru 'Arakan no rōsei'" 律蔵にあらわれる『阿羅漢の漏精』[The impurity of the Arhat in the Vinayapiṭaka]. *Hanazono Daigaku Kenkyū Kiyō* 花園大学研究紀要 23: 1–20.

———. 1996. "Biku ni narenai hitobito" 比丘になれない人々 [Those who cannot become monks]. *Hanazono Daigaku Bungakubu Kenkyū Kiyō* 花園大学文学部研究紀要 28: 111–148.

———. 1997. "Oshō to Ajari" 和尚と阿闍梨 [Upadhyāya and ācārya]. *Hanazono Daigaku Bungakubu Kenkyū Kiyō* 花園大学文学部研究紀要 29: 1–43.

———. 1998. "Buddhist Sects in the Aśoka Period (7): The *Vibhāṣā* and the *Śāriputraparipṛcchā*." *Bukkyō Kenkyū* 佛教研究 27: 1–55.

———. 2000. *Indo bukkyō hen'iron: Naze bukkyō wa tayōka shita no ka* インド仏教変移論・なぜ仏教は多様化したのか. Tokyo: Daizō shuppan 大蔵出版.

Satō Mitsuo 佐藤密雄. 1963. *Genshi bukkyō kyōdan no kenkyū* 原始仏教教團の研究. Tokyo: Sankibō 山喜房.

Schiefner, Antonius [Franz Anton von]. 1868. *Târanâthae de Doctrinae Buddhicae in India Propagatione. Narratio. Contextum Tibeticum*. Petrograd: Imp. Academiae Scientiarum Petropolitanae.

Schlesinger, Benjamin. 1982. *Sexual Abuse of Children: A Resource Guide and Annotated Bibliography.* Toronto: University of Toronto Press.

Schmidt, Hanns-Peter. 1987. *Some Women's Rites and Rights in the Veda.* Post-Graduate and Research Department Series 29. Poona: Bhandarkar Oriental Research Institute.

Schneider, Mark A., and Lewellyn Hendrix. 2000. "Olfactory Sexual Inhibition and the Westermarck Effect." *Human Nature* 11, no. 1: 65–91.

Schopen, Gregory. 1995. "Death, Funerals, and the Division of Property in a Monastic Code." In *Buddhism in Practice,* ed. Donald S. Lopez, 473–502. Princeton, NJ: Princeton University Press.

———. 1997. *Bones, Stones, and Buddhist Monks: Collected Papers on the Archaeology, Epigraphy, and Texts of Monastic Buddhism in India.* Honolulu: University of Hawai'i Press.

———. 2001. "Dead Monks and Bad Debts: Some Provisions of a Buddhist Monastic Inheritance Law." *Indo-Iranian Journal* 44: 99–148.

Schreiner, Peter, and Renate Söhnen. 1987. *Sanskrit Indices and Text of the Brahmapurāṇa.* Purāṇa Research Publications, Tübingen 1. Wiesbaden: Otto Harrassowitz.

Sedlar, Jean W. 1980. *India and the Greek World: A Study in the Transmission of Culture* Totowa, NJ: Rowman and Littlefield.

Senart, Émile Charles Marie. 1882–1897. *Le Mahāvastu.* Sociéte Asiatique, Collection d'Ouvrages Orientaux, Seconde Série. Paris. Reprint: Tokyo: Meicho Fukyūkai, 1977.

Sharf, Robert. 1996. "The Scripture in Forty-two Sections." In *Religions of China in Practice,* ed. Donald S. Lopez Jr., 360–371. Princeton, NJ: Princeton University Press.

Sharma, Ramanand. 1997. *Kāmasūtram of Sri Vatsyayana Muni, with the Jayamangala Sanskrit Commentary of Sri Yashodhara.* Bitthaldas Sanskrit Series. Varanasi: Krishnadas Academy.

Shāstrī, Haraprasād. 1931. "Chips from a Buddhist Workshop." In *Buddhistic Studies,* ed. Bimala Churn Law, 818–858. Calcutta. Reprint: Delhi: Indological Book House, 1983.

Shepher, Joseph. 1983. *Incest: A Biosocial View.* New York: Academic Press.

Shields, William M. 1993. "The Natural and Unnatural History of Inbreeding and Outbreeding." In *The Natural History of Inbreeding and Outbreeding: Theoretical and Empirical Perspectives,* ed. Nancy Wilmsen Thornhill, 143–169. Chicago: The University of Chicago Press.

Siegel, Lee. 1978. *Sacred and Profane Dimensions of Love in Indian Traditions as Exemplified in the Gītagovinda of Jayadeva.* Oxford: Oxford University Press.

Silk, Jonathan A. 1990. "Oedipal Calumny and Schismatic Rhetoric in Indian Buddhism: A Study in the Narrative Structure and Doctrinal History of Heresy." *Kushāna: Indo koten bunka keisei katei no kenkyū* クシャーナ: インド古典文化形成過程の研究 4, no. 4: 1–3. [Published by the Kushāna kenkyūkai クシャーナ研究会, Kyoto University, director Kobayashi Nobuhiko 小林信彦.]

———. 1997. "The Composition of the *Guan Wuliangshoufo-jing*: Some Buddhist and Jaina Parallels to Its Narrative Frame." *Journal of Indian Philosophy* 25, no. 2: 181–256.

———. 2002a. "Possible Indian Sources for the Term *Tshad ma'i skyes bu* as *Pramāṇapuruṣa*." *Journal of Indian Philosophy* 30, no. 2: 111–160.

———. 2002b. "What, If Anything, Is Mahāyāna Buddhism? Problems of Definitions and Classifications." *Numen* 49, no. 4: 355–405.

———. 2002c. "*Cui bono*? or Follow the Money: Identifying the Sophist in a Pāli Commentary." In *Buddhist and Indian Studies in Honour of Professor Sodō Mori*, 129–183. Hamamatsu: Kokusai Bukkyoto Kyokai.

———. 2003a. "Dressed for Success. The Monk Kāśyapa and Strategies of Legitimation in Earlier Mahāyāna Buddhist Scriptures." *Journal Asiatique* 291, nos. 1–2: 173–219.

———. 2003b. "The Fruits of Paradox: On the Religious Architecture of the Buddha's Life Story." *Journal of the American Academy of Religion* 71, no. 4: 863–881.

———. 2006. "Xuanzang's Portrayal of the Buddhist Mahādeva." In *Hokekyō to Daijō kyōten no kenkyū* 法華経と大乗経典の研究, ed. Mochizuki Kaishuku 望月海淑, 193–213 (622–602). Tokyo: Sankibō busshorin 山喜房佛書林.

———. 2007a. "Bauddhavacana: Notes on Buddhist Vocabulary." *Sōka Daigaku Kokusai Bukkyōgaku Kōtō Kenkyūjo Nenpō* 創価大学国際仏教学高等研究所年報/*Annual Report of the International Research Institute for Advanced Buddhology at Soka University* 10: 171–179.

———. 2007b. "Good and Evil in Indian Buddhism: The Five Sins of Immediate Retribution." *Journal of Indian Philosophy* 35, no. 3: 253–286.

———. 2007c. "Garlanding as Sexual Invitation: Indian Buddhist Evidence." *Indo-Iranian Journal* 50, no. 1: 5–10.

———. 2008a. "Forbidden Women: A Peculiar Buddhist Reference." In *Aspects of Research into Central Asian Buddhism*, ed. Peter Zieme, 371–378. Silk Road Studies 30. Turnhout: Brepols.

———. 2008b. "Maternity Homes and Abandoned Children in Buddhist India." *Journal of the American Oriental Society* 127, no. 3.

———. 2008c. "The Indian Buddhist Mahādeva in Tibetan Sources." *Indo Tetsugaku Bukkyōgaku Kenkyū* インド哲学仏教学研究 / *Studies in Indian Philosophy and Buddhism* 15: 27–55.

———. 2008d. "Incestuous Ancestries: On the Family Origins of Gautama Siddhārtha, Interpretations of Genesis 20.12, and the Status of Scripture in Buddhism." *History of Religions* 47, no. 4: 253–281.

———. Forthcoming a. "Putative Persian Perversities: Buddhist Condemnations of Zoroastrian Close-Kin Marriage in Context." *Bulletin of the School of Oriental and African Studies* 71, no. 3.

———. Forthcoming b. "The Story of Dharmaruci: In Kṣemendra's *Bodhisattvāvadānakalpalatā* and Its Source the *Divyāvadāna*."

———. Forthcoming c. "Dharmaruci in the South: Ceylonese Sectarianism and Indian Calumnies."

———. Forthcoming d. "The *Jifayue sheku tuoluoni jing*: Translation, Non-translation, Both, or Neither?" To appear in a special volume of the *Journal of the International Association of Buddhist Studies* dedicated to Chinese translations of Buddhist scriptures.

Silva, Lily de. 2001. "Mother Concept in the Hindu and Buddhist Traditions." *Bukkyō Kenkyū* 佛教研究/*Buddhist Studies* 30: 1–17.

Sircar, D[ines] C[handra]. 1961. "Some Brahmi Inscriptions." *Epigraphia Indica* 34, no. 4: 207–212.

Skilling, Peter. 2003. "The Three Seals Code on Crimes Related to Relics, Images, and Bodhi-trees." In *Sichamai-achan: Phiphit niphon chert chu kiat satsadachan dr. prasert na nakhon—satsadachan wisuth butsayakun nuang nai okat mi ayu 84 pi nai pho. so 2546*, ed. Winai Phongsipan, 287–307. Bangkok: Fuang fa Printing.

Smith, Helmer. 1916–1918. *Sutta-Nipāta Commentary, being Paramatthajotikā II*. London: The Pali Text Society.

Snellgrove, David L. 1987. *Indo-Tibetan Buddhism: Indian Buddhists and Their Tibetan Successors*. London: Serindia Publications.

Söhnen, Renate, and Peter Schreiner. 1989. *Brahmapurāṇa. Summary of Contents, with Index of Names and Motifs*. Purāṇa Research Publications, Tübingen 2. Wiesbaden: Otto Harrassowitz.

Spain, David H. 1987. "The Westermarck-Freud Incest-Theory Debate." *Current Anthropology* 28, no. 5: 623–645.

———. 1988. "Taboo or Not Taboo: Is That the Question?" *Ethos* 16, no. 3: 285–301.

Speyer, Jacob Samuel. 1902. "Critical Remarks on the Text of the Divyāvadāna." *Wiener Zeitschrift für die Kunde des Morgenlandes* 16: 103–130; 340–361.

———. 1906–1909. *Avadānaçataka: A Century of Edifying Tales Belonging to the Hīnayāna*. Bibliotheca Buddhica 3. Indo-Iranian Reprints 3. St. Petersburg. Reprint: The Hague: Mouton, 1958.

Sponberg, Alan. 1992. "Attitudes toward Women and the Feminine in Early Buddhism." In *Buddhism, Sexuality, and Gender*, ed. José Ignacio Cabezón, 3–36. Albany: State University of New York Press.

Stearns, Cyrus. 2001. *Luminous Lives: The Story of the Early Masters of the Lam 'bras Tradition in Tibet*. Boston: Wisdom Publications.

Stephens, Winifred. 1911. *Legends of Indian Buddhism. Translated from "L'Introduction à l'Histoire du Buddhisme Indien" of Eugène Burnouf*. London: John Murray.

Stern, Jacob. 1992. *Parthenius: Erotika Pathemata: The Love Stories of Parthenius*. New York: Garland.

Sternbach, Ludwik. 1953. *Gaṇikā-vṛtta-saṁgrahaḥ or Texts on Courtezans in Classical Sanskrit*. Vishveshvaranand Indological Series 4. Hoshiarpur: Vishveshvaranand Vedic Research Institute.

———. 1965. *Juridical Studies in Ancient Indian Law*. Part I. Delhi: Motilal Banarsidass.

Strong, John S. 1983. *The Legend of King Aśoka: A Study and Translation of the* Aśokāvadāna. Princeton, NJ: Princeton University Press.

———. 1992. *The Legend and Cult of Upagupta: Sanskrit Buddhism in North India and Southeast Asia*. Princeton, NJ: Princeton University Press.

Sugimoto Takushū 杉本卓洲. 1993. "Inkai o megutte" 婬戒をめぐって [A study on the prohibition from engaging in sexual intercourse]. In *Tsukamoto Keishō kyōju kanreki kinen ronbunshū: Chi no kaikō – bukkyō to kagaku* 塚本啓祥教授還暦記念論文集· 知の邂逅 – 仏教と科学, eds. Tsukamoto Keishō Kyōju Kanreki Kinen Ronbunshū Kankōkai 塚本啓祥教授還暦記念論文集刊行会, 207–222. Tokyō: Kōsei shuppansha 佼成出版社. Reprinted in *Gokai no shūhen: Indoteki sei no dainamizumu* 五戒の周辺: インド的生のダイナミズム, 195–215. Kyoto: Heirakuji shoten 平楽寺書店, 1999.

Sukthankar, Vishnu S., S. K. Belvalkar, and P. L. Vaidya. 1933-1966. *The Mahābhārata for the First Time Critically Edited.* Poona: Bhandarkar Oriental Research Institute.

Sullivan, Lee R. 1998. "The Hanging of Judas: Medieval Iconography and the German Peasants' War." *Essays in Medieval Studies* 15: 92–102. Available at: http://www.luc.edu/publications/medieval/vol15/sullivan. html. [accessed August 23, 2003].

Suzuki, Daisetz Teitaro, and Hokei Idzumi. 1949. *The Gandavyuha Sutra.* Kyoto: The Society for the Publication of Sacred Books of the World. Revision of 1934 edition.

Swan, Charles. 1876. *Gesta Romanorum: or, Entertaining Moral Stories; Invented by the Monks as a Fireside Recreation, and Commonly Applied in their Discourses from the Pulpit: Whence the most Celebrated of our own Poets and Others, from the Earliest Times, have Extracted their Plots.* Revised and Corrected by Wynnard Hooper. Reprint: New York: Dover Publications, 1959.

Takai Kankai 高井觀海. 1928/1978. *Shōjō bukkyō gairon* 小乗仏教概論. Expanded reprint with supplements by Miyasaka Yūshō 宮坂宥勝. Tokyo: Sankibō busshorin 山喜房佛書林.

Takakusu, Junjirō, and Makoto Nagai, (with Kogen Mizuno). 1924–1947. *Samantapāsādikā: Buddhaghosa's Commentary on the Vinaya Piṭaka.* London: The Pali Text Society.

Tambiah, S[tanley] J. 1969. "Animals Are Good to Think and Good to Prohibit." *Ethnology* 8, no. 4: 423–459.

Tāranātha. 1985. *The Collected Works of Jo-naṅ Rje-btsun Tāranātha. Reproduced from a set of prints from the Rtag-brtan Phun tshogs-gliṅ blocks preserved in the library of the Stog Palace in Ladak.* Smanrtsis shesrig dpemzod 16. Leh, Ladakh: C. Namgyal & Tsewang Taru. The *Dam pa'i chos ring po che 'Phags pa'i yul du ji ltar dar ba'i tshul gsal bar ston pa dgos 'dod kun 'byung* reproduced here is an independently paginated handwritten copy and does not belong to the xylographed sTog palace set otherwise reproduced in these collected works.

Tatelman, Joel. 2000. *The Glorious Deeds of Pūrṇa: A Translation and Study of the Pūrṇāvadāna.* Richmond, Surrey: Curzon Press.

Tawney, Charles Henry. 1895. *The Kathākośa; or Treasury of Stories.* Oriental Translation Fund, new series 2. London: Royal Asiatic Society.

Taylor, Archer. 1938. "Riddles Dealing with Family Relationships." *The Journal of American Folklore* 51: 25–37.

Teiser, Stephen. 1988. *The Ghost Festival in Medieval China*. Princeton, NJ: Princeton University Press.

Teramoto Enga 寺本婉雅 and Hiramatsu Tomotsugu 平松友嗣. 1935. *Zōkanwa sanyaku taikō Ibushūrinron, Ibushūseishaku, Ibusesshū* 藏漢和三譯對校· 異部宗輪論· 異部宗精釋· 異部説集. Kyoto: Mokudōsha 默働社.

Thomas, Edward J[oseph]. 1949. *The Life of Buddha as Legend and History*. Reprint: London: Routledge & Kegan Paul, 1975.

Thompson, Stith. 1956–1958. *Motif-index of Folk Literature*. Bloomington: Indiana University Press.

———, and Jonas Balys. 1958. *The Oral Tales of India*. Bloomington: Indiana University Press.

Thornhill, Nancy Wilmsen. 1990. "The Evolutionary Significance of Incest Rules." *Ethology and Sociobiology* 11: 113–129.

———. 1991. "An Evolutionary Analysis of Rules Regulating Human Inbreeding and Marriage." *The Behavioral and Brain Sciences* 14, no. 2: 247–293.

———, ed. 1993. *The Natural History of Inbreeding and Outbreeding: Theoretical and Empirical Perspectives*. Chicago: The University of Chicago Press.

Thorslev, Peter L., Jr. 1965. "Incest as Romantic Symbol." *Comparative Literature Studies* 2, no. 1: 41–58.

Trachtenberg, Joshua. 1943. *The Devil and the Jews: The Medieval Conception of the Jew and its Relation to Modern Antisemitism*. New Haven, CT. Second paperback edition: Philadelphia: Jewish Publication Society, 1983.

Trautmann, Thomas R. 1973. "Consanguineous Marriage in Pali Literature." *Journal of the American Oriental Society* 93, no. 2: 158–180.

Trenckner, Vilhelm. 1880. *The Milindapañho: Being Dialogues between King Milinda and the Buddhist Sage Nāgasena*. Reprint: London: The Pali Text Society, 1986.

———, et al. 1924–. *A Critical Pāli Dictionary*. Copenhagen: Royal Danish Academy.

Tsukamoto Keishō 塚本啓祥. 1965. "Daiten no denshō to sōga no kōsō" 大天の傳承と僧伽の抗争 [On the connection between Mahādeva and saṁghabheda]. *Indogaku Bukkyōgaku Kenkyū* 印度学仏教学研究 13, no. 1: 106–115.

———. 1980. *Shoki bukkyō kyōdanshi no kenkyū* 初期仏教教団史の研究. Tokyo: Sankibō Busshorin.

Tucci, Giuseppe. 1949. *Tibetan Painted Scrolls*. Rome. Reprint: Bangkok: SDI Publications, 1999.

Twitchell, James B. 1987. *Forbidden Partners: The Incest Taboo in Modern Culture*. New York: Columbia University Press.

Ui Hakuju 宇井伯壽. 1924. "Butsumetsu nendai-ron" 佛滅年代論 [On the date of the Buddha's death]. *Gendai Bukkyō* 現代佛教. Reprinted in *Indo tetsugaku kenkyū* 印度哲學研究 II, 3–111. Tokyo: Kōshisha 甲子社, 1933.

Uryū Tōshō 瓜生等勝. 1973. *Minobusanbon Hōbutsushū to kenkyū* 身延山本宝物集と研究. Mikan Kokubun Shiryō 未刊国文資料 4. Toyohashi, Japan: Mikan Kokubun Shiryō Kankokai 未刊国文資料刊行会.

Vallauri, Mario. 1938. "Sommari dello 'Skandapurāṇa': Il 'Brahmakhaṇḍa.'" *Aevum* 12, no. 2–3: 369–410.

van den Berghe, Pierre. L. 1983. "Human Inbreeding Avoidance: Culture in Nature." *The Behavioral and Brain Sciences* 6, no. 1: 91–123.

———, and Gene M. Mesher. 1980. "Royal Incest and Inclusive Fitness." *American Ethnologist* 7, no. 1: 300–317.

Vassilief [Vasil'ev], V[asiliĭ] P[avlovich]. 1865. *Le Bouddhisme: Ses dogmes, son histoire et sa littérature*. Trans. G. A. La Comme. Paris: Auguste Durand. Original Russian edition 1857.

Voragine, Jacobus de. 1941. *The Golden Legend*. Trans. and adapted by Granger Ryan and Helmut Ripperger. New York: Longmans, Green and Co.

Waldschmidt, Ernst. 1944, 1948. *Die Überlieferung vom Lebensende des Buddha: Eine vergleichende Analyse des Mahāparinirvāṇasūtra und seiner Textentsprechungen*. Abhandlungen der Akademie der Wissenschaften in Göttingen, Philosophisch-historische Klasse, Dritte Folge 29, 30. Göttingen: Vandenhoeck & Ruprecht.

Walleser, Max. 1927. *Die Sekten des alten Buddhismus*. Die buddhistische Philosophie in ihrer geschichtlichen Entwicklung 4. Heidelberg: Carl Winter's Universitatsbuchhandlung.

———, and Hermann Kopp. 1924–1957. *Manorathapūraṇī: Buddhaghosa's Commentary on the Aṅguttara-nikāya*. London: The Pali Text Society.

Walter, Alex. 2000. "From Westermarck's Effect to Fox's Law: Paradox and Principle in the Relationship between Incest Taboos and Exogamy." *Social Science Information* 39, no. 3: 467–488.

Watanabe Baiyū 渡邊楳雄. 1954. *Ubu Abidatsumaron no kenkyū* 有部阿毘達磨論の研究. Tokyo: Heibonsha 平凡社.

Watters, Thomas. 1904–1905. *On Yuan Chwang's Travels in India*. Oriental Translation Fund New Series 14–15. London. Reprint: New York: AMS, 1971.

Weinstein, Stanley. 1959. "A Biographical Study of Tz'ŭ-ên." *Monumenta Nipponica* 15, nos. 1–2: 119–149.

Weisfeld, Glenn E., Tiffany Czilli, Krista A. Phillips, James A. Gall, and Cary M. Lichtman. 2003. "Possible Olfaction-based Mechanisms in Human Kin Recognition and Inbreeding Avoidance." *Journal of Experimental Child Psychology* 85: 279–295.

Wenzel, H[[einrich]. 1893. "Dr. Serge D'Oldenburg 'On the Buddhist Jātakas.'" *Journal of the Royal Asiatic Society of Great Britain and Ireland* 1893: 301–356.

Westermark, Edward. 1921. *The History of Human Marriage*. 5th ed. 3 vols. London: Macmillan and Co.

Willemen, Charles. 1994. *The Storehouse of Sundry Valuables*. BDK English Tripiṭaka 10–I. Berkeley, CA: Numata Center for Buddhist Translation and Research.

Willner, Dorothy. 1983. "Definition and Violation: Incest and Incest Taboos." *Man* 18, no. 1: 134–159.

Wilson, Liz. 1996. *Charming Cadavers: Horrific* Figurations *of the Feminine in Indian Buddhist Hagiographical Literature*. Chicago: University of Chicago Press.

Winternitz, Maurice. 1927. *A History of Indian Literature*. Vol. II: *Buddhist Literature and Jaina Literature*. Calcutta. Reprint: New Delhi: Oriental Books Reprint Corporation, 1972.

Wisdom, Cathy Spatz. 1989. "The Cycle of Violence." *Science* 244 (4901): 160–166.

Wogihara Unrai. 1932–1935. *Abhisamayālaṁkārāloka Prajñāpāramitāvyākhyā*. Tōyō Bunko Publications Series D, 2. Tokyo. Reprint: Tokyo: Sankibō Busshorin 山喜房佛書ら林, 1973.

———. 1936. *Sphuṭārtha Abhidharmakośavyākhyā: The Work of Yaśomitra*. Reprint: Tokyo: Sankibo Bookstore, 1989.

Wolf, Arthur P. 1995. *Sexual Attraction and Childhood Association: A Chinese Brief for Edward Westermarck*. Stanford: Stanford University Press.

Woodward, Frank Lee. 1929–1937. *Sārattha-ppakāsinī: Buddhaghosa's Commentary on the Sanyutta-nikāya*. London: The Pali Text Society.

———. 1940–1959. *Paramattha-Dīpanī Theragāṭhā-Aṭṭhakathā: The Commentary of Dhammapālācariya*. London: The Pali Text Society.

Yamada Yoshio 山田孝雄 et al. 1959. *Konjaku monogatarishū* 今昔物語集 I. Nihon Koten Bungaku Taikei 日本古典文学大系 22. Tokyo: Iwanami Shoten 岩波書店.

Yamazaki, K., G. K. Beauchamp, D. Kupniewski, J. Bard, L. Thomas, and E. A. Boyse. 1988. "Familial Imprinting Determines H-2 Selective Mating Preferences." *Science* 240 (4857): 1331–1332.

Young, Mary de. 1985. *Incest: An Annotated Bibliography*. Jefferson, NC: McFarland & Company, Inc.

Yuyama, Akira. 2001. *The Mahāvastu-Avadāna: In Old Palm-Leaf and Paper Manuscripts*. I. Palm-Leaf Manuscripts. Bibliotheca Codicum Asiaticorum 15. Tokyo: The Centre for East Asian Cultural Studies for UNESCO; actually published 2003.

Zimmer, Heinrich. 1925. *Karman: Ein buddhistischer Legendkranz*. Munich: F. Bruckmann.

Index

Mūlasarvāstivāda Vinaya, 65, 72, 123–124, 187; celibate marriage story, 135; *Cīvaravastu* (Section on Robes), 180, 265n24; ordination prohibitions, 30–34, 241n45; *Pravrajyāvastu* (Section on Monastic Ordination), 30–33, 35–36, 92, 117–118; *Saṁghabhedavastu* (Section on Schism), 130–133, 272n32; sibling incest stories, 129, 130–133; *Vinayavibhaṅga* (Vinaya Exegesis), 137, 139–158, 162–163, 200
Mulian, 240n40. *See also* Mahā-Moggallāna/Mahā-Maudgalyayana
Müller, Éduard, 119
murder: of Jesus, 290n13; by Mahādeva, 19–23, 25–26, 42, 48–49, 73–74, 82, 163, 169, 217. *See also* arhat murder; arsons; parricide

Nanda and Mahāpadma, kings, 58–59, 251n3
Nārada, 158–160, 181–184
Nattier, Janice, 40
New Testament, and Judas, 192
Nichiren-shū, 13
Nikāyabhedavibhaṅgavyākhyāna (Commentary on the Classification of the Divisions of Buddhist Monastic Communities), 58, 245n7, 251n2
nirvāṇa, 26, 240n39

Obeyesekere, Gananath, 127–128, 220, 269n5
"Oedipal fantasy," 3–4
Oedipal Judas, 189–201, 290n13
"Oedipal wish," 118
Oedipus complex, 2, 5–8, 164–170, 299n50; defined, 164, 171; directionality of aggression and desire, 165–172, 167–169*figs*, 178–179, 217, 222–224, 282n8, 286n41; Tantric, 125; universality, 2, 64, 164. *See also* Greek Oedipus; Indian Oedipus; mother-son incest; parricide
Oedipus the King, 95. *See also* Greek Oedipus

Ohly, Friedrich, 197, 290n17, 291n24
Okkāka. *See* Ikśvāku, King
ordination, 238n22; *Ajita, 114; Aśvadatta, 104; Dharmaruci and, 74, 94, 255nn18,23, 292n29; Mahādeva, 24, 42–44, 49, 74; Meghadatta, 116, 118; preceptor qualifications, 43; sins prohibiting, 29–34, 42, 74, 232n7, 241n45, 242n55; Utpalavarṇa, 152–154
"outbreeding depression," 210
Ovid, *Metamorphoses*, 206

Padmāvatī, 173–174, 284n14
Paduma, Prince, 172–173
pakatatta, 238n18
Pāla, Prince, 174–175
Pālagopālakathānakam (Small Tale of Pāla and Gopāla), 174–175
Pāli *Cullavagga* (Lesser Division of the Vinaya), 23
Pāli Theravāda Vinaya, 23, 27, 33–34, 62, 129–139, 156
Pāṇini, 220
Pāpapraṇāśana (Destruction of Evil), 184
Parañcōtimuṉivar, 219
Paramārtha, 38–39, 41–42, 170, 247nn15,18,19, 248n27
Paramatthajotikā (Illuminator of the Ultimate Meaning), 126–128
parricide, 229n1, 299n45; Judas, 190, 193, 199; Mahādeva, 19–20, 22, 48–49, 73–74, 169, 217; Mahā-Moggallāna, 27–29. *See also* matricide; patricide
Parthenius, 95–97
Pārvatī, 184–186
Pāṭaliputra, Council of, 14
Patañjali, 220
patricide, 2, 30, 217, 229nn1,4; Ajātaśatru, 180; Aśvadatta, 103, 107–108, 109; Dharmaruci, 73, 166–169, 217; directionality of aggression, 168–169*figs*, 169, 217; Hindu texts, 220; incest more heinous than, 302n19; Judas, 190, 199; Mahādeva, 19–20, 22, 42, 73–74, 169, 217; matricide more severe than, 21–22,

upādhyāya, 33–34
Upagupta, 36, 244n69, 255n23
Uppalavaṇṇa. *See* Utpalavarṇa
Urban II, Pope, 194
Utpalavarṇa, 137, 200, 274n1; *Aṅguttara-Nikaya* and, 216, 280n40; conversion, 152–154, 156–157, 160–161, 281n53; father's logic, 139, 275n7; mother-son incest, 137, 139–163, 184, 276n9; murder, 236n6; propinquity hypothesis and, 214; prostitute/courtesan, 144–150, 156–158, 184, 276n14, 277n19, 281n53
*Uttaraśaila, 39–40, 43, 245n7

Vapu (Apsaras), 159–160
Vasubandhu, 35, 85
Vasugupta, 121–122, 122*fig*
Vasumitra, 38–41, 239n30
Vātsyāyana, 105
Vibhāṣā. *See* **Abhidharma-Mahāvibhāṣā*
victimhood, incest, 76–81, 88–98, 224, 259n7
Vimalā, 156
Vinayas, 13, 30, 192. *See also* Mūlasarvāstivāda Vinaya; Pāli Theravāda Vinaya
Vinayavibhaṅga (Vinaya Exegesis), Mūlasarvāstivāda Vinaya, 137, 139–158, 162–163
violence: antisemitic, 194; bedtrick and, 90, 97; child sexual abuse reaction, 80–81, 258n19; intergenerational, 171. *See also* arsons; murder; rape
Virūḍhaka Ikśvāku. *See* Ikśvāku, King
Voragine, Jacopo da, 189–190, 196, 293n33
Vyāsa, 185

Wang Och'ŏnjuguk chŏn (Account of Travels to the Five Countries of India), 85–86
Westermarck, Edward/Westermarck hypothesis, 77, 208, 211–215, 298n42
women: adultery by, 93, 99, 107, 277n14; Indian Buddhist misogynistic views of, 83–85, 102–103, 127, 223. *See also* mother; prostitutes/courtesans; sibling incest

Xuanzang, 38–42, 85–86, 246nn8,11, 247nn15,16
xwaētwadatha ("next-of-kin marriage"), 86–87

Yaśomitra, 25, 239n30
Yasuyori, Taira, 45, 248nn30,33
Yibuzonglunlun shuji (Expository Account of the Treatise [called] The Wheel of Tenets of Diverse Sects), 41, 245n8, 247n27
Yogācārabhūmi (Stages of the Yoga Practitioner), 25–26
Young Man Luther (Erikson), 215
Yuqieshidilun lüezuan, 231n9

Zabaozang jing (Storehouse of Sundry Treasures), 177–178
Zapiyu jing (Scripture of Miscellaneous Exemplary Stories), 122–123
Zhetatuo, 110–111
Zoroastrians, and incest, 85–87, 134

About the Author

Jonathan Silk is a professor in the study of Buddhism at Leiden University. Trained at the University of Michigan and in Japan, he has taught at Yale University and the University of California, Los Angeles. He has published widely on the Buddhist traditions of India, especially on Mahāyāna scriptures. Recent works include *Body Language* and *Managing Monks.*

Production Notes for SILK | RIVEN BY LUST

Text design by Paul Herr, University of Hawai'i Press
with display in Black Chancery and text in Minion

Text composition by Binghamton Valley Composition

Printing and binding by The Maple-Vail Book
Manufacturing Group

Printed on 60 lb. Glatfelter Offset B18, 420 ppi